W9-DDI-211

Methods of Instruction
for Severely Handicapped Students

Methods of Instruction for Severely Handicapped Students

Edited by

Wayne Sailor, Ph.D.
Professor, Department of Special Education
San Francisco State University

Barbara Wilcox, Ph.D.
Division of Special Education and Rehabilitation
University of Oregon, Eugene

Lou Brown, Ph.D.
Department of Studies in Behavioral Disabilities
University of Wisconsin, Madison

·P·A·U·L·H·
BROOKES
PUBLISHERS

Baltimore • London

117701

Paul H. Brookes, Publishers
Post Office Box 10624
Baltimore, Maryland 21204

Copyright 1980 by Paul H. Brookes Publishing Co., Inc.
All rights reserved.

Typeset by The Composing Room of Michigan, Inc. (Grand Rapids)
Manufactured in the United States of America by Universal
Lithographers, Inc. (Cockeysville, Maryland)

Library of Congress Cataloging in Publication Data
Main entry under title:

Methods of instruction for severely handicapped
    students.

    Bibliography: p.
    Includes index.
    1.   Handicapped children—Education—Addresses,
essays, lectures.   I.   Sailor, Wayne.
II.   Wilcox, Barbara, 1947-   III.   Brown,
Lou, 1939-
LC4015.M48   371.9   80-16668
ISBN 0-933716-06-0

Contents

117701

Contributors

Donald Baer
Department of Human Development
University of Kansas
Lawrence, KS 66045

Marylud Baldwin
Department of Special Education
San Francisco State University
1600 Holloway Avenue
San Francisco, CA 94132

Diane Baumgart
427 Education Building
University of Wisconsin
Madison, WI 53706

William Bricker
Department of Special Education
Kent State University
Kent, OH 44242

Lou Brown
427 Education Building
University of Wisconsin
Madison, WI 53706

Pansy Brown
427 Education Building
University of Wisconsin
Madison, WI 53706

Philippa Campbell
Molly Stark Center
Children's Hospital of Akron
Akron, OH 44308

Glen Dunlap
Speech and Hearing Center
University of California
Santa Barbara, CA 93106

Andrew Egel
Department of Special Education
College of Education
University of Maryland
College Park, MD 20742

Mary Falvey
427 Education Building
University of Wisconsin
Madison, WI 53706

Robert Gaylord-Ross
Department of Special Education
San Francisco State University
1600 Holloway Avenue
San Francisco, CA 94132

Lori Goetz
Department of Special Education
San Francisco State University
1600 Holloway Avenue
San Francisco, CA 94132

Lee Gruenewald
Division of Specialized Education
Services
Madison Metropolitan School District
545 West Dayton Street
Madison, WI 53703

Doug Guess
Department of Special Education
University of Kansas
Lawrence, KS 66045

Norris Haring
WESTAR, JD-06
University District Building
1107 Northeast 45th Street
Seattle, WA 98105

Robert Koegel
Social Process Research Institute
University of California
Santa Barbara, CA 93106

Kathleen Liberty
EEU, CDMRC, WJ-10
University of Washington
Seattle, WA 98195

Steve Lyon
Special Education Department
University of Kansas
Lawrence, KS 66045

Michael Powers
Department of Studies in Behavioral
Disabilities
University of Wisconsin
Madison, WI 53706

Ann Rogers-Warren
Department of Human Development
University of Kansas
Lawrence, KS 66045

Wayne Sailor
Department of Special Education
San Francisco State University
1600 Holloway Avenue
San Francisco, CA 94132

Christine Salisbury
Director of Educational Services
Kansas City Regional Developmental
Disabilities Center

610 East 22nd Street
Kansas City, MO 64141

Jack Schroeder
Madison Metropolitan School District
545 West Dayton Street
Madison, WI 53703

Adriana Schuler
Department of Special Education
San Francisco State University
1600 Holloway Avenue
San Francisco, CA 94132

Bonnie Utley
Bay Area Severely
Handicapped/Deaf-Blind Project
Sunshine School
2730 Bryant
San Francisco, CA 94110

Lisbeth Vincent
427 Education Building
University of Wisconsin
Madison, WI 53706

Gail Walter
Department of Studies in Behavioral
Disabilities
University of Wisconsin
Madison, WI 53706

Steven Warren
Department of Human Development
University of Kansas
Lawrence, KS 66045

Owen White
EEU, CDMRC, WJ-10
University of Washington
Seattle, WA 98195

Barbara Wilcox
Division of Special Education and
Rehabilitation
University of Oregon
Eugene, OR 97403

Introduction

Education of severely handicapped persons as a national mandate and as a coordinated effort of the U.S. Office of Education is now five years old, and there are significant changes in the wind. The Public Law that in 1975 enfranchised the nation's educationally deprived, the severely handicapped, created much more than a flurry of new educational activity. It created a new and important socio-political *movement*. Conference goers who attend the national meetings of The Association for the Severely Handicapped (TASH) along with other national conferences each year come away with a strong impression that there is a difference with this group. The difference seems to take the form of higher energy and a stronger sense of purpose. The national meeting agenda is well attended. A group with a national membership of 5,000 mobilizes up to 50% of its members for its national conference each year, most of whom must pay their own way to attend. These are remarkable feats for a young educational association.

Historians tell us that to predict where we are going we must understand the implications of where we have been. Five years is a short history upon which to build projections for the future, yet we can in this short time frame discern some definite trends which have major implications for our efforts and planning in the 1980s. The portent signaled by these trends is at once exhilarating and frightening. The exhilaration is in the realization that a common thread binds these trends, a thread that represents an even more significant piece of civil legislation, the Civil Rights Act. If one thing is clear from analysis of our short history it is that we are moving into the new decade as proponents for and architects of a national movement to integrate the services for our clients in the *mainstream* of society. The fear comes from the realization that all similar integration movements in the history of our nation have met with great resistance. Our professional task would indeed be an easier, happier one if all we had to do was teach. The difficulty is that our responsibilities under the Public Law also require advocacy. We have just emerged from a decade that has cost the general teaching profession in the United States a much greater psychological tithe than has any period in history. At times, the nation has seemed to have entered what some have called the "new dark ages." Standards of classroom education have significantly and rapidly eroded. Teachers have watched their profession slide economically below that of many blue-collar and skilled labor jobs. Universities have witnessed a staggering decline in the degree of literacy of incoming freshmen classes. States have allowed their school systems to close for long periods of the school term rather than legislate adequate funding with which to operate. The "new generation" has seemed to be willing at times to sacrifice the future to attain pleasure in the present, and education has frequently been the sacrificial lamb.

The challenge for the 1980s for education of severely handicapped persons is to provide educational services to more than one hundred thousand persons nationwide who many people believe cannot profit from that effort and for whom many people will be unwilling to allow use of *the public schools* to achieve that goal. No one ever said it would be easy; that is the legacy of our social movement. The purpose of this book is to begin to reveal the changes in direction that will influence this process and to place this evolution in the perspective of ongoing scientific research.

To understand better the emerging service delivery model we should examine that model as it emerged in its infancy five years ago. Haring and Brown (1976) provided the first text on the education of severely handicapped students. This book attempted to lay down the foundations of assessment, curriculum development, and measurement as the state of the art existed then. Chapters on educational programming for handicapped infants and toddlers were included because of their obvious relevance for prevention of later severely handicapping conditions. Two important issues repeatedly surfaced in these chapters: 1) severely handicapped persons should and could be defined by their common characteristics, and 2) those characteristics would form the basis for the determination of what to teach. To this end, assessment systems were developed and reviewed that attempted to pinpoint small, specific, behavioral skills that, when ultimately placed in some (unknown) sequence, would provide for the movement of severely handicapped persons from a state of near total dependence to a state of relatively independent functioning. The models for assessment prerequisite to educational program development were the large, comprehensive checklists that had been evolved years earlier for purposes of standardized testing in state hospitals for the retarded.

The second text to appear was a landmark of its genre and continues to serve today as a standard reference for teachers in the field: Sontag's *Educational Programming for the Severely and Profoundly Handicapped* (1977). This text represents a shift of population definition away from categorical or behavioral descriptors (e.g., seizures, aberrant behavior, lack of toilet regulation, etc.) to service need characteristics (e.g., basic skill development curriculum) and focuses on the goals of deinstitutionalization and community-based service delivery.

We began our task with a clear understanding that severely (or profoundly, if you still will) handicapped persons could benefit from systematic, measured instruction that used prompting, shaping, and fading techniques, was guided by task analysis, and employed the heightened external and artificial motivation that characterized a decade of operant conditioning research. Earlier work done in state hospitals for mentally retarded persons, in special schools for handicapped students, and in day care centers had given us that hopeful start. What remained for us, in 1976, was to implement the technology in a fully *educational* program distinct from a *treatment* program. We were less concerned with what to teach than with how to teach it, and were largely unconcerned with where to teach. We believed then that the careful study of the ontogeny of normal child development would provide us with a sequence of instructional objectives that would move severely handicapped students, in a development pattern parallel, albeit significantly delayed, to normal children, toward relative independence in self-help, motor, social, and communication domains. We believed that our students would "graduate" into programs for the so-called trainable retarded. We were, at this early time, relatively unconcerned with parents, their needs and level of understanding and expertise, and with the environment in which students lived and received their education. If we assessed, instructed, and measured with steadily increasing precision, we would accomplish the mandate of PL 94-142.

At this writing, we have a significantly altered perspective on these issues for we have grown from infants to five-year-olds. There has been striking progress in the level of development of our technology. The process of how to teach severely handicapped students has reached a very satisfactory level of development in a relatively short period of time. The current changes in direction have more to do with what we teach and where the process is to take place. This book is intended to reveal those changes and to equip the teachers of the 1980s with a new set of tactics for the delivery of educational programs in public schools and the community. This text, like its earlier predecessor, Haring and Brown (1976), is organized into ten chapters that address assessment, instruction, measurement, and research. The first section, "Assessment and the Establishment of Objectives," highlights the sense of new directions. The chapter by Bricker and Campbell raises the question of the nature of the assessment that leads to the selection of instructional objectives. They argue that the process is necessarily interdisciplinary (or "multidisciplinary" or "transdisciplinary") and that appropriateness and functionality are often overlooked. Their alternative to traditional checklist, skill-assessment inventories is a tentative list of 19 dimensions that are basic to educational and therapeutic intervention. These dimensions go well beyond the standard skill-sequence based on normal development.

The chapter by White presents a similar perspective from a slightly different vantage point. He calls for a shift in emphasis away from teaching specific skills toward meeting the demands of an individual's environment and the functions required to maintain self-help skills in that environment. Too much attention has been placed, White argues, on the specific form that skills to be learned take. Should we teach a student to count nickels, dimes, and quarters? Counting change is a *form,* argues White, the *function* of which is the purchase of goods and services. If we concentrate on teaching the functions required by independent living, we find that the forms selected for instruction may well be quite different from those dictated by checklists derived from hypothetical sequences of normal development.

This thesis is also basic to the chapter by Sailor, Guess, Goetz, Schuler, Utley, and Baldwin on the teaching of communication skills. These authors offer a decision model intended to help the teacher to select a communication system that is maximally appropriate and functional for a particular severely handicapped student. Their approach to assessment is again based on the requirements of functioning in the normal, or normalized, environment rather than upon an analysis of discrepancies between normal language users and severely handicapped persons.

Taken together, these three chapters guide the educator into a different realm in selecting the specific content to be taught to the severely handicapped student. All assume that students will need to function in the mainstream of society and that the skills needed immediately are those that are appropriate and functional in such an integrated context. Pointing to color cards and pegs in pegboards are "out"; wheelchair mobility, basic speech, manual signs or communication board vocabulary, and appropriate social adaptations are "in."

The second section, "Instruction and Measurement," brings into focus more clearly the underlying reason for the shift in assessment methodology. What we choose to teach to our students is critically affected by the environments in which they will eventually function. In the 1980s, this clearly assumes the orderly transition of our clients out of hospitals and special segregated schools into the mainstream of public education and community living.

No center of development for education of severely handicapped students has been more community oriented than the group at Madison, Wisconsin. The chapter by Falvey, Brown, Lyon, Baumgart, and Schroeder represents a continuation of this thrust with a focus on how to teach. The authors provide an analysis of skill-shaping techniques that are consistent with functional skills taught in natural settings. Stress is placed on the utilization of cues and consequences that occur in the natural environment, a theme that also surfaces in the chapters on communication instruction by Guess, on research and instructional methods with autistic children by Koegel, Egel, and Dunlap, and the communication assessment chapter by Sailor and his colleagues.

The focus on the natural environment is extended from another perspective in the chapter by Gaylord-Ross. He presents an analysis of approaches to the management of aberrant behaviors in natural settings that culminates in a practical decision model to guide the teacher in the selection of appropriate techniques. This chapter also reveals a significant turn away from the isolated targeting of behavior problems for reduction. Gaylord-Ross calls for an analysis of the learning environment and the selection of a management system that is consistent with and utilizes the positive motivational factors extant in instructional situations.

Haring, Liberty, and White present an important outgrowth of research on the rates with which severely handicapped students acquire objectives under tightly controlled, highly programmed instructional conditions. The result of these efforts is a data-based decision model to guide teachers about what to do when things go wrong. This chapter supplies a critical missing link in the developing educational technology for the severely handicapped population. Over the past five years teachers have become proficient data collectors but have had little guidance to dictate tactical shifts when the data reveal a failure to teach a skill successfully. Should the reinforcer be changed? Is the problem a poor task analysis, or poor instructional technique? Haring, Liberty, and White rely on the results of a large scale research program to provide guidelines to the teacher on the utilization of data collected on-line to select the most probable tactical shift to produce success when trouble is encountered.

The third section of the book, "Evaluation of Outcome: Current Research," is intended to acquaint the reader with the status and implications of current research into the educational process with severely handicapped persons. The chapter by Guess provides a critical analysis of current research in communication instruction for severely handicapped students. It provides the teacher with a source of empirical justification for the selection or rejection of a particular programmatic approach. Guess points again to research support for the continuing theme of this book: that skills selected for instruction should be functional, should occur in a natural environment such as a public school cafeteria or playground, and should be appropriate for the individual's interactions with that environment.

The chapter by Warren, Rogers-Warren, Baer, and Guess presents a preliminary analysis of the data from a large, multiple setting research program. With language acquisition as the focus of the research effort, they offer suggestions to facilitate the generalization of newly acquired skills. Support for the notion that generalized language usage must include instructional elements placed at key points in the students' environment is presented. Teaching becomes more than a teacher-student relationship, and focuses on inducing changes in the total system in which the teaching is embedded. A linguistic social skill will become functional for the student, for example, only to the extent that the skill is supported by persons in environments other than the classroom.

Koegel, Egel, and Dunlap provide a comprehensive update on the results of years of extensive research into efforts to establish communication skills and to reduce behavior problems with autistic children. The work of the Santa Barbara group represents one of the nation's most exciting long-term child research projects, the results of which have immediate importance for instructional programming with all severely handicapped students, not just those labelled autistic. Major innovations in stimulus-control techniques and the recent data in support of the sensory reinforcement hypothesis are just two of the outcomes of this research having immediate applicability for classroom teachers.

In the final chapter, Vincent, Salisbury, Walter, Brown, Gruenewald, and Powers provide a vehicle for leaving the reader of this book with strong feelings of satisfaction and optimism for continuing the struggle that we know as advocacy for the educational rights of severely handicapped persons. From their work with infants and toddlers, the authors supply research data on the development of curricula in early childhood education based on an analysis of the successes and failures of handicapped students as they advance into kindergarten and later school years. The authors find, for example, that traditional instruments for screening admission to post preschool nonhandicapped programs fail to predict with any accuracy handicapped students' actual adaptation to these settings. Handicapped infant intervention programs must, by this analysis, carefully consider whether the curriculum employed at the preschool level is preparing the student to function effectively in a restrictive setting, with highly structured cues and consequences, or to function in a least restrictive, integrated setting, with a more unstructured curriculum that demands greater self-reliance.

We hope that this volume will provide the reader with a feeling for the significant new directions being taken in the education of severely handicapped students, and with an initial set of decision models and tactics with which to effect change. The research chapters were selected with an eye toward bolstering the teacher's confidence in implementing new approaches and in letting go of old assessment tools and outdated program models.

Assessment of severely handicapped students must be based on analysis of the requirements for an individual to succeed in both immediate and later environments, and decisions regarding the specific forms of objectives should be made only after a clear understanding has been reached of the function of the skill for the individual. The skills to be taught must be appropriate to performance in natural, integrated environments. Instructional methods must be closely monitored with data, and decisions for change of tactics to be applied must be contingent upon a present criterion of failure to progress. Teachers' objectives must maximize the student's overall progress toward independence and must be functional outside the classroom training setting. In short, the mandate for the next decade is to provide teachers with the tools with which to educate severely handicapped persons alongside their nonhandicapped peers on public school campuses and in the mainstream of the community. The model for this decade cannot continue to be an analysis based upon discrepancy with normal development, but must rather be an environmental analysis that promotes reciprocal adaptation: natural environments accommodate the special needs of severely handicapped students as students learn to perform successfully in those adapted environments.

REFERENCES

Haring, N., & Brown, L. (eds.). *Teaching the severely handicapped* (Vol. 1). New York: Grune and Stratton, 1976.

Sontag, E., Smith, J., & Certo, N., (eds.). *Educational programming for the severely and profoundly handicapped*. Reston, Virginia: Council for Exceptional Children, 1977.

Methods of Instruction for Severely Handicapped Students

Section I
ASSESSMENT AND THE ESTABLISHMENT OF OBJECTIVES

Chapter 1

Interdisciplinary Assessment and Programming for Multihandicapped Students

William A. Bricker and Philippa H. Campbell

> The schools are in serious trouble. And when the institution that is responsible for preparing the next generation for adulthood is in trouble, the whole country is in trouble.
>
> There is enough responsibility to go around. Too many parents, if they are still at home, send their children to school in the hope that the teachers will do for them what the parents have been unwilling or unable to do: love and discipline them, motivate and instruct them. Too many teachers and administrators have given up in the face of teaching the undisciplined and unmotivated. And too many children have given up because they are tired of waiting for adults to act like adults. I can't find any segment of our society which is satisfied with the state of your profession. Oh yes, I do find people who accept it, but the difference between acceptance and satisfaction is the difference between Egypt and the Promised Land: a grim resignation to things as they are versus a hope fulfilled (Jackson, 1977, p. 1).

The Reverend Jesse Jackson directed these statements to regular educators in an address at the 36th biennial conference of Phi Delta Kappa. Special educators would be in a position to share this criticism significantly except that special education has, through enactment of PL 94-142, the Education for All Handicapped Children Act, been singled out by Congress to become one of the first professions to be told how to behave professionally by a legislative body. The definition of an appropriate education for any handicapped student has largely been taken from the special education profession and placed in the hands of the court. Jackson (1977) also addressed this issue:

> I am aware that some states have legislated competency-based education. But I say to you, isn't it a shame you waited for the politicians to force it on you? Educators should be out in the front toning up their own profession. Your professional literature is filled with debate over competency-based education. I understand that debate is essential. It is a prerequisite for getting things right. But the debate doesn't seem to be how to do it, but rather if it can be done at all.

If professional educators are going to argue about whether it is possible to decide what students should know, and whether it is possible to find out if they know it, then you must not be surprised if the public's faith begins to waiver. To lay people, it translates as: 1) they don't know what to teach, and 2) even if they did, they don't know how to find out if the students have learned it (p. 18).

The recent professional debate (Burton & Hirshoren, 1979a, 1979b, versus Sontag, Certo, & Button, 1979) over the education of children with severe and profound handicaps is an illustration of Jackson's points. The essence of this debate concerns the extent to which severely handicapped students can benefit from programs that emphasize the "traditional goals of education." Burton and Hirshoren (1979a) believe that educators should not delude themselves into thinking that a zero reject system of public education will "ultimately lead to the development of productive, independent individuals." They define any attempts to teach severely handicapped students to talk or write as an "egocentric wish" performed only "in the interest of our own professional edification." Sontag, Certo, and Button (1979) have countered by referencing over 30 research and demonstration reports in language and reading instruction, to which Burton and Hirshoren (1979b) have the following rebuttal:

Our major error was perhaps in the use of the definition directed toward a more generic and heterogeneous population, that is, the severely and profoundly handicapped, rather than one more specific to the issue at point—the education of the severely and profoundly retarded. We concede that in a general population of handicapped children there will be those with sufficiently intact intellect to participate successfully at some level of academic instruction (p. 619).

Education for this population (whether labeled handicapped or retarded) has been *mandated* by law, but arguments continue to center on whether these students can be educated, rather than on the development of innovative practices that will guarantee the appropriate education granted by law. Furthermore, issues that center on curriculum content, teacher preparation, supportive services, and instructional settings can only be meaningfully resolved through a series of clear, empirical student demonstrations of achieved educational goals resulting from validated intervention procedures.

The purpose of this chapter is to look beyond the basic and isolated issues raised by Burton and Hirshoren (1979a, 1979b) and to illustrate useful assessment and programming strategies to educate severely handicapped students. These strategies are discussed using data derived from interdisciplinary programming that has been provided to a group of institutionalized, severely multihandicapped adolescents who have been participants in the Molly Stark demonstration project funded by the Bureau of Education for the Handicapped (Campbell, 1977b, 1978a, 1979a). The initial 17 students in this project resided in a nursing care facility and ranged in age from 11 to 21. All of the group had been placed in this long term convalescent setting for at least 6 years prior to the initiation of the project, and the majority had lived in some sort of residential institution since early childhood. None had ever received formal or systematic training through any sort of therapeutic or educational programming. The major focus of the project was to provide interdisciplinary expertise and adaptive/ training equipment necessary to enable this multihandicapped group of students to be transported to and educated in community environments. A second focus was to provide the degree of systematic and comprehensive intervention needed to enable residents to reside in less restrictive living environments within the community. The initial year of the project was devoted to implementing age-appropriate programming, which resulted in acquisition of functional skills required for adequate performance in community-based settings. During the second project year (as well as since that time), these 17 students were absorbed into local public educational programs. Each student's individual education plan was coordinated with a residential program plan which was carried out during nonschool hours by residential staff and trained volunteers.

Before the initiation of programming for these students, all were nonambulatory, nonverbal, incontinent, unable to dress or wash themselves, unable to engage in any sustained or appropriate activity, and, in all but two cases, unable to feed themselves. The multiple handicapping conditions present in combination with age, length of institutionalization, and absence of previous programming would lead many to question whether this group of students could benefit from provision of appropriate educational and related services. Such students may represent one of the least optimistic targets for comprehensive programming, but provide a basis for discussing issues in interdisciplinary assessment and programming in relation to both theory and data.

MULTIFACTORED ASSESSMENT

Most professionals would be hard pressed to define severely or profoundly handicapped people on any single behavioral dimension since many of these individuals have problems in more than one area of basic functioning. People with severe handicaps are likely to have difficulties in mobility, self-care, language, social interaction, health, or any combination of areas. To attempt to differentiate those in this extremely diverse group who are retarded from those who are otherwise severely handicapped is unwarranted. No theory of intellectual development assumes that development occurs in the absence of vision, hearing, movement abilities, and other means of human interaction with the environment. When numerous disabilities are present, no professionally trained person would assume automatic developmental progress in the absence of intervention by highly trained specialists working both in the classroom and in close coordination with the parents on an intensive and longitudinal basis. Thus, the starting point for the provision of special education and related services is a multiple dimension evaluation system performed by members of various disciplines as each becomes relevant to the problems of a given child. In Ohio, this process is called multifactored assessment and has some merit as a generic descriptor of the process.

The role and functioning of teams of professionals have been described in the literature with differentiation between team functions of evaluation and treatment programming (Haynes, 1976; McCormack & Goldman, 1979). Whether the process is labeled *multidisciplinary, interdisciplinary,* or *transdisciplinary,* the initial responsibility of team members is to utilize expertise in such a way as to determine the degree and types of dysfunction present in the individual being assessed and the resultant intervention needs to be met through placement and programming (Hart, 1977). Various distinctions have been made in the evaluation responsibilities of team members by pinpointing differences in the composition of the team, the length of time the evaluation process takes, and the methods by which individual expertise of various team members relates to the subsequent programming provided for the handicapped individual. Issues that are seldom mentioned in a discussion of the team approach are the training and level of expertise of each team member, the responsibilities of each member in relation to areas of functioning to be assessed, and the validity and reliability of the typical clinical assessment procedures used in the evaluation process.

The evaluation process used with the Molly Stark project students was designed to follow the exact specifications and implementation regulations of PL 94-142. All of these students were previously unserved educationally and therefore constituted the highest priority group in terms of implementation of the law. The team assessment provided multidisciplinary evaluations from two separate sources before the development of the individualized education program (IEP) and the initiation of programming. The purpose of these assessments was not simply to identify educational placement but to determine the long and short range objectives that could constitute the basic focus of each student's programming. The local Regional Resource Center diagnostic team, consisting of a psychologist, occupational therapist, speech-language therapist, and educator, generated a team evaluation with a coordinated set of recommendations for subsequent programming. The second team assessment was completed by project staff (occupational therapist, physical therapist, and special educator) supplemented by medical specialty, audiological, and speech-language assessments provided by members of the staff of the Children's Hospital Medical Center of Akron. Assessments were conducted over a period of several weeks and included those formal or informal observational measures and/or checklists or other testing aids judged to be appropriate by the individual conducting the evaluation. Those evaluations provided by the therapy and medical staffs of the Children's Hospital were supplemental to those required by law and would not have been provided to this group of students under standard practice. The evaluations made by the Regional Resource Center followed referral of these students to the local school district for completion of evaluation and placement procedures.

Each of the completed assessments contained recommendations for treatment, further evaluation, equipment utilization, and individualized educational or therapy activities. A total of 476 such recommendations were made of which only 79, or 16.5%, were duplicates. This was a surprising finding since each team contained some overlap in disciplines. For instance, the expectancy that the occupational therapist from the project staff would make recommendations similar to those of the occupational therapist on the Regional Resource Center team was not realized when recommendations were analyzed and compared. A total of 397 unique recommendations remained when duplicates were subtracted.

Further analysis of the recommendations is presented in Table 1. Initial categorizations were based on dividing recommendations into those that required follow-up from another specialist but were not related to specific programming for the student and those that directly related to ongoing therapeutic and educational interventions. Approximately one-third of all recommendations made did not relate to programming but required further medical evaluation or treatment (17.8%) or purchase of adaptive equipment of other types of devices (14.9%).

The remaining 267 recommendations (67.3%) involved programming. These recommendations were classified into either vague or specific programming goals. Recommendations that were so general as to be difficult to translate into relevant long or short term goals constituted 107 (27%) of the total number of recommendations made. Examples of vague recommendations included suggestions for "language" or "sensory stimulation," passive forms of positioning ("place side-lying"), contact with parents or parent surrogates, and opportunities for environmental stimulation, peer interaction, vocal play, assisted dressing, or other forms of general and passive activity.

Specific recommendations, on the other hand, were characterized as those activities that could be easily translated into appropriate programming by a

Table 1. List of recommendations made by the multidisciplinary evaluation teams

Recommendation	Number	Percent
Follow-up Recommendations		
Recommendations for medical treatment and/or further medical evaluation	71	17.8
Prosthetic equipment and other device recommendations	59	14.9
Total follow-up recommendations	130	32.7
Programming Recommendations		
General or vague program recommendations that were impossible to implement as written	107	27.0
Definite and specific recommendations but inappropriate for the designated student	41	10.4
Specific and appropriate recommendations that were attempted in programming	45	11.3
Specific and appropriate recommendations that were not attempted after 18 months of programming	74	18.6
Total programming recommendations	267	67.3
Total number of recommendations*	397	100.0

*Seventy-nine additional recommendations were made which were duplicates of the above for a total of 476 recommendations.

parent, teacher, residential care aide, or volunteer, as well as by the physical, occupational, and speech-language therapists. A recommendation to "provide sensory stimulation" was classified as vague and nonspecific, whereas one that specified provision of "visual stimulation through use of a brightly colored object, held at midline with the student lying on his back, and moved slowly from side to side to encourage visual tracking" was judged as definite and specific. No attempt was made to judge the relevance of the recommendations in terms of age appropriateness or relationship to future functional behavior of the student. The clarity of the recommendation formed the basis for classifications of general or vague and definite and specific. A total of 160 recommendations (40.3%) were classified as specific and were further judged as appropriate or inappropriate for the specific student for whom each definite programming recommendation was made.

An extremely conservative approach was taken in classifying these recommendations in terms of appropriateness. Inappropriate recommendations were those that were specific enough to be carried out with a given student but that could not possibly have an effect on the student's behavior because of physical, sensory, or motivational deficits. Recommendations classified as inappropriate included suggestions for specific training to teach the student to perform an activity that the student could already do. Examples of this category included a suggestion to use a head control training apparatus with a student who had excellent head control under minimal conditions of motivation and training wheelchair transfer with a sliding board for a student who was able to stand and walk with minimal assistance. Other recommendations that outlined instructional techniques that were inappropriate given basic sensory, physical, or motivational deficits of students were also classified as inappropriate. Teaching a totally blind child to communicate using a picture communication board and training spoken language skills to a totally deaf student through verbal imitation procedures were examples of recommendations judged as inappropriate. Issues of relevance or professional agreement about instructional activities were not used to make classifications of appropriateness, such that any recommendation that was clearly enough written to be part of an outlined intervention procedure and that was not precluded by basic deficits of the student was classified as appropriate.

One hundred nineteen recommendations (29.9%) were judged to be adequate to formulate long or short term goals and appropriate in relation to basic information known about each particular student. The number of specific and appropriate recommendations made for each student ranged from 2 to 14. However, only 45 of all programming recommendations were attempted at any level of programming during the 18 months of intervention that followed the multidisciplinary evaluations. The reasons for this low rate of implementation (11.3%) are not fully clear. In several instances, recommendations were not implemented because more appropriate objectives were formulated by members of the project multidisciplinary team after months of working with a student. For example, a goal of walking long distances with a walker and extensive assistive devices was replaced with training a severely physically handicapped student to operate an electric wheelchair. In other instances, the team members were unable to achieve a necessary prerequisite to implementation of the recommended activity. Designing and identifying a toilet chair for a 20-year-old severely physically disabled young woman that would enable her to be toilet trained has still not occurred despite prolonged attempts by team members to find one and thereby solve this problem. However, in most instances, many of the recommendations made, while not classifiable as inappropriate, were still not within the behavioral range of reaction of many students even after 18 months of programming. This observation is substantiated by the fact that the proportion of implemented recommendations on a student by student basis correlated with the severity of handicap with a value of $r = -0.498$ ($P < 0.05$). Thus, the greater the degree of handicap, the fewer the number of programs implemented.

Several other interesting points emerged from this analysis of the multidisciplinary evaluations. This group of students resided in a medical facility; however, few had ever been evaluated by medical specialists and none had received a complete medical diagnostic work-up within the preceding 5 years. The students in this group represent a national population of individuals with multiple handicaps who are often maintained in custodial living facilities. However, the medical services provided in most custodial facilities are geared toward providing day to day health care rather than information from diagnostic specialists that could be related to the educational and therapeutic programming of these students. The medical specialty evaluations provided for the Molly Stark project students resulted in critical programming information concerning the nature of vision, hearing, and other sensory systems deficits, the prescription of medication, and possible surgical procedures to correct a variety of problems demonstrated by these students. The neurology evaluations identified several students who, although having received seizure medication for a number of years, had normal EEG patterns. Eight students were diagnosed as blind from either optic nerve atrophy or cataracts, in opposition to previous medical records that indicated "possible blindness" for only two of the students. Only one student had been previously noted as "possibly deaf," although audiological assessments (despite not being fully complete because of lack of response-based testing) of the total group identified 12 students with sensorineural, conductive, or mixed hearing losses. Legal requirements are unclear for assessment of handicapped students with respect to the collection of medical evaluative information, an essential component to appropriate programming. However, these results would indicate that physicians can provide information that is not only useful but essential to programming efforts with multihandicapped students and should, therefore, become an integral part of the education mandate.

A related point is that, although all students received a full medical diagnostic work-up independent of recommendations for assessment from the two diagnostic teams, the recommendations suggested a complete medical assessment for only one student. Individual types of medical follow-through were suggested for other students. However, these individual specialty recommendations were made only where the student showed clear evidence of problems in relation to orthopedics, neurology, vision, or hearing. For example, ophthalmological and audiological examinations were recommended for the students with previously suspected vision and hearing problems but not for the other students in the group. Orthopedic evaluations were recommended for those students whose deformities were so severe as to be observable by even an untrained individual but not for the students with slight or visually undetectable deformities or abnormal patterns of movement. Clearly, *all* multihandicapped students should have a complete medical diagnostic work-up; to rely on recommendations from the basic multidisciplinary team may be an insufficient means of meeting the educational needs of these students.

Cost of the total process of assessment by project staff, the Regional Resource Center, and the medical and related therapy staff was conservatively estimated at approximately $1,500 per student, not including inpatient admission costs. Such costs can be readily justified when tests or assessments that require no active participation on the part of the student (such as laboratory tests, passive audiometry, and structural vision assessment) constitute the methods used for assessment. However, accurate assessment of current levels of functioning with this sample of severely handicapped students was not possible in the initial period of the project because of problems of motivation and behavioral control. Perhaps the fact that programming recommendations with this group of students were limited to only 29.9% of all recommendations is understandable in the absence of controlled and motivated responses from these students. The fact that only 11.3% of those recommendations were implementable in programming begins to illustrate major deficiencies with current conceptualizations of the role and functioning of multiple-discipline teams within educational settings and in particular in relation to cost-outcome factors.

The limitations of outcome of the multifactored evaluation did not derive from either naiveté or lack of effort on the part of the two assessment teams. The therapists used traditional clinical observational approaches to assess functioning levels and degrees of dysfunction in such areas as motor processes, self-care, response to sensory stimulation, oral-motor responding, and vocal processes as well as in receptive language. Information included in the initial assessment was based on observational probes over varying lengths of time and in a variety of circumstances or from interviews with the residential care staff. Methods of eating and drinking were assessed for each student during two or more meals. Bathing was observed and probed relative to the degree of contribution to the task that could be made by the student. Aspects of grooming, dressing, and mobility were observed under a variety of motivating conditions. The various reflexes that relate to motor dysfunction as well as muscle strength and active and passive range of motion were evaluated. However, none of the members of the assessment teams attempted to establish test-retest reliabilities even though most of the behavioral aspects being evaluated were observed on two or more occasions. The outcomes were a series of written reports that described each student and included the recommendations outlined above.

Standardized testing was attempted using such instruments as the Columbia Mental Maturity Test, the Peabody Picture Vocabulary Test, the Bayley Scales of Infant Development, the Denver Developmental Screening Test, the Balthazar Scales, and the Vulpe Assessment Battery. Developmental checklists deemed most relevant to this group of students included the TARC (Sailor & Mix, 1975), the Pennsylvania Training Model Assessment guide (Somerton & Turner, 1975), a system of rating developmental pinpoints (Cohen, Gross, & Haring, 1976), and the Behavior Characteristics Profile (Vort, 1973). All of this was done over a period of 2 months and with only 17 students. The results were confused and confusing due to the confounding of motivational problems and interference of learned forms of institutional, stereotyped behavior. The effort directed toward deriving meaningful assessment results may have been better spent in teaching and training the students rather than in such extensive and ultimately meaningless testing. One is hard pressed to advocate substantial financial resources for services that yield such limited results.

INDEX OF QUALIFICATION FOR SPECIALIZED SERVICES

An alternative to conventional forms of multidisciplinary assessment was devised in response to the limited and nonfunctional results obtained with the Molly Stark project students (Campbell & Bricker, 1979). This alternative was based on observations of the students who, under their long and untutored residence in an institution, were out of the realm of immediate behavior control and evidenced such severe forms of stereotyped behavior that standard forms of assessment were meaningless. A list of 19 dimensions along which behavior could vary and according to which behavior could be directly influenced through education and therapeutic intervention was formulated. These dimensions, presented in Table 2, were selected to represent the "bedrock" of subsequent behavioral development. For example, one of the dimensions selected for assessment, *surviving and thriving,* was in the medical realm. To assess the first aspect of this dimension, the question being asked by the various medical specialists who examined the Molly Stark students was whether the student had an active disease process that could be treated medically. Was there a degenerative or progressive disease process that might be influenced through medical treatment? If so, then the status of an individual student could be altered through medical treatment. The latter aspect of *thriving* was intended to cover such factors as nutrition, seizure control, or activity level relative to the medical condition of the student. Was the dosage level used in the control of seizures necessary or, if necessary, so high that behavior was impaired? Was the diet received by the student effective from a nutritional standpoint? Would greater amounts of movement or exercise be ap-

Table 2. Dimensions included in the index of qualification for specialized services

---

1. *Surviving and Thriving:* This initial dimension is rated by the physician and attempts to summarize the health of the individual in terms of disease processes, medication status, growth, and nutrition.
2. *Tonicity:* The degree of tension in the body musculature provides the basis for all movement. Deviations in tone, ranging from hypotonicity to hypertonicity, are rated on this dimension and derived from physical and/or occupational therapy evaluations.
3. *Visual Acuity:* Scale values on this dimension are derived from ophthalmological examination and relate to abnormalities in the visual structures as well as overall measures of visual acuity.
4. *Auditory Ability:* Abnormalities in the aural structures and disease processes are rated on this dimension from the ear-nose-throat specialist. Auditory acuity and presence of conductive, sensorineural, and mixed hearing losses identified through audiological examination are also represented on this dimension.
5. *Motor Quantity:* The amount of movement that is possible in relation to both automatic and goal-directed (voluntary) movements is rated on this dimension by the physical and/or occupational therapist. Deviations in the amount of movement, ranging from excessive movement to absence of movement, are represented on this dimension.
6. *Motor Quality:* Movement occurs in patterns made up of various components that are sequenced to produce functional automatic and goal-directed movement. Physical and/or occupational therapy evaluations provide the basis for rating the quality of the patterns produced both automatically and voluntarily.
7. *Oral-Motor/Feeding:* Tone and movement quantity and quality are rated by the occupational or speech-language therapist as those dimensions relate to the muscles of the head, neck, and mouth. Problems with food or liquid intake are represented as deviations.
8. *Oral-Motor/Vocalization:* The range of nonspeech and speech vocalization may be limited by problems with tone, movement quantity, and quality in the oral structures. The speech-language therapist rates deviations ranging from absence of vocalization to excessive (stereotypic) vocalizations.
9. *Mobility:* The extent to which an individual moves from location to location in the environment is related not only to the neuromotor dimensions but also to motivational conditions. This dimension rates the degree of mobility present regardless of the specific form that the mobility takes.
10. *Manipulation:* The competence of the hand in interacting with objects can range from basic contact with an object to very complex assemblies. Both motor skill and motivational conditions intersect for the manipulative function to occur. Deviations ranging from lack of grasp through the sometimes very complex manipulation schemes present in stereotypic behavior are rated by the occupational therapist or special educator.
11. *Consequence Preference:* The extent to which a hierarchy of potentially reinforcing events can be empirically defined for an individual is rated by the psychologist or special educator. The range of reaction reflected is from limited (or lack of) preference for any objects, foods, or activities through fixation on a single class of reinforcing events.
12. *Primary Circular Reactions:* A reinforcer can be operationally defined as a consequence that increases the rate of behavior for which that consequence is provided. Piaget has described this condition as a temporary increase in behavior that produces interesting consequences. The extent to which the interesting consequences derived from the preceding dimension can be used to increase behavior is rated by the psychologist or special educator.
13. *Secondary Circular Reactions:* When a particular set of events operates repeatedly as the basis for a particular response, the child is said to be secondary circular reactive (Piagetian) or under the control of antecedent conditions.

Continued

Table 2.—*continued*

14. *Social Responsiveness:* The degree of interest that the handicapped person shows toward his parents, caregivers, and other individuals is rated by the special educator on a range from limited or absence of social responding to high interest in a variety of persons.
15. *Compliance:* The "willingness" of an individual to respond to instruction, such as following directions, making appropriate responses to environmental cues, or allowing physical guidance, is rated by the special educator.
16. *Memory:* There is no reference to this process in the majority of writings about education and training of severely handicapped persons. However, many students who have learned a task need to be retaught after several days without practice. The maintenance of behavior over time is rated by the psychologist or special educator.
17. *Production of Intentional Chains:* When single components of behavior are linked together in order to produce a desired outcome, an inference can be made that the behavior is intentional. The degree of intentionality demonstrated through participation in classroom or programming activities is rated by the educator or psychologist.
18. *Motor Imitation:* The degree of imitation that a student demonstrates is critical both to the selection of intervention strategies and to rapid learning of new skills. Competence in imitation of motor actions allows skills to be taught through demonstration without extensive shaping through physical guidance. The student's competence in imitation of motor actions on the basis of demonstration only is rated.
19. *Verbal Imitation:* This dimension is an extension of the motor imitative dimension in that the student's skill at reproducing verbalizations from a model is rated by the educator or speech-language specialist.

propriate or harmful for a given student? These and other questions established a biological status indicator apart from survival that could be influenced through revised treatment or care and that would have a direct effect on the extent to which the student could benefit from other forms of therapy and special education. This first dimension is generally outside the education mandate for handicapped students but set the basis for other aspects of the system.

Neuromotor Dimensions

Several dimensions were defined to represent the basic components of movement and neuromotor functioning and their relationship to other forms of behavior. The most basic dimension is *tonicity* in that the degree of tension in the muscles of the body underlies the production of all movement. More important is that when tone deviates from "normal," movement of the body is restricted or confined to limited and stereotypic ways of interacting with the environment. Prolonged tone deviations may also result in permanent tightness in individual muscles or groups of muscles, which can produce orthopedic deformities. These deformities in turn produce even greater limitations of movement.

Movement is a component of all forms of responding to the environment. Basic motor movements that are typically automatic rather than goal directed, or voluntary, maintain the body parts in alignment with gravity and maintain balance in relationship to changing gravity. Behavior such as head lifting is the result of muscle groups working together automatically to right the body in space. The body musculature works in concert rather than as isolated muscle movement to maintain balance in various positions against gravity. Being able to maintain a sitting position or to stand independently without support is the result of automatic movements that occur to maintain balance in these positions. When muscle tone is abnormal, the body musculature may be prevented from producing the patterns of movement that automatically produce the righting and balancing functions. Balance may not be maintained not because the response is not within the student's repertoire but because the response is blocked (or prevented) because of abnormal muscle tone. Instituting intervention procedures that normalize tone as much as possible and then maintain that normalized tone is an essential prerequisite to training a student to perform automatic movements.

Tone also underlies production of goal-directed movements. However, goal-directed movements are typically voluntary (at least in the acquisition stage) and, as such, are more closely related to conditions of motivation and basic sensory intactness than are the more automatic response movements. In other words, sensory deficits in vision or hearing do not influence the production of automatic movements where antecedents are more internal than external. (*Visual acuity* and *hearing ability,* although involved in neuromotor functioning, are therefore discussed with regard to application of the Index in relation to the dimensions of learning.) To seek an object or food or a specific location within a room relies more heavily on motivational states and sensory intactness than does the maintenance of balance against gravity. However, a student may be motivated to perform a goal-directed activity, such as feeding himself or herself or walking or reaching and grasping a particular object, but may be prevented from performing the necessary movement response as a result of tonal deviations that act to block the production of those movements. Normalizing tone becomes an antecedent to performing the required movement to obtain the desired consequence. In this sense, without procedures that both normalize tone and maintain normalized tone over time, the desired movement response cannot be considered to be within the behavioral repertoire of the student.

Muscle tone is not a static entity but rather a dimension that changes in response to environmental events. These events can be contrived (as in therapeutic intervention techniques) or can be spontaneous changes in reaction to ongoing events within the student's environment. The changes in muscle tone that occur can act to increase or decrease tonal deviations. Thus, a student who is very stiff may be made less so through appropriate interventions or may be made more stiff when positioned incorrectly or in response to being talked to suddenly or when attempting to produce a difficult movement.

Both the quantity and the quality of movement patterns are directly related to tone. A student whose muscle tone is very low may have difficulty moving in any way against gravity. The resultant movement patterns will be very low in *motor quantity* since movement will be restricted to only those specific movements that are possible with gravity eliminated. A student with very high muscle tone (spasticity or hypertonicity) may also have very few possible movements due to the blocks to movement that result from severe hypertonicity. Both of these students will have limited movement, but the reasons for the limitations are sufficiently different to warrant different forms of intervention procedures. *Motor quality* is related to the specific components of a movement pattern that can be performed by a student under varying conditions. For instance, a student with athetoid or uncontrolled movements may be successful in not falling when balance is disturbed but may use extremely inefficient and disorganized ways of preventing falling. The same student may, in fact, manage to get the spoon into the mouth but may require many attempts and many arm movements before the spoon actually reaches the mouth. In both of these instances, the quality of movement is atypical and inefficient.

Movement of the muscles in the mouth was represented as two separate dimensions, although the dimensions of tonicity, motor quality, and motor quantity are incorporated in *oral-motor/feeding* and *oral-motor/vocalization*. These three basic dimensions of movement influence the more specific and detailed movements required to eat and to vocalize or speak. However, the use of the oral muscles for various activities is also influenced by conditions of motivation and prelanguage abilities which must be taken into consideration when planning appropriate intervention strategies. There is no basis for an assumption that normalizing tone in the general body musculature will be sufficient to enable a student to eat more efficiently or to vocalize or speak. Therefore, these dimensions were included not only to represent two important programming targets but also to reflect the differences in specificity and influence of other dimensions of behavior.

Two final dimensions were included in the neuromotor group. These are *mobility* and *manipulation*. These dimensions were differentiated as being important prerequisite developments to other types of behavior responding and as forming the bridge between automatic–goal-directed movement and neuromotor and motivational groupings. Tone and motor quality and quantity must be sufficiently intact for a student to become mobile in his or her environment— regardless of the form which that mobility takes. However, the use of sufficient movements for true mobility requires motivation to move from one location to another in the environment. A similar relationship holds for manipulative abilities. Both the motivation to manipulate and the ability to move must be present for any contact between the hand and an object to occur. Thus, the function of mobility is to move from one place to another even though the form of that mobility may range from rolling to running or to such situations as operating an electric wheelchair. The function of manipulation is to bring the hand into contact with an object, an action that can range from basic swiping movements to very fine and precise movements of the hand such as those required in detailed assembly tasks. Neither of these dimensions attempts to rate the forms of mobility or manipulation demonstrated by a handicapped student but rather seeks to assess the extent to which these dimensions are present in any form in the repertoire of the student.

Dimensions of Motivation

Motivation is a term that is used so often and in such a loose manner that in many circumstances it has no operational meaning. At the simplest level of description, the child can be assumed to be motivated to do whatever the child happens to be doing at that moment. In an educational context, when a child is directed to make a particular movement or evidence a given skill, the issue of motivation comes in at the point where the child can perform the required response but does not, as opposed to a problem of learning in which the child cannot perform the required response. To differentiate these two "states of being" with a severely handicapped student, the process is started by establishing a hierarchy of consequence preferences. Such preferences can be inferred from the various probabilities of freely emitted response forms across time using the principle established by Premack (1965).

A student who spends the bulk of available free time engaged in stereotypic forms of behavior, such as rocking, repetitive object flipping, hand or light gazing, or string twirling, can be assumed to be highly motivated through these forms of behavior. However, a student who immediately ceases the stereotypes in order to receive a bite of food, a drink, or simply to look at some new social event in another part of the room has a broader range of motivated behavior and a substantially larger hierarchy of consequence preferences. Among severely handicapped students, the major problems are seen with students who do not engage in much of any type of behavior and who do not respond easily or quickly to food, fluids, music, or any other of a range of stimulating events. A second problem area is the student who appears fixated on a specific form of stimulation. The one who will not cease a stereotypic form of behavior regardless of outside stimulation or one who looks only for edibles provides a fixed and very narrow range of consequence preferences. These two extremes set the boundaries of the dimension of *consequence preference*.

Once a hierarchy of consequence preference has been established, the next step is to determine whether the consequences can be used to increase the rate or probability of specific responses upon which they are made contingent. This is a standard procedure in behavioral technology to establish the validity of a particular consequence as a positive reinforcer. However, among severely handicapped persons, several problems are apparent. The first is that reinforcement is defined operationally in that it is an event that does alter the rate or probability of behavior that it follows closely in time. If such changes do not occur, then the consequence is not a positive reinforcer.

With Molly Stark project students, a number of instances have been observed in which an event that is high on the list of consequence preferences will not function as a positive reinforcer. For example, in giving a student a preferred corn curl immediately following the release of a block into a cup, the student will eat the item, but the rate of block dropping does not accelerate as predicted. On the other hand, the same student has learned to quickly lift a cup in order to obtain an edible hidden underneath it. Thus, the same consequence provided alternately in two different tasks operates as a positive reinforcer in one task but not in the other during the same relative period of time. Another example of this process is illustrated by a student who has a very high rate of a stereotypic behavior, pursing the lips and emitting a sucking response at a rate of 20 times a minute. Following the Premack principle, if sucking is prevented for periods of time, then sucking should become a positive reinforcer for some other forms of behavior that can be followed immediately with allowable sucking. This was tried with the student, using vocalizations as the response to be followed immediately with allowable sucking. Over a large number of trials during several sessions there was no increase in the rate of vocalization.

The initial designation that was to be used for this dimension was "responsiveness to positive reinforcement." However, the behavior of the students indicated the difficulty of this designation since positive reinforcement always works by definition. If a consequence fails to function in an accelerating manner, then it is not a positive reinforcer. If no acceleration is demonstrated with a given student, then the assumption is made to continue the search for reinforcers. If a given consequence functions in some circumstances to produce acceleration, but not in others, then it is a positive reinforcer in only those circumstances where it does accelerate behavior.

To alleviate these problems, a decision was made to adopt another term to represent this state of affairs. Piaget described several stages of sensorimotor development (Piaget, 1952), the second of which was called the stage of *primary circular reactions*. In that stage, a child (actually, infants between the ages of 1 and 4 months using Piaget's age guidelines) is observed to repeat a form of behavior that produces "interesting" consequences. Piaget indicates that such reactions are temporary in that they must be rediscovered during subsequent encounters with the interesting consequence. To say that a student is primary circular reactive is to imply that a number of response-consequence interactions resulting in acceleration of behavior have been observed, although this does not imply that the child is totally responsive to positive reinforcement. The difference is subtle and not readily apparent to those trained in behaviorism. The selection of a term such as *primary circular reactive* implies that conditions have been found under which behavior can be changed as a function of consequences and their relative frequency based on a variety of consequences can indicate their dimensionalized value. A related term, but one that is even less operational than *primary circular reactive,* is *contingency awareness* (Watson & Ramey, 1972), which implies knowledge on the part of an infant concerning a casual relationship between a response and a consequence. While not acceptable to most behaviorists, this implication seems to apply to the Molly Stark student who has learned to lift a cup to obtain a corn curl but has not learned to drop a block into a cup to get the same outcome. The first situation is causal and the second is not, without the interaction of a social agent.

Dimensions of *social responsiveness* and *compliance* were also assessed in the motivational domain.

Dimensions of Learning and Language Prerequisites

At the next level of behavioral organization, relative to motivation, is a dimension that has been called *secondary circular reactions,* based on Piaget's third stage of sensorimotor development. In this stage, objects are used differentially from session to session without any relearning as implied in primary circular reactions. For example, a rattle is picked up by the older infant and shaken while a pacifier is taken immediately to the mouth. In this situation, motivation is linked to antecedent properties of the situation itself. Skinner (1969) has characterized this situation as the "three-term contingency of reinforcement," which includes a specification of "(1) the occasion upon which a response occurs, (2) the response itself, and (3) the reinforcing consequences" (p. 7). Where the occasion is defined and repeatedly operates as the basis for a predictable form of behavior, then the child is said to be under the control of the antecedent conditions. This is a secondary circular reaction. The difference between the behavioral term *three-term contingency of reinforcement* or an operant and Piaget's use of *secondary circular reactions* is in the assumption of control by generic, rather than specific, properties of the behavioral "occasion." In a secondary circular reaction, many different stimuli that share some particular group of properties may all operate as an effective occasion for a particular form of behavior. The results of this process form "schemes," in the language of Piaget, as in schemes of sitting, pushing, eating, drinking, throwing, kicking, climbing, and so on. Different objects are "sittable" and each may require a modification in the act or process of sitting, but they are a unified organization of antecedents in relation to response forms at a generic or generalized level. Thus, a student who is secondary circular reactive is "capable of generalizations" or "able to form concepts at a functional, although nonverbal, level" (Piaget, 1952).

Several other dimensions of learning were used with this group of students, including *memory, motor imitation,* and *verbal imitation,* which are readily understood among psychologists and teachers who have read aspects of the experimental and behavior analysis literature that pertain to handicapped students. The dimension that needs additional clarification is the one entitled *production of intentional chains.* The term *intention* is evasive because it can be used in a mentalistic sense by referring to an unobservable process that takes place somewhere in the nervous system. However, relative to the education of severely handicapped persons, it refers to an outcome of relatively specific forms of training. For instance, looking for bread in a grocery store in order to match a word or a picture to a loaf of bread on the grocery list is an example of an intentional chain. This operation entails several different schemes that must be sequenced in a flexible manner. One scheme relates to seeking and getting an empty grocery cart. A second scheme involves pushing it up and down the store aisles. A third scheme involves tracking and scanning the items on the shelves until a match to the word or picture is found. Finding an empty cart is discriminated from finding any cart (one that may be in use by another person, for example), and pushing it in a systematic pattern is a higher order scheme than simply pushing it. Tracking, scanning, and matching are all additional examples of secondary circular reactions or schemes that are now chained into a single sequence.

Piaget claims, and the data from Molly Stark students substantiate, the fact that teaching a student to chain schemes in a flexible manner is somewhat different and more difficult than teaching the schemes themselves. An example from one of the students was given by the case where the student had to ring a bell to have a teacher bring over a language board which was then used by the student to signal some activity, such as having a drink or going to the bathroom. Planning and flexibility in the selection of schemes that are relevant to the plan are essential components of use of intentional chains. In another example, wanting something sweet that is not now visible chains into systematic searching (object permanence scheme), which may or may not include the scheme of climbing depending on the height at which sweets might be found, and then matching objects through a series of discriminations in order to match the initial intention. Thus, edibles are discriminated from nonedibles and sweet edibles are discriminated from nonsweet edibles. This dimension is viewed as pivotal in the language prerequisites since functional language can be best understood as a verbal or symbolic equivalent of an intentional chain of behavior.

Taken together, the Index of Qualification for Specialized Services involved only those 19 dimensions that were deemed relevant to the group in the Molly Stark project. Other dimensions such as receptive language (nouns, verbs, adjectives, or other aspects of language), as well as expressive forms of language, aspects of quantity, time, conversational language, reading and writing, were beyond the competencies of these students.

APPLICATION OF THE INDEX

Each student was rated on each of the 19 dimensions using a 5-point scale where a scale point value approximated 1 standard deviation. A point value of 1 was used to indicate that the performance or behavior on that dimension was in the normal range relative to either an age norm (as in verbal imitation), or a more general scale of human performance (as in tonicity). In tonicity, there is not a condition that would be known as "3-year-old normal tone" but, rather, a more general requirement of degree of tension in the motor process relative to a particular movement. A value of 2 was used to specify a mild deviation from the norm, or standard, for which a relatively small amount of specialized intervention might be necessary to assist in making progress on this and on related dimensions. A value of 3 was used to scale moderate degrees of deviation, indicating placement from 1½ to 2½ standard deviations from the norm. A value of 4 was assigned to severe degrees of deviation that would have a value and a frequency of incidence in a general population of children of that associated with an average of 3 standard deviations from the mean level of performance on that dimension. A value of 5 was used to indicate profound handicap in terms of being 4 or more standard deviations from the average or norm on that dimension.

Each of the students was rated independently on each dimension by two raters who had been in contact with the students for several months and who had reviewed all medical, psychological, educational, and therapy evaluations. Reliability of the ratings was established by counting the number of identical scores across the 17 students in each dimension. The percentage of agreement ranged from 65 (11 of 17 values were identical) on the dimension of motor quantity to 94 (16 of 17 values in agreement) for visual acuity. The average value was 88% agreement for the 19 dimensions.

The scale values for each student on each dimension are represented in Table 3 and are "negotiated" scores in the sense that an agreement was reached through discussion at points where scale values differed. The means and standard deviations of the column indicate the relative degree of difficulty presented in the individual dimension. For example, on thriving, four of the students were scaled as having severe or profound difficulties. These are the students for whom careful incorporation of medical intervention into home and school programming was clearly indicated. However, the other three students did not have scores as significantly discrepant in thriving and were not in need of the degree of medical care and surveillance provided by their current place of residence. Nine of the students were determined to be as healthy as anyone else their age and required, at most, minimal assistance in mobility and care that could be provided by a parent surrogate.

The means and standard deviations of the rows in Table 3 describe the number and degree of problems that are of a severe nature for each student and the extent to which the student demonstrates isolated or a more general range of problems. All but three of the students were scaled as having severe or profound problems on 10 or more of the 19 dimensions, and, of the 323 total ratings, 200, or 62%, of those ratings were scaled in the severe or profound ranges. The remaining three students, students P, D, and N in Table 3, were rated as having severe/profound problems on one, four, and eight dimensions, respectively. Although one student in the Molly Stark group had only one area of severe handicap, if the assessment were extended to include language, quantitative skills, and more complex forms of social development, this student would be rated as severely/profoundly discrepant on these more complex forms of behavior as a result of the absence of a measureable receptive language and minimal verbal imitation skill. Thus, utilization of the scale can signal severe problems in any dimension of behavior in which special education or therapeutic interventions are required. The number of dimensions on which severe/profound ratings were made dictates both the range and the relative need for specialized services for the students in this group.

Table 3. Ratings for each student on each dimension

Student	Thriving	Auditory Ability	Visual Acuity	Tonicity	Motor Quantity	Motor Quality	Manipulation	Oral-Motor/ Feeding	Oral-Motor/ Vocalization	Consequence Preference	Primary Circular Reactions	Mobility	Secondary Circular Reactions	Social Responsiveness	Compliance	Memory	Production of Intentional Chains	Motor Imitation	Verbal Imitation	Mean	Standard deviation	Number of 4 and 5 ratings
A	1	3	5	4	3	3	3	3	2	4	4	5	4	5	4	5	5	3	3	3.63	1.15	10
B	1	2	3	2	4	2	2	4	4	5	3	2	5	4	4	5	5	5	5	3.52	1.35	11
C	1	4	5	2	3	3	2	3	3	4	3	3	5	5	5	5	5	5	5	3.74	1.28	10
D	1	2	4	4	3	4	3	4	3	1	2	4	2	1	2	1	2	2	3	2.37	1.12	4
E	1	5	1	3	3	4	4	3	5	5	4	3	5	5	5	5	5	5	5	4.42	1.57	14
F	1	3	4	4	4	4	4	4	4	4	3	4	5	5	5	5	5	5	5	3.94	1.22	15
G	5	2	5	4	5	5	5	4	3	3	5	5	5	5	5	5	5	5	5	4.36	0.96	15
H	3	2	5	5	4	4	4	5	5	3	3	5	5	2	3	3	5	5	5	4.21	0.92	15
I	4	1	5	4	4	5	5	3	2	3	5	5	5	3	5	5	5	5	4	4.26	1.24	14
J	4	5	5	4	5	4	4	4	4	3	3	5	4	3	3	3	5	4	4	3.79	0.98	11
K	3	5	5	4	4	4	5	5	5	5	4	5	5	5	5	5	5	5	5	4.53	0.61	18
L	3	3	4	3	3	3	3	5	4	5	5	5	5	4	5	5	5	5	5	4.53	0.77	16
M	1	5	3	3	4	3	4	2	5	4	3	3	4	4	5	4	3	4	5	3.79	1.18	11
N	1	2	2	3	3	3	3	2	4	3	3	3	5	5	5	5	4	4	5	3.26	1.19	8
O	4	2	2	5	4	4	4	3	3	3	3	5	5	3	4	5	4	5	4	3.79	0.98	12
P	1	1	1	3	3	3	3	2	2	3	2	3/2	4	2	3	3	3	3	3	2.53	0.84	1
Q	2	2	5	3	4	4	4	4	4	3	2	5	5	5	3	3	3	5	3	4.26	1.04	15
Mean	2.18	2.70	3.47	3.52	4.35	3.65	4.18	3.94	4.35	3.70	3.88	4.12	4.59	4.29	4.35	4.47	4.53	4.41	4.53			
S.D.	1.42	1.35	1.66	0.87	2.34	0.78	2.21	1.82	2.91	1.10	1.32	1.05	0.79	1.57	0.93	1.12	0.69	0.94	0.80			

117701

A review of the visual and auditory variables represented in Table 3 indicates that 13 of the 17 students had no more than a mild problem in hearing. However, this is a deceptive finding in that only three of these students have been through a response-based audiometric procedure using pure tone stimuli and only two of the three gave reliable indices of being under the control of pure tone at the level of approximately 15 decibels. Assessment of the other 14 students was done entirely through passive audiometric procedures such as tympanic bridge audiometry and visual inspection. Only one of the two students who had been through and passed the response-based audiological assessment gave reliable responses on a receptive vocabulary task. However, this student could be readily confused by such contrasts as "Bill" and "bell," "horse" and "house," "Bev" and "give," and other minimally distinct phonological contrasts. The point is that when these students are moved into learning domains, such as receptive language training, that require precise rather than gross auditory discriminations, significant hearing losses will become more apparent.

The same caution would operate in the area of vision, which again is not a critical factor in the types of tasks currently being used in the education of these students, but will be when fine-grained discriminations are required. Eleven of the students have severe to profound problems in the areas of vision or hearing, with 5 of the 11 being both hard of hearing and partially sighted or blind (ratings of 3 or lower). However, none wears glasses or hearing aids. Thus, the available methods for assessing sensory processes of these students may be inadequate, and accurate outcomes derived from educational data have yet to provide indices of visual or auditory acuity.

As indicated earlier, the remainder of the dimensions can be distributed across three major domains of behavior, including neuromotor processes, motivation, and learning processes. The neuromotor processes provide the first set, including tonicity, motor quantity, motor quality, manipulation, oral-motor/feeding, oral-motor/vocalization, and mobility. One means for looking at the relationship among these dimensions is through an intercorrelation matrix. Table 4 presents the Pearson product-moment correlation coefficients and the average intercorrelation of each dimension with every other dimension. Only the oral-motor/vocalization dimension has no significant correlation with any of the other dimensions and has an average value of only $r = 0.220$. Manipulation has four of six correlations that are statistically reliable ($P < 0.05$) and an average intercorrelation of $r = 0.58$. Motor quality and mobility tend to have approximately equal correlations with manipulation, with the possible conclusion that each is measuring the same process.

The second set of dimensions pertains to aspects of motivation and learning and includes consequence preference, primary circular reactions, production of intentional chains, social responsiveness, and compliance, as well as secondary circular reactions and memory (also considered in the third domain of dimensions). The intercorrelation matrix of the scaled values for these dimensions is contained in Table 5. Examination of the table indicates a high degree of inter-

Table 4. Intercorrelation matrix of the dimensions related to motor process

	Motor Quantity	Motor Quality	Manipulation	Oral-Motor/Feeding	Oral-Motor/ Vocalization	Mobility	Average intercorrelation
Tonicity	0.451	0.653*	0.594*	0.327	−0.15	0.742*	0.411
Motor Quantity	—	0.431	0.571*	0.479*	0.06	0.518*	0.409
Motor Quality		—	0.800*	0.548*	0.251	0.657*	0.557
Manipulation			—	0.438	0.379	0.683*	0.578
Oral-Motor/Feeding				—	0.305	0.453	0.425
Oral-Motor/Vocalization					—	−0.177	0.220
Mobility						—	0.538

*P < 0.05.

correlation among the dimensions, which is produced in part by the heterogeneity of this particular group in combination with the large number of students who have an assigned scale value of 5 on these dimensions. At this point in their educational program, the students who have shown more complex forms of behavior did so almost across the board, while those who failed to respond adequately on one dimension also failed to respond to the other dimensions of this group. Consequence preference, secondary circular reactions, and memory have the highest average intercorrelation values. However, the overall matrix tends to be hierarchical in structure, indicating that the left–right and top–bottom progression demonstrates an increasing level of behavioral difficulty in the order of the scales. This is consistent with the mean values for each of the dimensions presented in Table 3.

The final set of dimensions provides analysis of those aspects of behavior and learning processes that are frequently judged to be prerequisite to language acquisition. These dimensions are represented in Table 6 and include auditory ability, visual acuity, manipulation, oral-motor/vocalization, secondary circular reactions, social responsiveness, memory, and motor imitation. The intercorrelation matrix provides a bridge with the other two sets of dimensions by having some overlapping dimensional content. For example, manipulation has the highest average intercorrelation value among the motor items (Table 4), but has no statistically reliable correlation with this set of prelanguage dimensions. However, the high intercorrelation values for secondary circular reactions and memory indicate a great deal of overlap with the motivation and learning related domains, which is not totally unexpected with this group of students. The correlation of oral-motor/vocalization with motor imitation provides the first basis for a statistically reliable relationship of the oral-motor dimension with any of the other dimensions.

Table 5. Intercorrelation matrix of dimensions related to motivation

	Primary Circular Reactions	Secondary Circular Reactions	Production of Intentional Chains	Social Responsiveness	Compliance	Memory	Average intercorrelation
Consequence Preference	0.461	0.782*	0.699*	0.799*	0.702*	0.758*	0.700*
Primary Circular Reactions		0.642*	0.488*	0.301	0.388	0.373	0.442
Secondary Circular Reactions			0.828*	0.614*	0.653*	0.780*	0.716*
Production of Intentional Chains				0.523*	0.693*	0.836*	0.678*
Social Responsiveness					0.866*	0.763*	0.644*
Compliance						0.846*	0.691*
Memory						—	0.726*

*$P < 0.05$.

The use of the scale in this context illustrates an initial means for both identifying necessary resources and determining programming priorities. There is no mention made of cognitive development, self-help skills, language, or fine and gross motor skills among the dimensions. Tonicity, quantity and quality of movement, manipulation skill, and oral-motor processes are the basic ingredients of which more complex behavior is made. Unless special educators and related services personnel contend with these processes in a substantive way, either through the use of prosthetic devices or through systematic intervention, or through a combination of the two approaches, there is relatively little hope for enabling these students to attain the larger and more socially visible educational objectives.

Ten of the students in the Molly Stark project had severe problems in motivation (see Table 3) in that no clear evidence of a consequence preference hierarchy was obtained even though the 10 students had provided evidence of behavioral acceleration in response to contingent consequences. In other words, the behavior of these students was responsive to limited numbers of consequences at any given point in time. In general, however, responses to consequences were of low intensity and brief duration with little carryover from day to day. Satiation occurred frequently. The problem was compounded by the fact that these students were well fed, protected from most discomfort, and through the years of residential living had grown accustomed to long periods of inactivity or self-stimulation. Despite 20 months of systematic attempts to identify effective reinforcers, the staff has failed to discover any sustaining motivators for seven of the students. There is little need to consider short term objectives in cognitive,

Table 6. Intercorrelation matrix of the dimensions that are prerequisites to language

	Visual Acuity	Manipulation	Oral-Motor/ Vocalization	Secondary Circular Reactions	Social Responsiveness	Memory	Motor Imitation	Average intercorrelation
Auditory Ability	0.239	−0.02	0.400	0.422	0.556*	0.439	0.204	0.326
Visual Acuity	—	0.260	0.046	0.687*	0.348	0.476*	0.428	0.355
Manipulation		—	0.379	0.314	−0.065	0.142	0.366	0.221
Oral-Motor/Vocalization			—	0.392	0.288	0.120	0.534*	0.308
Secondary Circular Reactions				—	0.614*	0.780*	0.755*	0.566*
Social Responsiveness					—	0.763*	0.713*	0.478*
Memory						—	0.702*	0.529*
Motor Imitation							—	

self-help, or other domains until the problem of motivational events has been solved.

As a consequence of these findings, educational plans may have to be reconstituted in the direction of a "learning to learn" or test-teach system of the type suggested by a number of investigators (W. A. Bricker, 1976; Budoff & Hamilton, 1976; Feuerstein, 1972; Haywood, Filler, Shifman, & Chatelanat, 1975). Assessment on relevant dimensions must be interactive with intervention on a daily basis to be educationally useful.

INTERDISCIPLINARY PROGRAMMING STRATEGIES

The fundamental question in the education of severely handicapped persons is whether an individualized education program (IEP) including a specification of necessary related services can be devised that will assist a student to change behavioral form and functions in the direction of ultimate independent living as a free person in our society. In the language of PL 94-142, what system of intervention will meet the unique needs of the severely handicapped student? This leads to the second question which is, what knowledge and what skills from the existing reservoir of information about human health and human development must be combined to meet those needs? Relative to physical survival and behavioral development, the care and nurturance of a parent or a parent surrogate is assumed. In our society—at long last—a teacher is a mandated assistant in this process for at least part of the developmental period. In the main, medical assistance is readily available, at least at the level of diagnosing and treating acute diseases. What else is needed in meeting the criterion of ultimate functioning? The answer to this last question becomes the operational definition of interdisciplinary programming. Prefixes like *trans, inter,* and *multi* are of little consequence if the operational definition is fulfilled in terms of combining separate domains of professional and personal expertise into a unified program of health and developmental assistance.

An interesting example is provided by the student identified as M in Table 3. A review of the profile provided by the index indicates that her health is reasonably good, she has mild spasticity in tone, she is reasonable in both quantity and quality of motor movements, she has a profound hearing loss, she is mobile to the extent of being able to manipulate her wheelchair from one place to another, and, while she is reasonably social, she is tremendously resistant to contingency management in terms of response to primary circular reactions and compliance. She is totally mute. She was the first student to learn to eat without assistance, but also the only one who has gone on hunger "strikes" when her routine was changed as, for example, when she went to school on the bus for the first time. The strikes lasted for days, but she never rejected fluids, and in each attempt to reintroduce self-feeding a system of alternation of a preferred fluid with a "bite" of food was used and this method was then systematically shifted to more bites per drink. Neither increased food deprivation nor mild aversive consequences in the form of "forced" bites facilitated the process. However, the important fact about M, that provides an interdisciplinary programming example, was her foot deformity.

The deformity prevented M from weight bearing on her feet, for which the orthopedic surgeon prescribed corrective foot surgery. M's mother would not sign a surgical release, since there was no guarantee that surgery would allow her to bear weight and ultimately to walk. The mother viewed the surgery as "experimental" and could not justify the risk and pain with such uncertain consequences. The physical therapist, teacher, surgeon, and parent negotiated a solution which enabled a better judgment to be made of the outcome of surgery. The program was one of teaching M to bear weight initially in a tall-kneeling position to demonstrate that weight bearing on the lower extremities could be acquired with the body in a fairly upright position. Once M demonstrated this skill, the program was modified to include walking in a kneeling position, as a demonstration of reciprocal movement of the legs in a weight-bearing position. The third programming phase required M to stand supported, bearing weight on her deformed feet. Initially, this skill was trained with as upright a posture as possible, and gradually the demands for correct posture were increased until M was able to stand with the support of one hand on a table, with upright posture, and with as correct foot placement as was allowed by the deformities. The program was successful and, in fact, improved the outcome of surgery by training weight bearing to the extent allowed by physical limitations prior to surgery. The mother signed the release, the surgery was performed, and M is now able to walk with the use of some adaptive aids.

The surgery alone required a surgeon, an anaesthesiologist, a nurse, and other hospital-staff support personnel. Was a physical therapist required for this case? Would an occupational therapist provide a unique contribution to both the presurgery training and the postsurgery rehabilitation process? Was the teacher necessary? Clear-cut answers to these questions are not available since all of these professionals assisted in developing and providing the training activities along with a psychologist who defined the shaping and motivational processes required to make this motor program successful. Most children who had foot deformities like M would have had surgery when they were much younger, and many would have received surgery to prevent the development of those deformities before spasticity in the legs produced contractures. Instead, M had the surgery when she was 20 years old. On the other hand, if she had had proper therapy as a toddler, she would have been walking at an early age and surgery would not have been required at all.

These principles of interdisciplinary team structure and function, emphasis on basic processes of behavior, and attention to programming strategies were applied in providing a replication of M's program in the mobility training of F. This multihandicapped student began her education at the age of 12 years, having been institutionalized in custodial settings since the age of 11 months. Ratings on the dimensional system (see Table 3) indicated significant problems in the key components of behavior involving motor and motivational processes. Difficulties with motor processes related directly to spasticity throughout the body, but to a greater degree in the legs than in the arms and trunk. Deformities were present in the feet, knees, hips, trunk, and elbows. Active movement was limited to rolling from her side to her stomach or back, which was achieved with a qualitatively poor pattern or full body rotation in combination with excessive movement of the head, to hitting herself on the side of the head or on the chin repeatedly, and to rolling her head from side to side in a self-stimulatory fashion. Weight bearing on her extremities was present on bent arms, but was not demonstrated on extended arms or on her feet. Oral-motor processes for eating were restricted to a very primitive suckle pattern that enabled her to take strained foods and liquids. Food was frequently rejected by hitting the arm of the person feeding her or by pushing the food out of the mouth with the tongue. Initial consequence preference attempts by project staff yielded limited data on positive events that might be preferred by F. Nonfunctional potential reinforcers, such as stroking, soft talking, and blowing on F's face, elicited generalized responses such as temporary cessation of self-stimulatory head rolling, but did not change behavior under contingency circumstances.

The critical components of behavior that were deficient (as indicated by the Index) became the initial targets for programming by the interdisciplinary team. Programming that related to several of these basic processes was generated around an initital objective of mobility. General mobility options possible for F included: rolling, prone mobility, crawling, assisted ambulation, and independent ambulation. Independent ambulation was initially ruled out due to the number of deformities present in the lower extremities combined with lack of weight bearing on the legs and feet. Assisted mobility in an upright position (e.g., a wheeled walker with a seat) was judged inappropriate since such forms of ambulation would increase the already-present spasticity and exaggerate existing deformities. Hand-knee crawling was also eliminated because the position also increased spasticity and further orthopedic deformity. Prone positioning for mobility was selected because such an activity required weight bearing on the arms, allowed the legs to be passively positioned to decrease tone and deformity, and increased the quantity of motor movements to include basic motor patterns that were not currently present in her repertoire. Although prone mobility is not a typical activity of 12-year-old children, careful consideration of the strengths and weaknesses of both upright (age-appropriate) and prone forms of mobility led the team to select training in the prone position during the initial phase. Prone was selected because it was the only position that allowed mobility, facilitated normalized tone, maintained (not increased) the current status of orthopedic deformities, and increased the quantity of movements in her motor repertoire while allowing new movement patterns to be performed with qualitatively normal patterns of movement.

Incorporating additional processes that relate to motivation, such as consequence preference and primary circular reactions, were critical to the success of the training strategies. Mobility in and around one's environment is simply a motor expression of a function which presupposes motivation to get to another location (with any form of motor skill) and reinforcement when one successfully arrives. A number of reinforcers were tried in conjunction with training this task, and ultimately food reinforcers such as peanut butter and ice cream were used. These were not fed to F but were made available to her on a tongue blade to which she gained access after completing the required movement. The tongue blade was used at the beginning of training since F was not able to control a spoon adequately enough to ensure that the food reached her mouth, but was later replaced with a spoon as she acquired skill in self-feeding through additional and separate training. The interdisciplinary team had observed that she tended to reject foods when fed to her but not when she controlled the blade or spoon.

Training prone mobility was initiated by placing F on her stomach and encouraging her to move forward in that position to gain access to the food reinforcers. Under these conditions, movement increased but frequently resulted in increased postural tone, rolling, and ending up on her back rather than moving forward. Further task analysis of the motor requirements of the activity made by the physical therapist indicated the following sequences:

1. Maintain symmetrical weight bearing on the hands with flexed elbows
2. Shift weight to one side (arm) to free the other arm for movement other than passive weight bearing
3. Forward reach of the released arm
4. Placement of the hand (or fist) on the floor
5. Shift weight to the forward arm
6. Forward pull toward the body with that arm
7. Maintain symmetrical weight bearing on the hands with flexed elbows
8. Repeat sequence with the other arm

A more careful analysis of F's performance in relation to the requirements of the task indicated that increased tone resulted from attempts to move, and that this increased spasticity prevented symmetrical weight bearing on the arms and the necessary weight shift to free one arm for movement and resulted in increased use of rolling patterns which were previously in her repertoire. As a result, F was unsuccessful in moving forward from the prone position. However, the more specific and careful observations of her responses under these conditions provided the interdisciplinary team with the additional information required to re-structure the task requirements.

Training was then modified so that F was placed prone on a full-length scooterboard with some adaptations to prevent increased tone at the shoulders. The scooter prevented rolling and allowed more precise maintenance of normalized tone in her legs through passive positioning. Programming involved shaping of weight shift from arm to arm which, when achieved, was replaced with training in the more complex component of forward reach under conditions of normalized postural tone. Plungers were placed on the floor so that the forward reach was performed with the shoulders in a neutral position rather than in a posture of increased flexor tone, which had previously been demonstrated by F when she was required to place her hand on the floor. The plungers also decreased the complexity of the pulling action by providing leverage against which to pull. After F was successful in pulling forward by her arms with the plungers, she was required to pull forward with normalized tone in her arms without the aid of plungers. Programming was continued through increasing distances of movement for each access to food. Ten opportunities for movement were presented daily. The scooterboard was then eliminated and the task again restructured to require movement of the legs with tone as normalized as possible as well as normal patterns of movement in the upper extremities.

The sequence of steps used to train F to move around her environment, and her performance under each of the training conditions are presented in Table 7. The success of the program was based not only on the careful attention to selection of programming targets and training strategies but also on the ongoing interaction among members of the interdisciplinary team. The structure of the team was flexible throughout program implementation to ensure that team members with the relevant expertise were brought together for problem solving at the point that the student appeared to be making no further progress. Such flexibility was required in order to modify the mobility program at one point in order to decrease head hitting. Table 7 illustrates the decrease in distance moved at the

Table 7.   Mobility training program for student F

Program conditions	Distance required per SR+	Average distance traveled per session
On stomach—no adaptations	Baseline (none)	0
Weight shift of arms on scooterboard	None	0
Scooterboard—use of plungers	1 movement cycle (1 foot)	8.06 feet
Scooterboard (no plungers)	1 movement cycle (1 foot)	9.33 feet
Scooterboard	2 movement cycles (2 feet)	16.00 feet
Scooterboard	3 movement cycles (3 feet)	29.01 feet
Scooterboard	4 movement cycles (4 feet)	32.89 feet
Scooterboard	5 movement cycles (5 feet)	29.34 feet
Scooterboard	18 inches	50.00 feet
Scooterboard	24 inches	80.00 feet
Scooterboard	30 inches	80.00 feet
Scooterboard	36 inches	102.00 feet
Scooterboard	42 inches	96.00 feet
Scooterboard	48 inches	66.00 feet
Scooterboard	42 inches	28.00 feet
Scooterboard (restraint for head hitting)	42 inches	98.10 feet
Scooterboard (restraint for head hitting)	48 inches	108.00 feet
Scooterboard (no restraint)	54 inches	162.00 feet
Scooterboard	60 inches	160.00 feet

point that access to the food was made contingent on 48 inches of distance rather than 42 inches. The program was adjusted by dropping back to the previously required 42 inches of distance and attempting to reinstate behavior. However, performance continued to decrease. At that point, the psychologist was brought in to reevaluate the program and added a deceleration strategy to decrease her head hitting. This strategy was employed for several additional training sessions until head hitting was stopped. Performance then increased, and the complexity of the task was subsequently altered by dropping the scooter and moving to independent prone mobility.

I was a 12-year-old with severe spasticity throughout her body, limited movement, optic nerve atrophy resulting in total blindness, excellent hearing, and social responsiveness. Her program is an interesting third example of interdisciplinary programming. Among all of her major difficulties, the single biggest problem was I's inability to take foods or liquids by mouth, requiring all food to be given through a gastrostomy tube. Several attempts had been made since infancy by her parents and nursing staff to teach her to eat properly, but all efforts were discontinued due to weight loss and dehydration which resulted from inadequate intake, choking, and aspiration which frequently produced pneumonia, as well as the significant amount of time required to feed a minimal amount of food or liquid. Effective programming required not only intake of foods within reasonable amounts of time per meal but also sufficient intake to prevent the development of resultant medical problems through complex enough intervention procedures to reduce choking and aspiration significantly. The necessary and sufficient members of the team needed to solve this fairly complicated programming problem consisted of the physical, speech-language, and occupational therapists, teacher, nurse, physician, and nutritionist, each of whose skills were critical to developing effective intervention strategies. Procedures included careful and systematic monitoring of nutritional intake, both in relation to food values as well as to motivational properties, careful recording of medical and general health status, and specific programming to reduce overall tonicity, facilitate movement in the oral structures, and focus on the coordination of breathing with movement in the oral structures. The resultant programming was successful, and within 10 months the gastrostomy tube was permanently removed and I was able to eat strained foods and liquids with reasonable efficiency.

Another illustration of required processes of the interdisciplinary team can be demonstrated through reviewing several programs that were conducted with B, who is among the least handicapped in this group of students. Table 3 shows an average deviation score for this student of 3.52 and a rating of severely/profoundly handicapped on 11, or 58%, of the 19 dimensions of the Index. B has a relatively slight degree of motor impairment which includes mild flexor spasticity in all four extremities compounded by general muscle weakness produced through years of lack of motor activity and confinement to a crib. Eating is a major preoccupation, which places both foods and fluids high on a list of consequence preferences. Self-stimulation and activities such as hand-in-mouth, induced regurgitation, rocking, moaning, and toe flicking are in second place in terms of probability of behavior. Her performances to date all involve primary circular reactions with only a few preliminary versions of behavior moving in the direction of more complex secondary circular reactions.

Training was begun by teaching her to feed herself. This objective was selected not so much because it was a self-help skill but because it was a functional skill that depended upon her high degree of interest in food and preoccupation with eating. The program was initiated using the procedures outlined in Figure 1. All components except scooping of the food in the overall spoon-to-mouth-to-plate movement cycle were acquired using physical guidance and fading over a period of 10 meals. A number of additional training sessions failed to produce independent scooping, and a decision was made to bring the process under more precise analysis.

When she was allowed to bring the food to her mouth independently at the beginning of each meal, she attempted to use the spoon to scoop then reverted quickly to using the fingers of her other hand. After two or three attempts, she would lapse into a major temper tantrum. Two principles appeared to operate. First, she had adjusted to a specific rate of being fed (approximately 10 bites per minute when fed by hospital aides) so that, from the framework of a Premack (1965) probability analysis, the rate generated through her own efforts was below the required level and constituted a deprivation state rather than a reinforcing one. This provided an operational definition of learned helplessness (Seligman, 1975). If rate of eating was the critical factor, then being fed by the hospital aide was most reinforcing, being physically guided through scooping less reinforcing, and total independence not reinforcing at all. Precise analysis yielded information about discrepant rates under the various conditions of full independence, training, and total dependence, and highlighted the need to identify more precisely those factors that were contributing to her slow rate of eating under fully independent conditions.

Specific observation of her scooping indicated that primitive flexion patterns of movement in the arms produced a movement pattern of attempting to scoop with a fully flexed wrist in combination with undifferentiated movement in the hand. B was thus able to maintain a firm grip on the spoon, and the swing of her hand by the food tended to bring the blade of the spoon through the food in a vertical (rather than horizontal) plane. Consequently, when the spoon was taped into her hand, there was some acceleration of success to approximately 60%. When the splint was taped underneath her wrist to prevent wrist flexion, her performance increased to 100% accuracy with a rate of response stabilizing at about 6 bites per minute. These data are depicted in Figure 2. However, an even more effective position was initiated later by placing the spoon in the standard position used by most adults. This position countered the flexion patterning in the arms (including the flexed wrist induced by holding the spoon in a palmar grasp) by facilitating shoulder external rotation and inhibiting the pattern of shoulder-elbow-wrist-finger flexion which had previously been used.

Of central importance to the issues being discussed is the fact that physical

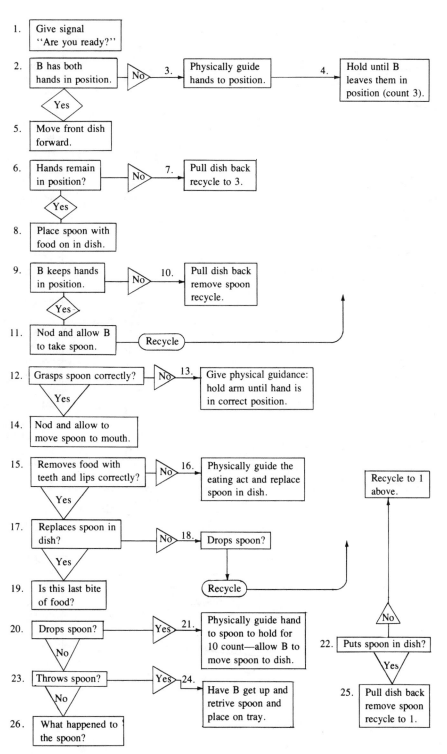

Figure 1. Profile of a feeding program.

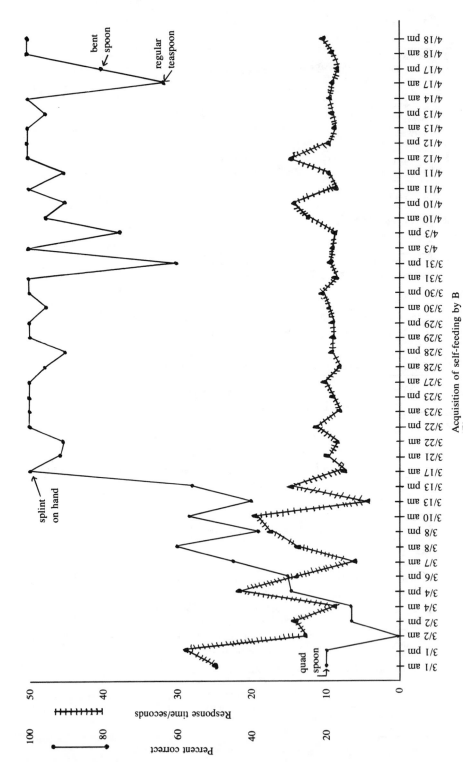

Figure 2. Acquisition of self-feeding by student B.

guidance over a sustained period prior to the use of the splint resulted in no improvement in her performance. Careful observation and analysis of her performance when eating yielded an atypical intervention strategy that matched the critical block to progress, which in this case was the presence of qualitatively poor motor patterns. One of the principal factors in training severely handicapped students to acquire skills at reasonable rates is the accurate identification of the critical block to success. It is in this identification process that the input of the interdisciplinary team is most essential.

Additional training programs that were attempted with B emphasized object permanence in a primary circular reactive process and in discriminated performances (secondary circular reactions). Object permanence was first described by Piaget (1952) and has been used by a number of investigators as one prerequisite to language and other aspects of complex human behavior (W. A. Bricker, 1976; Robinson & Robinson, 1978). Performances in object permanence can be chained into two-choice discriminations in order to assess visual acuity and to deal with a variety of processes involving receptive language (Bricker & Bricker, 1970; Vincent, Bricker, & Bricker, 1973). This particular chain is an excellent example of both secondary circular reactions and a form of generalized behavior which meets the criterion of ultimate function. To seek something that is needed provides the basis for verbal mands (Skinner, 1957), and choices among various events are commonplace. Selecting the correct button on an elevator, choosing items of foods on store shelves or in restaurants, or selecting articles from a dispenser are all examples of discriminated performances requiring object permanence.

Neither object permanence nor secondary circular reactions were evidenced by B. She would quickly reach for and take an edible from the table but would cease reaching if the edible was covered during the reaching process. Similarly, she did not seek to retrieve an object that fell from her hand to her lap. Her training program started with a simple requirement of lifting a flexible plastic cover from over an edible, which required holding the cover with one hand while reaching to retrieve the edible with the other hand. Physical guidance was used to establish the preliminary lifting of the lid. However, on the first five trials, B dropped the lid in order to retrieve the edible with the same hand that she had used to lift the lid. This occurred even though her other hand was free and in close proximity to the edible. She required additional physical guidance for several trials to establish the coordination of two hands so that one hand was used to lift and the other to retrieve the edible. Full retraining was necessary 24 hours after having learned this skill, and additional trials were required to generalize coordinated use of the two hands to other situations requiring manipulation of different materials.

Several different approaches were then taken to restructure this basic form of object permanence into a situation where two different containers were presented and selection of the container under which the edible was placed constituted a correct choice. Table 8 briefly outlines the training strategies that were

Table 8. Sequence of approaches tried in teaching student B a two-choice discrimination task

Materials	Strategy	Results
One container; edible underneath	Physical guidance	Successful with generalization to various containers.
Two containers; edible placed under one, randomized for position	Physical guidance	Unsuccessful. After 400 trials, strategy was to select container closest to hands.
Two containers; edible placed under one, randomized for position	Physical guidance with hands held equidistant to cups; hand opposite cup that included edible released after 5-second count.	Unsuccessful. After 100 trials, selected cup on side of initial hand movement (did not cross body midline).
Two containers; edible placed under one, position held constant and changed to other side after correct selection	Physical guidance with hands held equidistant to cups; hand opposite cup that included edible was released after 5-second count.	Unsuccessful. After 100 trials, accuracy still below chance.
Two containers; edible placed under one, randomized for position	Container under which edible is placed has red covering; physical guidance.	Unsuccessful. After 100 trials, accuracy still below chance.
Two containers; edible placed under one, randomized for position	Container under which edible is placed has red cover; cup with edible placed forward of empty cup.	Unsuccessful. After 460 trials, strategy was to sweep arm across table such that forward cup was always selected on basis of first physical contact.
Two containers; edible placed under one, randomized for position	Container under which edible is placed has red cover; physical placement of edible is made obvious; physical guidance.	Initial success with progress increasing (see Figure 3).

attempted in order to enable B to make a discriminated response in one situation. The training situation was contrived in order to control the variables necessary to train this form of more complex behavior. Requirements were that various forms of containers could be used as long as those containers were distinctly different. Figure 3 shows B's performance on the final approach tried with her, which is described in Table 8. To date, 628 training trials have been presented in order to bring B under the control of color as a cue in two-choice discriminated performances. Each training approach has required careful analysis of her performance under specified conditions by members of the interdisciplinary team and generation of approaches that might help overcome the primary obstacle to successful performance in each situation.

The goals with B have in every case of training involved a generalized form of behavior rather than a specific skill. Her eating is still not characterized by secondary circular reactions or object permanence. Her scoops across the plate are not fully controlled by the location of food, and scooping is actually more of a scanning movement than a motion directed to specific food locations on the plate. The scanning is a programming "compromise" and is being shifted through training by moving into the use of a fork in conjunction with more solid foods. She is still unable to discriminate independently between two choices (without a specific cue), even though she has now been through several thousand trials involving various cueing and prompting procedures. She has acquired several forms of behavior over the past 20 months of programming, but these newly acquired skills were easily trained in isolation. For instance, she has moved from being relatively nonmobile to being able to explore the environment on her hands and knees. She is able to walk with a walker and minimal supervision and to take a few steps independently but does so only in the presence of edible reinforcers. Manipulation skills have become more varied in that she is now able to use several types of intermediaries (such as rakes, cloths, strings) to bring food reinforcers to her or to manipulate various types of boxes, containers,

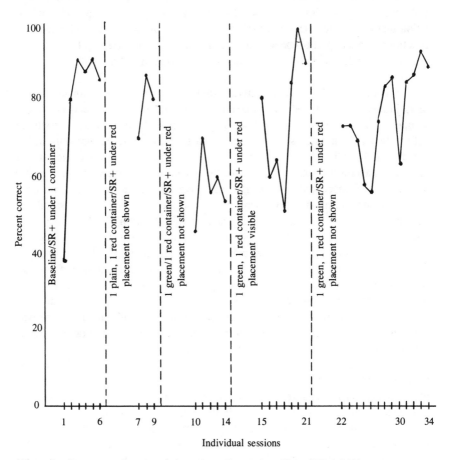

Figure 3. Percentage of correct choices of container under which edible is hidden.

and objects to retrieve edibles in an object permanence situation. Her rates of self-stimulatory behavior have decreased significantly, but such activities have been replaced by sitting quietly rather than by more complex forms of interactive behavior. Objects no longer are mouthed to the extent that this previously occurred. However, objects are not manipulated in any meaningful or functional way in nonstructured situations. After several months of training in dressing, she is still unable to complete any part of the dressing sequence without some form of physical guidance.

The basic problem with B relates to performance in basic processes and is consistent across all activities. When her movements are causally linked to an edible, the skill is acquired with less stringent training. Physical guidance has typically not brought B's behavior under the control of the correct dimension of the stimulus unless the edible is part of the stimulus situation. In other words, where any training activity can be structured such that her activity is geared toward obtaining an edible, B has acquired independent performance in simple tasks such as self-feeding, walking, object permanence, means/end, and manipulation tasks. Activities that are high priority for training where food cannot be functionally made part of the activity (such as dressing or toileting) have still not been acquired despite several different approaches toward training these forms of behavior.

A concluding example of interdisciplinary programming with the Molly Stark students is provided by student D. This student is a 21-year-old young woman with such severe spasticity throughout her body and extensive resultant deformities and limitations to movement that she has functional use only in her left arm and hand. Spasticity in her left hand prevents a pincer grasp so that grasping is accomplished through use of the outside three fingers against the heel of her hand. Consequently, a primary objective throughout the duration of the project to date was to have her always properly positioned with her feet stabilized and an abductor block between her legs. In this position she had maximum utilization of her left hand. She had also lost her front teeth as a consequence of a continuing suckling reflex and was being fed strained food up to the beginning of the project. Shortly thereafter, she was fitted with proper dentures and her diet was changed to regular foods. Adaptive equipment was used to enable her to feed herself and to drink fluids from a glass. As indicated in Table 3, her only areas of severe handicap were dimensions involving movement. In all other areas she was alert, attentive, compliant, and social. Consequently, the primary target of education with D was training in language processes.

D's vocalizations were completely restricted to vowels, which were of varying length and tonal contour. Through her vocalizations and her facial expressions, she has been able to communicate at a fairly primitive level with those in contact with her. Assessment was initiated using a large sample of pictures including the items contained in the Oregon Teaching Research picture list which has several hundred nouns and verbs. These were presented using a two-choice paradigm. The assessment took several days during which each item was presented twice as a named choice and twice as an unnamed distractor. In this way, 700 words were checked relative to her receptive vocabulary level. Her overall percentage correct score was 92. She did as well in verbs as in nouns. However, when adjectives such as size and color were used as items, her performance dropped to chance. Additionally, her use of *yes* and *no* at the receptive level was also at chance relative to two types of questions. In the one type, she was asked to indicate something she wanted such as a cup of coffee or a donut. Her response was typically a yes-like nod of her head and a random choice of the yes and no cards available to her. A training situation was started in which she was asked if she wanted a blanket (on a warm summer day) and if she indicated the yes card, the blanket was gently wrapped around her. Later she was asked if she still wanted the blanket and if she again selected yes, she was allowed to keep it on. If she indicated no, then the blanket was removed and she was asked another question which could be a repeat of the blanket question or whether she wanted a drink of Coke. The blanket and the Coke were repeated in a systematic yes/no manner over a series of five sessions at which point she was indicating an appropriate choice of yes or no 100% of the time. The contrast was then shifted to one that was less intrusive but still differed on the dimension of probably wanting one of the items and probably not wanting the other.

Retrospectively, this system was used more to teach the teacher to ask her instructionally relevant questions in a more systematic and data-based way. In fact, up to the point of the systematic assessment of yes and no, people in contact with her felt certain she had the differentiation. What they failed to observe was that everyone was asking her only yes-type questions. Consequently, she nodded yes to everything and was generally reinforced for doing so. On the second dimension of yes/no, she was asked whether a given item was what it was named, with half of the answers being correct in the affirmative and the other half correct in the negative. For example, she was shown a picture of a dress and asked if the item was a "shoe." Again she demonstrated chance performance across a range of items. However, she again mastered the distinction after about 15 training sessions that lasted approximately 30 minutes each.

A special language system was then designed for D. Based on the fact that her vocal processes were difficult for her to control after several highly motivating sessions involving verbal imitation and the fact that her limited manipulative capability rules out signing as an alternative, a picture language was developed with the name or phrase to be expressed by each card written along the bottom. These pictures were mounted on 2 by 2 inch cards with a beveled piece of soft plastic on the bottom in order to accommodate her method of grasping. In other words, a lip was created along the edge of each card so that she could pick it up readily using her palmar grasp. The pictures, including people, actions, and objects, were drawn in her presence and at the time that they would be relevant to the situation. Line drawings were sufficient for most of the representations. She was then given sequences to "read" which included items such as "Bill give D Coke," "D point to car," and "Lisa push D to room" (designated by various cards). Some were expressive in that she was asked to construct the sequence, while others were receptive in that they required actions by D. The system broke down quickly in relation to the action words. Simple differences, such as that between *give* and *point to*, were at a chance level when they were embedded in a relevant sentence. Training again dropped back to a two-choice situation using only the verb contrasts, and over 500 trials were used with a variety of prompting methods before D finally made the distinction without an error. The key to the success of the program was derived from the use of a camera shot of "D pointing" and "D giving" using an instant camera and letting her watch the picture develop. She made only two errors after that and proceeded to be correct not only in that context but also in the context of sentences. Her program is now being expanded to put D into expressive contact with the people around her.

Two outcomes from this are important. The first is that the language program was not constructed haphazardly. The items, their representation, and their various combinations were based on a knowledge of language as a process including the linguistic distinctions involved in the yes/no training. Knowledge about her motor processes was important also in being able to make an informed judgment about the probable success of a verbal imitation training program. The conclusion from both the occupational and the speech therapists is that she would probably not acquire consonant production capabilities except in extremely abnormal and generally unintelligible ways. Finally, the methods for systematically evaluating her language repertoire were extremely precise and not like those generally used in educational assessment or in speech therapy. In other words, the program represented a cooperative interdisciplinary effort.

The second outcome is more devastating. D is at the end of her qualification for mandatory education. She has spent the bulk of her life in residential facilities and has learned to become a "pet" of the ward aides. Everyone likes her, talks to her, and provides pretty much what she wants each day. However, no one taught her to want something that was not available in the institution. No one taught her to state her requests; they only taught her to say yes to things that they were then willing to provide. The project provided an electric wheelchair and a language system. The problem that remains is that she has so much more to learn and exhibits so much competence in learning what she is taught. Won't it be a shame if her education stops now?

CONCLUSIONS

There appears to be tremendous agreement among professionals who are associated with the education of severely handicapped persons concerning both the goals of instruction and the procedures that should be used in attempting to reach those goals. For instance, five classic phases of learning, including acquisition, strengthening, maintaining, generalizing, and application of the new skill, have been described (Haring & Bricker, 1976). These phases are expanded by describing procedures of shaping behavior by means of differential reinforcement of successive approximations, imitation, prompting, cueing, stimulus generalization, and response differentiation. Similar intervention strategies are discussed at even greater length by Snell and Smith (1978), who define issues of reinforcement, schedules of reinforcement, shaping, chaining, discriminative stimuli, priming or prompting, imitation, response cost, and other relatively common procedures that have become classified as behavior modification techniques. Of course, such procedures were also discussed in relation to this population of students prior to mandatory education and as the basis for programming for severely handicapped persons in institutional environments (Bensberg, Colwell, & Cassel, 1965; Girardeau & Spradlin, 1964; Gorton & Hollis, 1965; and Larsen & Bricker, 1968). To these descriptions of behavioral approaches and techniques can be added those methods that are derived from therapeutic procedures used in the treatment of children with cerebral palsy and other forms of neuromotor involvement. Extensive descriptions of how to teach children to move, become independent in eating, dressing, and toileting, and even to talk through use of neurophysiological facilitation and inhibition procedures are available in several books (Bobath & Bobath, 1975; Finnie, 1975; Pearson & Williams, 1972) as well as in numerous therapist-developed but unpublished materials. The emphasis on intervention approaches that derive from the neurophysiological perspective is on replication of the normal developmental sequence through stimulation of the senses, facilitation of normal movement patterns, and use of adaptive equipment to replace and to train movement.

The most successful instructional programs that have been used with the students at Molly Stark have been generated and implemented by interdisciplinary team members who have carefully applied instructional strategies to the unique learner characteristics of each student. However, typical approaches to interdisciplinary programming have recommended a structure where the educator is assigned the role of synthesizing the often general recommendations made by various specialists into some sort of organized programming for the student (D. Bricker, 1976; Haynes, 1976). One might question the extent to which most teachers of severely handicapped students are sufficiently well trained in enough instructional areas to instruct students effectively on this basis. This point is further highlighted by McCormack and Goldman's (1979) data, which indicate that between 18% and 39% of classroom time is spent in instructional activities which results in approximately 1 to 2 hours of daily programming time. Into this limited time, the teacher is expected to fit programming objectives generated from education, psychology, the therapies, and any other disciplines represented on the team. To assume that the average classroom teacher has either the time or the necessary expertise to provide precise programming in each relevant instructional area with every student is to advocate a programming structure that underestimates the complexities of effective interdisciplinary programming.

Progress demonstrated by the Molly Stark students on selected intervention targets has come about through careful assessment of basic processes within the context of ongoing programming. The instructional targets have been selected by the team members to represent those skills that are necessary and sufficient to function maximally in adult environments. Each team member lends his or her expertise to developing the instructional strategies that will overcome deficits in basic processes and ensure demonstration of the desired behavior. Thus, the precision of behavioral instructional strategies, which is the knowledge base of the psychologist and special educator, becomes merged with the neurophysiological perspective of the occupational, physical, and speech-language therapists around a behavioral outcome formulated for a specific student. The resultant intervention plan is therefore responsive to the specific neuromotor and motivational characteristics of that individual student. This is not to suggest a team model in which each team member provides individual programming for students but an approach where the time of each specialist is spent in careful analysis of student performance, development of precise training strategies, and training of other individuals to implement established programs.

REFERENCES

Baer, D., Wolf, M., & Risley, T. Some current dimensions of applied behavior analysis. *Journal of Applied Behavior Analysis*, 1968, *1*, 91–97.

Bensberg, G. J., Colwell, C. N., & Cassel, R. H. Teaching the profoundly retarded self-help activities of behavior shaping techniques. *American Journal of Mental Deficiency*, 1965, *69*, 674–679.

Bobath, B., & Bobath, K. *Motor development in the different types of cerebral palsy.* London: Wm. Heinemann, 1975.

Brewer, G. D., & Kakalick, J. S. *Handicapped children: Strategies for improving services.* New York: McGraw-Hill Book Co., 1979.

Bricker, D. Educational sythesizer. In M. A. Thomas (ed.), *Hey, don't forget about me!* Reston, Virginia: Council for Exceptional Children, 1976.

Bricker, W. A. Principles of assessment from the interdisciplinary team. In N. Haring (ed.), *Developing effective individualized education programs for severely handicapped children and youth.* Columbus, Ohio: Special Press, 1977.

Bricker, W. A. Service of research. In M. A. Thomas (ed.), *Hey, don't forget about me!* Reston, Virginia: Council for Exceptional Children, 1976.

Bricker, W., & Bricker, D. A program of language training for the severely language handicapped child. *Exceptional Children*, 1970, *37*, 101–111.

Brown, L., Nietupski, J., & Hamre-Nietupski, S. Criterion of ultimate functioning. In M. A. Thomas (ed.), *Hey, don't forget about me!* Reston, Virginia: Council for Exceptional Children, 1976.

Budoff, M., & Hamilton, J. Optimizing test performance of moderately and severely mentally retarded adolescents and adults. *American Journal of Mental Deficiency*, 1976, *81*, 49–57.

Burton, T. A., & Hirshoren, A. The education of severely and profoundly retarded children: Are we sacrificing the child to the concept? *Exceptional Children*, 1979, *45*, 598–602. (a)

Burton, T. A., & Hirshoren, A. Some further thoughts and clarifications on the education of severely and profoundly retarded children. *Exceptional Children*, 1979, *45*, 618–625. (b)

Campbell, P. H. Daily living skills. In N. Haring (ed.), *Developing effective individualized education programs for severely handicapped children and youth.* Columbus, Ohio: Special Press, 1977. (a)

Campbell, P. H. Molly Stark project proposal. Bureau of Education for the Handicapped, Programs for Severely Handicapped, 1977. (b)

Campbell, P. H. Annual report: Molly Stark project. BEH Severely Handicapped Program (OE-300-77-0249), 1978. (a)

Campbell, P. H. Measuring motor behavior. In P. W. Bailey (ed.), *Ongoing data collection in the classroom*. Seattle, Washington, WESTAR, 1978. (b)

Campbell, P. H. Annual report: Molly Stark project. BEH Severely Handicapped Program (OE-300-77-0249), 1979. (a)

Campbell, P. H. Basic considerations in programming for students with motor problems. In *Proceedings of the Southeastern Regional Training Coalition*. Nashville: George Peabody College, 1979. (b)

Campbell, P. H., & Bricker, W. A. Programming for the severely/profoundly handicapped person. In J. Gardner, et al. (eds.), *Program issues in developmental disabilities*. Baltimore: Paul H. Brookes, Publishers, 1980.

Cohen, M., Gross, P., & Haring, N. Developmental pinpoints. In N. Haring & L. Brown (eds.), *Teaching the severely handicapped* (Vol. I). New York: Grune and Stratton, 1976.

Faris, J. A., Anderson, R. M., & Greer, J. G. Psychological assessment of the severely and profoundly retarded. In R. M. Anderson & J. G. Greer (eds.), *Educating the severely and profoundly retarded*. Baltimore: University Park Press, 1976.

Feuerstein, R. A dynamic approach to causation, prevention and alleviation of retarded performance. In H. C. Haywood (ed.), *Social-cultural aspects of mental retardation*. New York: Appleton-Century-Crofts, 1972.

Finnie, N. *Handling the young cerebral palsied child at home*. New York, Dutton, 1975.

Gentry, D., & Haring, N. Essentials of performance measurement. In N. Haring and L. Brown (eds.), *Teaching the severely handicapped* (Vol. I). New York: Grune and Stratton, 1976.

Girardeau, F. L., & Spradlin, J. E. Token rewards in a cottage program. *Mental Retardation*, 1964, *2*, 345–351.

Gorton, C. E., & Hollis, J. H. Redesigning a cottage unit for better programming and research for the severely retarded. *Mental Retardation*, 1965, *3*, 16–21.

Guess, D., & Baer, D. M. Some experimental analyses of linguistic development in institutionalized retarded children. In B. Lahey (ed.), *The modification of language behavior*. Springfield, Illinois: Charles C Thomas, 1973.

Guess, D., Sailor, W., & Baer, D. M. To teach language to retarded children. In R. L. Schiefelbusch and L. L. Lloyd (eds.), *Language perspectives—acquisition, retardation, and intervention*. Baltimore: University Park Press, 1974.

Guess, D., Sailor, W., & Baer, D. M. A behavioral-remedial approach to language training for the severely handicapped. In E. Sontag, N. Certo, and J. Smith (eds.), *Educational programming for the severely and profoundly handicapped*. Reston, Virginia: Council for Exceptional Children, 1977.

Guess, D., Sailor, W., Keogh, B., & Baer, D. M. Language development programs for severely handicapped children. In N. Haring and L. Brown (eds.), *Teaching the severely handicapped* (Vol. I). New York: Grune and Stratton, 1976.

Haring, N. (ed.). *Developing effective individualized education programs for severely handicapped children and youth*. Columbus, Ohio: Special Press, 1977.

Haring, N. *Team programming*. Keynote Address, Statewide Institute for Education of the Severely and Profoundly Handicapped, Chicago, February, 1979.

Haring, N., & Bricker, D. Overview of comprehensive services for the severely/profoundly handicapped. In N. Haring and L. Brown (eds.), *Teaching the severely handicapped* (Vol. I). New York: Grune and Stratton, 1976.

Hart, V. The use of many disciplines with the severely and profoundly handicapped. In E. Sontag, N. Certo, and J. Smith (eds.), *Educational programming for the severely and profoundly handicapped*. Reston, Virginia: Council for Exceptional Children, 1977.

Haynes, U. (ed.). *The first three years of life: Final project report of the Comprehensive Infant Project*. United Cerebral Palsy Associations, 1976.

Haywood, H. C., Filler, J., Shifman, M., & Chatelanat, G. Behavioral assessment in mental retardation. In P. McReynolds (ed.), *Advances in psychological assessment* (Vol. 3). San Francisco, Jossey-Bass, 1975.

Hobbs, N. *Issues in the classification of children* (Vols. I and II). San Francisco: Jossey-Bass, 1975.

Hobbs, N. *The futures of children*. San Francisco: Jossey-Bass, 1976.

Jackson, J. 36th Biennial Conference of Phi Delta Kappa, October, 1977.

Keen, R. A., & Sullivan, S. *Programming for motorically handicapped children*. Harrisburg: Pennsylvania Training Model, 1976.

Larsen, L. A., & Bricker, W. A. *A manual for parents and teachers of severely and moderately retarded children*. Nashville, Tennessee: Institute on Mental Retardation and Intellectual Development, George Peabody College, 1968.

McCormack, L., & Goldman, R. The transdisciplinary model: Implications for service delivery and personnel preparation for the severely and profoundly handicapped. *AAESPH Review*, 1979, *4*, 152–161.

Pearson, P., & Williams, C. *Physical therapy services in the developmental disabilities*. Springfield, Illinois: Charles C Thomas, 1972.

Piaget, J. *The origins of intelligence*. New York: Norton Books, 1952.

Premack, D. Reinforcement therapy. In D. Levine (ed.), *Nebraska symposium on motivation*. Lincoln, Nebraska: University of Nebraska Press, 1965.

Robinson, C., & Robinson, J. H. Sensorimotor functions and cognitive development. In M. Snell (ed.), *Systematic instruction of the moderately and severely handicapped*. Columbus, Ohio: Charles E. Merrill Publishing Co., 1978.

Sailor, W., & Horner, R. D. Educational assessment strategies for the severely handicapped. In N. Haring and L. Brown (eds.), *Teaching the severely handicapped* (Vol. I). New York: Grune and Stratton, 1976.

Sailor, W., & Mix, B. J. *The TARC assessment system*. Lawrence, Kansas: H & H Enterprises, 1975.

Salek, B. Movement, learning, and the cerebral palsied child. Suffolk Rehabilitation Center, 1977.

Sarason, S., & Doris, J. Mainstreaming: dilemmas, opposition, opportunities. In M. Reynolds (ed.), *Futures of education for exceptional children*. Reston, Virginia: Council for Exceptional Children, 1978.

Seligman, M. E. *Helplessness: On depression, death, and development*. San Francisco: W. H. Freeman, 1975.

Skinner, B. F. *Verbal behavior*. New York: Appleton-Century Crofts, 1957.

Snell, M., & Smith, D. Intervention strategies. In M. Snell (ed.), *Systematic instruction of the moderately and severely handicapped*. Columbus, Ohio: Charles E. Merrill Publishing Co., 1978.

Somerton, E., & Myers, D. Educational programming for the severely/profoundly mentally retarded. In N. Haring and L. Brown (eds.), *Teaching the severely handicapped* (Vol. I). New York: Grune and Stratton, 1976.

Somerton, E., & Turner, K. *Pennsylvania training model: Individual assessment guide*. Reston, Virginia: Council for Exceptional Children, 1975.

Sontag, E., Certo, N. & Button, J. On a distinction between the education of the severely and profoundly handicapped and a doctrine of limitations. *Exceptional Children*, 1979, *45*, 604–616.

Sontag, E., Smith, J., & Certo, N. (eds.). *Educational programming for the severely and profoundly handicapped*. Reston, Virginia: Council for Exceptional Children, 1977.

Stone, C. Motor skills. In N. Haring (ed.), *Developing effective individualized education programs for severely handicapped children and youth*. Columbus, Ohio: Special Press, 1977.

Vincent-Smith, L., Bricker, D. D., & Bricker, W. A. Receptive vocabulary: Performances and selection strategies of delayed and nondelayed toddlers. *American Journal of Mental Deficiency,* 1973, *77,* 579–584.

Vort. *Behavior characteristics progression.* Palo Alto, California: Santa Cruz School District, 1973.

Watson, J. S., & Ramey, C. T. Reactions to response contingent stimulation in early infancy. *Merrill-Palmer Quarterly,* 1972, *18,* 219–227.

Wehman, P. *Curriculum design for the severely and profoundly handicapped.* New York: Human Sciences Press, 1979.

Williams, W., & Fox, T. (eds.). *Minimal objective system for pupils with severe handicaps.* Burlington, Vermont: University of Vermont, Center for Special Education, 1977.

York, R., & Edgar, G. *Teaching the severely handicapped* (Vol. IV). Columbus, Ohio: Special Press, 1979.

Chapter 2

Adaptive Performance Objectives
Form Versus Function

Owen R. White

Individualized goals and objectives that reflect the unique needs and abilities of each pupil have been a part of good special education programs since long before they were mandated by PL 94-142 (Education for All Handicapped Children Act) in late 1975. Still, we are only beginning to understand what meaningful individualization actually entails. Far more than simply coming up with a different list of objectives for each child, it involves a delicate balance between the unique needs of the individual and the common demands of the world in which that individual lives. It is the purpose of this chapter to examine that task and to outline at least a few ways in which meaningful individualized goals and objectives might be achieved. Moreover, since individualized programs must rest on careful assessments of individual talents and needs, additional attention is focused on methods for adapting evaluation procedures to better reflect the abilities of severely handicapped students.

COMMON DEMAND

While each child may be unique, the demands placed upon children in general by the environments in which they find themselves are not. For example, all of the workers in a particular sheltered workshop may be expected to work independently for periods of at least 30 minutes; those living in a group home might have to accept at least some of the responsibility for dressing themselves, keeping their rooms in order, and helping in the preparation of their food. Even individuals

The development of material presented in this chapter was supported in part by grant G00772139 to the Consortium on Adaptive Performance Assessment (CAPE)/American Association for the Education of the Severely/Profoundly Handicapped from the Bureau of Education for the Handicapped, U.S. Office of Education (Note 1). For additional information concerning CAPE, contact Dr. Dale Gentry, CAPE Chairperson, Department of Special Education, University of Idaho, Moscow, Idaho 83843.

confined to a residential institution are likely to have demands placed upon them. Typically, for example, institutionalized people are expected to occupy themselves nonaggressively and nondestructively (even if that means they only "self-stimulate") and show extraordinary patience while waiting for food or other services. Regardless of whether or not such demands are reasonable, ignoring them will certainly reduce the probability that the individual will be allowed to remain in any but the most restrictive of living environments.

In order to account for the probable demands that will be placed on a pupil, farsighted educators have usually tried to identify potential future placements, analyze the basic skill requirements for maintenance in those placements, and then develop a general curriculum to teach those skills. As pupils enter the training program, they are assessed with respect to the curriculum, and those skills that they lack are targeted for instruction (White & Haring, 1978). Other attempts might be made to further "individualize" the program. Inappropriate objectives, such as visual discrimination tasks for blind students, may be dropped from the curriculum. Objectives may be broken down into smaller steps if they appear too complicated for the pupil to master all at once. Other objectives may be combined if the pupil shows particular talent in a certain area, and still other objectives may be added to account for special sensorimotor deficits or to deal with behavior problems. Overall, however, the student's program will only be appropriate if it reflects the behavioral demands of his or her potential future placements. The degree to which meaningful program individualization can take place will depend heavily upon the manner in which those demands are identified.

BEHAVIOR MODELS VS. CRITICAL FUNCTIONS

Ideally, the skills required for successful functioning in any given situation would be identified by a careful analysis of environmental demands and consequences. That is, careful experiments would be devised to determine which behaviors are absolutely necessary in order for a person to be "successful" in a given placement option. Since such analyses are rarely possible, educators turn more often to an analysis of what seems "typical." For programs serving older handicapped pupils, the models of behavior are likely to be actual individuals who have proved successful in the next placements being considered. For example, the behavior of "good" busboys might be observed if food service employment is being considered; "successful" residents in a group home could serve as models if the home is a viable living arrangement for one or more graduates of a program. With younger handicapped pupils, where eventual adult placements are far less certain, the models are more likely to be general in character, like a model of normal sensorimotor development of Piagetian stages of concept development. In those cases, the "model" essentially represents what one would typically expect of a pupil's chronological peers. Alternatively, for students of any age, the models could be selected from the people involved in programs that represent the next "least restrictive" environment to which it would be desirable to transfer the student. In any case, it is assumed that the eventual success of our pupils is a function of the degree to which they can approximate the behavior of those "previously successful" models. That may be true in principle, but in practice too much attention has been given to the specific *form* of model behavior.

The "do exactly as they do" approach to goal setting overlooks the possibility that there may be more than one way to accomplish the same basic end. For example, since people who function well in an independent living situation are able to count money and make change, it seems reasonable that those skills would be part of an "independent living" curriculum. Imagine, however, working with a trainee who is 20 years old. He can count objects to match numbers up to 20, but has no addition skills and cannot even discriminate between different denominations of coins and paper money, let alone group them according to equivalent value. Based upon experience with the trainee, it is concluded that at very best he could be taught to identify one or two denominations of money in the time before he must leave the program. Is it worth it? Many would give up and begin searching for placements where the individual would not be expected to handle his own money. Brown (Note 2) felt differently. The true *critical function*[1] or purpose of counting money is simply to facilitate the purchase of items and services. Perhaps there are ways of accomplishing that end with specific behaviors that differ in *form* from those traditionally used. He designed a new program that involved only a few basic discriminations:

1. Discriminating the difference in appearance between "one-dollar bills" and "other money"
2. Identifying the number to the right of the decimal point in a price tag
3. Counting objects to match numbers
4. Responding to statements of "one more," "not enough," and "too much" when applied in very specific situations

Now, in order to buy something, the trainee is taught to put those skills together:

1. Go into a store carrying a roll of dollar bills and locate the item to be purchased.
2. Identify the "whole dollar price" (the number to the left of the decimal).

---

[1]The notion of defining skills or behaviors in terms of their consequences is really quite old (cf. Skinner, 1938). White (1971) gave a name to that process when he talked about defining skills in terms of their *critical effects* and, later, described the use of critical effect definitions in special education (White & Haring, 1976; White & Liberty, 1976). Brown (1976) expanded the concept somewhat and coined the term *criterion of ultimate functioning*. Finally, the Consortium on Adaptive Performance Evaluation (CAPE), in attempting to devise an adaptive curriculum-referenced assessment instrument for use with severely and profoundly handicapped persons settled on the term *critical function* (Note 6). Although the specific meaning of each term may be somewhat different, all attempt to focus attention on the definition of behaviors, skills, goals, or objectives in terms of the function or purpose the behavior is supposed to serve, rather than on the specific form of the motor act used to achieve that effect.

3. Count out the required number of dollar bills from the roll.
4. Take one more dollar bill (to account for any "cents" listed to the right of the decimal on the price tag).
5. Go to the checkout counter, place the dollar bills and the item in front of the clerk, and wait for change.
6. If the clerk responds by saying anything that might be interpreted as "not enough," as might be the case if taxes or other extra charges are added to the price, the trainee responds by placing another dollar on the counter.
7. Following the transaction, the trainee places the change (if there is any) in one pocket, any dollar bills in another pocket, picks up the item (ideally, with a polite "thank you"), and leaves.

If the trainee wishes to purchase more than one item, the same counting rules are applied to each item and the accumulation of bills is kept in a separate pocket. That may result in a "too much" statement from the clerk, but the trainee can respond just as he would when receiving change. When he begins to run out of dollar bills, the individual goes to a bank, drops the change on the counter and says, "Dollar bills, please."

Such an approach to training is certainly not without limitations. The procedure is dependent upon a printed price (or the ability of the trainee to count bills to match a spoken number); the honesty of the clerk is important (but how often does *anyone* count change?); and, unless training is extended to "dimes vs. non-dimes," the trainee could not use vending machines. Still, the trainee *could* purchase items with a minimum of assistance and without needing to know monetary equivalences or addition. There is even a bonus: the trainee is actually likely to look *less* handicapped! Rather than laboriously counting out nickels, dimes, and quarters at the counter, he simply strides up, hands the clerk some bills and patiently awaits his change—very much like anyone else might do. All-in-all, it would seem a very attractive approach.

By placing emphasis on what he wanted the individual to *accomplish,* rather than on the specific form of the behavior most people employ to accomplish the same thing, Brown was able to identify alternative behavior patterns that the trainee could master more easily. Actual training still concentrates on the development of specific forms of behavior (e.g., discriminating the number to the left of the decimal point in a price tag and matching that number to dollar bills), but those behaviors differ from what we would typically expect from a trainee (e.g., matching the entire price to the least number of bills and coins that will meet the price). The only meaningful relationship between those sets of behaviors lies in the fact that they both *accomplish* the same thing; that is, they allow the person to purchase an item.

"Making a purchase" is a relatively discrete act with an easily identified purpose. Some of the skills a child should learn may be more abstract. What could be done, for example, to modify a preschool objective like "puts together a three-piece puzzle" for a child who has no arms or legs? What is the critical function the child should achieve? There are several possibilities. The puzzle might serve as one way for the child to occupy himself or herself "constructively" during free-play, as a means of developing some combination of eye-hand coordination or fine motor skills, or as a means of developing some concept (e.g., space-object relationships). If the value of the puzzle is primarily recreational, then alternative forms of entertainment and leisure time activities should be found that are more appropriate for the child's limited motoric skills (e.g., listening to story records; watching educational television; working with objects that can be manipulated with a head stick or very gross body movements). If the purpose of the objective is to develop eye-hand coordination or fine motor skills, then training in the use of prosthetic limbs should be explored. Most likely, however, the purpose of working with puzzles is to encourage the development of certain concepts like space-object or part-whole relationships. Having the child manipulate the puzzle is only a convenient way of accomplishing that end. The same thing might be accomplished if the teacher rotated each piece of the puzzle in turn and had the pupil nod when they were positioned properly to be put in place. Alternatively, a puzzle with one missing piece could be placed on the table. The teacher could then point to each piece in a random assortment of pieces (only one of which fits) until the child blinks to indicate that the piece that will complete the puzzle has been found. There are any number of possibilities. Of course, most alternatives for completing the puzzle might be more clumsy than the method used with normal children (i.e., having the child actually perform the manipulations), but at least the alternatives allow some chance for the motorically handicapped pupil to develop and demonstrate the same concepts.

IDENTIFYING THE PURPOSE OF AN INSTRUCTIONAL OBJECTIVE

Clearly, defining skill objectives in terms of their critical functions can be very useful in deciding which specific forms of behavior should be developed or used in order to achieve that delicate balance between an individual's personal abilities and environmental demands. Before attempting to list all of the critical functions served by several possible curricular objectives, however, it will help to have some sort of organizational schema. The basic behavioral paradigm seems to suit that purpose well. Any discrete interaction between an individual and the environment can be described as some sort of stimulus, followed by some sort of response, resulting in some sort of effect:

STIMULUS ----►	RESPONSE ----►	EFFECT
(cues that	(behavior or	(result,
define how	motor act	outcome, or
and when the	of the	consequence
individual	individual)	of the
should behave)		interaction)

As it turns out, most curricular objectives are primarily concerned with part, but not all, of the specific elements in the above paradigm. For example, some objectives will be concerned with the development of a wide range of *physical response patterns* (e.g., wrist rotation, arm flex, head lifting), but less concerned with the specific stimuli that one might use to generate those responses or the specific effects (consequences) of those movements in any given situation. Other objectives are interesting in developing *concepts* (i.e., differential responding to complex stimuli like printed words), but will accept a wide range of response types for demonstrating those concepts (e.g., vocalizations, pointing, signing, or even staring at the appropriate word when it is read). Finally, other objectives are mainly interested in the *outcome* or *effect* of an interaction, and are only secondarily interested in how that outcome might be achieved. For example, if a worker is paid to sort electronic parts, it is irrelevant whether a pincer grasp is used to pick up the parts or whether the worker simply slides the parts over the counter and into bins suspended below. Similarly, a color discrimination, size/shape discrimination, or a match-to-picture process to identify the parts might all be equally acceptable, just as long as the parts get into their proper bins. That is not to say that the form of the behavior used to demonstrate a concept, or the concepts employed in achieving a certain critical function, is of no importance. Only certain aspects of any interaction are likely to be *critical,* however, so each of the other elements can be adapted to place the individual at his or her best advantage. In the following sections, each element of the paradigm is examined in detail.

Physical Ability

The purely physical abilities of an individual to receive information through the senses and to move the various parts of the body define the "forces" that can act upon that person and which, in turn, that person can bring to bear to act upon the environment. Any given sensory mode or motor movement might be used to achieve a virtually infinite range of critical effects. For example, sight is useful for guiding a person's movement through space and for such receptive communication skills as reading print, but it can also serve the receptive communication function of reading sign language or even help in guiding an expressive function like staring at objects in response to the question "What do you want?" Since the range of those potential functions is so broad, it is probably best to simply work with the development of the visual sense per se rather than to tie instructional or therapeutic efforts to any single type of interaction. Similarly, one might work to improve the general form of a pincer grasp, the form of a leg extension, or the ability to discriminate low volume sound—all on the assumption that, if those basic physical abilities can be improved, a wide range of critical effects will be more easily achieved. The three basic concerns regarding an individual's physical development are reflexive behavior, sensory abilities, and voluntary motor behavior.

Reflexes   The reflexive behavior of an individual is determined by basic neurological development and represents a necessary relationship between very specific environmental stimuli and muscular responses:

STIMULUS – – – – – – – – – – – ► RESPONSE
(specific)   (specific)

If, for example, we tap a child's knee in a particular way, the patellar reflex should cause the leg to jerk up. The absence of certain reflexes may indicate neurological damage; for example, the absence of a direct light reflex (the contraction of the pupil in response to light) may indicate a visual deficit with neurological origins. Other reflexes may either help or hinder development, or even both, depending upon when they emerge and fade. For example, the tonic neck reflex (the tendency of one arm to extend and the other to flex when the head is turned to one side) is presumed to help an infant develop asymmetrical movement. If the tonic neck reflex does not fade, however, it will eventually inhibit the development of voluntary arm movements. It is generally not possible to develop a "true reflex" where it does not exist, nor to completely eliminate one that does exist, short of surgery. Still, there are reasons for the educator to be concerned with them.

First, knowledge of an individual's reflexive behavior may influence the desirability of certain other programs. If, for example, a child still has a tonic neck reflex, special considerations must be made for programs involving head and arm movements. Second, although it may not be possible to change the basic reflex, special programs may still be successful in training a person to inhibit or replace them. If an infant does not display the grasp reflex, for example, extra attention will be required to generate a voluntary grasp later in the child's development. Some reflexes may be directly assessed by teachers or parents with a little instruction and guidance, but for a complete examination and list of program implications, it is best to consult a qualified physician, occupational therapist, or physical therapist.

Sensory Abilities   Appropriate educational programs emphasize the use of an individual's preferred sensory modality and avoid a heavy reliance on weak modalities (White & Haring, 1976). For example, if a child has a visual deficit, supplementary auditory cues should be used when presenting new or complex learning material. At the same time, of course, the usefulness of an individual's weaker senses should be improved wherever possible, either by training or prosthetic devices. In the organizational schema presented here, the evaluation of sensory abilities is concerned primarily with the stimulus component; virtually any response might be used to indicate a reaction to the stimulus and any special consequence that is effective in maintaining the individual's interest in the assessment or program would be acceptable:

STIMULUS – – – ► response – – – – – –► effect

(selected   (any behavior   (any consequence
light   that can be   that maintains
or   used to indicate   the individual's
sound)   that the individual   work with
                      hears or sees   the task)
                       the stimulus)

Preliminary screening for visual or auditory deficits may be made by simply noting whether an individual is "startled" or reacts in any consistent way to high intensity light or sound. Complete examinations can be more difficult. Traditional methods for testing sight and hearing rely upon the subject to indicate (usually verbally or by pressing some button) when something can be seen or heard. It is assumed that the individual will want to respond appropriately. Severely and profoundly handicapped individuals may fail to respond in such situations because they lack the actual motor behavior requested, because they have not learned to respond to the directions provided, or simply because there is insufficient reinforcement for their actions. It may be necessary, therefore, to select special responses that are already exhibited by the individual—anything from pointing to standing up or even staring right or left—and train the person to engage in that behavior in response to at least *some* sound or light in order to earn a special "treat." Training can then be extended to lights and sounds of varying intensity or frequencies to determine their sensory limits. With a little ingenuity and a lot of patience, individuals may demonstrate surprising abilities. For example, Stolz and Wolf (1969) actually trained a moderately retarded person who had been formally diagnosed as organically blind to discriminate a wide range of visual stimuli; Decker and Wilson (1977) were able to conduct meaningful auditory evaluations with 19 of 28 profoundly retarded children and adults previously thought to be "untestable"; and Fulton and Spradlin (1971) were able to ascertain the auditory thresholds of 5 out of 6 severely retarded children.

Body Movements   While it is possible for a child with very limited muscle and joint movement to accomplish a great many things (for example, a child with no use of his arms or legs might still type out words with a head stick), it is also true that a child with normal movement is generally far more effective and efficient. Therefore, regardless of the availability of prosthetic devices and adaptive procedures, some attempt should always be made to expand and refine continually the range and quality of a child's gross and fine motor behavior. Many of the tasks traditionally used to assess or encourage such development also involve the use of some discrimination or concept (e.g., putting puzzles together or building three-block bridges). That's fine, if they work. If the individual appears to have any difficulty, however, then it should be remembered that the only critical component of the instructional paradigm when developing motor behavior is the *response*. Virtually any cues or consequence that can be used to evoke and encourage the response should be acceptable:

stimulus– – – ►RESPONSE – – – ►effect

| (any cue that prompts or guides the individual, nonphysically, to emit the desired response) | (the specific motor act of concern) | (any consequence that will maintain the individual's performance) |

Generally, a teacher should try to use whatever cognitive skill the individual may already have (e.g., the concept of imitation following the command "Do as I do . . .'') and should try to arrange situations that are naturally reinforcing or highly motivating. In one case, for example, a teacher was having no success in getting a child to hold an object. When attempting to place an object in the child's hand, it would drop out almost immediately. It could not be decided whether the child was having a problem understanding what to do, simply did not want to cooperate, or really lacked the coordination and strength required to perform the task. To find out, the teacher put the child on a tricycle and gently pushed her forward. The child quickly grasped the handle bars to support herself. Now the teacher knew that the child had the motor behavior to grasp objects and only needed further instruction or encouragement to follow the command "hold" (Note 3).

Once an individual's basic reflexes, senses, and gross/fine motor behavior have been assessed, a list should be prepared of programmatic concerns. At the very least, the following should be noted:

1. Sensory modalities (hearing, sight) that are of no functional use and should be avoided when designing instructional programs
2. Sensory modalities that are weak but that might be enhanced with practice or the use of prosthetic devices (e.g., hearing aids)
3. Sensory modalities that are preferred (i.e., strongest, even if all are relatively weak) and should therefore be used whenever possible for the presentation of new or complex learning material
4. Motor skills that cannot or should not be developed now, because of a total lack of physical attribute (e.g., arms), the presence of inhibiting reflexes (e.g., the tonic neck reflex), or the lack of prerequisite skills (e.g., the lack of the head balance needed for walking); and the conditions under which those skills might be developed later (e.g., after the tonic neck reflect fades)
5. Motor skills over which the individual has good (or at least reasonable) control and that might be most useful in building and demonstrating other skills (e.g., if the child has little other than good eye control, "staring" and "looking-at" might be used as behaviors for indicating the solutions to discrimination problems)
6. Special health conditions that should be considered when working with the child, like seizure patterns, medication, or special handling considerations for a "fragile" child

Putting all of that information together, appropriate goals and objectives can be developed for the individual's physical development. The highest priority should be given to the development of at least one or two "tool movements"— behaviors that the individual can control with some certainty and use to interact with the world (White & Haring, 1976). It is hoped that those tools will include such things as the formation of discrete vocalizations and fine motor movements, but even if they amount to little more than eye movements or gross pointing responses, each individual must have *some* behavior with which to work. After a few basic tool movements are intact, attention can be turned to the improvement of other gross or fine motor behaviors that show some promise for development, would expand the range of "tools" available to the individual, and would allow the individual to appear more normal.

Conceptual Skills

Cognitive, or conceptual, skills represent the nonphysical tools that an individual may use to interact with the environment. Like the purely physical skills discussed above, any given concept may be useful in accomplishing a wide variety of critical functions. Being able to respond differentially to the color *green,* for example, may be useful for knowing when to walk across a street, finding the appropriate wire in the assembly of an electronic device, or even knowing what to expect when someone says, "I'll be by in a green car at 10 to pick you up." Since the useful expression of a concept may take such a wide variety of forms, the specific forms or types of motor behavior and consequences used to develop the concept are more a matter of convenience or expediency than anything else:

STIMULUS — — —► response — — — — —► effect

| (cues that represent the conceptual problem to be solved) | (any that can be used to indicate the solution of the problem) | (any that will encourage the individual to work) |

It should be possible for an individual to respond differentially to complex environmental situations, solve problems, and self-direct his or her own behavior or the behavior of others by controlling only one differential motor act. True, it may be easier to assess problem-solving ability if a child can also move normally, but there are usually many alternatives. Mindy, for example, could only control her eyes. After 7 years of intensive physical therapy, she still could not control any other part of her body with certainty. Using eye movements as her tools, however, she was able to communicate to her teacher by staring at objects on a board—first pictures, and then words and letters. After only 6 months of work (and with no previous "academic" instruction), she was able to read at the first-grade level. The teacher would prop the book up in front of Mindy. If Mindy had difficulty with a word, she would blink her eyes to guide the teacher to the problem. To indicate when she was finished with a page, Mindy would close her eyes. After a story, she would spell out the answers to comprehension questions by staring at the words and letters on her communication board (Note 4). In short, it is not necessary to wait for a child to move normally before attempting to develop complex concepts and cognitive behavior. If normal movements are available, then fine. If not, the teacher should work with *any* movement that the individual can control with some certainty. Similarly, if it helps to make a "game" out of some instructional task or if the pupil can earn "points" or food while developing a concept, those tactics certainly do not detract from the expression of the concept itself. Once the concept is established, control of the program can be faded to natural consequences and cues.

The type of success that Mindy enjoyed is still more the exception than the rule, but there are at least two basic guidelines that can be followed when setting goals for concept development:

1. Eliminate any mention of specific motor acts whenever possible. As mentioned earlier, physically manipulating the pieces of a three-piece puzzle is only one way of indicating space-object or part-whole relationships. Similarly, a child with no arms or legs should not be required to recover a hidden object to demonstrate object permanence. Any means of indicating the location of a hidden object should be acceptable, such as staring at its location in response to the question "Where is _____?" Use common or normal movements whenever possible, but do not hesitate to deviate from them if it will increase the chances of the individual's successful mastery of a concept.

2. Define the materials or stimuli required for the concept in the broadest terms possible. In an attempt to provide useful guidelines for people in the assessment of certain concepts, educators often become overly specific in their description of materials. It is common, for example, to suggest that object permanence be assessed by covering a child's favorite toy with a cloth and seeing if he or she will recover it. Such suggestions can be helpful, but they sometimes unnecessarily limit the imagination of the teacher or tester. *Any* object of interest to the child should be acceptable. In one case, a tester capitalized on a child's fascination with his beard by covering *himself* with a blanket. It worked. The child reached out immediately and uncovered the tester's face (Note 5). Some care must be taken, however, to ensure that the basic difficulty of the concept being tested is not altered by changes in materials or stimuli. It may be easier to locate a large, breathing human being under a blanket than to find a small, motionless ball under a towel.

If it is necessary to use an adaptation that changes the level of difficulty of a concept, an increase in difficulty is generally more acceptable than a decrease in difficulty. For example, hiding an object by covering it with a towel would be meaningless for a blind child. The child might feel the object through the towel, but even if the object were recovered it might only reflect simple curiosity concerning the object to which the child's attention had been directed, not that he or she actually knew that it was the same object recently felt without the towel. Alternatively, a ringing bell (or some other sound-making object of interest) could be moved around the child and silenced at a particular point to see if the child could find it. Since auditory localization is generally more difficult than visual localization, it might take longer for the child to learn the skill. When the child did, however, the teacher could be quite sure that the pupil had really demonstrated object permanence at a level of complexity at least equal to that expected of a "normal" child.

Whenever possible, the selection of concepts for assessment and instruction should be based upon an analysis of potential future placements. If most tasks in a sheltered workshop are structured in a left-to-right sequence and use a match-to-sample procedure, then certainly those basic concepts should be included as part of the curriculum. Similarly, if an individual will have to interact with customers in a cafeteria, then at least some basic concepts in social behavior should be considered. If the pupil is too young to be considering definite future placements, general concepts might be identified by analyzing available developmental sequence charts and/or norm-referenced instruments. Care must be taken, of course, to abstract the basic concepts implied by the items on those scales and to restate them in broader, adaptable terms. One might still suggest the use of standard procedures as one means of determining whether a child has a concept, but it should be made clear that alternative procedures and criteria may serve equally well.

Whenever an individual's conceptual skills have been assessed, at least the following should be noted for use in program planning:

1. Concepts that the child has demonstrated using "standard" procedures (e.g., demonstrating space-object relationships with the usual three-piece puzzle). Since standard assessment procedures were employed, it will be easier to use the results of those assessments for any comparative analyses one might want to perform, like deciding whether the skill emerged at the age when it would be most commonly expected and whether the skills seem to be emerging in the same sequence expected with most children.

2. Concepts that the child has demonstrated using "adapted" procedures, like demonstrating space-object relationships with a head nod when the teacher points to the piece that will fit a puzzle. If care has been taken to maintain at least the same level of difficulty with the adapted procedures, one can be sure that the individual *does* have the concept involved and that the concept can be used in the development of other skills. However, since the adapted procedures may not be of equivalent difficulty, results of those assessments should not be used for comparisons with "normal" developmental expectancies.

3. Concepts that the individual failed to demonstrate, but that may simply be delayed due to basic physical limitations, as would be the case if a blind child failed to find a silenced bell to demonstrate object permanence. Attempts to retest those concepts should be postponed until the requisite physical behavior has been developed. For example, the teacher would first train the individual to find *ringing* bells, thereby demonstrating auditory localization skills. Then the individual would be directed to find a *silenced* bell to demonstrate object permanence.

4. Physical skills and sensory modes that were found most useful as "tool" behaviors for the adapted demonstration of concepts. For example, "staring at objects" might be listed if the individual was able to use that skill to

indicate which blocks in a row were blue and which were red. That list of skills may prove useful in deciding how to arrange new adaptations for the instruction or assessment of other concepts.

The information is then analyzed to determine how well the individual is progressing, what concepts remain to be developed, and how they might be developed or assessed more successfully in the future.

Critical Effects

Although it is important to develop an individual's physical and cognitive tool behaviors, it is equally important to remember that they *are* just tools. At some point, the teacher must consider how those tools will be blended and orchestrated to accomplish something of significance for the individual. That leads to the consideration of skills where the effect of an interaction is of primary concern. The specific nature of the concepts or physical behaviors that the individual will use to accomplish that critical effect will be of some concern, but virtually anything that accomplishes the critical effect should be acceptable:

stimulus – – – – → response – – – → EFFECT

(concepts	(some forms	(the result
using	of behavior	of the
certain	may be	interaction
types of	preferred,	is of
cues or	but virtually	primary
materials may	any response	concern)
be preferred,	that works	
but virtually	will be	
any concept	acceptable)	
that works		
will be		
acceptable)		

Many critical effects will be fairly obvious. If, for example, an individual is to be placed in a sheltered workshop to sort electronic parts, then the teacher must find that combination of physical skills and concepts that will enable the trainee to accomplish that end. A normal person may use a pincer grasp to pick up the parts and sort them on the basis of color. If necessary, however, the trainee could use a palmar grasp or simply slide the parts over the edge of the countertop into bins suspended below the edge. Similarly, if the trainee were color blind, a size/shape discrimination or match-to-picture approach might work. In either event, it is fairly obvious what the trainee must accomplish.

In other cases the critical function of a skill will be somewhat obscured. "Independent walking," for example, is a common goal in many curricula for severely and profoundly handicapped persons. At first glance, it would seem like a physical tool behavior. Most tool behaviors, however, have a virtually infinite range of purposes. For example, wrist rotation allows a child to eat soup with a standard spoon, write with a pencil, turn an electronic part to fit into a circuit board, and use standard sign language. Walking, on the other hand, actually represents a complex combination of tool physical behaviors, including balance and flexion/extension of the legs, that has a relatively narrow range of purposes, i.e., the transportation of an individual from one place to another. If an individual does not have the tool behaviors that enable normal walking, alternative ways of accomplishing the same critical effect should be considered (e.g., crutches, wheelchairs, scooter boards, or even directed rolling). That does not mean that any method of accomplishing the same critical effect will be as desirable as any other method. There are several factors to consider.

1. Efficiency and effectiveness. It is most important that the individual accomplish the critical effect is *some* manner, even if that manner is highly unusual. Once the critical effect can be achieved, emphasis is usually placed on the development of those concepts and motor behaviors that will increase the individual's efficiency. If the individual has all requisite tool behaviors and concepts, the most efficient method is frequently the "normal" method, but there are many examples where a simple task analysis of the skill has led to the elimination of redundant or inefficient steps (e.g., Crosson, Youngberg, & White, 1974; White, 1968). Efficiency might also be increased through the use of special cues, artificial limbs, or mechanical devices, but care must be taken in the selection of prosthetic aids so as not to limit the generalizability of the skill or to make the individual any more dependent upon those aids than is absolutely necessary.

2. Generalization. Having targeted a general critical effect as an instructional target, like "locomotion," the teacher should then try to identify the various situations in which that critical function might be important. Adaptations useful in some situations may fail utterly in others. The basic motions involved in walking over level ground, for example, are readily adapted by the normal individual for locomotion over rough ground, up and down ramps or stairs, and up or down ladders. The use of a wheelchair may help an individual over the level ground and ramps, but, at the least, crutches or braces would be necessary for most stairs and rough ground, and the strong application of the individual's arms would be necessary to overcome ladders unless some very special prosthetic devices were developed. Finally, the variables of distance and time might be important. Over what distances might it be important to move? How rapidly? A motorized wheelchair might be almost as fast as a normal individual's walking gait, but would the battery carry the individual as far as a lighter wheelchair that the individual could move by himself or herself? Obviously, there is no "best" answer. The particular needs of the individual must be considered. As with the issue of basic efficiency, however, the behavior that most closely approximates that of normal individuals is also likely to prove the most generalizable.

3. External dependencies. Teachers should always strive to make an individual as independent as possible. In selecting adaptations, therefore, attempts should be made to minimize the individual's dependence on other people or special devices. The best possible adaption is one that involves neither another person nor a special device, such as using a shape discrimination instead of a color discrimination to sort electronic parts. If that is impossible, or for some reason inadvisable, the use of prosthetic devices or procedures that the individual can obtain, arrange, and use without help should be considered. The individual might, for example, pick up one part, place it in a bin, and then find all similar parts with a match-to-sample procedure before selecting another part to sort. If the individual is not able to arrange the prosthetic device, the teacher should then try to find an adaptation that someone else might have to set up, but that the individual would at least be able to maintain without continued assistance. Perhaps the teacher could place one of each part in a separate bin or prepare pictures ahead of time for the individual to use as samples in the sorting task. A prosthetic device or procedure that requires the continued assistance of someone else is least desirable, as would be the case if the trainee needed someone to help pick up each part before it could be placed in the appropriate bin.

In some cases the need for "continued assistance" is rather subtle. Successful expressive communication depends, for example, on the existence of another person with the appropriate *receptive* communication skills. An English-speaking child needs to talk to another English-speaking person. Little can be done about that. With some adaptations, however, dependence is increased by narrowing the range of people who have the appropriate reciprocal skills. If a nonverbal child is taught to sign, he or she will only be able to use that skill with other signing people. That may also be an acceptable level of dependence, in view of the alternatives, but the teacher should be aware that the dependence exists and work to minimize its impact whenever possible. For example, the teacher might make sure that the deaf child can also communicate at least essential needs with pictures, written words, or common gestures that might be more commonly understood.

4. Other development. Certain adaptations, while providing immediate benefit of some sort, may have detrimental effects on the development of other skills. O'Brien, Azrin, and Bugle (1972) found that they had no success in teaching a group of profoundly handicapped children to walk until they were prohibited from crawling. Crawling had simply become so efficient for these children that they saw no reason to walk. In the same way, a child taught to dress himself or herself with specially designed clothes may lag in the development of more generalizable skills involving the type of clothing worn by most children and most readily available in most stores. Similarly, the physically impaired person who is given a "swivel-spoon" has little reason to develop the wrist control necessary for using standard eating utensils. Certainly there is a place for crawling, special clothes, or swivel-spoons, but care must be taken to balance their immediate usefulness with long term goals.

5. Appearance. The importance of appearance cannot be overestimated. Even if an individual cannot function normally, if he or she *appears* normal, there is likely to be less adverse reaction to his or her behavior. One of the best features of the approach discussed earlier for "purchasing an item" was that the individual appeared far more normal than if the exact change were laboriously counted, one coin at a time, or if the trainee continuously asked people to rummage through his or her money. Whenever possible, teachers should try to devise adaptations that are unobtrusive and normal in appearance.

It will be difficult or impossible in many situations to find the ideal adaptation that balances all of the concerns listed above. The relative importance of each concern in most situations is reflected by its order in that list, but there are several factors that may alter those priorities:

1. The immediate usefulness of the skill. If a skill will be of immediate usefulness to an individual, then emphasis should be placed on the development of that skill in the most efficient and effective manner possible, even if all of the other factors (i.e., generalizability, dependency, other development, and appearance) are adversely affected. For example, if an individual has an opportunity to gain paid employment contingent upon the ability to accomplish some particular task, then any prosthetic devices or other adaptations that can be developed to help that individual accomplish that task should be considered. Similarly, if the parents of a young child complain that they cannot wait long enough for their child to dress independently in the morning, it would be highly desirable to investigate the use of special clothing or prosthetic devices that will speed up the self-dressing process so the child continues to develop *some* independence. Work should, of course, proceed at other times of the day to develop more generalizable dressing skills.

2. Time available. If many years remain to work with an individual before he or she must leave the educational system, then emphasis should be placed on developing the most widely generalizable and adaptable skills possible. For example, the development of fine motor skills should be emphasized in assembly tasks rather than the use of prosthetic devices that avoid the need for those more common movements. As an individual nears the time for transfer to an adult placement, however, emphasis should be placed on the identification of those critical functions that will be most important for success in that placement and instruction should concentrate on the development of the most efficient means by which those critical functions might be achieved—regardless of how nongeneralizable or nonadaptable those behaviors might be.

3. Consistency of demands. The relative importance of efficiency and generalizability/adaptability will depend on the consistency of the demands that will be placed on an individual. If, for example, an individual is likely to be employed to perform the same basic assembly task for a period of several months or years, the use of prosthetic cues or devices to facilitate that task is not likely to pose a major problem. Special picture-cards might be used that illustrate each step in the assembly sequence, or special devices could be built to hold each part in the assembly task in the proper position until it is needed. If, on the other hand, the nature of the assembly task is likely to change quite frequently, it may not always be possible or economically feasible to prepare new prosthetic devices or cues continually for each task. Emphasis must then be placed on the development of somewhat more generalizable skills, like the skill to pick up and assemble any set of objects in a particular sequence, regardless of what those objects might be.

4. ***The availability or "portability" of devices or persons required by external dependencies.*** External dependencies in the demonstration of a skill might be acceptable in some situations, but not others. For example, in a classroom where one teacher and one aide must divide their attention among six or eight children, a dependency on special prosthetic devices may be acceptable, but a dependency upon the continued attention of another person would pose serious problems. Similarly, prone-boards or waterbeds for support of the body, vision enhancement devices like large-screen televisions for the presentation of reading material, and special head-stick typewriters for expressive communication might be easily accommodated in a special classroom, but such devices will usually not be available in regular classrooms, on a street corner, or at most community-based job sites. Even the use of a common prosthetic device like a wheelchair is frequently restricted by the architectural barriers of a world designed by and for nonhandicapped people. If interaction with the nonhandicapped world is a high priority, then programs to reduce dependencies on "nonportable" prosthetics should also be a priority.

ANALYZING EXISTING CURRICULA

As mentioned earlier, an attempt should be made to define potential future placements for each pupil or group of pupils, to analyze the environmental demands of those situations, and then to develop a general curriculum to teach the skills that will meet those demands. Rather than concentrate on the specific behaviors that "successful models" in each of those placements demonstrate, however, the teacher should first isolate the critical effects that those models are accomplishing, identify all of the various tool skills that might be used to achieve those same critical functions, and order the alternatives from most to least desirable according to the criteria discussed above. Programs could then be individualized in a rational manner. The teacher would know exactly what critical effects the individual must accomplish in order to be reasonably successful, would have a list of various skills that might be arranged to accomplish those effects, and would have a set of basic criteria for judging the usefulness of new adaptations if the set of "standard adaptations" proves unusable in any given case.

The development of such a curriculum is far from easy, however. In many cases the teacher will not know exactly where an individual might be placed as an adult. Also, most curricula are arranged according to some general "hierarchy" that describes the sequence in which skills might be developed. If a skill is radically adapted at one point in the hierarchy, however, what effect will that have on the development of subsequent skills? A child must have head control before learning how to walk, but is head control also necessary for locomotion in a motorized wheelchair? If a child is allowed to move about in a motorized wheelchair, what effect will that have on related objectives like the development of crawling skills or the use of braces? What about objectives with completely different critical functions, like the development of social skills? These and other questions are currently being addressed by the Consortium on Adaptive Performance Evaluation (CAPE) (Note 6), but they are still a long way from providing complete answers. In the interim, the following may serve as guidelines:

Identify specific needs whenever possible. If specific placement options are known, then of course every attempt should be made to identify the general skills that will be required by those placements. If that is not possible or specific placement options are unknown, the teacher should begin by analyzing whatever curriculum guides or assessment devices have been used in the past. Presumably, the skills listed in those materials are representative of the skills that will be required in most situations.

Identify the critical elements in each skill. Try to decide whether the purpose of the task, curricular item, or assessment item is to demonstrate some concept (e.g., "space-object relationships"), to attain some sensorimotor tool skill (e.g., "head control"), or to achieve some important critical effect (e.g., "obtain an object" through whatever means).

Rewrite each skill description to reflect its important elements. If the time and resources are available to rewrite each item in the general curriculum, then that should be done. The descriptions should be translated into statements that emphasize the critical elements of the skill to be developed. For example, "picks up raisin" might be translated into "demonstrates pincer grasp." If time is not available to rewrite the descriptions, at least a little code might be used to indicate which elements of the skill are believed to be critical. For example, a little c, m, s, or e could be placed next to each item to indicate whether the objective of the skill is to demonstrate a concept, a motor skill, a sensory skill, or simply to achieve some critical effect. Those codes will then provide people with at least a general idea of the elements in the skill that might be adapted and those that should remain standard.[2]

Describe at least a few ways in which the skill might be demonstrated. Ideally, describe how a "normal" individual would usually demonstrate the skill and then one or more "standard adaptations" that might be used for children with common handicapping conditions. For example, describe how object permanence might be tested with a normal child by covering an object with a towel, and then how a bell might be used with a blind child. If some procedures for development or assessment of the skill are preferred, be sure to indicate those preferences. It might, for example, be better for a child to demonstrate certain expressive communication skills orally than with sign, if both behaviors are equally possible.

---

[2]Some instruments are already available with "critical element" codes for each skill. One such instrument, the Uniform Performance Assessment System (UPAS, birth to 6-year scale) is available from the Experimental Education Unit, Child Development and Mental Retardation Center, WJ-10, University of Washington, Seattle, Washington 98195.

Indicate the basic parameters that should be considered when developing "nonstandard adaptations." Try to identify those stimulus or response dimensions that will make a concept more or less difficult, increase or decrease the efficiency of a motor response, or make a skill for obtaining a critical effect more or less generalizable or adaptable. For example, when describing an object-permanence objective, it should be noted that finding an object through auditory localization will be more difficult than finding an object through visual localization. Similarly, if the size of an object used in demonstrating a pincer grasp makes a difference, that should be explained; and if an individual will be able to work on a wider range of assembly tasks if he or she uses size/shape discriminations instead of match-to-picture discriminations, those differences in preference should be described. These notes will be helpful in devising new adaptations whenever they are required.

Develop a systematic way for people to record the results of adaptive assessments or program planning. The form illustrated in Figure 1 developed by CAPE provides an example of one way in which that information might be recorded.[3]

Item listings. Space is provided on the left-hand side of the form to list the items or objectives being assessed. Only key words are usually put in that space (e.g., "head control") and a much more detailed description of the desired skill is provided elsewhere.

Assessment data. Next to the item listing, space is provided to record the individual's performance on several assessment trials. The teacher might, for example, ask a child to sort 10 blocks according to size and note his or her success on each trial in the boxes provided. Those trials are then analyzed to determine whether the individual met the criteria established for skill mastery (e.g., three correct trials in a row) and the final score is recorded in the "results" section.

Standard results. Unless it is quite apparent that an individual cannot perform a skill using "standard procedures" (e.g., a child with no arms will not be able to use a pincer grasp to pick up a pencil), some attempt to assess "normal behavior" should be made. The results of that assessment are recorded in the two columns labeled "standard." One column, labeled "assess," is reserved for indicating whether the individual met the criteria for success in a formal assessment situation, that is, a time when a trained person carefully set up a special situation and directly observed whether the individual responded appropriately. The other column, labeled "report," is reserved for recording whether the individual has ever been observed, however casually, to demonstrate what appeared to be the skill in question. Perhaps, for example, the parents of a child say that they have seen their child rotate a doorknob without moving his arm, or the

---

[3]The form shown in Figure 1 represents only a preliminary draft of the forms under development for use with CAPE's assessment instrument. It does not necessarily reflect the actual forms that will be included in the final instrument.

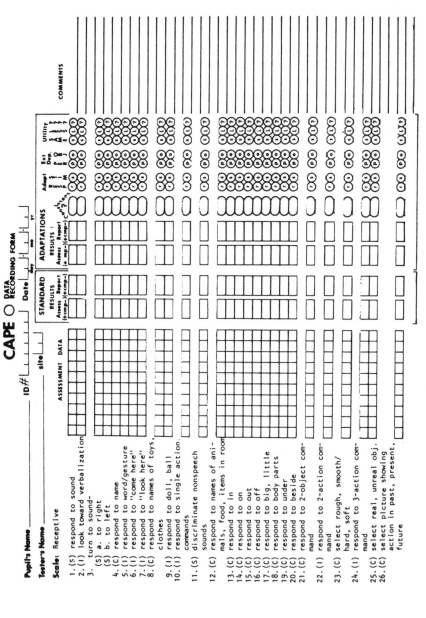

Figure 1. Consortium on Adaptive Performance Evaluation (CAPE) data recording form.

child's teacher has noted that the child is able to eat soup with a regular spoon without spilling—implying that he must have wrist rotation. Those observations would be noted in the column labeled "report." An apparent discrepancy between the results of formal assessment and reported observations will be very useful information for program planning. For example, the child who does not pick up an object when told to do so, but who has been seen to pick up objects on his own, probably only needs continued instruction in the meaning of "pick up" or needs to be motivated to apply the skill, rather than instruction in the physical skill per se. If the cues or prompts used to evoke the individual's responses are important for determining how useful the skill is likely to be, then a special coding system can be devised to record the type of cues used. For example, CAPE allows the tester to code four different conditions: +, if the individual displayed the skill without any form of artificial cues whatsoever; *c,* if extra verbal or gestural cues were necessary in order to evoke the response; *p,* if it was necessary to physically prompt the individual; and −, if the individual failed to display the appropriate response under any circumstances. If one or more of those cues is unacceptable (as, for example, a complete physical prompt might be when trying to test the individual's physical ability per se), then the code for that type of assistance is removed from the list of acceptable codes provided on the form.

Adaptations. If the individual fails to reach criterion on the nonadapted, standard task, then adaptations should be attempted. Again, space is provided for recording the results of both a formal assessment of the skill (using standard or nonstandard adaptations) and the observations of people who are familiar with the child. If a standard adaptation is employed (e.g., the use of sign language for the demonstration of expressive communication skills), then a number is recorded that corresponds with the number of the adaptation on a list of possible adaptations provided elsewhere.

If a nonstandard adaptation is employed, like having a child stare up to indicate yes and down to indicate no as a means of meeting the requirements for an expressive communication skill, then the implications of that adaptation are noted by checking one or more of the boxes provided to the right of the results section. First, the adapted element of the interaction is indicated by checking either *r* for response (e.g., staring up or down instead of saying yes or no) or *s* for stimulus (e.g., using sign language to make a request of the child instead of verbalizing instructions in a receptive communication task). The tester then notes whether the adaptation increased the individual's dependency on a person or object. For example, the up and down eye movements for yes and no require a person who knows what the code means, so *p* would be checked in the "external dependency" column. If a special body brace were used to maintain correct posture while walking, the *o* for "object" would be checked. If certain types of adaptations are unacceptable, then the boxes that correspond to those adaptations are deleted from the form. When testing for a purely physical response, adaptations in the nature of the response would be unacceptable, so the *r* box would be deleted from the form. Similarly, if dependency on a person were not acceptable for some type of interaction, the *p* would be removed from the "external dependency" columns on the form.

Next, the overall "utility" of the adapted skill is noted. If the adapted skill will be just about as useful as the unadapted skill in most situations, *s* for "same" is checked. For example, the usefulness of a color discrimination is not reduced just because the child had to nod his head to indicate that he could find the green blocks. If the adapted skill is likely to be somewhat less useful than the nonadapted skill should have been, *l* for "less" is checked. For example, the skill of picking up a small object with a prosthetic limb is likely to be less adaptable to other situations than the use of a pincer grasp. If the implications of the adaptation are simply not known, as might be the case when trying to decide whether finding a man under a blanket is really the same as the locating of a small object under a towel for the demonstration of object permanence, the *?* is checked. Finally, space is provided for a few key comments that might help in the interpretation of results.

By scanning down the assessment form after the results are recorded, it should be possible to tell at a glance which skills remain to be developed, which skill elements (stimulus or response) are most likely to require adaptations when those skills are developed, and which adapted skills may require additional attention (either because of increased external dependency or because of reduced utility). Moreover, by looking at just the results of the "standard" (unadapted) assessments, the teacher can determine the degree to which the individual appears to be behaving "normally" (even if those normal behaviors were delayed in development); and by taking the best of the assessments—whether standard or adapted—the teacher can determine the degree to which the individual is able to *accomplish* the same things as a normal person, even if the individual does so in an abnormal way. Those comparisons will help to place the individual's development in a meaningful perspective.

IN CONCLUSION

Much remains to be learned about the concepts and procedures involved in adaptive goal setting, assessment, and instruction, but there seems to be no lack of places to begin. Even if the teacher begins with only a single skill and approaches it from the perspective of "critical function" instead of "usual form," the benefits to the individual may be great. The teacher begins by asking *why*, why should an individual learn this skill? What will the pupil accomplish with it? And if the pupil cannot accomplish that end by using the tools a normal individual might use, what are the alternatives? The answers to such questions can be crucial in the development of individualized programs that truly help handicapped people meet the environmental demands of the world in which they live.

REFERENCES

Brown, L., Nietupski, J., & Hamre-Nietupski, S. *The criterion of ultimate functioning and public school services for severely handicapped students.* Madison, Wisconsin: University of Wisconsin and Madison Public Schools, 1976.

Crosson, J. E., Youngberg, C. D., & White, O. R. Rehabilitating the mentally retarded: A behavioral approach. In P. L. Browning (ed.), *Mental retardation rehabilitation and counseling.* Springfield, Illinois: Charles C Thomas, 1974.

Decker, T. N., & Wilson, W. R. The use of visual reinforcement audiometry (VRA) with profoundly retarded residents. *Mental Retardation,* 1977, *15*(2), 40–41.

Fulton, R. T., & Spradlin, J. Operant audiometry with severely retarded children. *Audiology,* 1971, *10,* 203–211.

O'Brien, F., Azrin, N. H., & Bugle, C. Training profoundly retarded children to stop crawling. *Journal of Applied Behavior Analysis,* 1972, *5,* 131–137.

Skinner, B. F. *The behavior of organisms.* New York: Appleton, 1938.

Stolz, S. B., & Wolf, M. N. Visually discriminated behavior in a "blind" adolescent retardate. *Journal of Applied Behavior Analysis,* 1969, *2,* 65–77.

White, O. R. *The analysis and programming of vocational behavior.* Working paper #17, Rehabilitation Research and Training Center in Mental Retardation, University of Oregon, 1968.

White, O. R. *The glossary of behavioral terminology.* Champaign, Illinois: Research Press, 1971.

White, O. R., & Haring, N. G. *Exceptional teaching: A multimedia training package.* Columbus, Ohio: Charles E. Merrill Publishing Co., 1976.

White, O. R., & Haring, N. G. Evaluating educational programs serving the severely and profoundly handicapped. In N. G. Haring & D. D. Bricker (eds.), *Teaching the severely handicapped* (Vol. 3). Seattle: American Association for the Education of the Severely/Profoundly Handicapped, 1978.

White, O. R., & Liberty, K. A. Evaluation and measurement. In N. G. Haring & R. L. Schiefelbusch (eds.), *Teaching special children.* New York: McGraw-Hill Book Co., 1976.

REFERENCE NOTES

1. AAESPH (American Association for the Education of the Severely/Profoundly Handicapped), Consortium on Adaptive Performance Evaluation (CAPE), Committee on Infant Assessment (CIA). *Adaptive assessment for evaluating the progress of severely/profoundly handicapped children functioning between birth and 2 years.* A field-initiated research proposal, submitted to the Bureau of Education for the Handicapped, grant number G00772139, 1977.

2. Dr. Lou Brown, personal communication, fall, 1976.

3. Mike Day, personal communication, 1976.

4. Jean Kelly, personal communication, 1977.

5. Ann Hogan, Jeff Siebert, and Diane Bricker, personal communication, 1977.

6. AAESPH (American Association for the Education of the Severely/Profoundly Handicapped), Consortium on Adaptive Performance Evaluation (CAPE), Committee on Infant Assessment (CIA). *Adaptive assessment for evaluating the progress of severely/profoundly handicapped children functioning between birth and 2 years.* The annual report of a field-initiated research project funded by the Bureau of Education for the Handicapped, grant number G00772139, 1978.

Chapter 3

Language and Severely Handicapped Persons
Deciding What to Teach to Whom

Wayne Sailor, Doug Guess, Lori Goetz,
Adriana Schuler, Bonnie Utley, and Marylud Baldwin

Literature on the teaching of language to severely handicapped persons is burgeoning, and yet in any given classroom serving severely handicapped students the probability remains high that some students will lack systematic language instruction and that others will fail in their language programs despite dedicated teaching efforts. The term *severely handicapped* is used here to refer to those students whose educational needs center primarily on the development of basic skills (Sontag, Smith, & Sailor, 1977). There is particular concern for those students who do not evidence any consistent form of communication, often even after intensive programming, and who in addition may evidence single or multiple sensory deficits and mild to severe neuromuscular involvement. This population can be described as *prelinguistic* because of their frequent failure to develop any functional speech and language.

Professional concern, therefore, is not directed to remediating deficiencies in already established patterns of communication, but rather to facilitating the emergence of language through alternative means. Language assessment and instruction for these students present very complex sets of problems. A major decision confronting any programming team is the identification and selection of a mode for presenting information to and receiving responses from each student in order to maximize the probability of functional communication. Despite reports of successful language instruction in nonspeech modes including gestural language (Topper, 1975), simultaneous communication (Stremel-Campbell, Cantrell, & Halle, 1977), and graphic symbols (LaVigna, 1977), there are few systematic attempts to specify particular communication modes that are most likely to be successful with particular subgroups of severely handicapped students.

This chapter reports the initial development of an assessment model that can be used to make decisions in the selection of modes of language instruction for individual severely handicapped students. Before presenting the assessment model, however, some broad issues related to language instruction are discussed. These issues are relevant to *any* form of language or communication assessment and instruction. For purposes of clarity, some basic terms are defined below.

Communication is used to refer to social interactions in which some information is exchanged, but participants do not necessarily share complex systems of grammatical or syntactic rules governing the interchange. For example, a student may reliably indicate "want food" through gestures, vocalizations, or even words without sharing the rule system that would allow specification of a particular amount or kind of food, from a specific person, and so on.

Language is used to refer to interactions in which participants share highly differentiated and structurally complex systems of symbolic reference, and systems of rules governing the form of the interchanges. Prelinguistic severely handicapped students must begin instruction with forms that establish the function of *communication* before a longer range goal of complex *language* may begin to be realized.

Mode is used interchangeably to refer to the form in which the content of a message is expressed. Speech, manual signs, or pressing buttons on a communication board are all *modes* of communicating.

Input refers to the mode in which a student receives messages.

Output refers to the mode in which a student expresses messages.

Modality is used to refer to the individual's sensory channel (auditory, visual, or tactile) that receives information from the environment during any communication exchange.

PREREQUISITES TO LANGUAGE INSTRUCTION: CURRENT ISSUES

Cognitive Prerequisites

The question of the existence and nature of prerequisites to language instruction is widely debated in the literature. Relying primarily upon the developmental theory of Piaget (1962), Bricker and Bricker (1970) have argued that one specific prerequisite to language is the learner's ability to separate himself or herself from physical objects and to act upon these objects in purposeful ways. Object permanence, means-ends relationships, and functional object use are considered *cognitive prerequisites* to language, and the child is taught to use objects functionally before learning to give them linguistic labels.

Reichle and Yoder (1979) have recently extended this line of observation further by citing evidence (Reichle & Yoder, 1976a, 1976b) that suggests that severely handicapped students learning to communicate fail to exhibit spontaneous, *intentional* communicative forms prior to reaching Piagetian sensorimotor Stage 5 (means-end). Similarly, Kahn (1975) reported the observation that severely handicapped persons use no verbal referents prior to evidence of functioning in sensorimotor Stage 6. Reichle and Yoder conclude that a model of normal language development provides the best prediction of the sequence of stages in which a severely handicapped student will progress through the attainment of early communication skills. They argue that other models (e.g., Guess, Sailor, & Baer, 1978) succeed in establishing the rudiments of communication, but inevitably fail to produce generalized *initiated* behavior in addition to substantially cued responses. Reichle and Yoder (1979) then suggest that behavioral intervention models fail to produce an active communication use system and, instead, teach a passive, responsive communicative system because these intervention systems fail to teach or follow the emergence of cognitive prerequisites.

Guess, Sailor, and Baer (1978), on the other hand, reported the failure to turn up any hard evidence to support the arguments for cognitive prerequisites to communication instruction. Guess (this volume) reviews a number of studies in which communicative structures were successfully taught to severely handicapped students in the absence of their presumed prerequisites. With respect to the Reichle and Yoder (1979) conclusion on communication initiation, Gee (Note 1) successfully taught the initiated, spontaneous use of noun-referent manual signs to a severely handicapped student who was learning a first-time communication system. Gee's method was to train a generalized use of signs across various persons, settings, and noun objects *from the outset* rather than following initial acquisition in a tightly cued, instructional situation.

Hollis and Carrier (1975, 1978) make a careful distinction between the information exchange process (communication) and language itself. They argue that communication is a *prelinguistic* phenomenon and prerequisite to language development. Language, in contrast, involves a set of semantic and syntactic rules that permit a correlation between the representational systems of two or more persons. According to Hollis and his associates, simultaneous attempts to teach both the information exchange *process* and *language* to a communication-deficient child are likely to result in failure. Training should begin with the cognitive prerequisites to language and, when the child is proficient in the *process* of information exchange, then proceed to training the more complex production and reception characteristics of language. It is Hollis's assertion that cognitive prerequisites to language (learning to exchange specific symbols) do exist and must be taught prior to language instruction. Nonspeech symbol systems such as Non-SLIP (Carrier & Peak, 1975) are believed by these theorists to provide a learning sequence that should facilitate the later development of speech and receptive language.

Other authors (Mahoney, Crawley, & Pullis, in press) have suggested that the prerequisites to language are *social* in nature. They stress the importance of communication as a social act and suggest that natural patterns of language interaction should be more closely analyzed in order to provide information about social interactions that might facilitate language learning. Their emphasis is upon the social context in which language is likely to be evidenced.

Table 1. Different language systems in terms of processing modes, modalities, and stimulus arrangements

Language system	Primary input modality	Primary output mode	Stimulus arrangement
Speech	Auditory	Verbal	Temporal
Signing (all systems)	Visual	Manual	Temporal/Spatial
Direct selection aids (e.g., communication boards)			
Rebuses/Pictures	Visual	Motor (various forms)	Spatial
Blissymbols	Visual	Motor (various forms)	Spatial
Three-dimensional objects	Tactile	Motor (various forms)	Spatial

Processing Constraints and Overselectivity

Research (Koegel, Egel, & Dunlap, this volume; Lovaas & Schreibman, 1971) suggests that some severely handicapped individuals may respond differentially or overselectively to input from specific modalities (i.e., auditory vs. visual) and that autistic children in particular may evidence specific processing constraints dependent upon whether stimuli presented to them are arranged temporally or spatially (Schuler, 1979). To expand on this, speech, for example, is arranged temporally such that each word, once presented, is "lost" in time to be replaced by the next word, and so on. Writing, on the other hand, is arranged spatially and each word in a sentence remains fixed in time and space. Initial investigations (Schuler, 1979) suggest that it may be possible to improve communication of autistic individuals by shifting from temporal to spatial input arrangements. While additional replication of these findings is of course necessary, the work does suggest that severely handicapped learners may have *processing preferences* that remain unknown due to currently incomplete or imperfect assessment techniques.

Table 1 presents an evaluation of different language systems in terms of the processing modalities and stimulus arrangements involved. A student with a strong temporal processing preference, for example, might respond poorly to instruction that is heavily dependent upon transient auditory cues, such as speech. The detection of early processing preferences awaits future refinements in assessment techniques.

ASSESSMENT

Different Input and Output Modes

Although it may at first appear surprising, it is quite likely that practical application of an assessment-decision model will result in different input and output modes for a severely handicapped student. Hollis, Carrier, and Spradlin (1976) and Hollis and Carrier (1978) provide extensive discussion of variables related to selecting input and output modes for communication and language training. On the input side, the student may receive information transmitted in the visual, auditory, tactile, and even the olfactory modality as a primary basis for communication. On the output side, the learner may express language by means of a motor activity, including manual sign systems, or may be taught a fine motor transmission system, such as directional eye movements. While graphic expression (writing or printing) and speech are, of course, the more common output modes, they may not be immediate options for the severely handicapped individual. Communication may have to occur using manual sign systems or even idiosyncratic motor movements such as gestures or directed eye movements. Thus, *sensory efficiency* and *discriminative ability* are primary considerations in the selection of an *input* mode, while *motoric capabilities* become primary to the identification of an *output* mode.

Combinations of various input and output modes over the course of communication training are possible. For example, a student may initially require a communication board–Blissymbol input–output system with instruction geared to shifting from board-generated input to speech. It is critical to remember that input and output are two separate systems and that each requires separate assessment and training. A student may express himself or herself to others using a communication board, but if he or she can use speech as an input mode, he or she will be able to understand a much broader language community than if the input system is also necessarily tied to the communication board. The determination and preliminary teaching of the output mode should *precede* selection of an input system, since the *output* channel will be needed to evaluate the success of input efforts. In order to determine if initial information is received there must first be a form of reliable, and differentiated actions (expression) based on input.

Reichle and Yoder (1979) have recently presented a concise discussion of some of the key issues in the determination of input and output formats for early communication instruction with severely handicapped persons. Table 2, reprinted from their chapter, presents a sample of communicative acts as a function of the relationship between input modality and mode of output.

Assessment Strategies

Assessment prior to initial instruction is basic to the determination of a communication strategy for severely handicapped persons. It must necessarily result in a prediction of the most efficient utilization of scarce resources including student effort, teaching staff time, and possibly the cost of equipment.

At one level, the assessment examines the child's behavioral repertoire including aspects of cognitive and communicative development. If, for example, a student "communicates" his or her needs through temper tantrums, screaming, or other undesirable behaviors, then the teaching of more appropriate communicative means to bring about environmental changes would be a likely place

Table 2. Modality function

Stimulus input	Response output	Behavioral example
VISUAL	Visual	Natural gaze
		ETRAN Chart
VISUAL	Motor/Manual sign	Observing manual sign and signing
	Gesturing	response
VISUAL	Motor/Pointing	Picture on Command Board
		Blissymbolics
	Motor/Gross movement	Word boards/Language board
VISUAL	Vocal/Verbal	Naming pictures
		Reading words
		Oral response to manual sign
AUDITORY/Verbal	Visual	Visual glance at agent/object/action in response to request or command
AUDITORY/Verbal	Motor/Manual sign	Signed response to verbal stimulus
	Gesturing	
AUDITORY/Verbal	Motor/Pointing	Communication board response to verbal stimulus
Auditory/Verbal	Vocal/Verbal	Use of vocal/verbal response to verbal stimulus
VISUAL-MOTOR (Signing)	Visual	Visual glance at agent/object/action in response to manual sign or gesture
	Motor/Manual	
	Motor/Pointing	
	Vocal/Verbal	
VISUAL-Verbal	Visual	See examples above
	Motor/Manual	
	Motor/Pointing	
	Vocal/Verbal	
TACTILE	Visual	To touch stimulus the child responds with any of the usual means
	Motor/Manual	
	Motor/Pointing	
	Vocal/Verbal	

From Reichle and Yoder (1979); reprinted by permission.

to begin. Similarly, a student who relies on a gross gesture such as mouthing a clenched fist to signal hunger may be providing a valuable cue as to the most likely sign with which to begin instruction in manual communication.

Until very recently, there have been essentially no guidelines to assist the teacher or language interventionist in the selection of an appropriate communication system matched to the needs of the individual severely handicapped person. Commonly, teachers who favor speech models tend to attempt to teach words, input and output, in the *speech* mode to all of their students. Those who favor "total communication" select the simultaneous instruction model in all cases, and so on. Waldo, Barnes, and Berry (Note 2) have recently disseminated a total communication checklist and assessment which enables the teacher to collect reliable data across a broad spectrum of considerations in the selection of an initial communication system. Their manual provides a very useful guide to the systematic observation of prelinguistic communication acts with the severely handicapped population.

On a much more general conceptual level, the recent chapter by Shane (1979) provides a system for arriving at a decision between vocal and nonvocal instruction in early communication efforts. The goals of communication, by this analysis, are the ability to express wants and needs, and to describe the here and now. Shane's model suggests expansion of the child's options for expression and reception as the child progresses in instruction from simple declaration of wants and needs to descriptions of present events. The model places a strong emphasis on an analysis of the requirements of the language environment, including the prevalent communication systems of the people in the environment and the skills of the caregivers in providing relevant cues.

Assessment must also extend to the student's environment, for it is crucial that the extant environment support and reciprocate developing communication skills. If the critical others in a child's present or future environment are unable or unwilling to become proficient in signing, selection of manual signs as a language mode is unrealistic and inappropriate if other options are available.

Another aspect of assessment includes the way in which a child processes information, i.e., whether modality preferences are exhibited, and whether the child can attend to multiple-stimulus input, search, scan, and so on. Obviously, one must also examine gross and fine motor performance and determine the student's capability to produce oral movement and vocalizations, directed reaching, and other controlled body movements.

While clearly some assessment must occur prior to communication and language instruction, communication assessment is, in fact, a continuous process that cannot and should not be clearly differentiated from teaching. Assessment and teaching are closely interwoven processes, with assessment dependent upon data obtained through close monitoring of student responses to teaching efforts.

Communication System Possibilities

The basic communication modes available to severely handicapped persons include speech, manual signing, and communication boards with alternatives available within each mode. For example, possibilities for manual expression include American Sign Language (ASL), which is a complete linguistic system independent of spoken language; Signing Exact English (SEE), which corresponds to a manual system for spoken English; and gross gestures (cf. Hamre-Nietupski, Stoll, Holtz, Fullerton, Ryan-Flottum, & Brow, 1977). The reader is referred to the summaries by Wilbur (1976) and by Shane (1979) for analyses of various manual communication alternatives. Communication boards may vary in size, layout, symbols employed (e.g., pictures, miniature objects, printed words), and the response modality used.

Each of these systems can be evaluated against three criteria: portability, language capacity, and the potential communication audience. Speech is clearly the preferred mode because of its obvious portability (the oral musculature is always present). It has infinite language capacity, and is the dominant communication mode of our culture. Both manual signing and communication boards (or similar aids) have unique advantages and disadvantages for the student who is not a speech candidate. While signs are obviously portable and signing systems such as SEE have the potential for infinite language growth, environmental applications of signing are in general limited to settings where others sign to communicate or have extensive receptive sign repertoires. Communication boards present the disadvantage of requiring the user to always have the equipment available in order to communicate (a complex board may not travel well on the school bus, for example), and the potential for language growth is limited as a function of the symbol system selected, and by the physical capacity of the board. However, depending upon the type of symbol system needed, it is likely that the board user will be able to convey messages to any literate adult speaker simply by including small printed words along with the actual symbol, such as is done in Blissymbolics (Kates & McNaughton, 1974).

Sensory Evaluation

In order to determine if speech is an expressive possibility, one must begin with an assessment of the sensory capabilities of the student. While it is not at all unreasonable to expect an otherwise normal blind or deaf child to acquire speech, it is probably unreasonable to assume that a severely handicapped blind or deaf child has this capability. Speech production requires fine auditory and/or visual discriminations in order to produce a match to modeled stimuli in an imitation paradigm. Visual and/or auditory impairments in a severely handicapped individual need not rule out speech if efficiency in these modalities can be substantially improved through prosthetic devices.

Several new programs are currently underway to refine the visual and auditory assessment of severely handicapped students. One of the newest of these (Utley, Note 3) focuses on functional classroom assessment for the deaf/blind population. This particular project has developed a package of procedures to be used by teachers of severely handicapped students to determine the relative *efficiency* with which a student with sensory impairment functions in his or her environment. The idea is to enable a teacher to structure an individualized education program (IEP) for the student that will contain both *compensatory* and *remedial* teaching strategies. Compensatory strategies include objectives that are designed to compensate for sensory impairment in either the auditory or visual modality. They enable the student, usually with the aid of prostheses, to function effectively in a normalized environment at a low level of sensory efficiency. For example, a blind student is taught to orient to and localize the source of sounds that serve as cues for reinforced actions. At the same time, initial objectives are set to provide remedial treatment of sensory deficit where some residual hearing or vision exists. Objectives of this type are intended to teach the student, literally, to see and/or hear better by requiring use of information available through the impaired modality. For example, a student for whom a severe auditory loss has been prosthetized recently with hearing aids is now required to respond to auditory cues only to earn reinforcement in a teaching session. The combination of compensatory and remedial programming should progressively facilitate a student's reliance on impaired sensory modalities by a progressive shift from a ratio of many compensatory objectives and few remedial objectives to a ratio that maximizes the growth and development of sensory efficiency.

Auditory Assessment If the teacher of a severely handicapped student suspects a hearing loss, he or she might record the student's responses to a variety of situations (described below) and present the results to an audiologist to supplement audiological testing or to justify the need for such procedures. If the student vocalizes and imitates some sounds, the teacher can record the accuracy of vocal imitations under conditions when the teacher's face is available as a visual cue and under conditions where the visual cue is absent. A comparison of performance under these two conditions can be used to provide an indication of the relative reliance on auditory and visual input. For a nonverbal student, the teacher should record the student's response to sound. The test stimuli should generally include speech, environmental sounds (e.g., a spoon scraping the inside of a bowl or water pouring from a pitcher into a cup), and musical instruments (e.g., maracas, school bells, squeak toys). The teacher should position the sound stimulus no more than 12 inches away from the student's head and alternate presentations of the stimuli 3 to 4 inches on either side of the posterior midline. When presenting the stimulus, the teacher holds it in position for about 10 seconds before activation and then presents the sound stimulus for 2 or 3 seconds. The student may respond with an increase or decrease in activity; a startle, eye blink, smile, or head turn, with or without an accompanying reach for the object, and any response to sound should be recorded with differentiated scoring between stimulus presentations to the student's right and left sides. This procedure is continued until suitable reliability of response measurement is obtained.

Vision Assessment Visual functioning assessment ideally begins with a thorough ophthalmological examination by a pediatric ophthalmologist who has experience with severely handicapped individuals, and is willing to communicate and share data with other professionals. Teachers who do not have access to quality ophthalmological services or who wish to supplement ophthalmological examination may take classroom data on the following three classes of visual behavior.

Conjugate Eye Movements There are several informal techniques for evaluating how well a student's eyes work together. The student should be seated (or in a supine position with flexion at neck, hips, and knees if nonambulatory) with the teacher opposite, approximately 12–18 inches away. The teacher should be positioned so that the child's face is on the same "plane" with the teacher looking directly into the student's eyes. A brightly colored yellow or green object (a penlight inside a "pop" bead or finger puppet) is then introduced at nose level. The teacher can shake or tap the object to get the student's attention, but as soon as the student looks at the object the movement should cease. The teacher should then look quickly at the student's pupils, and if the eyes are working together, the bright object will be reflected exactly in the center of each pupil. To be used effectively, this technique must be practiced on another adult until the teacher is confident that he or she can make the necessary observation quickly and accurately. A careful record of the student's responses should be kept. Students who are very active or those suspected to be extremely visually impaired should be tested in a darkened room.

Similar observations should be made of the student's tracking movements. The same brightly lit objects may be used. After the student has fixated on an object, the teacher should move the object on a horizontal plane to both sides, and observe whether tracking occurs and whether both eyes follow the object smoothly. The wandering eye is probably not providing the student with meaningful input.

The final observation of the eyes' ability to work together again employs a brightly lit object. Fixation is obtained as in the first observation at nose level and at midline, but this time 18 inches in front of the student. The object is then moved quickly toward the tip of the student's nose. The object should continue to be reflected evenly in both pupils up to 4–6 inches from the tip of the student's nose.

Data on the student's responses to these tasks should ideally be shared with an ophthalmologist. For the nonambulatory student whose restricted range of motion gives little indication of visual functioning, poor responses on conjugate eye movements may indicate severe visual impairment. For active, severely handicapped individuals who are positioned upright, poor responses may indicate *strabismus* (poor coordination of the eye muscles). The assessment items are useful also as objectives for training. Control of eye muscles is, for some severely handicapped students, a learned behavior. Ophthalmological recommendations regarding corrective lenses and/or patching must be implemented conscientiously since failure to use both eyes may lead to degeneration in the function of the weaker eye. The primary educational implications of poor conjugate eye movements and resulting suppression of input from one eye are: 1) a limited field of vision, 2) no compensation for the blind spot in each eye, 3) uniocular visual acuity is usually less than combined binocular visual acuity, and 4) assessment of depth perceptions is less accurate with vision limited to one eye.

Visual Field The most common evaluation of visual field involves manipulation of two penlights in a darkened room. The test is done on one eye at a time with the other "occluded" with an eye patch or eyeglass frame with an occluder clipped over first one eye, then the other. The teacher sits facing the student, or straddling the nonambulatory student in a supine position, with both the student's and the teacher's faces on the same plane. One penlight is held at nose level approximately 18 inches from midline. The second penlight is held at the teacher's arm length in eight different positions, one at a time, forming a circle around the student's head. The teacher extends his or her arm out to the side at shoulder height, holding the second penlight. Both lights should be off at this point (also both lights should operate silently to avoid the confounding effect of a "click"). The centrally positioned penlight is then turned on (and flicked on/off a few times to get the student's attention if necessary) until fixation is obtained. Then, *simultaneously,* the central light is switched off while the light at arm's length is switched on. The student should shift fixation to the new source of illumination. That light is then turned off and, in darkness, the teacher extends his or her arm straight up over the head and the procedure is repeated. Measures of the student's shift in fixation are taken straight up, down, right and left, and at points midway. Two complete circles of the student's responses or failures to respond are charted. The evaluation is done first at the teacher's arm length, then 10–12 inches from the tip of the student's nose.

A failure to respond in the outer circle (as well as a failure to respond in a "slice" of the circle) may indicate a degenerative condition of the retina that may require medical intervention. The educational implication of a restricted visual field is primarily the limitation in mobility imposed by seeing within a "cone." Attempts to obtain the student's attention are ineffective unless done directly in front of the face. Visually scanning a display of stimuli (on a communication board, for example) may be inefficient for the student unless he or she is taught to use a head turn with the scan.

Visual Acuity   The third class of visual behavior to be assessed is visual acuity or central vision. An ophthalmologist working with a fairly cooperative student can measure acuity adequately with the use of drops to dilate the pupil and an ophthalmoscope. Corrective lenses can then be prescribed. There are also several testing procedures applicable for use by teachers with some severely handicapped students (Dunn & Smith, 1965; Lawson & Schoofs, 1971; Sheridan, 1969; Von Noorden & Maumence, 1973). For uncooperative students a teacher can make use of careful presentation of stimuli at measured distances to determine the distance appropriate for presentation of instructional materials. The distance each student holds objects to examine them visually is then observed and recorded. The educational implications of uncorrected central vision defects are results of "fuzzy" images that limit finer discriminations.

Vocal Proficiency

Consider a student who presently lives and receives education in an environment that is characterized primarily by speech as the dominant mode of communication, and suppose that within the year the student is expected to be moved from a special school and placed in a class for severely handicapped students in a public school where speech is not only prevalent, but more complex. It is clear that the attainment of competence in speech and receptive language would greatly facilitate this student's likely future success in his or her new placement. It has been determined that the student is fully efficient in the visual modality but suffers a hearing impairment that has only recently received prosthetic attention. As a result, auditory efficiency has been significantly delayed, but is steadily improving with instructional efforts. At this point, a decision to instruct toward proficiency in expressive speech remains a distinct possibility. The next task is to attempt an assessment and prediction of the student's capabilities for the physical aspects of speech production. For example, if the student manifests Down's syndrome, and is characterized by distended tongue and tongue-thrust, should speech be ruled out on the basis of improbable control over the vocal musculature? Not long ago the answer would have been an unqualified yes, and the same pessimism would have been applied to otherwise capable individuals with cerebral palsy. Today, the decision not to instruct speech is not so easily and readily made. Guess, Sailor, and Baer (1978) have reported summary results from a field-test effort with over 400 severely handicapped persons utilizing their speech and language instruction program. Many students within the field-test sample had Down's syndrome, and a significant number of the remainder were diagnosed as having cerebral palsy in addition to other multihandicapping conditions. Many of these students actually progressed through the program with a high degree of resultant articulation proficiency. With the Down's syndrome group, it appears that tongue control may well *follow* the establishment of speech production in a differential reinforcement paradigm with gradually increasing demands on articulation proficiency. Not long ago, tongue control was regarded as prerequisite to speech development.

McLean (1976) has recently provided a very useful and comprehensive analysis of issues surrounding speech production in language-deficient children. McLean argues that, before electing to establish language through the speech mode, the teacher should have some evidence for a student's awareness of vocalization as a linguistic mode, a factor that may be *prerequisite* to success in an instructional program to establish functional receptive and expressive speech. However, with severely handicapped students, it is often difficult to determine the extent of any *prior history* with vocal production. In some cases, reports exist of the emergence of limited speech at an early age, which subsequently disappeared. In other cases, no speech sounds have ever been reported. If the determination of a severely handicapped student's awareness of speech as a communicative mode is difficult, however, observations can be made of whether any vocalizations (pitch, inflections, grunts, etc.) are used for communicative purposes.

A principal criterion for the determination of speech production proficiency as an outgrowth of instruction is the potential for phonemic articulation. It is this criterion, unfortunately, that is least predictable with present methods. Clearly, a student who evidences speech sounds (phonemes), and particularly one who seems to approximate words, on occasion, with the *intent* of communicating, meets the initial criterion for speech instruction (other variables notwithstanding). For this student, McLean (1976) would advise a course of language instruction that uses a distinctive feature approach to the establishment of articulated speech, with initial instruction addressing at least the following issues:

1. *Confusion of similar articulation features:* Initial words taught should contain sounds that are dissimilar in voicing and manner features.

2. *Developmental errors of articulation:* Young children produce articulation errors that appear to be perceived as if correct articulation by adult listeners. Attempts to provide early correct substitutions are probably unnecessary and are possibly regressive.

3. *Attention to specific phonemic features as they occur in various places of articulation:* This approach will likely prove more fruitful than planning instruction according to the emergence of phonemes in normal development.

4. *Train consonant distribution in a phonemic chain as word chains become more complex:* This approach will preserve syllable integrity and facilitate speech articulation.

McLean's objective is to ascertain the probability of later *intelligible* speech from initial assessment data. Unfortunately, many severely handicapped students will need to be taught, at an extensive outlay of time and resources, a sufficient amount of initial speech in order to make the determination suggested by McLean.

At this juncture, it is safe to say that there are two somewhat contrasting viewpoints on the decision to instruct a severely handicapped student in speech. The more traditional position argues for the assessment and determination of prerequisites to speech and articulation with particular emphasis on evidence of cognitive ability. Hollis and Carrier (1978), for example, suggest that a "cognitive map" of that which is to be communicated about must be (figuratively) in place before its initial linguistic expressions. On the other hand, a behaviorist position puts much more stress on the *pragmatics* of communication, that is, what speech is likely to accomplish for the child that other communication modes may not. The importance of early articulation receives little emphasis in this perspective, while the selection of first words for their functional impact receives great emphasis.

Imitation Fortunately, nearly all of the contending factions in the beginning speech instruction issue are presently able to agree on one diagnostic point. If a student cannot be taught to imitate words, then that student cannot be taught to communicate in the speech mode. Of the original sample of severely handicapped students who were screened for instruction in the Guess, Sailor, and Baer (1976) program, 40% failed to progress to the *entry level* required by the program. This failure to teach imitation occurred despite nearly 2 years of intensive instruction with this group using the most sophisticated teaching methods known at the time. Why some severely handicapped students seem incapable of learning to imitate, when all other systems seem functional, remains an issue for ongoing research.

The role of imitation in the emergence of speech in normal infants remains a controversy in theoretical psycholinguistics (cf. Bloom & Lahey, 1978). Behavioral psychology has regarded imitation preceded by babbling as the initial fabric from which later coherent speech production is fashioned through differential reinforcement (Staats, 1968). Cognitive psycholinguists, on the other hand, have argued that "surface structures" such as imitation play a relatively minor role in subsequent language acquisition and emergence (Slobin, 1968). In the case of the language-deficient, severely handicapped student, however, it is safe at this point to say that verbal imitation is necessarily *prerequisite* to the subsequent development of speech as a mode of expressive communication. The problem of a decision model, then, is how to determine the propensity for verbal imitation where none is evidenced.

Bricker, Dennison, and Bricker (1975), working from within a Piegetian theoretical framework, investigated the establishment and maintenance of "vocal chains" as an avenue to instruction in imitation. Vocal chains are transactional events between the instructor (adult) and the child. The adult imitates the child who then "imitates" the adult if the adult's sound is immediately followed by a second effort by the child. Bricker et al. (1975) found that repetitive vocal chains could be lengthened only if the child imitated the chain in the early stages of instruction. Welch (Note 4) similarly found that vocal chains in nonimitative children could be lengthened, but could not, in her efforts, be transformed into single instances of child imitating adult phonemes.

Behavioral techniques and procedures have been used extensively to teach generalized imitation skills to nonimitative children. Typically, the strategy has been to present a model of the vocal stimulus to be imitated (e.g., "John, say 'Mama' "), wait briefly for the child's response, and reinforce the child for close approximations to the modeled vocalization. Training usually continues in this manner until the child begins to imitate new vocal sounds the first time they are presented. At this point, the child is said to have learned a *generalized imitative repertoire,* from which point the child can be taught to use words in a symbolic or functional manner.

Although operant procedures have been successful, most researchers and language teachers agree that more sophisticated methods must be developed to teach nonverbal children to imitate. The typical procedure described above is arduous and time consuming, requiring a language teacher to present the same vocal stimulus perhaps thousands of times until the child begins to imitate. Then a second sound must be trained and brought under imitative control; then a third sound, and so on. This method of instruction may continue for months or even years before the child becomes a skilled, generalized imitator. Recognizing the need for more efficient ways to teach this important prerequisite skill, various training strategies have been used to teach language-handicapped children to imitate. Baer, Peterson, and Sherman (1967) taught nonimitative retarded children to imitate a wide number of motor movements (e.g., the teacher raises his or her hand and says to the child, "Do this") before beginning training on vocal items. They reasoned that training motor imitations allows the teacher to physically assist the child through the desired imitation while this sort of prompting is not generally available when training vocal imitations. Sloane, Johnston, and Harris (1968), using much the same rationale as Baer et al. (1967), also required their subjects to master motor imitations that involved movements of the tongue and mouth. Once the subjects were imitating these motor movements (e.g., open mouth), training began to include a vocal component as well (e.g., the subject was required to open the mouth and say "ah"). Lovaas, Berberich, Perloff, and Schaeffer (1966) taught autistic children to imitate verbally by bypassing motor imitation and training a stimulus that possessed salient auditory and visual cues (i.e., "ma" instead of "ka") reasoning that some children learn to discriminate sounds with visual (lip closure) and auditory components more easily than those with auditory cues alone.

Much imitation training in use today fails to provide sufficient rationale for the type of response (either motor or vocal) to be trained. In many cases, attempts have been made to teach specific verbal imitations that have never been in a child's spontaneous vocal repertoire. Thus, children are required to emit new and often quite difficult phonological responses. Some sounds (e.g., [a], [ka], [i]), seem to be quite simple to most adults, but actually require complex coordination between the various voicing and musculature structures. Severely handicapped children often have a very difficult time trying to produce the more complex responses associated with speech sound production. In the past, operant techniques, especially shaping, prompting, putting-through, and fading have been invaluable tools in assisting severely handicapped children to learn specific utterances. However, for many nonimitative children, the language teacher might be premature in attempting to teach new sound production without first taking the necessary steps to ensure that prerequisites for the target behavior already exist. Sometimes the selection of phonological responses for imitation training might not be the appropriate starting point, especially for children whose spontaneous rate and diversity of sounds are very low. Bricker et al. (1975) emphasized the need to select vocal models that the child has been observed to produce spontaneously. Utilizing the child's own vocal repertoire as the primary indicator of what vocal stimuli should be trained ensures that the child possesses the phonological-response prerequisites necessary to produce the responses physically. The task that remains is to bring these responses under imitative stimulus control.

The two primary issues in initial attempts to teach verbal imitation have been: 1) *selection of initial phonemic stimuli,* and 2) the *role of nonvocal imitations* in the establishment of a vocal-verbal imitative repertoire. The historical perspective of these efforts to teach imitation is extensively discussed elsewhere (see Guess, this volume). In short, the selection of sound stimuli for initial training has progressed from: 1) lists of phonemes and phonemic combinations arranged by developmental norms in increasing difficulty and complexity, through multisyllabic words and phrases (Lovaas, 1977), 2) through similar stimuli hierarchically arranged by increasing complexity according to an analysis of distinctive features, particularly phonemic contrast (McLean & McLean, 1978), 3) through vocal chains of child-initiated stimuli (Bricker et al., 1975), to

4) direct imitation of simple words arranged in a hierarchy of practical utility to the student (Sailor & Guess, in press).

Turnbull (Note 5) examined a variant of this notion in a study that compared two methods of teaching imitation to normal 18-month-old infants. Baseline data were initially gathered on vocal frequency and diversity in the children. The stimuli to be trained were selected from the obtained probability of occurrence in the infant's natural repertoire. Turnbull then compared tapes of the infants' own vocal productions to tapes of the experimenter's *renditions* of those stimuli when used as training stimuli in a reinforcement imitation-training paradigm. The question of experimental interest was, "Will an infant learn to imitate an adult producing 'infant sounds' to be imitated, or will the actual 'infant sounds' provide more functional stimuli?" The issue is related to whether infants discriminate adult speech sounds as different from their own. The results, while somewhat equivocal, were suggestive of an enhanced generalization in vocal imitation when child-produced stimuli were in effect. Regardless of the adult-child speech discrimination issue, it was of interest in this study to demonstrate that 18-month-old infants could be taught generalized vocal imitation using sounds taken from their own initial babble repertoire.

Some further support for the selection of the student's own vocal output to use as vocal stimuli to be modeled comes from a recent study by Guess, Keogh, and Baer (Note 6). Analysis of sound tapes from three severely handicapped students led to groupings of training stimuli on the basis of "high frequency," "low frequency," and "zero production" conditions. Results of subsequent imitation training suggested that the high and low frequency sounds, with two of three students, were mastered more rapidly than equivalent new sounds not previously observed in the students' repertoires. The third subject of the study failed to learn to imitate any of the modeled stimuli.

A related issue is whether instruction in a nonvocal imitative repertoire precedes or facilitates the instructional effort in *vocal-verbal* imitation. Guess, Sailor, and Baer (1974) employed four different training procedures to establish generalized verbal imitation. One procedure taught a series of imitated motor activities such as clap hands, touch table, etc., *prior* to beginning instruction on sound-matching items. Two other procedures attempted to teach motor items mixed with vocal items in the same training sets, and a fourth procedure taught vocal imitation with no effort to utilize nonvocal training items. A subsequent comparative analysis of the relative success in training generalized verbal imitation accruing to each procedure yielded somewhat equivocal results but generally seemed to favor the vocal training procedure. It appeared from these data that vocal stimuli in an imitative instructional paradigm comprise a unique and separate stimulus set from that employing nonvocal motor acts. The resulting imitative repertoires develop separately, if at all, and motor imitation seemed not to facilitate progress in vocal imitation. Whether training in the motor repertoire actually *inhibited* progress in acquiring the vocal repertoire could not be ascertained from these data.

OPTIONS FOR COMMUNICATION OUTPUT

Speech Expression

It now appears that verbal imitation is *prerequisite* to successful instruction in speech communication with severely handicapped students. Success in teaching generalized verbal imitation may be predicted to some degree by the range of diversity and frequency of extant vocal expression. Further, if an effort is to be made to teach the prerequisite verbal imitation skill, that effort should probably concentrate upon teaching simple words that contain phonemes *already present* in the student's repertoire. Furthermore, success in teaching generalized verbal imitation may be a function of selection of initial stimuli that contain phonemes occurring at a high frequency within the student's vocal repertoire.

Suppose, for example, that the sound "uh" occurs with a high frequency in a severely handicapped student's babble repertoire. The teacher might elect to postpone a decision whether or not to instruct in the speech mode pending the outcome of an initial effort to instantiate prerequisite verbal imitation. This brings us to the issue of *first word* selection in imitation training. The teacher might, for example, elect to teach the word "tub" for reasons of phonemic contrast and distinctiveness. Or he or she might elect to teach the word "cup," which, while phonemically more advanced for some students and thus more difficult to produce, may well be the more functional word in the student's present environment. We would elect to teach the latter and use the success of the effort as a predictor of future success in speech instruction.

Before moving on from a discussion of assessment factors in the selection of speech as an expressive communication mode, it is necessary to consider the ramifications of an old and revered assumption in psycholinguistics, namely, that an individual must be able to comprehend an utterance as a prerequisite to producing it (Ingram, 1974). Bloom (1974) raised the issue of the relationship between the two linguistic processes as they bear on the initial language learner, who operates linguistically at Piaget's stage of concrete operations, versus the more sophisticated language user who operates at the stage of formal, logical operations. Bloom questions whether the assumption holds true in early stages of language development. Baer and Guess (1973) report a series of experiments which strongly support the conclusion that initial language training may proceed with instruction in the expressive mode first, with receptive acquisition in the second position. The two repertoires seem functionally independent, with acquisition of a linguistic structure (e.g., plurals) in one having virtually no effect on subsequent acquisition in the other.

The approach of this chapter to communication assessment with a severely handicapped student has begun with procedures to select an *output* channel: expressive language. It has elected to begin with a set of assessments aimed at determining the possibility for instantiation of expressive speech. It has called first for an examination of the child's environment—the social context in which the child presently lives and learns, as well as the next likely environment. It has called next for an examination of the child's sensory efficiency, his or her capacity for vocal expression, and the child's ability to learn to imitate sounds under ideal training conditions. Suppose as a result of one or more of these considerations, a teacher elects to rule out speech as the system to teach to a particular student. What then?

Manual Expression

Of all of the nonspeech language systems, manual signing certainly has the longest history and the widest social applicability, features that render it first place among alternative modes for communication with and for severely handicapped persons.

Ruling Out Manual Expression   Assessment considerations in deciding to instruct signs are substantially less formidable than for the decision to elect speech. For one thing, imitation is not prerequisite to sign language development as far as is known. Initial sign expressions may be started through a physical prompt and fade procedure consistent with many other types of instructional programs for severely handicapped students. As with speech, other primary considerations are with the physical aspects of language production and sensory efficiency. If a student is severely visually impaired in addition to showing severe, functional retardation, and visual efficiency cannot be substantially improved with prosthetic devices, then manual signing, above the level of gross gestures may not be successfully taught to the student. Functional deafness is, of course, not a problem for the acquisition of expressive signs. The most significant consideration, after vision, is *manual dexterity*. A student must be capable of performing relatively finely differentiated motor actions. A student, however, who is neither hypertonic nor hypotonic but who has poorly developed sensorimotor coordination, may be begun on a program of gestural communication (cf. Hamre-Nietupski et al., 1977) and guided, over time, toward manual signing by a combined motor-communication development educational program. A child with serious involvement of the upper extremities will not, in most cases, be a candidate for initial efforts to teach manual expression.

The most important distinction between speech components and *language* also holds for nonspeech systems. The choice of a particular manual linguistic system should be guided in part by expectations of linguistic proficiency. Many persons providing initial instruction to handicapped students in manual signing are relatively careless in the selection of initial signs to teach. In general, the first signs taught, unless gross-gestural in form, should be those signs that characterize or belong to the system in which the student is ultimately expected to become linguistically proficient and should also be signs that have an immediate utility for the student.

Kopchick and Lloyd (1976) have recently argued for use of a modification of Signed English proposed by Bornstein, Hamilton, Saulnier, and Roy (1975). This alternative has simplified the morphological-grammatical demand of the parent language by omitting the initial use of inflectional markers, thereby emphasizing semantic content without sacrificing syntax. This system is well suited to a "total communication" approach since it can be initially paired with reduced speech ("Tarzan talk") and the totality expanded later as the student becomes more proficient. Kopchick and Lloyd, however, go on to suggest that "total communication" (simultaneous instruction in both the speaking and signing modes) is the *preferred* method with all severely handicapped students, both expressively and receptively. They argue that simultaneous instruction will facilitate the later development of speech while leaving the child in the present with an alternative mode of expression and reception. They argue further that this approach is ideal for those students who have failed to evidence or to learn verbal imitation.

This conclusion, while compelling, seems a bit premature at this time. Common sense seems to suggest that language mastery of a system relatively easy to teach should facilitate later acquisition of the more complex system. Hollis and Carrier (1978) argue, for example, that mastery of the *linguistic* features of one system allows for a concentration on the surface features of the more complex system later. A student who has mastered the rules of language with signs (or symbols, as in Hollis and Carrier) should evidence later positive transfer to the content features of speech, through simple imitation. Research evidence on this issue to date is, however, confusing at best. While, for example, Stremel-Campbell, Cantrell, and Halle (1977) found a tendency for sign training to enhance speech with severely handicapped students, studies by McDonald (Note 7) and by Camozzi (Note 8) found no support for these efforts. Camozzi found instead that acquisition of receptive noun labels by three severely handicapped adults did not favor sign, speech, or "total communication" training. With two of three adult, severely handicapped subjects, a mild trend was established in a direction opposite to the usual prediction. Training in the simultaneous mode failed to enhance generalized effects to the same (untrained) nouns in response to either speech or sign requests. Rather, training in speech seemed to facilitate generalization to signed nouns! Apart from generalization effects, the results of the Camozzi study seemed also to suggest that simultaneous communication functions as a separate but equal system, not completely explainable by either of its two components. Training in the simultaneous mode, for example, did not seem to affect *acquisition* of the same noun-objects in either the sign or speech modes alone. Obviously, there is much to learn about application of the simultaneous communication approach to language instantiation with the severely handicapped.

Apparently, the information children use to acquire discriminations may be quite different from that which educators expect or hope for. This may especially apply to children whose perceptual idiosyncracies are among their most distinctive characteristics, as is the case with early childhood autism. Not only do autistic children often over- or underreact to sensory stimulation, but experiments have also recently shown that they seem generally unable to attend to multiple stimulus input when auditory and visual input are presented at the same time

(Lovaas & Schreibman, 1971; Schreibman & Lovaas, 1971). This deficit also appears when autistic children are presented with multiple stimulus input within either the visual (Koegel & Wilhelm, 1973) or auditory modality (Schover & Newsom, 1976). It is, therefore, at least questionable whether the simultaneous presentation of auditory and visual input as in total communication will benefit the severely handicapped student with autistic characteristics. In fact, Carr, Binkoff, Kolginsky, and Eddy (1978) found that in three out of four cases attention was only paid to the sign when signs and speech were presented conjointly in a language teaching program. Some current research suggests that autistic children may be better equipped to process visuo-spatial, i.e., nontransient stimuli (Schuler, 1979), but both speech and signs are transient stimuli. Schuler's study compared the rate of acquisition of receptive labels as a function of the stimulus characteristics of the labels used. She found that while no systematic discriminations were acquired between either spoken or signed labels with an adolescent autistic subject, written word labels were acquired with remarkable ease, as evidenced by fast acquisition rates and impressive generalization scores. In addition, efforts to use discrimination between written word labels as an aid in the acquisition of spoken and signed labels proved fruitless. Nevertheless, efforts to shift stimulus control from nontransient to transient stimuli were not exhaustive within this study. Signing, because it is coded both temporally as well as spatially, might be useful as an intermediary between a completely transient, temporal mode of processing, such as speech, and systems that are nontransient, such as communication boards, written word labels, and pictorial or abstract plastic symbols. Given that so many efforts to teach speech or signs to autistic-like students are met with limited or no success, the use of coding systems that incorporate a nontransient stimulus array should certainly be pursued. For instance, use of a communication board with autistic children might establish communicative intent, and possibly later serve as a stepping stone, through a stimulus-shift teaching paradigm, to a more transient system of communication.

Communication Boards

When neither speech nor manual signing is a viable possibility for expression, the language instructor may consider a wide variety of communication aids and techniques of which the *communication board* is the most widely researched and adapted. Much of the available technology and research in its development for severely handicapped persons had been conducted at the TRACE Center at the University of Wisconsin-Madison, and reported by Vanderheiden and Grilley (1977) and Vanderheiden and Harris-Vanderheiden (1976).

Vanderheiden and Grilley (1977) have distinguished three types of aids on the basis of the processing requirements needed for each: scanning, encoding, and direct selection, the latter being the least "sophisticated." Considering the severely handicapped population, concern here is primarily with *direct selection* aids, in which the child selects directly the symbols that convey a message.

Within this direct selection format, the symbol system used may be Blissymbols, rebuses, or pictographs (Woodcock, Clark, & Davis, 1968), or an idiosyncratic system such as might be developed for a deaf-blind severely handicapped student who selects a message via tactile feedback. Within a given symbol system, the particular type of motor response a student uses will depend upon sensory and motoric abilities; a head pointer, use of directional eye movements, or use of tactile feedback are all possibilities.

A communication board may range in complexity from the use of simple three-dimensional symbols representing a few basic needs to highly sophisticated electronic encoding and scanning boards. As with manual communication, the decision to adopt a communication board does not mean that attempts to train speech should discontinue. Concurrent instruction on lip closure, breath control, lateral tongue movements, and vocalizations should continue not only to control drooling where it occurs and to improve feeding skills, but to increase the possibility that functional speech may develop in the future through stimulus-shift instruction.

Selecting a Response Mode   There are many skills to be assessed and trained in preparation for communication board use. All of the visual behaviors described earlier need to be evaluated. Visual attention shown through facial orientation to the board, convergence of the eyes on training stimuli, and smooth visual scanning responses are all necessary for communication board use.

To assess and train board use, a severely handicapped student should be positioned to promote near normal muscle tone. The student should be seated with equal weight distribution, hips and knees at 90° angles, with the board positioned to avoid elicitation of primitive and abnormal reflex activity. For example, positioning might include restraint of an athetoid student's lower extremities by strapping or by placing sandbags next to (not on top of) the feet. The hypotonic student may need a chest harness to maintain an upright sitting position. Both hyper- and hypotonic students may need to have their shoulders rounded forward to enable the hands to make contact with training stimuli. Shoulders can usually be rounded forward by placing pillows or small wedges of foam behind them.

When the student is positioned well, an assessment can be made of the range of motion of the best upper extremity. This can be done by dividing a 12-inch by 18-inch piece of cardboard into quadrants. A potentially reinforcing stimulus such as an edible, or a series of small reinforcing toys can be placed in each of the quadrants on a trial basis. Data are then recorded on the student's range of motion as he or she reaches for the stimuli in the quadrants. The range of motion assessment information is used to determine placement of the symbols vertically and horizontally within the student's range. If the student has difficulty crossing midline, the display of stimuli can be centered at midline of the best extremity. Care must be taken, though, to make sure that placement of the training stimuli "off center" does not elicit an asymmetrical tonic neck reflex to that side or interfere with the student's functional vision. Just as teacher-collected data on visual assessment are shared where possible with a pediatric ophthalmologist, assessments of the type discussed here should be undertaken and shared, whenever possible, with a physical or occupational therapist.

While data are recorded on the range of motion of the student, two additional types of data may be recorded. One is the latency between delivery of the cue "touch toy" and the student's physical contact with the reinforcing stimulus. The other measure recorded is the student's ability to hold his or her hand (or finger, fist, etc.) in contact with the toy or edible. A response of 2 seconds' duration is the minimum required for interpretation of the movement as a discrete response. If the student lacks a controlled pointing response during assessment, it is highly desirable to train that behavior. A manual response is much preferred over any mechanical replacement (including a head stick) because the use of a mechanical response mode is often exhausting for physically involved students.

If it is necessary to use a head stick, the student must be taught control of it prior to introduction of the board itself. To make reinforcement contingent upon a correct communication response before the motor response is perfected may result in extinction of voluntary responses, or the appearance of associated reactions ("overflow" of abnormal muscle tone), which may interfere with an accurate response. A more extensive discussion of response mode options for use in adapting communication aids to severely handicapped students is available in Barnes, Murphy, Waldo, and Sailor (1979).

Board Construction and Symbol System Selection   An often overlooked element of many communication boards is the provision of a neutral position for the hands when the student is not attempting to communicate. The "hands ready" position should be trained as the first step of the student's expressive response. Departure from it then can serve as a clear cue to the trainer that an attempt at communication is being made.

The selection of symbols for the board is usually determined on an individual basis. To avoid the need for retraining with new symbols, consideration should be given to the flexibility and potential for linguistic expansion of the symbols chosen, as well as to their interpretability by nonboard users and their discriminability for the student. Simple high contrast (black on white), two-dimensional line drawings for vocabulary items are preferred by some teachers while photographs are preferred by others. The drawings then used should be done on paper with a flat finish to avoid the glare from high gloss paper. Photographic prints should have a flat finish for the same reason. A black and white line drawing of a glass, for example, can be trained to represent "drink" (of milk, juice, water) as an alternative to using a picture of a glass of orange juice. Photographs, however, have the advantage of greater representativeness (Shane, 1979). While Blissymbols are convenient symbols, it should be recognized that, just as with American Sign Language, Blissymbolics is a self-contained idiographic, linguistic system that uses discrete symbols to represent *concepts* rather than English words. The extent of cross-modal transfer from Blissymbolics to other forms of communication of English is unknown. Other systems, such as the Initial Teaching Alphabet (Clark & Woodcock, 1976), or rebuses, such as those represented in the *Peabody Rebus Reading Program* (Woodcock, Clark, & Davies, 1968), may in fact comprise more facilitative initial symbol systems in considering later linguistic development. Of course, functional considerations are of prime importance in the selection of content. The reader is referred to Clark, Davies, and Woodcock (1974) and Shane (1979) for a discussion of various symbol-system options.

Training Use of the Board   Once a response modality and a symbol system have been determined through the above procedures, two separate aspects of communication board use need to be trained. The first is discrimination among the stimuli on the board; the second is pairing of the symbols with the environmental objects or events they represent. The authors favor training these aspects separately, working first on discrimination and then later on symbolic representation. If an attempt is made to train representation and discrimination simultaneously, the student may form the discrimination without the trainer's knowledge and begin selecting stimuli according to his or her needs. For example, a student learning to discriminate a symbol for food from a symbol for drink may incorrectly choose drink when shown a bit of food in a teaching paradigm, simply because the student is thirsty and is communicating the need-request. The teacher may interpret the student's responses as a failure to discriminate. This is apt to occur particularly in situations where the relative reinforcement value between the training stimuli varies greatly. Some teachers attempt to correct for this by training representation of one symbol at a time; e.g., a sip of juice is contingent upon touching the "drink" symbol when *only* the drink symbol is within reach. Training one representative stimulus at a time either by presenting trials randomly with one choice available within each trial, or by massed trials on one stimulus before beginning instruction on a second representative stimulus, fails to produce discrimination. The student is not required to attend to the form on the board and, when presented with a choice, performance at "chance" level emerges. Several techniques can be employed to produce discrimination, with the most successful being a procedure to fade the intensity of visual stimuli (Bijou, 1968; Gollin & Savoy, 1968; Schelmoeller & Etzel, 1978; Schreibman, 1975; Sidman & Stoddard, 1967; Stoddard & Sidman, 1967). After a discrimination among stimuli is formed, the symbolic representation can then be trained in a free-choice situation. The student is allowed to select stimuli freely and the corresponding environmental event is delivered immediately.

Summary: Selection of an Output Mode

Figure 1 presents a schematic illustration of the major steps in the proposed sequence of assessment leading to the selection of an expressive communication system with which to begin initial instruction for a severely handicapped, nonlan-

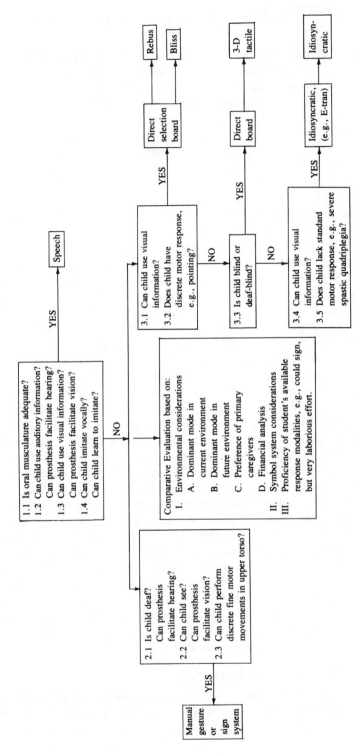

Figure 1. A schematic decision model for the output mode.

guage child. Systems for communication output are conceived in this decision model as a hierarchy, with speech at the top as the preferred mode of expression. A decision to begin instruction in speech is made unless various assessments, including auditory and visual efficiency, capacity for physical speech sound production, and the ability to learn to imitate vocally or verbally, rule speech out. Following a decision not to instruct in speech, a decision to teach manual signs is made unless this system, too, is ruled out by assessment of visual efficiency and/or sensorimotor functioning. If speech and manual communication (including "total communication" and gestural expression) have been ruled out, then the decision to instruct in a communication board or physical, adaptive-aid system is necessitated. Can all three systems be ruled out? The answer is no. Each severely handicapped student, no matter how extensive the involvement of handicapping conditions, is capable of learning to communicate expressively. Initial instruction in one of the three modes depicted in the schematic is appropriate for any student regardless of age and handicapping condition.

SELECTION OF AN INPUT MODE: LANGUAGE RECEPTION

This chapter began with the determination of an output mode with which to begin instruction and has stressed the *primacy* of output in the decision process because of the necessity of establishing a means for student self-expression and environmental control. While, obviously, the input-output modes are interdependent, this does not mean that an input channel must be selected that is the same as the output channel. Acquisition of skills in reception and expression has been determined to function initially as if reception and expression constitute separate response classes, and there is presently no basis to suggest that information transmitted *to* the child in speech cannot be used as the basis for transmission of information *by* the child in the manual sign or communication board modes. Furthermore, there is no hard evidence to suggest that initial instruction in one mode facilitates or in any way enhances production in any other mode during the early stages of communication skill acquisition.

Suppose a teacher wants to teach a child with no discernible communicative skills to learn receptively the name of the common noun-object "cup." Suppose further that it has been determined through the assessment-decision model to instruct in manual sign for output. This hypothetical student is efficient in the auditory and visual sensory modalities but has nevertheless failed either to demonstrate any imitation or to learn to imitate speech sounds or words. The teacher is now faced with a choice of instructing in sign, speech, a combination of the two, or symbolic representation through a physical aid. Here it is important to determine how much speech the student comprehends. If some experimental assessments in nonredundant (speech without visual cues) situations are indicative of a considerable degree of speech comprehension, teaching efforts should attempt to strengthen and expand these receptive skills. Such informal assessments might take the following form: A group of several objects is placed in front of the student, one of which is a cup. The student is then asked to pick up "cup" and the word "cup" is emphasized to stand out clearly. In this instance, the child may indicate reception of the message by reliably selecting the object cup. Subsequently, instructions of increasing complexity might be presented, such as "Give me cup and brush," "Put the brush in the cup," "Turn the cup upside down," "Show me the empty cup," "Show me the cup with milk in it," and so on. Each instruction would need to be devoid of visual cues from observing the teacher's mouth, or gestures, etc.

With severely handicapped students one will often find that the comprehension of speech becomes limited as soon as visual cues are eliminated and tasks are presented in a nonredundant manner. When a student is unable to make any consistent discriminations between words, information might have to be presented through different channels. In these cases it would need to be determined whether speech should be presented concomitant with signs or pictorial presentation, or written words, and so on. This might be accomplished by making comparisons between rates of learning when two systems are presented together and when they are not. Tests for the differential comprehension of two separate systems can be made once the student is making consistently correct responses. For some students, the ability to discriminate among various speech sounds may remain limited. In these cases, speech may in fact merely function to call attention to relevant visual stimuli.

There is little to guide the teacher in providing an answer to the question of an appropriate input channel for the child in the example above. Because speech was ruled out as the target for initial output instruction, it might be a temptation to rule out speech on the input side on the basis of sheer difficulty of speech discrimination relative to discrimination among signs. On the other hand, if this judgment is an error, and the student is fully capable of becoming linguistically proficient in speech reception, then the teacher will have denied the student a broader social context for the reception of language. Diagnostic factors may even complicate the issue. If the recent findings by Schuler (1979) find a wider replication, it may be that neither sign nor speech, nor even a combination of the two, is appropriate for receptive language in some children. Rather, a nontransient stimulus array may be necessary, such as can be symbolically or graphically displayed on a communication board.

Probably the best answer for the present is simultaneous speech-sign input coupled with sign-only output for the child in the previous example. While "total communication" has as yet failed to substantiate its promise as a facilitator of speech *output* in the severely handicapped, there is no experimental evidence to suggest that it does not provide a good basis for initial *language reception*. At best, the student learns two parallel systems and may eventually become proficient in reception in either system alone. At least, if stimulus overselectivity or other factors leads to reliance upon one of the two to the exclusion of the other, receptive communication is nonetheless established. Since there is no basis with which to predict the relative success of either speech or signs in the long run, the authors would elect to employ both but to assess continuously whether the speech component is, in fact, functional. The ultimate hope is, of course, that if the child learns to receive signs when paired with speech, speech reception will be more easily instantiated later by increasing response demand upon speech stimuli while selectively fading out signing.

The assessment factors in selecting an input channel begin with a consideration of the earlier decision on selection of an output system. If speech was selected as the output mode, then speech in most cases would also be selected as the mode of receptive instruction. This is because all of the assessment considerations that led to the decision to teach expressive speech would contribute even more strongly to a prediction of success in receptive speech instruction, with exceptions occurring only in relatively rare instances of aphasic disorders.

If the initial decision is *not* to teach speech production, then a decision must now rest upon the data from estimates of auditory and visual efficiency. Receptive speech is ruled out if the student is deemed to be auditorially insufficient. One may elect to instruct in receptive speech if a child is visually insufficient, but should recognize that auditory-tactile combinations may be required throughout instruction. If the decision not to teach speech was made solely on the basis of physical considerations, as with cerebral palsy, or the decision not to teach speech output was made solely on the basis of failure to establish vocal-verbal imitation, further evaluation of speech discrimination skills is warranted. At any rate, simultaneous use of speech and signs would in most cases be preferable if speech proves to be not interfering with the acquisition of signs.

The sole consideration in ruling out receptive manual sign instruction is visual insufficiency. Tactile signs, such as the palmar signing techniques used with some deaf-blind students, are almost certainly outside the range of likely discriminability as a linguistic mode for severely handicapped students.

A severely handicapped student who is also deaf-blind, that is, who is inefficient in both the visual and auditory modalities, will require a communication aid of the tactile board type for instantiation of receptive language skills.

A student who is efficient in both auditory and visual modalities, but for whom a decision was reached to teach communication board output on the basis of physical complications, as in cases of cerebral palsy, presents another difficult problem for a decision on receptive instruction. The student may be potentially capable of attaining receptive language in the speech mode but cannot show evidence for early skill attainment if all inputs are made solely through the board. For these students, a *pairing* of board input (e.g., rebus symbols) with speech is probably the most viable initial receptive effort. Consistent fading out of board stimuli to leave speech reception becomes a possible ongoing teach-test strategy.

To summarize, if a child is being instructed in expressive speech, teach receptive speech skills, too. Rule out speech input if the student is auditorially

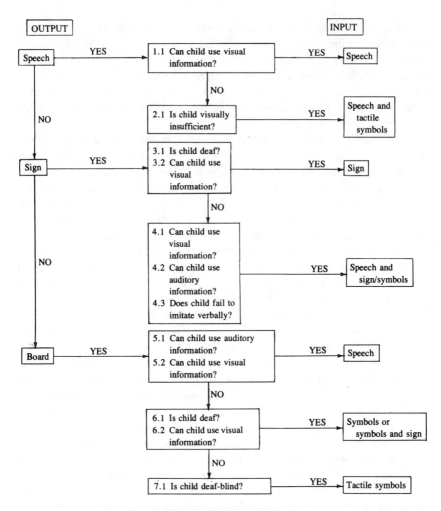

Figure 2. A schematic decision model for the input mode.

insufficient. Manual signs should be ruled out for receptive training if the child is visually insufficient. Finally, both speech and signs should be ruled out if the student is insufficient in both visual and auditory channels. Figure 2 presents a schematic illustration of these considerations. As the figure indicates, the initial step involves focusing upon a student's output mode. Pairings of two modes of communication, such as speech and sign for the child who could not imitate, or board and speech for the severely, motorically impaired student, are frequently recommended as possibilities for initial receptive language development. As a student begins to become proficient in receptive language characterized by paired systems, efforts may be begun to selectively reduce dependence upon the less preferred system (e.g., increase signs and reduce communication board). Both

Figure 1 and Figure 2 are meant to provide general guidelines for a logic of assessment, and are not intended to be programmatic in a "cookbook" sense. Often the best answer to one of the various questions posed in the two schematic models may be gotten from an initial effort to teach the more preferred system.

THE FIRST VOCABULARY

Having selected a tentative communication system, the first step is to validate the choice by teaching some initial communication responses to the student. A small body of recent literature suggests that the content of a communication program may have important facilitative effects upon learning. In particular, the *functionality* of the response for the student appears to be a major criterion for selection of responses, which implies that many first utterances should function as requests for relevant actions. Guess, Sailor, and Baer (1978), for example, have defined functional responses as ones that "...1) produce an immediate consequence for the child; 2) the consequence is potentially reinforcing; 3) the consequence is specific to the response, and 4) the response is natural to the child's interaction with the environment" (p. 114). Some examples of functional responses might include imitating swinging a small bell back and forth to hear the ringing sound, labeling a cup expressively in order to gain access to the juice in the cup, or tactile scanning and selection of a specific symbol for vibrator resulting in several seconds of sensory feedback from an actual vibrator. Experimental evidence supporting the use of functional responses in language training has been reviewed in detail elsewhere (Goetz, Schuler, & Sailor, 1979), but a few examples warrant discussion here. Saunders and Sailor (1979) trained three institutionalized retarded children on two-choice discrimination problems using toys to which nonsense labels had been assigned. Training involved three different reinforcement conditions: 1) *specific,* in which a correct response to the request "Point to X" resulted in an opportunity to play with the toy pointed to, 2) *nonspecific,* in which a correct point resulted in the opportunity to play with a third, uncorrelated toy, and 3) *variable,* in which a correct point provided access to either the toy pointed to or an uncorrelated toy 50% of the time, in randomized order, as a control for the effects of two reinforcers versus one reinforcer in the other conditions. Results for all three subjects favored the specific reinforcement condition, suggesting that response-specific reinforcers facilitate discrimination.

In an unpublished study that focused on the acquisition of motor imitation responses, Carpenter (Note 9) found that imitations involving actions with objects (i.e., squeezing a plastic bottle full of water) were learned faster than topographically similar imitations that did not use objects (i.e., imitating a squeezing motion), again suggesting that responses that are natural to the child's interaction with the environment and that also produce natural consequences may facilitate learning. Janssen and Guess (1978) have also provided data suggesting that experience in functionally manipulating an object, such as learning to staple with a stapler, may enhance discrimination among objects. These authors compared acquisition of receptive labels in four profoundly retarded subjects under two conditions. In one condition, subjects were taught to point to objects using standard reinforcement procedures; in a second condition, in addition to receiving reinforcement for a correct response, the subject was shown the function of an object and given the opportunity to perform it. Contingent upon an incorrect response, the student was required to imitate functional use of the object and he or she then received reinforcement. The general trend of the resulting data was suggestive of more rapid acquisition for those items concurrently trained in functional use.

In light of these data, what criteria should a teacher follow in selecting initial responses for communication training? A logical first step would be to obtain an inventory of both the child's school and home (or nonschool) environments, in search of objects and events that occur naturally with high frequency and that are of interest to and functional for the student. Nearly all severely handicapped students will have high frequency interactions with food objects, eating utensils, and the event of eating; many will also have regular interactions with self-help objects and events; for others, the experiences of being lifted up, positioned, laid down, and so on, will be frequent. Having rank ordered those objects and events in terms of frequency, a second step would be to analyze the most frequent items in terms of their reinforcement value for the student. Although many severely handicapped students will frequently experience being buckled into and out of wheelchairs, "seat belt" is probably not an event that is particularly reinforcing to the child. "Brush" used in the context of hair brushing may be a less frequently used object, but one that a particular student finds highly reinforcing. The result of this inventory should thus be a list of objects or events that occur with reasonable frequency and that have some intrinsic reinforcing properties for the student. Before making a final selection of vocabulary, however, the teacher should also consider whether some potentially highly reinforcing events have been overlooked precisely because the student lacks the communicative skill to request them. Thus, a severely spastic, low vision child may enjoy listening to music but, without communication skills, be unable to request this event. The teacher should, therefore, also explore reinforcement sampling (Striefel, 1974) with events that have reinforcement potential. In particular, events that provide sensory feedback, such as music, a bell, stroking the skin, vibration, and visual displays such as blinking Christmas lights, may be highly salient to the severely handicapped student (Rincover, Newsom, Lovaas, & Koegel, 1977). These events may not occur in the child's natural environment with high frequency but they are potentially ideal for teaching initial communicative responses because they do rely upon natural, response-specific, powerful reinforcers. Similarly, initial vocabularies can be employed as substitutes for aberrant behaviors. For instance, a student who displays high rates of self-stimulatory behavior, such as twirling objects, may be taught signs or words to request objects such as spinning toys or records to play. In these instances, rates of inappropriate behavior might be directly decreased by teaching functional communication. By tying language objectives more closely to a student's current behavioral repertoire, and by emphasizing *functional* rather than *structural* concerns, efforts to teach communication might well take on a much broader scope, helping to make progress toward normalization an objective of all teaching efforts.

CONCLUSION

The model presented in this chapter suggests that a decision to instruct in a particular communicative mode can be made on the basis of thoughtful and reliable evaluations of those factors that, taken together, make effective communication possible: the student's environment, extant communicative repertoire, processing preferences, sensory proficiency, and motoric capabilities. Many of the broad issues involved in communication assessment will require further data before firm conclusions can be drawn. In particular, the role of prerequisites to language instruction and the nature of the relationship between different communication modes are questions in need of clarification that may ultimately have a substantial impact upon effective communication assessment. Advances in the development of strategies for assessing sensory efficiency, processing preferences, and current communicative functioning level, as well as in teaching methodologies for developing critical skills such as vocal imitation, will also contribute substantially to improved methods of evaluation for communication instruction. The need for further data on these questions, however, is presently no reason for failure to assess *all* students in a given severely handicapped classroom. Deciding what to teach to whom is not always an easy task, but as the evidence presented here suggests, it is always both possible and necessary.

REFERENCES

Baer, D., Peterson, R., & Sherman, J. The development of imitation by reinforcing behavioral similarity to a model. *Journal of the Experimental Analysis of Behavior,* 1967, *10,* 405–416.

Baer, D. M., & Guess, D. Teaching productive noun suffixes to severely retarded children. *American Journal of Mental Deficiency,* 1973, *77,* 498–505.

Barnes, K. J., Murphy, M., Waldo, L., & Sailor, W. Adaptive equipment for the severely, multiply handicapped child. In R. L. York and E. Edgar (eds.), *Teaching the severely handicapped* (Vol. IV). Columbus, Ohio: Special Press, 1979.

Bijou, S. W. Studies in the experimental development of left-right concepts in retarded children using fading techniques. In N. R. Ellis (ed.), *International Review of Research in Mental Retardation.* New York: Academic Press, 1968, *3,* 65–96.

Bloom, L. Talking, understanding, and thinking. In R. L. Schiefelbusch and L. L. Lloyd (eds.), *Language perspectives—Acquisition, retardation, and intervention.* Baltimore: University Park Press, 1974.

Bloom, L., & Lahey, M. *Language development and language disorders.* New York: John Wiley & Sons, 1978.

Bornstein, H., Hamilton, L., Saulnier, K., & Roy, H. *The Signed English dictionary for pre-school and elementary levels.* Washington, D.C.: Gallaudet College, 1975.

Bricker, W., & Bricker, D. Development of vocabulary in severely retarded children. *American Journal of Mental Deficiency,* 1970, *74,* 599–607.

Bricker, D., Dennison, L., & Bricker, W. Constructive interaction-adaption approach to language training. *MCCD monograph series, no. 1.* Miami: Mailman Center for Child Development, University of Miami, 1975.

Carr, E. G., Binkoff, J. A., Kolginsky, E., & Eddy, M. Acquisition of sign language by autistic children. I. Expressive labeling. *Journal of Applied Behavioral Analysis,* 1978, *11,* 489–501.

Carrier, J. K., Jr., & Peak, T. *Non-speech language initiation program.* Lawrence, Kansas: H & H Enterprises, 1975.

Clark, C. R., Davies, C. O., & Woodcock, R. W. *Standard rebus glossary.* Circle Pines, Minnesota: American Guidance Service, 1974.

Clark, C. R., & Woodcock, R. W. Graphic systems of communication. In L. L. Lloyd (ed.), *Communication assessment and intervention strategies.* Baltimore: University Park Press, 1976.

Dunn, L. M., & Smith, J. O. *Peabody language development kit.* Circle Pines, Minnesota: American Guidance Service, 1965.

Goetz, L., Schuler, A., & Sailor, W. Teaching functional speech to the severely handicapped: Current issues. *Journal of Autism and Developmental Disorders,* 1979, *9,* 325–344.

Gollin, E. S., & Savoy, P. Fading procedures and conditional discrimination in children. *Journal of the Experimental Analysis of Behavior,* 1968, *11,* 443–451.

Guess, D., Sailor, W., & Baer, D. To teach language to retarded children. In R. L. Schiefelbusch and L. L. Lloyd (eds.), *Language perspectives—Acquisition, retardation, and intervention.* Baltimore: University Park Press, 1974.

Guess, D., Sailor, W., & Baer, D. *Functional speech and language training for the severely handicapped.* Vol. 1: *Persons and Things.* Lawrence, Kansas: H & H Enterprises, 1976.

Guess, D., Sailor, W., & Baer, D. Children with limited language. In R. L. Schiefelbusch (ed.), *Language intervention strategies.* Baltimore: University Park Press, 1978.

Hamre-Nietupski, S., Stoll, A., Holtz, K., Fullerton, P., Ryan-Flottum, M., & Brow, L. Curricular strategies for teaching selected non-verbal students. In L. Brown, J. Nietupski, S. Lyon, S. Hamre-Nietupski, T. Crowner, & Lee Gruenewald (eds.), *Curricular strategies for teaching functional object use, non-verbal communication, problem solving and mealtime skills to severely handicapped students,* Vol. VII, Part 1. Madison, Wisconsin: Madison Metropolitan School District, 1977.

Hollis, J. H., & Carrier, J. K., Jr. Research implications for communication deficiencies. *Exceptional Children,* 1975, *41,* 405–412.

Hollis, J., & Carrier, J. K., Jr. Intervention strategies for nonspeech children. In R. L. Schiefelbusch (ed.), *Language intervention strategies.* Baltimore: University Park Press, 1978.

Hollis, J. H., Carrier, H. K., Jr., & Spradlin, J. E. An approach to remediation of communication and learning deficiencies. In L. L. Lloyd (ed.), *Communication assessment and intervention strategies.* Baltimore: University Park Press, 1976.

Ingram, D. Phonological rules in young children. *Journal of Child Language,* 1974, *1,* 49–64.

Janssen, C., & Guess, D. Use of function as a consequence in training receptive labeling to severely and profoundly retarded individuals. *AAESPH Review,* 1978, *3,* 246–258.

Kahn, J. V. Relationship of Piaget's sensorimotor period to language acquisition of profoundly retarded children. *American Journal of Mental Deficiency,* 1975, *79,* 640–643.

Kates, B., & McNaughton, S. *The first application of Blissymbolics as a communication medium for nonspeaking children: History and development, 1971–1974.* Toronto: Blissymbolics Communication Foundation, 1974.

Koegel, R., & Wilhelm H. Selective responding to multiple visual cues by autistic children. *Journal of Experimental Child Psychology,* 1973, *15,* 442–454.

Kopchick, G. A., & Lloyd, L. L. Total communication for the severely language impaired: A 24-hour approach. In L. L. Lloyd (ed.), *Communication assessment and intervention strategies.* Baltimore: University Park Press, 1976.

LaVigna, G. Communication training in mute autistic adolescents using the written word. *Journal of Autism and Childhood Schizophrenia,* 1977, *7,* 135–149.

Lawson, L. J., & Schoofs, J. G. A technique for visual appraisal of mentally retarded children. *American Journal of Ophthalmology,* 1971, *72,* 622–624.

Lovaas, O. *The autistic child: Language development through behavior modification.* New York: John Wiley & Sons, 1977.

Lovaas, O. I., Berberich, J., Perloff, B., & Schaeffer, B. Acquisition of imitative speech by schizophrenic children. *Science,* 1966, *151,* 705–707.

Lovaas, O. I., & Schreibman, L. Stimulus overselectivity of autistic children in a two stimulus situation. *Behavior Research and Therapy,* 1971, *2,* 305–310.

McLean, J. E. Articulation. In L. L. Lloyd (ed.), *Communication assessment and intervention strategies.* Baltimore: University Park Press, 1976.

McLean, L., & McLean, J. A language training program for non-verbal autistic children. *Journal of Speech and Hearing Disorders,* 1978, *39,* 186–193.

Mahoney, G., Crawley, S., & Pullis, M. Language intervention: Models and issues. In B. K. Keogh (ed.), *Advances in special education; an annual compilation of research* (Vol. 2). Greenwich, Connecticut: J. A. I. Press. In press.

Piaget, J. *The language and thought of the child.* New York: World Publishing, 1962.

Reichle, J. E., & Yoder, D. E. *The Colony Project: Teaching SMR/PMR children to communicate.* Unpublished manuscript, University of Wisconsin, 1976. (a)

Reichle, J. E., & Yoder, D. E. *The intentional uses of early communicative behavior: A case for give, show, and point.* Unpublished manuscript, University of Wisconsin, 1976. (b)

Reichle, J. E., & Yoder, D. E. Assessment and early stimulation of communication in the severely and profoundly mentally retarded. In R. L. York & E. Edgar (eds.), *Teaching the severely handicapped* (Vol. IV). Columbus, Ohio: Special Press, 1979.

Rincover, A., Newson, B., Lovaas, I., & Koegel, R. Some motivational properties of sensory reinforcement with psychotic children. *Journal of Experimental Child Psychology,* 1977, *24,* 312–323.

Sailor, W., & Guess, D. *The severely handicapped: An educational model.* Boston: Houghton Mifflin Co. In press.

Saunders, R., & Sailor, W. A comparison of three strategies of reinforcement on two-choice learning problems with severely retarded children. *AAESPH Review,* 1979, *4,* 323–333.

Schelmoeller, K. J., & Etzel, B. C. An experimental analysis of criterion-related and noncriterion-related cues in "errorless" stimulus control procedures. In B. C. Etzel, J. M. LeBlanc, & D. M. Baer (eds.), *New developments in behavioral research: Theory, method, and application. In honor of Sidney W. Bijou.* Hillsdale, New Jersey: Lawrence Erlbaum Associates, 1978.

Schover, L. I., & Newsom, C. D. Overselectivity, developmental level and overtraining in autistic and normal children. *Journal of Abnormal Child Psychology,* 1976, *4,* 289–297.

Schreibman, L. Effects of within-stimulus and extra-stimulus prompting on discrimination learning in autistic children. *Journal of Applied Behavior Analysis,* 1975, *7,* 91–112.

Schreibman, L., & Lovaas, O. I. Overselective responses to social stimuli by autistic children. *Journal of Abnormal Child Psychology,* 1971, *1,* 152–168.

Schuler, A. L. *An experimental analysis of conceptual and representational abilities in a mute autistic adolescent: A serial vs. a simultaneous mode of processing.* Unpublished doctoral dissertation, University of California, Santa Barbara, California, 1979.

Shane, H. C. Approaches to communication training with the severely handicapped. In R. L. York & E. Edgar (eds.), *Teaching the severely handicapped* (Vol. IV). Columbus, Ohio: Special Press, 1979.

Sheridan, M. *Manual for the STYCAR vision tests (screening tests for young children and retardates).* Berks, England: NFER Publishing Co., Limited, 1969.

Sidman, M., & Stoddard, L. J. The effectiveness of fading in programming a simultaneous form discrimination for retarded children. *Journal of the Experimental Analysis of Behavior,* 1967, *10,* 3–15.

Sloane, H., Johnston, M., & Harris, F. Remedial procedures for teaching verbal behavior to speech deficient or defective young children. In H. Sloane & B. MacAuley (eds.), *Operant procedures in remedial speech and language training.* Boston: Houghton Mifflin Co., 1968.

Slobin, D. I. Imitation and grammatical development in children. In N. S. Endler, L. R. Boulter, & H. Osser (eds.), *Contemporary issues in developmental psychology.* New York: Holt, Rinehart and Winston, 1968.

Sontag, E., Smith, J., & Sailor, W. The severely handicapped. Who are they? Where are we? *Journal of Special Education,* 1977, *11,* 5–11.

Staats, A. W. *Learning language and cognition.* New York: Holt, Rinehart and Winston, 1968.

Stoddard, L. J., & Sidman, M. The effects of errors on children's performance on a circle-ellipse discrimination. *Journal of the Experimental Analysis of Behavior,* 1967, *10,* 261–270.

Stremel-Campbell, K., Cantrell, D., & Halle, J. Manual signing as a speech initiator for the nonverbal severely handicapped student. In E. Sontag, J. Smith, and N. Certo (eds.), *Educational programming for the severely and profoundly handicapped.* Pennsylvania: CEC Division on Mental Retardation, 1977.

Striefel, S. *Behavior modification: Teaching a child to imitate.* Lawrence, Kansas: H & H Enterprises, 1974.

Topper, S. Gesture language for a nonverbal severely retarded male. *Mental Retardation,* 1975, *13,* 30–31.

Vanderheiden, G. C., & Grilley, K. *Non-vocal communication techniques and aids for the severely physically handicapped.* Baltimore: University Park Press, 1977.

Vanderheiden G., & Harris-Vanderheiden, D. Communication techniques and aids for the nonvocal severely handicapped. In L. L. Lloyd (ed.), *Communication assessment and intervention strategies.* Baltimore: University Park Press, 1976.

Von Noorden, G. K., & Maumence, S. E. *Atlas of strabismus.* (2nd ed.) St. Louis, Missouri: C. V. Mosby Co., 1973.

Wilbur, R. B. The linguistics of manual languages and manual systems. In L. L. Lloyd (ed.), *Communication assessment and intervention strategies.* Baltimore: University Park Press, 1976.

Woodcock, R. W., Clark, C. R., & Davies, C. O. *Peabody rebus reading program.* Circle Pines, Minnesota: American Guidance Service, 1968.

REFERENCE NOTES

1. Gee, K. *Assessment, analysis, and training of generalization in the usage of two manual signs with three non-verbal severely retarded students.* Unpublished master's thesis, San Francisco State University, Department of Special Education, San Francisco, California 94132, 1979.

2. Waldo, L., Barnes, K., & Berry, G. *Total communication checklist and assessment.* Kansas Neurological Institute, 1979. (Available at cost from: Lois Waldo, Speech Therapy Department, Kansas Neurological Institute, 3107 W. 21st St., Topeka, Kansas 66604.)

3. Utley, B., Project Director; Sailor, W., Principal Investigator. Bay Area Severely Handicapped Deaf/Blind Project. USOE contract #300-78-0338 to Department of Special Education, San Francisco State University, 1600 Holloway Ave., San Francisco, California, 94132.

4. Welch, P. *Vocal imitation as a consequence in imitation training for the severely handicapped.* Unpublished master's thesis, University of Kansas, Lawrence, 1978.

5. Turnbull, W. *An examination of two stimulus control methods in training generalized vocal imitation in infants.* Unpublished master's thesis, University of Kansas, Lawrence, 1975.

6. Guess, D., Keogh, W., & Baer, D. *Imitation training for difficult to teach severely handicapped children: An analysis of new procedures (final report).* Social and Rehabilitation Services, State of Kansas, Topeka, 1977.

7. McDonald, L. *A comparison of three methods of word imitation training with Down's syndrome children under six years of age.* Unpublished master's thesis, University of Manitoba, 1977.

8. Camozzi, L. *A comparison of the rates of receptive language acquisition across three modes of training with three developmentally disabled adults.* Unpublished master's thesis, San Francisco State University, Department of Special Education, San Francisco, 1979.

9. Carpenter, J. *An experimental comparison of acquisition rates of motor imitation items with and without manipulable consequences in a group setting.* Unpublished manuscript, Kansas Neurological Institute, Topeka, 1975.

Section II
INSTRUCTION AND MEASUREMENT

Chapter 4

Strategies for Using Cues and Correction Procedures

Mary Falvey, Lou Brown, Steve Lyon,
Diane Baumgart, and Jack Schroeder

This chapter essentially extends and consolidates earlier positions by the authors and their colleagues regarding how best to prepare severely handicapped students to function in complex, least restrictive, and natural post-school environments (Brown, Branston, Hamre-Nietupski, Pumpian, Certo, & Gruenewald, 1979; Brown, Certo, Belmore, & Crowner, 1976; Brown, Nietupski, & Hamre-Nietupski, 1976; Brown, Nietupski, Lyon, Hamre-Nietupski, Crowner, & Gruenewald, 1977; Brown, Wilcox, Sontag, Vincent, Dodd, & Gruenewald, 1977; Williams, Brown, & Certo, 1975). Specifically, the chapter offers a rationale for selecting *cues* and *correction procedures* to use when teaching severely handicapped students to perform age-appropriate and functional skills in natural environments. A *cue* refers to initial information provided to a student *before* an action is performed. A *correction procedure* refers to supplementary or corrective information to communicate to a student that a response *already performed* is inappropriate or that a different action is needed.

In the past, the cues and correction procedures used in many educational programs for severely handicapped students have been exceedingly artificial (Brown, Bellamy, & Sontag, 1971; Brown, Scheuerman, Cartwright, & York,

This chapter was supported in part by grant no. G007801740 to the University of Wisconsin-Madison from the Department of Health, Education, and Welfare, U.S. Office of Education, Bureau of Education for the Handicapped, Division of Personnel Preparation, Washington, D.C., and in part by contract no. 300-78-0345 to the University of Wisconsin-Madison and the Madison Metropolitan School District from the Department of Health, Education, and Welfare, U.S. Office of Education, Bureau of Education for the Handicapped, Division for Innovation and Development, Washington, D.C.

Appreciation is expressed particularly to the following persons who contributed substantially to the production of this chapter: Julie Benike, Ric Conroy, Agnes Daun, Nancy Dodd, Vicki Gammeter, Anneke Houtsma, Sharon Radbil, Wayne Sailor, Paul Sevett, Sue Stoxen, Mark Sweet, Kathy Tuttle, and Barbara Wilcox.

1973; Brown & Sontag, 1972; Guess, Sailor, & Baer, 1977). If severely handicapped students are to be prepared to function in many of the same natural environments and participate in many of the same activities as nonhandicapped persons, it is crucial that they acquire as many of the skills required by those environments as possible. Unless severely handicapped students are taught to perform skills in response to many *naturally occurring cues and naturally occurring correction procedures,* it is likely that they will continue to require excessive degrees and kinds of assistance and supervision. Therefore, it is not only important for teachers to possess the instructional repertoires necessary to teach severely handicapped students to perform potentially functional skills in instructional environments such as a classroom, but it is also imperative that teachers engage in longitudinal and systematic efforts to ensure that severely handicapped students are taught to perform these skills in response to the cues and correction procedures that occur *in natural environments.*

CONSIDERATIONS FOR SELECTING
CUES AND CORRECTION PROCEDURES

Cues and correction procedures range from those that provide maximal assistance to those that offer minimal guidance, and from those that occur exclusively in instructional environments to those that occur exclusively in natural environments. There are a number of factors to consider when generating hierarchies of cues and correction procedures for individual students in specific contexts because the kind and degree of assistance required may vary with the particular student, the target skill, and the features of the natural environment.

First of all, it is important to consider the cues and correction procedures that nonhandicapped persons typically utilize when performing a particular skill in a natural environment since those stimuli and consequences define at least in part the conditions under which severely handicapped students will need to perform that skill. Stated another way, if particular cues and correction procedures are commonly used by nonhandicapped persons in natural environments, it may be critical to include those cues and correction procedures in an instructional program for severely handicapped students.

A second important consideration may be the motor responses required to perform a particular skill. For example, some skills, such as opening a door, require primarily gross motor actions, and the acquisition of these skills is well suited to cues and correction procedures that involve direct physical guidance. However, other skills, such as verbalizing, require few if any gross motor actions, and thus cues and correction procedures that include direct physical guidance may be nonfunctional or even counterproductive.

It is also critical that teaching procedures not train severely handicapped students to respond only to a sequence or hierarchy of cues and correction procedures that may not exist in natural environments. For example, a very frequent training strategy is for the teacher to first provide the student with a verbal cue to perform the desired response. If the student does not respond appropriately, the teacher reissues the verbal cue and models the correct action. If there is still no correct response, the teacher reissues the verbal cue and physically guides the student through the desired actions. Extensive use of this sequence can be expected to teach students that there is no reason to respond to an initial cue since eventually they will be physically guided through the desired response. Adherence to ritualistic teaching hierarchies may severely limit students' ability to function in natural environments where such hierarchies are not available. Traffic police directing traffic from the middle of a street will issue a verbal direction but generally will not model standing on a curb; a bus driver generally will not physically guide a person to the back of the bus if that person fails to respond to a verbal cue. Perhaps the basic positions offered here can be summarized by the following points:

1. School environments are preparatory in nature and should be designed to enable severely handicapped students to function as independently as possible in a variety of current and subsequent *natural* environments.
2. One cannot *infer* that because a severely handicapped student can perform a particular skill in response to one set of cues and correction procedures he or she will also perform when different cues and correction procedures are employed.
3. Severely handicapped students should be taught to respond to as *few* as necessary cues and correction procedures that are operative in *instructional* simulated or artificial environments, and should be taught to respond appropriately to as *many* as possible cues and correction procedures that are operative in as many current and subsequent *natural* environments as possible.

DEFINITIONS AND EXAMPLES OF INSTRUCTIONAL AND NATURAL CUES AND CORRECTION PROCEDURES

Definitions of cues and correction procedures that might be used to teach severely handicapped students to perform chronological age-appropriate and functional skills are provided below. The reader is cautioned that the categories and descriptions discussed here are not unique, exhaustive, or mutually exclusive, and is alerted to the fact that other programs may use different labels or organize cues and correction procedures according to a different plan.

Cues and correction procedures can be viewed as either *instructional* or *natural. Instructional cues* and *instructional correction procedures* are used here to refer to providing information that is not generally available to persons in natural environments. Such information may be in addition to what is available in the natural environment or may reflect a difference in intensity, duration, or frequency of the information that is available. *Natural cues* and *natural correction procedures,* on the other hand, refer to information that is typically available to persons in natural environments and that is also equivalent in intensity, duration, and frequency to that which is naturally occurring.

Generally, although not exclusively, instructional cues and correction procedures are provided in instructional environments, while natural cues and correction procedures are provided in natural environments. *Instructional environments* is used here to refer to any setting where the education of others is the explicit concern. *Natural environments* is used here to refer to those settings where the actual performance of a skill is the primary concern. In addition, natural environments are those in which nonhandicapped persons function and in which severely handicapped students should be taught to function.

The following examples are provided in an attempt to illustrate some of the distinctions between instructional cues and correction procedures and their naturally occurring counterparts.

Instructional Cue: Rick is learning to functionally use a pocket calculator. His teacher *verbally directs* him to touch the following buttons on the calculator: *5, plus sign,* and *6.*

Instructional Correction Procedure: Joe is learning to use an electronic communication board. His teacher *verbally directs* him to touch the picture of a sandwich. Joe touches the picture of a glass of milk. His teacher then *touches* the picture of a sandwich as he watches and reissues her initial verbal direction. Joe then touches the picture of a sandwich.

Natural Cue: Mark intends to cross a street at a corner where traffic lights are present. Mark *looks at* the traffic light, waits for the green light to appear, and when the traffic light turns green he crosses the street.

Natural Correction Procedure: Chris intends to enter a store with automatically opening doors. She *steps* on the floor mat in front of the door, but the door does not open. Chris then steps off the floor mat and *observes others* entering the store through a different door, the door with IN printed on it. She then enters through the appropriate door.

Instructional cues and correction procedures can be effective vehicles for teaching severely handicapped students to acquire and perform many skills. However, if severely handicapped students are to function in natural environments, they must be able to perform in response to cues and correction procedures available in those environments.

While there are undoubtedly a large number of cues and/or correction procedures that teachers use when teaching students particular skills, only the following classes are of concern here:

1. Primed correction procedures
2. Modeled cues and/or modeled correction procedures
3. Direct verbal cues and/or direct verbal correction procedures
4. Indirect verbal cues and/or indirect verbal correction procedures
5. Gestural cues and/or gestural correction procedures
6. Pictorial cues and/or pictorial correction procedures

It is the considered judgment of the authors that these six kinds of cues and correction procedures are, at this time, the most relevant and functional for teaching severely handicapped students a variety of skills.

Primed Correction Procedures

Primed correction procedures is used here to refer to providing physical contact in order to assist or guide a student through part or all of the performance of a desired action. A primed correction procedure could involve direct contact with any part of a student's body, or contact through an artificial extension of the body of a student or a teacher.

> Aaron and Julie were seated at the table during lunch at school. Aaron scooped food from his plate with his fork. While lifting the loaded fork toward his mouth the food fell back onto his plate, but he continued to direct the fork to his mouth. Julie, who was seated next to Aaron, placed her hand over his and physically guided his hand toward the plate so that the piece of food was again speared with the fork.

The corrective information provided by Julie, physically guiding Aaron's hand so that he speared the piece of food, was 1) a *correction procedure* because assistance was provided *after* he performed an incorrect action, and 2) a *primed* correction procedure because the corrective information was provided by *physically guiding* Aaron through the desired action.

Teachers who generally use primed correction procedures in their instructional programs are almost always placed in paradoxical situations. On the one hand, the use of primed correction procedures might be a functional and critical component of the best available instructional strategy. On the other hand, teachers should realize that primed correction procedures are not typically available in community environments. Furthermore, primed correction procedures are viewed as increasingly stigmatizing by most nonhandicapped persons. The less obvious the handicaps and the older the student, the more stigmatizing the effect. Before relying on primed correction procedures, at least several points should be considered.

First, while initially relatively intense primed correction procedures might be used, it is usually critical that their intensity be faded or gradually removed. Intensity is used here to refer to the magnitude or the strength with which a primed correction procedure is provided. More specifically, a teacher might initially correct a response by firmly grasping and moving a student's hand and arm through a desired action. Subsequently, the teacher might fade or attenuate the intensity of this procedure by gently touching or shadowing the student's hand as the response is performed.

Second, in order for some severely handicapped students to acquire and perform even the most rudimentary actions correctly, it may be vital that teachers provide intensive and frequent primed correction procedures over long periods of time. Hence, if teachers are reluctant to provide the intense and/or frequent physical interactions required for affective instruction or find such interaction aversive, perhaps they should seriously consider a different profession.

Priming is viewed here as a correction procedure rather than as a cue. Teachers should be cautioned against using physical priming before allowing students the opportunity to perform actions without such assistance. Stated another way, if students can functionally use cues and correction procedures other than primed correction procedures, then primed correction procedures should not be provided. For example, if a severely handicapped student is being taught to walk and can walk without physical guidance, it would be counter-productive for the teacher to support the student physically or otherwise provide more assistance than is needed.

Modeled Cues and/or Modeled Correction Procedures

Modeled cues and/or *modeled correction procedures* are used here to refer to providing the student with a demonstration of actions that are expected of him or her. While the use of still pictures, movies, and other kinds of media may be used to present cues and correction procedures, and might well be considered "models," this discussion emphasizes live demonstrations. The intent of modeled cues and correction procedures is that the student imitate the behavior that is demonstrated. Imitation is said to occur if the student performs an action that is topographically similar to the actions modeled, if the student performs the topographically similar actions after the modeled cues or correction procedures were provided, if the student performs the topographically similar actions be-cause the model was provided, and if the student performs the topographically similar actions within an instructionally reasonable period of time following the model (Peterson, 1968).

> Jerry wants a soda from the pop machine during his break at work. He observes another employee insert money, press a panel, and remove and open a can of soda. Jerry then performs the same response sequence.

The information provided by the other employee, a live demonstration of obtaining a soda, was 1) a *cue* because information was provided to Jerry *before* he himself responded, and 2) a *modeled* cue because the information provided was a *live demonstration* of an action.

> When directed to label a photograph of a particular street sign verbally, Paul responded by saying "Go home." His teacher then modeled the desired action by verbally labeling the picture "Main Street."

The information provided by the teacher was 1) a *correction procedure* because assistance was provided *after* Paul performed an incorrect action, and 2) a *modeled* correction procedure because the corrective or supplementary infor-mation provided was a *live demonstration* of the desired action.

It is appropriate here to raise some general considerations in the use of modeled cues and correction procedures. First, in order to increase the probabil-ity that a student's action occurs in response to modeled antecedents or conse-quences, the person modeling the action must secure and maintain functional visual attending while the target action is being demonstrated. Responses should be modeled within the student's visual field in a way that ensures his or her attention. While teachers often enthusiastically perform excellent modeled actions, many of these demonstrations are functionally irrelevant because the target student is not attending.

A second consideration in the use of modeling procedures is the distinction that models can be presented continuously or intermittently. *Continuous modeling* is used here to refer to the ongoing performance of an action until the student imitates. For example, a teacher might stir cookie batter in a bowl and continue stirring until the student begins stirring the batter in his or her bowl. *Intermittent modeling* is used here to refer to completing one full sequence of the desired response. For example, a teacher might say "Do this" and complete one full circle of the spoon through the cookie batter in the bowl and then wait for the student to stir the cookie batter in his or her bowl. Continuous modeling strategies are potentially more effective for teaching some skills, while intermittent modeling may be more effective for other skills.

Teachers should consider using various kinds of graduated or cumulative modeling strategies. For example, a teacher intending to teach a student to imitate "jacket" verbally might initially model the sound [j]. When the student consistently imitated [j], the teacher might then model "jă," then "jăk," and then "jakut" until the student could produce the entire word. Cumulative modeling is analogous to shaping a complex response from its components, while graduated modeling is analogous to fading out the necessary model detail.

A fourth issue is related to the acceptance of approximations. A teacher might model an entire action sequence but accept imitated actions that are approximations of the entire sequence. For example, assume a teacher intends to teach a student the manual sign for "come." The teacher might model the sign for "come" using two hands, but reward the student even if he or she only moves one hand toward his or her body. The student's action of moving only one hand toward the body is considered an imitative approximation of the two-handed sign for "come."

Teaching skills necessary to learn from observing the mistakes and successes of others are seldom included in curricula designed for severely handicapped students. Instructional plans that emphasize the extensive use of one-to-one arrangements may effectively preclude the development of functional and generalizable observational learning skills. Teachers must be aware of and demonstrate skills in the use of the many modeling and imitative learning paradigms if they are to assist their severely handicapped students to learn truly functional skills. (The reader interested in more detailed discussions of imitation and other observational learning strategies is referred to Bandura, 1969; Horner, Holvoet, & Rinne, 1976; Lovaas, Freitas, Nelson, & Whalen, 1967; Peterson, 1968.)

Direct Verbal Cues and/or Direct Verbal Correction Procedures

Direct verbal cues and/or *direct verbal correction procedures* are used here to refer to verbal directions or commands that require relatively specific actions.

> Sally's mother tells her, "Take off your coat."

The verbal information provided by Sally's mother was 1) a *cue* because information was provided to Sally *before* the desired action was performed, and 2) a *direct verbal* cue because the information provided was communicated through a relatively *explicit verbal direction or command.*

> The bell rings indicating recess time, and Chris, a blind severely handicapped student, continues to play with paint. The teacher then says, "Chris, get up, follow the railing through the door and down the hall, open the door, and go outside for recess."

The corrective information provided by the teacher was 1) a *correction procedure* because corrective or supplementary information was provided to Chris *after* he performed an incorrect action, and 2) a *direct verbal* correction procedure because the corrective or supplementary information provided was communicated through relatively *explicit verbal directions or commands.*

There are at least two major points teachers might consider when using direct verbal cues and/or direct verbal correction procedures. First of all, it is important that direct verbal cues and correction procedures provide all the information a student needs to perform the desired action. Certainly, different students in different contexts will require different degrees of explicitness. However, a direct verbal cue and/or direct verbal correction procedure generally should contain at least a subject, verb, and object. Second, when teaching severely handicapped students to perform actions in response to direct verbal cues and correction procedures, teachers should provide minimal embellishment. Excessive and extraneous verbal information is unnecessary and may even be confusing. For example, consider the student who is hand flapping, foot shaking, nodding her head, and not working on her math worksheet. It is suggested here that the teacher verbally direct her to work on her math worksheet, rather than verbally directing her to *stop* hand flapping, *stop* foot shaking, *stop* nodding her head, and work on her math worksheet.

It is often extremely difficult to delineate precisely the critical differences between direct and indirect verbal cues and correction procedures. Nevertheless, for the purposes of communication and instruction, attempts at differentiation and delineation are made below.

Indirect Verbal Cues and/or Indirect Verbal Correction Procedures

Indirect verbal cues and/or *indirect verbal correction procedures* are used here to refer to providing a student with covert and implicit verbal statements that require relatively specific actions. While both direct and indirect verbal cues and correction procedures can be used to elicit the same actions, there are subtle differences. For example, if a student is in a warm classroom wearing a heavy coat, the teacher might say, "Take off your coat" (a *direct verbal cue*), or she might say, "Isn't it warm in here?" (an *indirect verbal cue*).

> Saul is riding a public bus to his sheltered workshop. The driver announces "Johnson Street," which is the bus stop at which Saul must get off in order to go to work. Saul gets off the bus at Johnson Street.

The information provided by the bus driver announcing, "Johnson Street," was 1) a *cue* because information was provided to Saul before the desired action was performed, and 2) an *indirect verbal* cue because the information provided to Saul was a statement *implying* that those needing to get off at Johnson Street should get off at the next stop.

> A teacher begins preparing lunch for his students. Jenny, one of the students, does not respond by getting ready for lunch but instead continues to play. The teacher then verbally states, "It's time to eat."

The information provided by the teacher's statement, "It's time to eat," was 1) a *correction procedure* because corrective or supplementary information was provided to Jenny *after* she performed incorrect actions, and 2) an *indirect verbal* correction procedure because corrective or supplementary information provided to Jenny was an *implicit* statement not explicitly describing the desired actions.

Since indirect verbal cues and correction procedures are used by many persons in a variety of natural environments, it is crucial that teachers eventually use indirect verbal cues and correction procedures when interacting with students in instructional settings. For example, waiters and waitresses generally will ask a person intending to order food or drink, "What would you like?" or "Yes, may I have your order?" instead of saying, "Tell me what you want to eat and drink."

Gestural Cues and/or Gestural Correction Procedures

Gestural cues and/or *gestural correction procedures* are used here to refer to physical, nonverbal motions or movements that indicate that certain actions should be performed. Gestural cues and correction procedures may include waving, manually indicating "hi" or "good-bye," shaking one's head to indicate yes or no, frowning to indicate displeasure or disapproval, and smiling to indicate pleasure or approval.

> Bonnie is riding her bike and intends to cross an intersection where a policewoman is directing traffic. Observing the policewoman beckoning with her hand, Bonnie crosses.

The information provided by the policewoman was 1) a *cue* because the information was provided *before* the action was performed, and 2) a *gestural* cue because the information provided was as a *nonverbal motion* indicating a desired action.

> Robert uses the toilet at the shopping center appropriately and begins to wheel out of the bathroom before washing his hands. His father then points to the sink to indicate that Robert should wash his hands before leaving the bathroom. Robert does so.

The information provided by Robert's father, pointing to the sink, was 1) a *correction procedure* because supplementary information was provided *after* Robert performed an incorrect action, and 2) a *gestural* correction procedure because the corrective or supplementary information provided was a physical, *nonverbal motion* indicating what response should be performed.

The opportunities of a severely handicapped student to function effectively in natural environments are severely limited if he or she is unable to or has not been taught to function in response to basic gestural cues and corrections. A point to be emphasized here is that teaching the skills necessary to function from a variety of commonly available gestural cues and correction procedures should be a part of the curriculum of each severely handicapped student.

Teachers need to consider the following points when using gestural cues and correction procedures. To increase the probability that an action occurs in response to gestural cues and/or correction procedures the person providing the gesture must secure and maintain the student's functional visual attention while gesturing. Furthermore, gestures intended to communicate that certain actions should be performed must be provided within the student's visual field in ways that allow the student to distinguish those actions.

Pictorial Cues and/or Pictorial Correction Procedures

Pictorial cues and/or *pictorial correction procedures* refer to providing representational, two-dimensional pictures, numbers, or other symbols to indicate that students should perform specific actions. Pictorial cues and/or pictorial correction procedures may include such diverse forms as price tags on retail items, pedestrian signs on street corners, symbols on communication boards, illustrations in a book, numbers on a digital clock, or picture sequences for cooking and assembling recipes.

> Mark intends to purchase a pencil at a variety store. The clerk rings up the purchase on the register and the total amount of the purchase appears on the top of the register. Mark gets an appropriate amount from his coin holder.

The information provided by the cashier on the cash register was 1) a *cue* because the information was provided to Mark *before* the desired action, and 2) a *pictorial* cue because the information provided to Mark consisted of *representational symbols* (numbers) which communicated to him how much money he had to produce.

> Gerry, a nonvocal student, uses a lap tray communication board on his wheelchair. Gerry's teacher verbally directs him to go to the cafeteria. Gerry continues to work on his math worksheet. The teacher then points to a referent on his communication board representing "cafeteria."

The information provided by Gerry's teacher was 1) a *correction procedure* because the corrective or supplementary information was provided *after* he performed an incorrect action, and 2) a *pictorial* correction procedure because the information indicating the desired action was provided through a *picture*.

In instructional settings, pictorial cues and correction procedures are frequently presented in conjunction with gestural, direct verbal, or indirect verbal cues or corrections. It is critical to secure and maintain attending at the time the pictorial cue and/or correction procedure is presented. Gestural, direct verbal, or indirect verbal cues or correction procedures often are valuable aids in the direction and maintenance of attending.

AN ECOLOGICAL INVENTORY STRATEGY

A major purpose of educational programs for severely handicapped students is to prepare them to function as independently and effectively as possible in a variety of least restrictive current and subsequent natural environments. It is therefore only logical that teachers secure vital information about those natural environments. One set of procedures that can be used to secure this information is an ecological inventory strategy. The term is used to refer to actions undertaken to secure critical information about the school and community environments in which a severely handicapped student is currently functioning, and the variety of least restrictive school and community environments in which that student might function in the future. Specifically, the inventory consists of identifying and listing the components of behaviors demonstrated by nonhandicapped persons in natural environments (e.g., the specific topology, rate, frequency, intensity, and duration). The concept has been extended to include identifying and listing naturally occurring cues and correction procedures normally available to nonhandicapped persons. The information obtained through the use of ecological inventory strategies can assist teachers in designing and implementing functional and effective preparatory educational programs for severely handicapped students.

Recently, there has been an increase in the degree of importance ascribed to the performance criteria required of nonhandicapped persons functioning in natural environments as a guide to establishing performance criteria in educational programs for severely handicapped students (Brown et al., 1976; Gaylord-Ross, 1979; Williams et al., 1975). For example, Belmore and Brown (1976) used one version of an ecological inventory strategy to determine many of the critical skills needed by severely handicapped students to function in selected community vocational environments, while Lyon, Baumgart, Stoll, and Brown (1977) used a different version of an ecological inventory strategy to determine the functional object use skills and performance criteria required to function in a variety of home, school, and community recreational/leisure environments.

In summary, if longitudinal educational services are going to prepare severely handicapped students to function in a variety of natural community environments, the ecological inventory strategy is an important tool that can be used to provide teachers with information on the actual skills necessary for functioning in those natural environments, and the naturally available cues and correction procedures under which those skills are typically performed. There are several points to consider in the design of such inventories. First, there are some environments in which a number of different cues and/or correction procedures are available that are functionally related to the performance of a specific skill. For example, at some intersections a severely handicapped student might be given the option to respond to at least the following naturally occurring cues and correction procedures: a signal light that has just turned green, an electrified sign that indicates WALK, the absence of cars in the pedestrian walk path, other pedestrians crossing the street, and people bumping into or pushing the student waiting at the curb. In such situations, it is often most efficient to take an inventory of the repertoire of the student as well as to take an inventory of the natural environment, and then decide upon the most functional and teachable cues and correction procedures for an individual student in a particular natural environment.

On the other hand, there are some natural environments in which only one cue and/or correction procedure (rather than many) that is functionally related to the performance of a specific skill may be available. For example, at some intersections the only reliable cue that it is safe to cross is the absence of cars traveling on that street.

It is important to realize that the naturally occurring cues and correction procedures that are functionally related to the performance of a particular skill might be different across different environments. In some grocery stores, for example, modeled cues (i.e., observing other people going to an appropriate cash register) and pictorial cues (i.e., observing the total cost of the purchase on the cash register) may be available, while in other grocery stores, a gestural cue (i.e., the cashier gesturing for the shopper to come to an available cash register) and indirect verbal cues (i.e., the cashier verbally stating the total cost of the purchase) may be the only natural cues. It is obviously critical that teachers be aware that cues and correction procedures vary across natural environments and ensure that each severely handicapped student is taught to function appropriately in the presence of variations appearing in his or her most significant natural environments.

In some natural environments, a variety of different naturally occurring cues and correction procedures might be functionally related to the performance of a sequence of different skills. For example, riding a public bus appropriately involves the performance of a sequence of skills such as identifying the correct bus, boarding the bus, placing the correct change in the fare box, locating a seat, sitting down, not bothering others, and so on. Performing such a complex skill sequence requires appropriate responding to a variety of cues and correction procedures.

These are only examples of some of the factors that must be considered when attempting to teach severely handicapped students to perform functional skills in natural environments. Since probably the most effective procedure for identifying appropriate cues and correction procedures is to observe the activity taking place in the natural environment, it is suggested that teachers engage in the following ecological inventory procedures:

1. List the current and anticipated least restrictive natural environments in which a severely handicapped student might function.
2. List the functional skills that are performed in those environments.
3. Identify the naturally occurring cues and correction procedures available to nonhandicapped persons in those environments.

Once a teacher has determined the cues and correction procedures that are naturally available, the existing performance repertoires of the student can then be assessed. In an attempt to determine the instructional cues and correction procedures that a particular student needs to be taught, a teacher might employ the following steps:

1. List the skills that are required in a particular natural environment.
2. List the cues and correction procedures required to function appropriately in that natural environment, and if possible and/or reasonably safe.
3. Take the student to the natural environment and determine if he or she performs appropriately in response to the naturally occurring cues and correction procedures.
4. If it is not reasonable to take the student to the natural environment, assess the student's skills in a simulated classroom setting. If it is necessary to use a simulated rather than a natural environment during initial instruction, then it is critical that strategies be designed to reduce the gap gradually and systematically between performance in simulated environments and performance in natural environments.

FADING INSTRUCTIONAL CUES AND CORRECTION PROCEDURES

In general, if a severely handicapped student has demonstrated the skills necessary to function appropriately in response to the cues and correction procedures available in a natural environment, fading strategies are not of concern. However, severely handicapped students have often been taught to perform skills in response to cues and correction procedures that are either unavailable or are less intense or frequent in natural environments. In such situations the use of fading strategies (i.e., strategies that allow the students to change from responding to instructional to responding to natural cues and correction procedures) is in order. The progression from performing skills in response to instructional cues and correction procedures to performing skills in response to natural cues and correction procedures is referred to here as fading from one cue and/or correction procedure to another. White (1971) refers to fading as

> ... the operation of gradually changing a stimulus, reinforcer, or contingency controlling an organism's performance to another stimulus, reinforcer, or contingency usually with the intent of maintaining the performance without loss or alteration, but under the new conditions. Quite frequently in reference to the operation of removing (gradually) stimuli, reinforcers, or contingencies which have been artificially imposed in an environment, to bring the behavior under

the control of the stimulus, reinforcers, and contingencies which existed in that environment prior to experimental or therapeutic manipulation (p. 62).

Strategies that teachers might use to fade cues and correction procedures are discussed briefly below. There are two major ways that teachers might fade the *number* of cues and/or corrections provided. While initially a teacher might provide a variety of cues or corrections in order to build a complex performance, once the chain is established the teacher could systematically decrease the number of cues provided. Consider the following example. Larry, a 6-year-old Down's syndrome child who is currently unable to walk, likes to watch "Sesame Street" when he arrives home from school at 4:00 p.m.; however, he does not yet have the series of skills in his repertoire necessary for turning on this favorite show. When the digital clock provides the natural cue by indicating 4:00 p.m., Larry's brother physically guides Larry through the skills necessary to turn on the program: crawling to the set, turning the set on, locating the appropriate channel, and adjusting the volume. Once Larry is able to perform the sequence with physical guidance at each step, the brother might announce that it is 4 o'clock and verbally direct Larry to go to the set and turn it on while he continues to provide Larry physical guidance in finding the appropriate channel and adjusting the volume. When Larry has demonstrated the skills necessary to locate the appropriate channel and adjust the volume, the assistance provided for the entire sequence might be faded to the single verbal cue "Turn on 'Seasame Street.'" When Larry performs appropriately in response to verbal instruction, the instructional cues can also be faded so that Larry is required to perform the entire series of actions in response to naturally occurring cues and corrections in that natural environment, i.e., observing the clock indicating 4:00 p.m. and then enjoying or missing his favorite program.

A second way to manipulate the number of cues and/or corrections would be to provide initially a number of concurrent cues when requesting a student to perform a *single* skill and then to eliminate systematically the redundant information. For example, a teacher intending to teach Saul to zip up his jacket zipper might announce, "It's time for recess," model by putting on her own coat, and provide verbal directions for zipping a jacket, *as well* as physically guide Saul through the zipping movements. Once Saul is able to zip his jacket consistently with these three kinds of assistance, the teacher might then provide only modeled and direct verbal cues. If Saul performs appropriately, the teacher might then fade the modeled cue until Saul is able to zip his jacket in response to the naturally occurring cue, the announcement of recess period.

Cues and/or correction procedures can also be faded in terms of their location or intensity. For instance a teacher might physically guide a student by *firmly* grasping and moving the student's hand and arm through the desired action or by gently touching the student's hand to facilitate the desired actions. The former constitutes a much more intense priming correction procedure than the latter. Teachers often fade the location and the intensity of cues and correction procedures concurrently. For example, a teacher who wants to teach Janet to place a quarter in a drink vending machine when it is break time at the workshop (natural cues) might initially firmly grasp Janet's thumb and forefinger and guide her hand in order to insert the coin in the appropriate opening. When Janet consistently performs with this level of assistance, the teacher might then gently hold her wrist and guide her hand to insert the coin in the appropriate opening. Subsequently, the teacher might lightly touch her elbow. Such gradual change in location and intensity will continue until Janet performs appropriately in response to the naturally occurring cues of seeing the drink machine in the break room.

There are several points that should be considered when teachers use fading procedures during instruction. In general, teachers should not begin to fade cues and/or correction procedures until the student performs the skills of concern at acceptable criteria. In addition, it is critical that students continue to perform the skills of concern at acceptable criteria *throughout the fading process*. For example, the teacher, intending to teach a student, Mark, to wipe his nose with a tissue initially might physically guide him to obtain a tissue from a tissue box, move his hand with the tissue to his nose, and guide him in the process of wiping his nose with the tissue. As the teacher fades the assistance, she must ensure that Mark continues to perform within an acceptable criterion range as the amount of assistance decreases.

Second, fading strategies should not prevent, or interfere with, critical affective interactions between teachers and students. Adhering to rigid sequences for fading cues and/or correction procedures may often interfere with warm, emotional, and natural ways of interacting. Thus, teachers concerned with the entire educational life space of severely handicapped students must make informed and sophisticated professional judgments over time as to what and how to fade cues and/or correction procedures and at the same time socially and emotionally interact with their students in warm and natural ways. Under certain conditions a student's increases in skill performance might result in depriving that student of physical and social contact from the teacher. Physical contact and social interactions should not be provided to students only in relation to cues and/or correction procedures. Teachers should provide their students throughout the school day with physical contact and social interactions that are not necessarily related to or contingent upon providing cues and/or correction procedures.

In summary, if severely handicapped students are to function as independently as possible in normal environments, teachers must fade their instructional assistance in a way that facilitates the performance of skills in response to the cues and/or correction procedures that routinely occur in natural environments. It is not always possible or practical to use natural environments to teach all severely handicapped students to perform all the skills they need to learn. Therefore, teachers will find it necessary to simulate some natural environments in classrooms and teach the skills of concern in those simulated environments. However, it is not sufficient for a student to perform a skill in a simulated environment even in response to naturally occurring cues and/or correction procedures. Teachers must systematically arrange an instructional plan that allows for empirical verification that the student can perform the skills of concern in response to naturally occurring cues and/or correction procedures in the actual target environments.

COOPERATIVE PLAY SKILLS:
ILLUSTRATION OF AN INSTRUCTIONAL STRATEGY

The following instructional program is included to provide the reader with an example of one method of developing instructional programs based on naturally occurring cues and correction procedures. The program focuses on training age-appropriate and functional skills in natural environments, and follows the format delineated by Williams et al. (1975).

Component 1: Why Should the Teacher Require
That a Student Acquire and Perform the Skills of Concern?

1. Instructional Objective The student will appropriately play on a teeter-totter, a swing, and a merry-go-round (manual) with another person. Performance must occur at appropriate times, in various natural environments (i.e., school playgrounds, neighborhood playgrounds, and backyards) and with a variety of partners.

2. Rationale In addition to learning skills required to perform in natural environments, severely handicapped students must develop the skills needed to *interact* with other handicapped and nonhandicapped persons. The purpose of this instructional program was to provide strategies that could be used to teach severely handicapped students to perform chronological age-appropriate playground skills that require both the use of selected playground equipment and interactions with others.

Ecological inventories can be used to determine the appropriate chronological age for the use of a skill. For example, when making inventories of playground environments, it was noted that playgrounds in parks, schools, and backyards were used by a wide range of nonhandicapped persons. More specifically, playground equipment was utilized by a high percentage of primary school–age children, children who were generally 10 years old and younger. The game areas of playgrounds and parks were used primarily by intermediate and secondary school–age children and adults (10 years of age and older) for ballgames and other recreational team sports, bike riding, and running. Thus, it would be more age appropriate to teach primary school–age severely handicapped students to use playground equipment, and intermediate and secondary school–age and adult severely handicapped students to use the game areas. Therefore, this instructional program was designed to teach primary school–age severely handicapped students to use selected playground equipment. It is critical that primary school–age severely handicapped students be taught to perform the skills necessary to interact and to use functionally playground equipment and the opportunity to interact with nonhandicapped peers. This instructional program was intended to be taught in those environments where the skills would be utilized, such as school playgrounds, neighborhood parks, and backyards.

Component 2: What Are the Specific
Skills the Teacher Intends to Teach a Student?

1. Task Analysis   This component calls for a task analysis delineating the specific components skills required to perform the educational objective. One possible task analysis for the playground objectives of concern is presented in Table 1.

2. Prerequisite and Correlate Skills   This component requires the teacher to identify skills prerequisite to the target skills or skills that might be taught along with the main training objective. The following skills are prerequisite of correlate skills to the sample program:

A.   Student A will sit in an upright stable position when seated on a teeter-totter, swing, or merry-go-round.
B.   Student B will sit in an upright stable position when seated on a teeter-totter.
C.   Students A and B will grasp the equipment in such a manner as to be able to maintain balance and remain in a safe position on the teeter-totter, swing, or merry-go-round.
D.   Student B will stabilize his or her body in a safe manner when pushing the swing or the merry-go-round.

Component 3: How Will the Teacher
Teach a Student to Perform the Skills of Concern?

1. Ecological Inventory   The ecological inventory delineates the naturally occurring cues and correction procedures available on school playgrounds, at neighborhood parks, and in backyards to primary school–age nonhandicapped persons when using teeter-totters, swings, and merry-go-rounds.

Figure 1 represents an example of an ecological inventory delineating the naturally occurring cues and correction procedures often available when nonhandicapped students use a teeter-totter within the environments described above. An inventory should be completed for each piece of equipment (swing and merry-go-round) to be trained since the cues and available forms of feedback may be different on each.

For each skill shown in Figure 1, the cues and correction procedures that were provided to the student are recorded. In some instances more than one cue and/or correction procedure was provided in assisting in the performance of the skill, while for other skills only one cue or correction procedure was provided. For example, the following types of assistance were provided for Phase 3: *other cues, direct and indirect verbal cues,* and *primed correction procedures.* For

Table 1.   Sample task analysis for playground skills

Skill Cluster I: Teaching students to play cooperatively on a teeter-totter for an appropriate play period at a playground.

Phase 1:   The student will locate another person and ask that person to play with him or her on the teeter-totter.

Phase 2:   The student will move to the teeter-totter with a partner.

Phase 3:   The student will approach the teeter-totter and level the board to enable the person on the opposite side to get on the teeter totter.

Phase 4:   The student will grasp the bar on the teeter-totter.

Phase 5:   The student will communicate who is to get on the teeter-totter first.

Phase 6:   The student will straddle the board of the teeter-totter, sitting with one leg on each side of the board, facing the center of the board.

  Part a: Student A will stabilize the board, then maintain a level position while student B straddles the teeter-totter.

  Part b: Student B will stabilize the board while student A straddles the teeter-totter.

Phase 7:   The student will maintain a grasp on the bar of the teeter-totter to maintain a secure position.

Phase 8:   The student will cooperatively play on the teeter-totter.

  Part a: Student A will push up with both legs or straighten both legs and push off the ground.

  Part b: Student B will guide his or her end of the teeter-totter to the ground in a safe manner.

Phase 9:   The student will communicate that he or she wishes to get off the teeter-totter.

Phase 10:   The student will cooperatively level the teeter-totter and take turns getting off the equipment.

  Part a: The student will cooperatively level the teeter-totter.

  Part b: Student A will get off the teeter-totter and slowly help lower the teeter-totter to the ground, release the handle, and move away from the board.

  Part C: Student B will get off the teeter-totter, release the handle, and move away from the board.

Skill Cluster II: Teaching students to play cooperatively on swings for an appropriate play period at a playground.

Phase 1:   The student will locate another person and ask that person to play with him or her on the swing.

Phase 2:   The student will go to the swing with a partner.

Phase 3:   The student will decide who will push and who will swing first.

Phase 4:   The student will play cooperatively on the swing.

  Part a: Student A will sit on the swing and grasp the right swing support with the right hand and the left swing support with the left hand.

  Part b: Student A will communicate that he or she is ready to swing.

  Part c: Student B will stand behind the swing and, grasping the seat of the swing, pull it back so the swing moves back. Student B will then release the swing so it moves forward.

  Part d: Student B, standing in a safe place and manner, will continue pushing the swing by pushing on the seat of the swing or the back of the person so the swing continues to move back and forth.

  Part e: Student B will stop pushing the swing after an appropriate play time or when student A communicates a desire to stop swinging.

Phase 5:   The student will exchange roles when the swing has stopped moving back and forth.

  Part a: Student B will grasp the seat of the swing and pull on the swing to stop the swing from moving back and forth. Student A may drag his or her feet to slow the motion of the swing.

  Part b: Student A will grasp the swing supports and stand up when the swing is in a stationary position.

Continued

Table 1.—*continued*

Part c: The student will reverse roles and continue to play on the swing. (Begin again at Phase 1.)

Skill Cluster III: Teaching students to play cooperatively on a merry-go-round for an appropriate play period at a playground.

Phase 1: The student will locate another person and ask that person to play with him or her on the merry-go-round.

Phase 2: The student will go to the merry-go-round with a partner.

Phase 3: The student will decide who will push and who will ride the merry-go-round first.

Phase 4: The student will play cooperatively on the merry-go-round.

Part a: Student A will get on the merry-go-round seat or platform.

Part b: Student A will grasp a support bar on the merry-go-round and maintain a sitting position.

Part c: Student A will communicate that he or she is ready for a push.

Part d: Student B will push the merry-go-round by grasping the support bar or seat while walking or running so that the merry-go-round moves in a circular motion.

Part e: Student B will stop pushing the merry-go-round after an appropriate play period or when student A communicates his or her desire to get off.

Phase 5: The student will exchange positions when the merry-go-round is in a stationary position.

Part a: Student B will grasp the support bar or seat and pull back on the merry-go-round in a direction opposite of that in which it was being pushed.

Part b: Student B will stabilize the merry-go-round while student A gets off the merry-go-round.

Part c: The students will reverse roles and play on the merry-go-round. (Begin again at Phase 1.)

Phase 2, only *other cues* as assistance was provided. Thus, in teaching this skill cluster, students will need to be taught systematically to perform some skills in response to a *variety* of cues and correction procedures and other skills in response to only *one* cue or correction procedure. Figure 1 is not intended to be an exhaustive listing of *all* the possible cues and correction procedures available to primary school–age children while playing on a teeter-totter. It is intended as an illustration of cues and correction procedures that were provided in the school playgrounds, neighborhood parks, and backyards that were studied.

2. Student Repertoire Inventory Once the naturally occurring cues and correction procedures are delineated, an inventory of the student's present ability to perform those skills in natural environments needs to be made, and the additional cues and correction procedures needed by that student should be identified. Figure 2 is an example of the assistance a student needed in order to use a teeter-totter on a playground. Figure 2 delineates the cues and correction procedures needed by a selected severely handicapped student to complete the performance requirements. The goal of the instruction would then be to teach the student to perform the skills in response to naturally occurring cues and correction procedures such as those noted in Figure 1. The instruction begins at the competency level of the student, as determined by the ecological inventory (Figure 1); then the instructional cues and correction procedures are faded until the student performs the skills within each phase in response to the naturally occurring cues and correction procedures.

ECOLOGICAL INVENTORY

Environment: _____

Student's name: _____

Skill cluster: _____

Cues and Correction Procedures

Phases	Primed correction procedures	Modeled cues and correction procedures	Direct verbal cues and correction procedures	Indirect verbal cues and correction procedures	Gestural cues and correction procedures	Pictorial cues and correction procedures	Other cues
1. S will seek out another person			Cue Given	Cue Given			Cue Given
2. S will go to the teeter-totter							Cue Given
3. S will get on the teeter-totter	CP* Given		Cue Given	Cue Given			Cue Given
4. S will play cooperatively on the teeter-totter	CP Given		Cue Given	Cue Given	Cue Given		Cue Given
5. S will indicate to partner he or she wants to get off			Cue Given		Cue Given		Cue Given
6. S will cooperatively get off teeter-totter	CP Given		Cue Given				Cue Given

*CP, Correction procedure.

Figure 1. Sample ecological inventory.

Component 4: Describe How the Teacher Will Empirically Verify That the Skills of Concern are Being Acquired.

Students will be pretested for each of the phases presented in the task analysis. If a student is not performing all the skills within a phase, student progress will be measured during teaching sessions. Student behavior will be recorded with a plus (+) when the skills contained in each phase are performed at criterion, and with a minus (−) when the skills contained in each phase are not performed at criterion. Figure 3 is a sample data sheet for Skill Cluster I.

In addition to verifying the student's performance on each of the skills in response to instructional cues and correction procedures, teachers should also evaluate student performance of each skill in response to naturally occurring cues and/or correction procedures. Figure 4 is a sample data sheet a teacher might use

STUDENT REPERTOIRE INVENTORY

Environment: _____
Student's name: _____
Skill cluster: _____

Cues and Correction Procedures

Phases	Primed correction procedures	Modeled cues and correction procedures	Direct verbal cues and correction procedures	Indirect verbal cues and correction procedures	Gestural cues and correction procedures	Pictorial cues and correction procedures	Other cues
1. S will seek out another person			CP* Needed				
2. S will go to the teeter-totter							Cue Used
3. S will get on the teeter-totter	CP Needed	CP Needed	CP Needed		CP Needed		
4. S will play cooperatively on the teeter-totter		CP Needed	CP Needed				
5. S will indicate to partner he or she wants to get off		CP Needed	CP Needed		CP Needed		
6. S will cooperatively get off teeter-totter							Cue Used

*CP, Correction procedure.

Figure 2. Sample student repertoire inventory.

DATA SHEET

Student's name: _____

Responses: + when desired response is performed

                 − when desired response is not performed

SKILL CLUSTER I: Teaching students to play cooperatively on a teeter-totter for an appropriate play period at a playground.

DATES

Phase 1						
Phase 2						
Phase 3						
Phase 4						
Phase 5						
Phase 6						
Part a						
Part b						
Phase 7						
Phase 8						
Part a						
Part b						
Phase 9						
Phase 10						
Part a						
Part b						
Part c						

Figure 3.   Sample data sheet for recording student's performance.

to collect data on a student's performance in response to the naturally occurring cues and/or correction procedures.

Component 5:   What Are Reasonable Characteristics of the Successful Performance of a Skill Cluster, i.e., Performance Criteria?

The ecological inventory strategy can be used to determine the rate at which nonhandicapped persons perform and engage in the skills of concern. The rate at which nonhandicapped persons performed and engaged in the skills of concern varied across ages and individuals. The inventory indicated that primary school–age nonhandicapped children spent more time engaged in activities using playground equipment than older persons and that time spent on any one piece of equipment varied from 2 minutes to 20 minutes.

In addition to determining the time nonhandicapped persons spent using playground equipment, it was critical to determine the time it took for non-handicapped persons to perform the skills of concern. The ecological inventory indicated that it took primary school–age nonhandicapped children 5 seconds to 1 minute to get ready to play. It took these same children 5 seconds to 2 minutes to locate another person to play with on the equipment. The rate at which non-handicapped persons perform the skill clusters in the task analysis can act as a criterion rate for handicapped persons to perform those same skills. The rate at which the skills are performed is evaluated as well as the qualitative aspects of performance of the skill cluster.

Component 6: What Instructional Materials Are to be Used?

The instructional materials for this program will be teeter-totters, swings, and merry-go-rounds. A variety of each piece of equipment will be used to teach students to perform the skills of concern using a variety of playgrounds.

DATA SHEET

Student's name: _____

P,   Primed
M,   Modeled
DV,   Direct verbal
IDV,   Indirect verbal
G,   Gestural
PT,   Pictorial
C,   Cue
CP,   Correction procedure

SKILL CLUSTER I: Cooperative play on a teeter-totter.

Dates

Phase 1									
Phase 2									
Phase 3									
Phase 4									
Phase 5									
Phase 6									

Figure 4.   Sample data sheet for recording student's performance in response to naturally occurring cues and/or correction procedures.

Component 7: How Will the Teacher Ensure That a Student Generalizes the Skills of Concern Across Relevant Dimensions (i.e., Persons, Places, Materials, Cues, etc.)?

To verify that a student can perform the skills of concern in a variety of circumstances, data will be collected in at least three different places and in the presence of three persons. For example, student performance might be measured on a school playground, at a neighborhood park, and in the student's backyard in the company of a school friend, a neighbor, and a brother or sister. If performance does not transfer to these natural settings, then additional instruction is necessary with careful attention directed to bring performance under the control of the features of those settings.

Component 8: How Will the Teacher Ensure That a Student Performs the Skills of Concern Independent of Instruction?

To determine if a student performs the skills of concern independent of instruction, the teacher will need to verify that the student can perform those skills in response to naturally occurring cues and/or correction procedures in natural environments. If the teacher includes, as a part of the instructional process, systematic fading of *instructional* cues and/or correction procedures to those cues and/or correction procedures that are usually available in the environment, then the ultimate independent performance of the skills of concern would be more readily ensured.

REFERENCES

Bandura, A. *Principles of behavior modification.* Chicago: Holt, Rinehart and Winston, 1969, 217–231.

Belmore, K., & Brown, L. A job skill inventory strategy for use in a public school vocational training program for severely handicapped potential workers. In L. Brown, N. Certo, K. Belmore, & T. Crowner (eds.), *Papers and programs related to public school services for secondary aged severely handicapped students* (Vol. 6, Part 1). Madison, Wisconsin: Madison Metropolitan School District, 1976. [Revised and republished: N. G. Haring & D. Bricker (eds.), *Teaching the severely handicapped* (Vol. 3). Seattle: American Association for the Education of the Severely and Profoundly Handicapped, 1978, 223–262.]

Brown, L., Bellamy, T., & Sontag, E. (eds.). *The development and implementation of a public school training program for trainable retarded and severely emotionally disturbed children* (Vol. I). Madison, Wisconsin: Madison Metropolitan School District, 1971.

Brown, L., Branston, M. B., Hamre-Nietupski, S., Pumpian, I., Certo, N., & Gruenewald, L. A strategy for developing chronological age appropriate and functional curricular content for severely handicapped adolescents and young adults. *Journal of Special Education,* 1979, *13*(1), 81–90.

Brown, L., Certo, N., Belmore, K., & Crowner, T. (eds.). *Madison's alternative for zero exclusion: Papers and programs related to public school services for secondary age severely handicapped students* (Vol. VI, Part 1). Madison, Wisconsin: Madison Metropolitan School District, 1976.

Brown, L., Nietupski, J., & Hamre-Nietupski, S. The criterion of ultimate functioning and public school services for severely handicapped students. In M. A. Thomas (ed.), *Hey, don't forget about me: Education's investment in the severely, profoundly and multiply handicapped.* Reston, Virginia: Council for Exceptional Children, 1976, 2-15.

Brown, L., Nietupski, J., Lyon, S., Hamre-Nietupski, S., Crowner, T., & Gruenewald, L. (eds.). *Curricular strategies for teaching functional object use, nonverbal communication, problem solving, and mealtime skills to severely handicapped students* (Vol. VII, Part 1). Madison, Wisconsin: Madison Metropolitan School District, 1977.

Brown, L., Scheuerman, N., Cartwright, S., & York, R. (eds.). *The design and implementation of an empirically based instructional program for young severely handicapped students: Toward the rejection of the exclusion principle* (Vol. III). Madison, Wisconsin: Madison Public Schools, 1973.

Brown, L., & Sontag, E. (eds.). *Toward the development and implementation of an empirically based public school program for trainable mentally retarded and severely emotionally disturbed students* (Vol. II). Madison, Wisconsin: Madison Public Schools, 1972.

Brown, L., Wilcox, B., Sontag, E., Vincent, L., Dodd, N., & Gruenewald, L. Toward the realization of the least restrictive educational environments for severely handicapped students. *AAESPH Review,* 1977, *2*(4), 195-201.

Gaylord-Ross, R. Mental retardation research, ecological validity, and the delivery of longitudinal education programs. *Journal of Special Education,* 1979, *13*(1), 69-80.

Guess, D., Sailor, W., & Baer, D. A behavioral-remedial approach to language training for the severely handicapped. In E. Sontag, J. Smith, & N. Certo (eds.), *Educational programming for the severely and profoundly handicapped.* Reston, Virginia: Council for Exceptional Children DMR, 1977, 360-377.

Horner, R. D., Holvoet, J., & Rinne, T. *Generalization and discrimination of operant behavior. Module J. Personnel training program for the education of the severely handicapped student.* Lawrence, Kansas: Department of Special Education, University of Kansas, 1976.

Lovaas, I., Freitas, L., Nelson, C., & Whalen, C. The establishment of imitation and its use for the development of complex behavior in schizophrenic children. *Behavior Research and Therapy,* 1967, *5,* 171-181.

Lyon, S., Baumgart, D., Stoll, A., & Brown, L. Curricular strategies for teaching basic functional object use skills to severely handicapped students. In L. Brown, J. Nietupski, S. Lyon, S. Hamre-Nietupski, T. Crowner, & L. Gruenewald (eds.), *Curricular strategies for teaching functional object use, nonverbal communication, problem solving, and mealtime skills to severely handicapped students* (Vol. VII, Part 1). Madison, Wisconsin: Madison Metropolitan School District, 1977, 14-68.

Peterson, F. Imitation: A basic behavioral mechanism. In H. Sloane & B. MacAulay (eds.), *Operant procedures in remedial speech and language training.* Boston: Houghton Mifflin Co., 1968, 61-74.

White, O. R. (ed.). *A glossary of behavioral terminology.* Champaign, Illinois: Research Press Co., 1971, 63.

Williams, W., Brown, L., & Certo, N. Basic components of instructional programs. *Theory into Practice,* 1975, *14*(2), 123-136.

Chapter 5

A Decision Model for the Treatment of Aberrant Behavior in Applied Settings

Robert Gaylord-Ross

Consideration of aberrant behaviors has had an important role in the diagnosis and treatment of severely handicapped individuals. Severely handicapped persons have been variously defined as a group having low intellectual functioning, limited adaptive behavior skills, and aberrant behaviors including self-injury, aggression, and other stereotypes (U.S. Office of Education, 1974). More formally, diagnostic instruments such as the AAMD Adaptive Behavior Scales have defined mental retardation in terms of deficiencies in a number of skill domains coupled with the prevalence of aberrant behaviors (Grossman, 1973). Autism, another severely handicapping condition, has as one of its primary defining characteristics the appearance of bizarre and aberrant behaviors. In fact, the term *autistic-like* has emerged to categorize some of these aberrant behaviors such as finger and object twirling, body rocking, and self-injury.

The term *aberrant behavior* is used to denote any behavior that is perceived to be clinically abnormal because of the response topography, the response frequency, or the situation in which the behavior occurs. For example, a behavior such as hand waving may be clinically normal when it appears in an appropriate context and/or with an acceptable frequency. However, the same behavior when occurring out of context or in excess, e.g., the self-stimulating behavior of hand flapping, may be considered aberrant. Other behaviors may be judged clinically abnormal in almost any context or frequency. Behavior such as head banging or stabbing others with sharp objects would fall into this category. The term *aberrant* is used interchangeably in this chapter with other terms that denote clinically

Work reported in this chapter was supported in part by grant G007603954 from the Bureau of Education for the Handicapped.

I would like to thank Marian Weeks and Luanna Voeltz for their input. The graphic work of Tom Haring is also appreciated.

abnormal behavior, viz., problem behavior, deviant behavior, or disruptive behavior.

There is little doubt that aberrant behaviors can interfere with and impede the instruction and development of severely handicapped persons. When an individual spends a disproportionate amount of time engaging in problem behaviors, it will be more difficult for that person to attend to instructional stimuli (Lovaas, Litrownik, & Mann, 1971). In turn, fewer correct responses will be made, and the acquisition rate for learning important skills will be decreased (Koegel & Covert, 1972). Since general development as well as educational progress will be impeded because of excessive engagement in aberrant behavior, it is important to eliminate or reduce significantly disruptive behaviors in order to protect the individual and others from potentially harmful acts, and to promote the developmental acquisition of important repertoires of motor, communicative, and social skills.

Fortunately for teachers, there has been a growing research literature that has documented techniques that effectively decelerate aberrant behaviors (cf. Baumeister & Rollings, 1976; Horner, Note 1; Schroeder, Mulick, & Schroeder, in press). Behavior modification techniques that either punish the problem behavior or positively reinforce alternative behaviors have been shown to reduce a number of problem behaviors significantly. While many of these experimental demonstrations have been impressive (e.g., Lovaas & Simmons, 1969), there is still a need to extend their findings and techniques to more applied and natural settings. Functional control of aberrant behavior has often been obtained over deviant acts in rather controlled, experimental settings where there is elaborate equipment and/or an abundance of staff members to record and treat the subject's behavior. In more natural settings like classrooms, however, it is not likely that such staff ratios and hardware will be available. Because of the constraints of reality, it is important to know not only which techniques are likely to be effective but also which can be efficiently carried out in the classroom. For example, Kelly and Drabman (1977) reported the successful application of an overcorrection procedure to reduce self-injurious behavior. In a follow-up to the research project, however, it was found that the staff members were not implementing the overcorrection procedure because it was physically exhausting, time consuming, and prevented attention to the other children in the class.

In an effort to develop procedures that are in fact useful in natural settings, it seems appropriate to explore alternative approaches to standard behavior modification. For example, an educational approach would focus upon building skill repertoires without directly treating the problem behavior (Gaylord-Ross, 1979). The successful performance of socially desirable and constructive skills would compete with the performance of deviant acts, and aberrant behaviors would be expected to drop out or never appear when socially acceptable behavior was being built. An advantage of the educational approach is that it falls within the framework of activities already being carried out in the classroom, namely, the implementation of instructional programs. In this sense the approach is more cost effective because it does not require "special" intervention programs. Rather, modifications in curriculum are made that should lead to concomitant reductions in problem behavior (cf. Weeks & Gaylord-Ross, Note 2).

A second alternative to a strict behavior modification approach is to make changes in the physical and social ecology that may affect the frequency of disruptive responses. For instance, Rago, Parker, and Cleland (1978) have shown that crowding is correlated with increases in aggressive behavior among profoundly retarded persons. It is conceivable that redesigning the spatial arrangements and social interaction patterns in classrooms or other settings could have positive effects in reducing aberrant behavior (cf. Hart & Risley, Note 3). Such ecological manipulations might also be cost beneficial since they would require little ongoing monitoring and program delivery. Once partitions are set up and students grouped into activities in designated zones, the ecological changes would be complete. There would be no need for additional special programming since activities would proceed within this new ecological context. Unfortunately, there has been little research to date to evaluate the effectiveness of different environmental adaptations.

Behavioral, curricular, and ecological techniques are not mutually exclusive. Rather, they constitute options available to teachers and other professionals responsible for the education of severely handicapped learners. The aim of this chapter is to offer a structured decision model that will guide professionals in the selection of procedures to deal with aberrant behavior. The sequence of steps in dealing with deviant behavior is justified on empirical and ethical grounds. Empirically, it is felt that after an initial assessment is made there exist a number of specific behavioral techniques that may be tried and that have been shown to result in rather immediate reductions in aberrant behavior (Baumeister & Rollings, 1976; Frankel & Simmons, 1976). Next, possible environmental and curricular modifications are suggested. Finally, it may be necessary to implement a punishment procedure in order to attain response suppression over more difficult behaviors. Punishment is used, and therefore is ethically justified, only after a number of "positive" approaches have been tried and evaluated. Ethical issues are considered in the discussion of punishment below.

DECISION MODEL

The basic components of the decision model are presented in Figure 1 and further analyzed in Figures 2–6. A flowchart format has been used to present the decision model. The flowchart is constructed so that the user first asks a series of questions to determine what factors are causing or maintaining the problem behavior. For example, a teacher would first examine the different reinforcement causes of a disruptive behavior (Component 2). If none of these factors appeared causal, the teacher would then move on to investigate the possible ecological

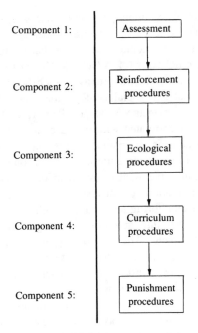

Component 1: Assessment

Component 2: Reinforcement procedures

Component 3: Ecological procedures

Component 4: Curriculum procedures

Component 5: Punishment procedures

Figure 1. A five-component decision model for the treatment of aberrant behavior.

causes of aberrant behavior. This procedure would continue until each component had been systematically examined. The flowchart offers the further advantage of recommending a particular intervention technique after a specific causal factor has been identified. The extent of empirical support for the treatment recommendations varies considerably. Strategies in the reinforcement and punishment components have received considerable experimental validation, while the ecological and curricular component interventions have received less experimental investigation and are more based on anecdotal evidence and unpublished reports. The decision model does not recommend specific treatments based on the response characteristics of the behavior, a limitation that, it is hoped, will be overcome by research investigating the best match between treatment and the intensity and type of problem behavior.

Assessment Component

The monitoring and implementation of behavior management programs often require efforts that can detract from instructional time and lead to unwanted staff fatigue. It is therefore imperative to make an accurate assessment of the severity of the behavior problem so that a proper decision can be made with respect to implementing a special program. This process, represented in Figure 2, includes both qualitative and quantitative procedures. The initial objective of the assessment component is to decide whether a particular deviant behavior necessitates

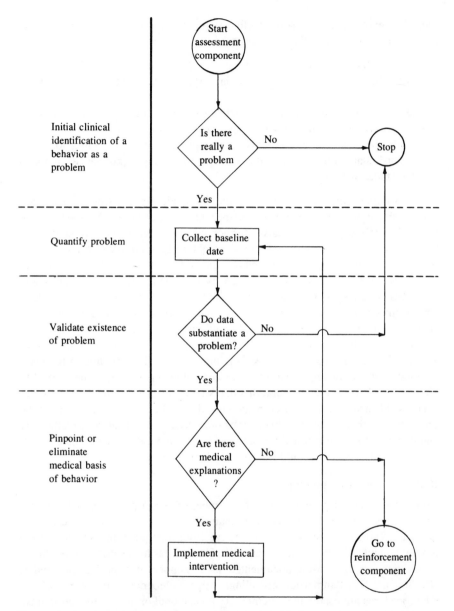

Figure 2. Flowchart of the *assessment* component. Circles indicate stop, start, or exit steps. Diamonds indicate a decision or branching step, e.g., *yes,* the behavior problem is clinically significant, or *no,* the behavior is not maintained by medical factors. A rectangle states the procedure to be implemented, e.g., collect quantitative data or institute a medical intervention.

special intervention. This sort of clinical judgment should consider both the obtrusiveness and harmfulness of the behavior and pose such questions as:

1. Is the behavior causing physical harm to the student or others?
2. Is the behavior disrupting overall classroom instruction to a significant degree?
3. Does the behavior appear to be triggering collateral emotional reactions, e.g., excessive crying or screaming, extreme withdrawal?
4. Is the behavior so contextually inappropriate that it is leading to social exclusion and a limitation in the number of places and experiences in which the student can engage?

An initial clinical judgment should be made by classroom personnel, perhaps in conjunction with a behavior specialist. If it is judged that the behavior is not clinically severe or obtrusive, further analysis is terminated. If an affirmative judgment is made, the next step is to obtain baseline data on the level of response. Baseline data are then used to validate the initial decision to intervene. If the behavior's rate, duration, or intensity is indeed high, the teacher should next consider possible medical causes of the behavioral problem. For example, a chronic inner ear infection might lead to ear digging which appears to be an aberrant behavior. Similarly, medical conditions can affect behavior, as in instances when changes in medication produce an increase in the frequency of stereotypic behavior (Baumeister & Forehand, 1973). This module in the decision model does *not* imply that pharmacological agents should be prescribed to eliminate problem behavior, but rather that when a specific biomedical factor has been established as causal, a corresponding biomedical intervention should be prescribed. When 1) the problem behavior has been judged to be clinically significant, and 2) biomedical factors have been ruled out (or manipulated without result), the teacher should proceed to Component 2.

Reinforcement Component

Component 2 presents an analysis of a number of reinforcement paradigms that can maintain deviant behaviors. The analysis focuses on consequence events. Specific treatment recommendations derive from manipulations on each of the possible maintaining variables (Figure 3). The success of the different treatment procedures has been well documented in a number of experimental studies (Bachman, 1972; Baumeister & Rollings, 1976; Schroeder et al., in press), and the procedures are usable in contemporary educational or habilitative programs.

Positive Reinforcement A variety of problem behaviors can be maintained by contingent social attention (Bandura, 1969). Often the persons in contact with the individual are not aware that they are providing contingent reinforcement for the undesirable behavior. The first module in Component 2 (see Figure 3) calls for a determination of whether the problem behavior appears to be maintained by social reinforcement. If repeated observations of behavior—consequence dyads do not indicate a functional relationship, one would proceed to the next module

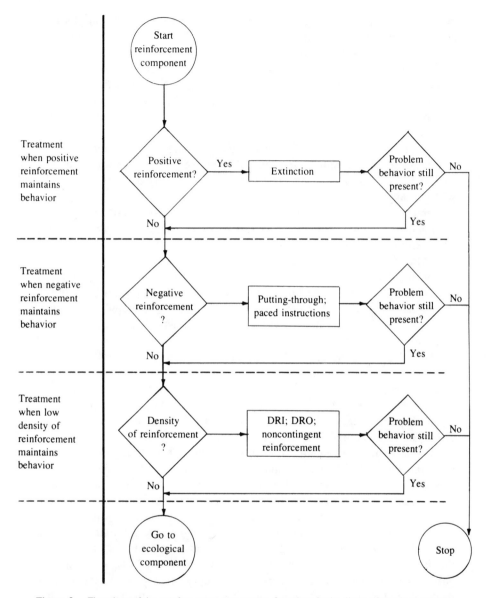

Figure 3. Flowchart of the *reinforcement* component. Questions in the diamonds evaluate whether a significant amount of problem behavior remains after the intervention has been implemented. *Yes,* there is still a significant amount of behavior, gives direction to the next maintenance variable to be considered. *No* means the behavior has been practically eliminated or reduced to socially acceptable level. The stop module declares that the special program can be terminated or faded out. (DRI, differential reinforcement of incompatible behavior; DRO, differential reinforcement of other behavior.)

in the decision process. If it were suspected or ascertained that some form of positive reinforcement maintained the aberrant behavior, the treatment recommendation would be extinction. Extinction requires that all persons having contact with the student would never attend (verbally or gesturally) to an occurrence of the deviant response. Extinction training should thus break the functional relationship between the inappropriate response and the target consequence. One problem with the use of extinction training in applied settings, however, is that caregivers may find it difficult or impossible to ignore the problem behavior consistently (Gilbert, 1976). The inconsistent ignoring of a behavior may actually result in an intermittent schedule of reinforcement that can maintain behaviors in a very powerful manner. Another problem with extinction is that there will typically be an increase in responding immediately after the procedure is implemented (Lovaas & Simmons, 1969). Increases in responding may be medically and ethically unjustified with certain behaviors that can result in extensive damage to the individual or others.

After extinction (or any other procedure in the decision model) has been carried out for a number of sessions or days (5–10 as a rule of thumb), the procedure should be evaluated by contrasting treatment with levels of occurrence during baseline. Reversal or other acceptable designs may be applied to further evaluate the scientific validity of the treatment effects. If extinction has not practically eliminated the aberrant behavior or reduced it to a socially acceptable level, one should proceed to the next decision point. If successful response suppression is demonstrated, the decision model would terminate. It would then be necessary to continue or fade out the program according to the particular characteristics of the case. The maintenance of program effects is not discussed in this chapter, but the interested reader can refer to Kazdin (1975) for a thorough discussion of this topic.

Negative Reinforcement   It is also possible for aberrant behavior to be maintained by negative reinforcement (Carr, 1977) when the emission of a response leads to the cessation of an aversive stimulus. Negative reinforcement operates as an attempt to escape from an undesirable state of affairs. Sometimes severely handicapped persons who have never participated in an educational program exhibit displeasure in engaging in instructional tasks. Carr, Newsom, and Binkoff (1976) and Gaylord-Ross, Weeks, and Lipner (in press) have shown that instructional commands (mands) for nonpreferred tasks lead to the appearance of self-injurious behavior. This relationship seemed to be maintained by a negative reinforcement paradigm. Sometimes caregivers will decrease their frequency of mands in order to obtain concomitant decreases in disruptive behavior. Limiting the educational involvement of the student can in fact strengthen the negative reinforcement relationship by correlating aberrant responses with fewer task demands. In an effort to eliminate this effect, Plummer, Baer, and LeBlanc (1977) used a "paced instructions" procedure that required teachers to deliver mands in a periodic and frequent way. Paced instruction was shown to reduce deviant behavior successfully in a group of preschool children. In a manner similar to paced instructions, a "putting-through" procedure would require the student to complete a task after a mand is presented. Manual or other prompts may be required to ensure that the task is completed. Teachers may find that regulating their rate of delivery of commands may effectively reduce disruptive behavior. Elimination of the negative reinforcement value of deviant behavior is important on two accounts. First, an undesirable behavior is eliminated, and second, the paced instructions and putting-through procedures guarantee that the student receives proper and undiminished amounts of educational stimulation.

Density of Reinforcement Even with a contemporary special education program in place, it may be possible that a student is experiencing little reinforcement, either because the environment itself supplies minimal positive consequences or because the student lacks skills to perform the behaviors that earn reinforcement. When there is minimal positive reinforcement for on-task or other appropriate behavior, there is a greater likelihood that aberrant behaviors will occur. This is especially likely when the aberrant behaviors themselves are intrinsically reinforcing, e.g., stereotypy (Lovaas et al., 1971), or when they themselves produce attention from the social environment. In order to design effective programming, it may be necessary to estimate the density of reinforcement a student receives over the different segments of the school day. If the density is low, a number of strategies may be employed to increase the availability of reinforcement. Simply providing reinforcement noncontingently may be sufficient to reduce the level of aberrant behavior. Bailey and Meyerson (1970), for example, found that noncontingent vibratory stimulation effectively reduced self-injurious behavior. An equally simple strategy may be to encourage staff and parents to increase the number of positive interactions they have with the target student. Whether using noncontingent or contingent procedures, the rate of reinforcement should be monitored to ensure that it has actually increased to an acceptable level.

The procedure of *differential reinforcement of incompatible behavior* (DRI) is one that reinforces a predetermined, on-task behavior. Theoretically, the repeated reinforcement of the on-task response increases its likelihood of occurrence, which concomitantly competes with, and decreases the likelihood of, the deviant response. DRI can entail the use of a task physically incompatible with the deviant response, e.g., shirt buttoning for a person who engages in hand mouthing, or any task that presents an alternative to the problem behavior (Bachman, 1972; Young and Wincze, 1974). The *differential reinforcement of other behavior* (DRO) is a procedure that delivers reinforcement for the nonoccurrence of the deviant response during a given time interval. For example, if a student does not slap his or her face for a 60-second period, he or she might be contingently reinforced with a bit of food. Repp and Deitz (1974) applied DRO to a group of institutionalized, severely retarded persons and successfully reduced aggressive and self-injurious behavior.

Implementation The ordering of variables in Component 2 is admittedly somewhat arbitrary since all three procedures have been shown to maintain aberrant behavior. In fact, it is possible for two or more variables to be maintaining several deviant behaviors simultaneously. For example, it might be found that whenever a student pulls other pupils' hair the teaching staff immediately talks to the student for at least a minute about why it is not nice to pull hair. The positive reinforcement of hair pulling through contingent teacher talk would be maintaining this undesirable behavior. It may also be found with this *same* student that whenever the child begins to scream during an instructional session the teacher terminates the session for the day. Here, screaming is being maintained by negative reinforcement. Thus, different behaviors are being separately maintained by positive and negative reinforcement. In addition, the density of reinforcement is likely to interact with other variables. A student receiving little positive reinforcement for on-task performance is likely to be more responsive to the social reinforcement of problem behavior. When nonpreferred instructional tasks are rarely reinforced it is more likely that deviant responses will be made to escape the mand or performance requirement. For example, a student might spend most of the day in a class in "down-time" isolation. When the student does receive instruction, the tasks used may have little intrinsic reinforcement value. Furthermore, correct task responses are not consistently consequated with an event of high incentive value. Under these conditions of low reinforcement density, the student might display face slapping during down-time to obtain social interaction with staff (positive reinforcement) and the student might finger bite during instructional sessions since the teacher immediately terminates the session, enabling the child to avoid engaging the nonpreferred task.

Perhaps the best rationale for the order of the variables relates to their ease of implementation. Extinction should be the easiest procedure to implement because it merely involves the consistent ignoring of certain behavior. Putting-through and the paced instruction interventions require active implementation of an instructional regime in a regulated fashion. That is, these procedures merely require that cues be delivered and the task be completed in the normal fashion without deviant responses obtaining escape/avoidance properties. Procedures involving reinforcement density may require even more effort because there must be changes in staff interaction patterns and the monitoring of response and/or time variables. For example, the application of DRO with high frequency behaviors can be difficult because it requires staff to count behaviors, keep track of DRO intervals, and carry out instruction simultaneously (Gaylord-Ross, Note 4). Regardless of the validity of the current ordering, the primary function of the decision model is to make professionals aware of important maintenance variables and the corresponding treatment procedures.

Ecological Component

There has been a growing interest among behavior scientists in human ecology, the systematic study of the interrelationships between humans and their environment (cf. Rogers-Warren & Warren, 1977), although there has been relatively little investigation of the effects of ecological variables on severely handicapped persons (see Berkson & Landesman-Dwyer, 1977). Still it seems evident that ecological variables should have important effects on their behavior and development. The types of environments in which severely handicapped persons have resided have often been characterized by a number of negative ecological factors such as crowding or an absence of objects to manipulate (Wolfensberger, 1972). An ecologist would hypothesize that if critical alterations were made in residential and educational environments, there would be increases in prosocial behaviors and decreases in aberrant behaviors. Component 3 points out potentially important ecological variables and recommends milieu changes to effect more desirable behavior.

Limited physical space can create a condition of crowding. Rago et al. (1978) demonstrated, for example, that increasing the amount of physical space can directly reduce aggressive behavior with severely handicapped persons. An appropriate intervention for problem behaviors would be to increase the size of the classroom or reduce the number of students per class (Figure 4). If it were impossible to increase classroom space or to lower the student-teacher ratio, alternative solutions would include shifting the students to different rooms throughout the school day so that the oppressiveness of a single crowded room could be varied and attenuated. Also, crowded space may be effectively "broken up" by partitioning the room into zones for different activities (Hart & Risley, Note 3).

A second ecological variable that may affect behavior is the number of objects in the setting that are available for the student to manipulate. A number of studies have documented an inverse relationship between the enrichment of the environment (presence of people or manipulable objects) and the degree of stereotypy exhibited (Baumeister & Forehand, 1973; Berkson & Mason, 1963; Hutt & Hutt, 1965). When objects are available for manipulation, the person's attention is engaged by the objects, thereby eliminating the aberrant behavior. An obvious implication of this finding is that classrooms and other environments should be designed so that there is an ample supply of objects with which students may interact. These objects should evoke the curiosity of the student and be readily available during noninstructional periods of the day, thus making more effective use of down-time periods. Such results, of course, are predicated on an assumption that students have the skills to interact effectively and appropriately with available objects. Obviously it may be necessary to provide prosthetic devices to permit a multiply handicapped child to interact with a particular object or to train students in appropriate play skills.

There is another very different set of environmental variables that could be labeled ecological "pollutants." Excessive noise, extreme heat or cold, and insufficient lighting are likely to have deleterious effects on learning and behavior. In the current times of fiscal cutbacks in education, urban decay and school deterioration, and the energy crisis, many of these ecological pollutants will be present. Although these variables have not been systematically studied, many ways to remediate these problems are apparent, including providing heat,

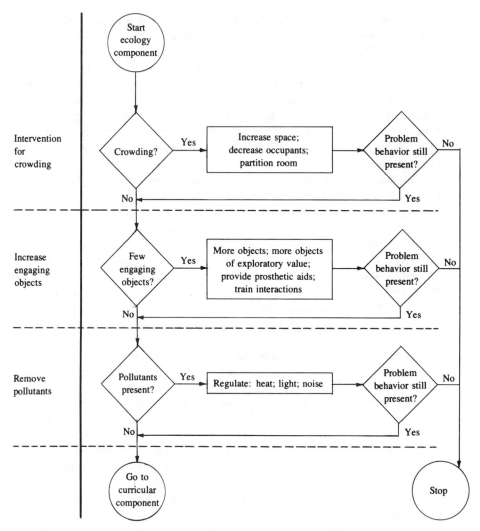

Figure 4. Flowchart of the *ecology* component.

insulating against sound, and so on, but they may be unobtainable because of limited funds. Nevertheless, the teacher should be aware of these variables and their potential effects on behavior, and take remedial action to eliminate them whenever possible.

Curriculum Component

Component 4 (Figure 5) presents an analysis of curriculum variables that may be manipulated in order to reduce problem behavior. Although the primary behavioral strategy to eliminate problem behaviors has been to manipulate consequence events, it may also be possible to produce desired changes through altering the task or activity the person is performing (an antecedent event). An increasing number of studies have shown a covariation between type of task and deviant behavior (Gaylord-Ross et al., in press; Schroeder & Humphrey, Note 5). Schroeder and Humphrey found consistently high rates of self-injury during fine motor activities in a severely retarded adult female. There were noticeably fewer self-injurious responses during other activity segments of the day. Gaylord-Ross et al., in a case study, showed the frequency of self-injury to be

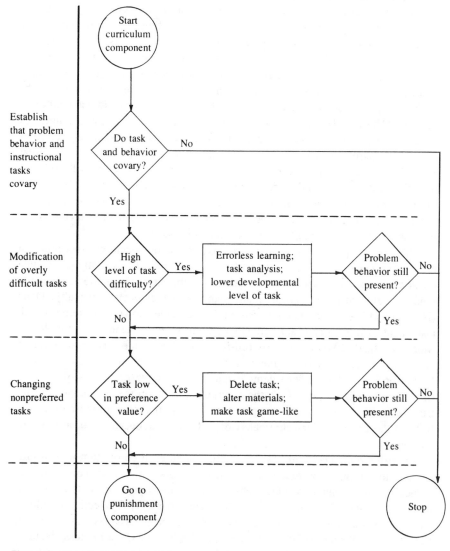

Figure 5. Flowchart of the *curriculum* component.

high when sorting buttons and low when assembling puzzles. Thus, such correlations suggest that the characteristics of the task may have important determining effects on the appearance of problem behavior. Furthermore, it would seem feasible that interventions focusing on the alteration of task properties hold promise as means to decrease aberrant behavior. What could be termed a curricular approach has the advantage over traditional behavior modification approaches of not adding an extra program or consequence event to existing activities. Rather, normal instructional sessions are conducted with adaptations built into the ongoing curriculum.

A curricular approach, therefore, asserts that an important way to reduce problem behaviors is through the process of skill building alone. Given the limited skill repertoires of severely handicapped persons, it is quite likely that deviant responses will be made due to their social, escape, or intrinsic reinforcement characteristics. As alternative, positively valued behaviors are taught, they will compete with disruptive behaviors, and as more and more skills are established, the probability of occurrence of problem behaviors should concomitantly decrease. This competing response notion is similar to the DRI strategy, although there is no monitoring of problem behavior(s) as a function of positively reinforcing an alternative response as in DRI; rather there is the delivery of a total educational program and the expectation that problem behaviors will drop out over time without the need of direct behavior management programs. In support of the curricular approach, Schroeder et al. (in press) and Voeltz (Note 6) have reported that programs showing the best maintenance of problem behavior reductions were those that taught a specific behavioral skill.

The first step in Component 4 is to observe and document whether problem behaviors appear to covary with particular tasks or activity settings. If such covariation is found, a series of maintenance-treatment variables should be examined. The first of these possible maintenance variables is task difficulty. Dehn (Note 7) and Weeks and Gaylord-Ross (Note 2) have shown that more difficult tasks tend to lead to aberrant behaviors among severely handicapped children. More specifically, Weeks and Gaylord-Ross found deviant behaviors to occur on error, not correct, trials. From a reinforcement perspective, Sailor, Guess, Rutherford, and Baer (1968) demonstrated the negative properties of difficult (high error) tasks by presenting them contingently upon the appearance of tantrum behavior. This punishment procedure, in combination with presenting easy tasks in the absence of tantrum behavior, effectively reduced the occurrence of tantrums.

Instructional Techniques   There are a number of curriculum-related procedures to eliminate or reduce performance errors which may concomitantly reduce problem behaviors. One technique is to select developmentally simpler tasks, which should produce fewer performance errors. Task selection should be based on some developmental theory that delineates task sequences, (e.g., Gesell, 1974; Piaget, 1970). For example, Weeks and Gaylord-Ross (Note 2) contrasted performance on developmentally prior and advanced, two-choice discrimination problems. The tasks were selected on the basis of Gibson's (1969) theory of perceptual development. Simple tasks involved visually discriminating between rudimentary figures like circles, triangles, and squares. Difficult tasks entailed discriminating between open-closed figures, and reversed figures. The investigation found that more errors were committed on difficult tasks, and that noticeably more aberrant behaviors appeared on error trials.

Task analysis is a second technique that can be used to reduce performance errors. Task analysis has been most frequently used to "slice" self-care, perceptual-motor tasks into their smaller components so that developmentally disabled learners can acquire those skills in a more efficient manner. Weeks and Gaylord-Ross (Note 2) extended the use of task analysis to the treatment of aberrant behavior. They first demonstrated that simple, one-step, perceptual-motor tasks produced few errors and few aberrant behaviors. Next, they showed that difficult, multiple-step tasks, like buttoning a shirt and buckling a belt, produced many errors and many associated deviant responses. Finally, these difficult tasks were task analyzed into graded steps so that the student was first brought to criterion on oversized shirts and buckles. Subsequently, the size of the garment was progressively decreased with the student(s) eventually reaching criterion on properly fitting clothes with few errors or problem behaviors appearing throughout the training sessions.

The technique of errorless learning (Sidman & Stoddard, 1967) may also be applied in an attempt to reduce performance errors and problem behaviors. Errorless learning entails the gradual fading in and/or fading out of properties of the stimulus so that error-free performance can occur. For example, a difficult task in the Weeks and Gaylord-Ross (Note 2) study demanded that the student discriminate a backward from a forward Z figure. In the difficult task (trial-and-error) condition, the student had to distinguish (point to) a forward and backward (not point to) Z on every trial. In the errorless condition, the student initially had to point to a forward Z (S^D) and not point to a card that was blank (S^Δ). When the student reached criterion on this discrimination, the blank S^Δ card was modified so that a few dots or parts of a backward Z were presented. When criterion was reached on this discrimination, more of the parts of the backward Z were filled in until the complete backward Z was presented on the S^Δ card. This training sequence produced relatively few performance errors and hardly any deviant responses. In summary, it seems that curricular modifications that eliminate errors in learning offer promising ways to diminish existing rates of aberrant behavior. It would, therefore, behoove teachers to be sensitive to the task difficulty variable not only for the purpose of refining their instructional delivery system, but also as a means for modifying disconcerting behaviors.

Task Preference Level It is also possible that the preference value of the task in addition to task difficulty may be correlated with problem behavior. Gaylord-Ross et al. (in press) observed high rates of self-injury when a subject engaged in a nonpreferred task and low rates when engaged in a preferred activity. The preference value of tasks is not always easy to determine, but free-choice techniques have been developed to infer the relative motivational value of different activities and stimuli (cf. Striefel, 1974).

It may be possible that a task is not preferred because of the low curiosity value of the stimulus materials (Berlyne, 1960). One might redesign the instructional materials to increase their curiosity and preference value in an attempt to influence disruptive behaviors. The curiosity value of instructional materials and activities could be increased by instituting game-like procedures or heightening the sensory stimulation of the objects. Solnick, Rincover, and Peterson (1977) demonstrated that contingent time-out from stimulating, enriched materials successfully reduced deviant behavior, while time-out from materials and activities that were low in curiosity value failed to suppress the same behaviors. Teachers, of course, have spent considerable time devising ways to make their instructional materials and activities more interesting. A great deal of effort is still needed from applied researchers to determine more systematic ways to increase the curiosity value of instructional materials and activities.

If it has been established that nonpreferred activities are correlated with problem behaviors, one obvious tactic would be to drop the nonpreferred task from the student's scheduled activities. If the maladaptive response was functioning to escape the unpleasant task demands, the problem behavior should disappear as a function of eliminating the task since the escape function of the problem behavior no longer serves a purpose. While in many cases the task deletion strategy may be warranted, it may not be appropriate when a critical skill such as manual communication or toileting is found to be correlated with aberrant behavior. It would hardly be educationally justifiable to stop instruction on such critical skills.

Punishment Component

Component 5 (Figure 6) deals with the use of punishment procedures to manage disruptive behavior. Punishment is defined as the contingent application of any consequence that leads to the deceleration of the target response. Punishment may involve the contingent presentation of an aversive stimulus or the contingent removal of a positive consequence (e.g., response cost). In either case, the contingency must result in a deceleration in the operant behavior.

The punishment component is the final choice point in the decision model for both ethical and programmatic reasons. Ethically, it is felt that in most cases punishment can only be justified if a number of more positive approaches (DRI, ecological, and curricular interventions) have already been attempted. When positive approaches have been tried and have failed to reduce the problem behavior significantly, certain types of punishment procedures may be implemented, although the type of punishment used may be circumscribed by regulations at the local site. Certain negative consequences, such as contingent electric shock, may be generally prohibited, while other forms of stimulation may be repugnant to staff members even if there is no legal stricture precluding their use. Programmatically, it is felt that the primary thrust of educational programs is to build

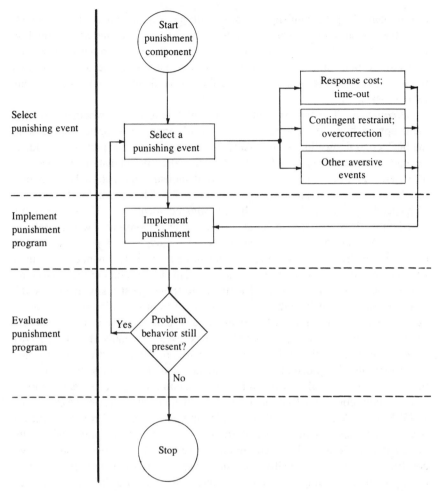

Figure 6. Flowchart of the *punishment* component.

skill repertoires. Therefore, the initial attempts at reducing aberrant behavior should revolve around the reinforcement of competing, desirable behaviors and the adaptation of curricular, antecedent events. When these positive approaches have been empirically shown to fail to reduce the problem behavior(s), it may become necessary to implement a punishment procedure. It can be anticipated that there will be occasions where positive approaches will fail and punishment is the only effective technique to suppress the behavior. For example, Koegel, Firestone, Kramme, and Dunlop (1974) found that autistic students could make little progress in learning discrimination tasks under a positive reinforcement contingency while relatively high rates of stereotypic behaviors were present. It appeared that the stereotypy was interfering with the students' attending to the discriminative stimuli of the task (also see Lovaas et al., 1971). It was only when a contingent slapping (punishment) of stereotypic responses procedure was instituted that the stereotypy disappeared and the students concomitantly learned the discrimination task. Thus, it would seem that there are a number of cases that will require punishment to suppress the problem behavior before the positive reinforcement contingencies can take effect to facilitate the acquisition of curricular tasks.

Sequence   The first step in Component 5 is to decide whether a punishment approach is appropriate (e.g., there are appropriate protections and no medical contraindications) and likely to succeed with the particular student. Second, it is necessary to select a potentially effective punishment procedure. There are a number of techniques that have demonstrated functional control over problem behaviors (Baumeister & Forehand, 1973). The criteria for the selection of a specific procedure has yet to be investigated adequately. If the selection is based on the least aversive technique, time-out or response cost would probably be the treatments of choice. Time-out is the removal of all potential positive consequences from the individual contingent upon the performance of the inappropriate behavior. Typically, this is accomplished by secluding the person in a time-out area apart from ongoing activity. Response cost takes away a single positive consequence from the person (e.g., a token or social interaction) contingent upon a deviant response. For example, a type of response cost that has been shown to eliminate self-injurious behavior is visual screening (Lutzker, 1978). Visual screening contingently blocks visual stimuli for a fixed period of time.

More intrusive procedures, overcorrection and contingent restraint, involve the exercise of physical control over the person committing the deviant response. The overcorrection of self-stimulatory and self-injurious behavior (Azrin et al., 1975; Foxx & Azrin, 1972, 1973) entails putting the person through a series of physical movements that either restore the environment to its previously undisrupted state (restitutional overcorrection) or require the practice of alternative, constructive behaviors (positive practice overcorrection). Contingent restraint merely involves holding the arm(s) or other body part in a fixed position for a given time interval (Gaylord-Ross, Note 4; Schroeder, Peterson, Solomon, & Artley, 1977). While positive practice overcorrection may have the appearance of teaching an alternative to the problem behavior, many persons actively resist the physical control of the overcorrection exercise, which supports an interpretation of the procedure as an aversive event (Rollings, Baumeister, & Baumeister, 1977). Foxx (1977) has more recently acknowledged the punishing characteristics of overcorrection.

Many questions can be raised concerning true controlling properties of overcorrection. Overcorrection can be viewed as a multicomponent treatment package that includes the characteristics of time-out, punishment, DRI, skill building, and response prevention. Which one or combination of these components is responsible for the reported success of overcorrection has yet to be determined. Furthermore, it can be argued that the internal and external validity of overcorrection has not been established in extant studies. A more comprehensive discussion of overcorrection with respect to causal components, efficacy, and so on, is beyond the scope of this chapter; the interested reader should refer to Axelrod, Brantner, and Maddock (1978) for a fuller treatment of the topic.

There exist a number of other negative consequences that have been shown to eliminate the aberrant behavior of severely handicapped persons. Some of these procedures include contingent electric shock (Lovaas & Simmons, 1969), aromatic ammonia (Tanner & Ziriler, 1975), and contingent imitation (Kauffman, LaFleur, Hallahan, & Chanes, 1975). The actual punishment procedure selected should be based on: 1) the individual characteristics of the student and the behavior problem, 2) the likelihood of the program being carried out in a consistent manner, 3) the probability of successfully eliminating the behavior, and 4) the ethical and legal legitimacy of using a specific procedure. If one punishment procedure has been implemented and has failed to eliminate the problem behavior, another punishment procedure can be implemented (Figure 6). As a general rule, whenever a punishing stimulus is presented, it should be paired with a verbal command such as "no" or "stop that" so that the verbal statement acquires conditioned negative reinforcement properties. Through repeated pairings, the verbal command may be able to suppress the aberrant behavior without the primary aversive stimulus. A program of such pairing places the student under the verbal control of the teacher and reduces the use of an aversive consequence. The critical point is that punishment is viewed as a last resort in a series of attempts to suppress aberrant behavior. The hasty application of punishment may lead to a "reactive" therapeutic strategy that fails to deal with the source of the behavior problem. Without a primary emphasis on skill building, it is likely that punishment procedures will be overused because they are effective and efficient.

CASE ILLUSTRATION

It should be useful to illustrate application of the decision model with a sample case study. The example, although hypothetical, represents a composite of a number of actual cases in which the five components of the decision model were sequentially considered for implementation of the model.

Tom was an 8-year-old severely retarded student attending a self-contained class for severely handicapped students in a regular elementary school. He was making considerable progress in vocal communication training and was already self-care capable in such areas as toileting, eating, and dressing. Although he was making nice gains in a number of skill domains, including communication, cognitive skills, and prevocational skills, it had been noticed that he was displaying increasing outbursts during instructional and free-play time. The outbursts consisted of jumping out of his chair, running around the room, screaming, mouthing his hand, and occasionally striking other students in the class. The assessment component of the decision model was applied by taking a 2-week baseline of the rate of these "tantrum" behaviors. It was found that there was an average of five incidents per day, but there appeared to be an increase of the behavior in the second week with some days having eight or nine incidents per day. It was decided that this "tantrum" response class constituted a serious behavior problem in need of intervention. It was further concluded that there were no known medical factors related to the problem. Tom was not on any medication and he had displayed no chronic or acute diseases or injuries in the past.

When examining the reinforcement component, it seemed that Tom's problem behavior might be maintained by positive reinforcement. It was observed that staff would usually go to Tom during a tantrum, tell him to return to his chair, and sometimes hold his arms down in a fixed position. It was also noticed that the other students would start laughing and jumping up and down while Tom was having a tantrum episode. His behavior did not seem to serve an escape/avoidance function, and he appeared to be getting a high density of reinforcement throughout the school day. An extinction program was devised where everyone was trained to ignore Tom's outbursts—a program that was carried out quite consistently by staff and students. During the 2 weeks of extinction the rate of tantrums dropped to two per day from the baseline level of five. It was felt by staff, however, that this rate could and should be driven down to a near-zero level. The ecological component was considered, but there seemed to be no factors that were in need of remediation. When examining the curriculum component, there seemed to be no major task-behavior covariance but it was noticed that Tom was having difficulty learning an assembly, prevocational task. The task was further task analyzed with the result that he learned it with few errors but there was no change in the tantrum rate during task assembly or throughout the day. The average rate remained at two responses per day during the 1-week curricular intervention. Finally, the punishment component was considered and it was decided that time-out might be an effective approach. Time-out was selected because it was surmised that, by placing Tom for 5 minutes behind a partition barrier in the corner of the room, it would have the aversive properties of isolating Tom from the rest of the class. Also, it had been noticed that not everyone was completely consistent in ignoring Tom during a tantrum. The time-out procedure ensured a break in social interaction during that 5-minute period. Data kept over a 2-week period indicated a rate of 0.2 aberrant behavior responses per day. During the next 3 months there were only three episodes of tantrum-like behavior. At that time it was decided to drop the time-out program because of the low response rate. Six months later, maintenance data were collected and showed that there were no tantrums over a 2-week period.

SUMMARY

The case of Tom illustrated how the decision model can be used in applied settings like classrooms. By guiding the actions of the professionals, the model ensured that a singular strategy approach to treatment of always using time-out, overcorrection, or another technique was avoided. Rather, a more systematic strategy was used of analyzing the behavior in terms of maintaining events and applying a corresponding treatment that should correct or remediate the maintaining events. Emphasis was placed on empirical evaluation of outcomes so that one would proceed to subsequent components if successful response reduction had not taken place. In this regard, there is certainly a need for future empirical validation of this model. As in all validation efforts, it is likely that the model will undergo revision in order to account for more parsimonious and convincing ways to approach the treatment of aberrant behavior. Better yet, the current model may generate alternative models from other investigators that may prove to be more effective in dealing with this matter. In this manner, an effective and efficient decision model approach to dealing with issues like curriculum development, communication training (cf. Sailor, Guess, Goetz, Schuler, Utley, & Baldwin, this volume), and eliminating aberrant behavior among severely handicapped persons can be developed. If such models are keyed to the developing needs of practitioners, they should make substantive contributions to the state of the science and art of providing services to severely handicapped persons.

REFERENCES

Axelrod, S., Brantner, J. P., & Maddock, T. P. Overcorrection: A review and critical analysis. *Journal of Special Education*, 1978, *12*, 367-392.

Azrin, N. H., Gottlieb, L., Hugart, L., Wesolowski, M. D., & Rain, T. Eliminating self-injurious behavior by educative procedures. *Behavior Research and Therapy*, 1975, *13*, 101-111.

Bachman, J. A. Self-injurious behavior: A behavioral analysis. *Journal of Abnormal Psychology*, 1972, *80*, 211-224.

Bailey, J., & Meyerson, L. Effect of vibratory stimulation on a retardate's self-injurious behavior. *Psychological Aspects of Disability*, 1970, *17*, 55-59.

Bandura, A. *Principles of behavior modification*. New York: Holt, Rinehart and Winston, 1969.

Baumeister, A. A., & Forehand, R. Stereotyped acts. In N. R. Ellis (ed.), *International review of research in mental retardation* (Vol. 7). New York: Academic Press, 1973.

Baumeister, A. A., & Rollings, J. R. Self-injurous behavior. In N. R. Ellis (ed.), *International review of research in mental retardation* (Vol. 8). New York: Academic Press, 1976.

Berkson, G., & Landesman-Dwyer, S. Behavioral research on severe and profound mental retardation (1955-1974). *American Journal of Mental Deficiency*, 1977, *81*, 428-454.

Berkson, G., & Mason, W. Stereotyped movements of mental defectives: III. Situation effects. *American Journal of Mental Deficiency*, 1963, *68*, 409-412.

Berlyne, D. E. *Conflict, arousal, and curiosity*. New York: McGraw-Hill Book Co., 1960.

Bucher, B., & Lovaas, O. J. Use of aversive stimulation in behavior modification. In M. R. Jones (ed.), *Miami symposium on the prediction of behavior 1967; aversive stimulation*. Coral Gables, Florida: University of Miami Press, 1968.

Carr, E. G. The motivation of self-injurious behavior: A review of some hypotheses. *Psychological Bulletin*, 1977, *84*, 800-816.

Carr, E. G., Newsom, C. D., & Binkoff, J. A. Stimulus control of self-destructive behavior in a psychotic child. *Journal of Abnormal Psychology*, 1976, *4*, 139-153.

Foxx, R. M. Attention training: The use of overcorrection avoidance to increase the eye contact of autistic and retarded children. *Journal of Applied Behavior Analysis,* 1977, *10,* 489–499.

Foxx, R. M., & Azrin, N. H. Restitution: A method of eliminating aggressive, disruptive behavior of mentally retarded and brain damaged patients. *Behavior Research and Therapy,* 1972, *10,* 15–27.

Foxx, R. M., & Azrin, N. H. The elimination of autistic self-stimulatory behavior by overcorrection. *Journal of Applied Behavior Analysis,* 1973, *6,* 1–14.

Frankel, F., & Simmons, J. Q. Self-injurious behavior in schizophrenic and retarded children. *American Journal of Mental Deficiency,* 1976, *80,* 512–522.

Gagne, R. M. *The conditions of learning.* (2nd ed.). New York: Holt, Rinehart and Winston, 1970.

Gaylord-Ross, R. J. Mental retardation research, ecological validity, and the delivery of longitudinal educational programs. *Journal of Special Education,* 1979, *13,* 69–80.

Gaylord-Ross, R. J., Weeks, M., & Lipner, C. An analysis of antecedent, response, and consequence events in the treatment of self-injurious behavior. *Education and Training of the Mentally Retarded.* In press.

Gentry, D., & Haring, N. G. Essentials of performance measurement. In N. G. Haring & L. J. Brown (eds.), *Teaching the severely handicapped* (Vol. I). New York: Grune & Stratton, 1976.

Gesell, A. L. *Developmental diagnosis.* (3rd ed.). New York: Harper & Row, 1974.

Gibson, E. *Principles of perceptual learning and development.* Englewood Cliffs, New Jersey: Prentice Hall, 1969.

Gilbert, G. O. Extinction procedures: Proceed with caution. *Mental Retardation,* 1976, *80,* 512–522.

Grossman, H. J. *Manual on terminology and classification in mental retardation.* Washington, D.C.: American Association on Mental Deficiency, 1973.

Hersen, M., & Barlow, D. H. *Single case experimental designs: Strategies for studying behavioral change.* New York: Pergamon, 1976.

Hutt, C., & Hutt, S. J. Effect of environmental complexity upon stereotyped behaviors in children. *Animal Behavior,* 1965, *13,* 1–4.

Kauffman, J. M., LaFleur, N. K., Hallahan, D. P., & Chanes, C. M. Imitation as a consequence for children's behavior: Two experimental case studies. *Behavior Therapy,* 1975, *6,* 535–542.

Kazdin, A. E. *Behavior modification in applied settings.* Homewood, Illinois: Dorsey, 1975.

Kelly, J. A., & Drabman, R. S. Overcorrection: An effective procedure that failed. *Journal of Clinical Child Psychology,* 1977, *6,* 38–40.

Koegel, R. L., & Covert, A. The relationship of self-stimulation to learning in autistic children. *Journal of Applied Behavior Analysis,* 1972, *5,* 381–387.

Koegel, R. L., Firestone, R. L., Kramme, K. W., & Dunlop, G. Increasing spontaneous play by suppressing self-stimulation in autistic children. *Journal of Applied Behavior Analysis,* 1974, *7,* 521–528.

Koegel, R. L., & Rincover, A. Treatment of psychotic children in a classroom environment: I. Learning in a large group. *Journal of Applied Behavior Analysis,* 1974, *7,* 45–59.

Lovaas, O. J., Litrownik, A., & Mann, R. Response latencies to auditory stimuli in autistic children engaged in self-stimulatory behavior. *Behavior Research and Therapy,* 1971, *9,* 39–49.

Lovaas, O. J., & Simmons, J. Q. Manipulation of self-destruction in three retarded children. *Journal of Applied Behavior Analysis,* 1969, *2,* 143–157.

Lutzker, J. R. Reducing self-injurious behavior by facial screening. *American Journal of Mental Deficiency,* 1978, *82,* 510–513.

Piaget, J. Piaget's theory. In P. H. Mussen (ed.), *Carmichael's manual of child psychology*. (3rd ed.). New York: John Wiley & Sons, 1970.

Plummer, S., Baer, D. M., & LeBlanc, J. M. Functional considerations in the use of procedural time out and an effective alternative. *Journal of Applied Behavior Analysis*, 1977, *10*, 689–705.

Rago, W. V., Jr., Parker, R. M., & Cleland, C. Effect of increased space on the social behavior of institutionalized profoundly retarded male adults. *American Journal of Mental Deficiency*, 1978, *82*, 554–558.

Repp, A. C., & Deitz, S. M. Reducing aggressive and self-injurious behavior of institutionalized retarded children through reinforcement of other behavior. *Journal of Applied Behavior Analysis*, 1974, *7*, 554–558.

Rogers-Warren, A., & Warren, S. (eds.). *Ecological perspectives in behavior analysis*. Baltimore: University Park Press, 1977.

Rollings, J. P., Baumeister, A., & Baumeister, A. The use of overcorrection procedures to eliminate stereotyped behaviors in retarded individuals. *Behavior Modification*, 1977, *1*, 29–46.

Sailor, W., Guess, D., Rutherford, G., & Baer, D. M. Control of tantrum behavior by operant techniques during experimental verbal training. *Journal of Applied Behavior Analysis*, 1968, *1*, 237–243.

Schroeder, S. R., Mulick, J. A., & Schroeder, C. S. Management of severe behavior problems of the retarded. In N. R. Ellis (ed.), *Handbook of mental deficiency*. (2nd ed.). New York: Lawrence Erlbaum Associates. In press.

Schroeder, S. R., Peterson, C. R., Solomon, L. J., & Artley, J. J. EMG feedback and the contingent restraint of self-injurious behavior among the severely retarded: Two case illustrations. *Behavior Therapy*, 1977, *8*, 738–741.

Sidman, M., & Stoddard, L. T. The effectiveness of fading in programming a simultaneous form discrimination for retarded children. *Journal of the Experimental Analysis of Behavior*, 1967, *10*, 261–270.

Solnick, J. V., Rincover, A., & Peterson, C. R. Some determinants of the reinforcing and punishing effects of time-out. *Journal of Applied Behavior Analysis*, 1977, *10*, 415–424.

Striefel, S. *Managing behavior, Part 7: Teaching a child to imitate*. Lawrence, Kansas: H & H Enterprises, 1974.

Tanner, B. A., & Zeriler, M. D. Punishment of self-injurious behavior using aromatic ammonia as the aversive stimulus. *Journal of Applied Behavior Analysis*, 1975, *8*, 53–57.

U.S. Office of Education, Bureau of Education for the Handicapped. Definition of severely handicapped children. Code of Federal Register, 1974, Title 45, Section 121.2.

Wolfensberger, W. *The principle of normalization in human services*. Toronto: National Institute of Mental Retardation, 1972.

Young, J. A., & Wincze, J. P. The effects of the reinforcement of compatible and incompatible alternative behaviors of the self-injurious and related behaviors of a profoundly retarded female adult. *Behavior Therapy*, 1974, *5*, 614–623.

REFERENCE NOTES

1. Horner, R. D. *A review of the application of operant techniques in the analysis and modification of self-injurious behavior*. Unpublished manuscript, 1978. Available from Don Horner, Department of Special Education, University of Kansas, Lawrence, Kansas 66045.

2. Weeks, M., & Gaylord-Ross, R. J. *The relationship between task difficulty and inappropriate behavior in severely retarded children*. Paper presented at the meeting of the American Association on Mental Deficiency, Denver, May, 1978.

3. Hart, B., & Risley, T. R. Environmental programming: Implications for the severely handicapped. In H. J. Prehm & S. J. Deitz (eds.), *Early intervention for the severely handicapped: Programming and accountability.* Eugene, Oregon: University of Oregon, Severely Handicapped Learner Monograph, No. 2, 1976.

4. Gaylord-Ross, R. J. *The development of treatment techniques for the remediation of self-injurious behavior in the classroom and home.* (Annual report no. G007603954.) New York: Yeshiva University, December, 1977.

5. Schroeder, S. R., & Humphrey, R. H. *Environmental context effects and contingent restraint time-out of self-injurious behavior in a deaf-blind profoundly retarded woman.* Paper presented at the meeting of the American Association on Mental Deficiency, New Orleans, May, 1977.

6. Voeltz, L. Discussant. In R. J. Gaylord-Ross (Chair), *Skill acquisition and aberrant behavior reduction through operant procedures.* Panel given at the meeting of the American Association on Mental Deficiency, Denver, May, 1978.

7. Dehn, J. *An investigation of the development and maintenance of the negative behavior of autistic children.* Unpublished doctoral dissertation, Washington University, 1969.

8. Gaylord-Ross, R. J. *The treatment of a self-injurious, Down's syndrome adolescent with omission training, overcorrection, and time-out procedures.* Paper presented at the congress of the International Association for Scientific Study of Mental Deficiency, Washington, D.C., August, 1976.

Chapter 6

Rules for Data-Based Strategy Decisions in Instructional Programs
Current Research and Instructional Implications

Norris G. Haring, Kathleen A. Liberty, and Owen R. White

Instructional programs designed to teach new behaviors or to improve performance of previously learned behaviors should be individualized and should provide for frequent collection of performance data and program modification based on those data (Baldwin, 1976). Information about designing individualized instructional programs is available to classroom teachers (e.g., Haring & Bricker, 1978; Smith, 1968; Snell, 1978; York & Edgar, 1979). Information regarding the collection of performance data is also available (e.g., Snell & Smith, 1978; White & Haring, 1976). However, information about how to use performance data to make strategy decisions in instructional programs for the severely handicapped is usually not available to teachers.

Researchers were generally the first to be interested in utilizing performance data to make decisions regarding the effects of experimental interventions. Performance data were analyzed visually rather than "statistically." Generally, the use of traditional statistical analyses was avoided for several reasons. First, such analyses seemed to mask the effects of treatments on individual subjects and, second, statistical significance was not always equivalent to practical significance (Kazdin, 1976; Sidman, 1960). Visual analyses of charted or graphed data generally replaced statistical analyses (Hersen & Barlow, 1976; Kazdin, 1976). Researchers emphasized the examination of trends or changes in performance over time in the analyses.

When classroom teachers began collecting data, they were taught to use

The research reported herein was performed pursuant to a grant from the Bureau of Education for the Handicapped, Project No. 443CH70564, Grant No. G007500593.

The authors wish to extend their thanks to the teachers who supported the research activities: Lestra Hazel, Joyce Weiss, Ellen Scheyer, Heather Carrell, Sara Liberty, Deanna Mar, Cathy Christianson, Linda Watson, and Glenna Hamasaki; and to thank the administrators who facilitated the research: Dale Gentry, Jane Rieke, Ralph Bohannon, Gordon Hauck, and Rick Seim.

visual analyses of charted or graphed performance data in order to make decisions about the effects of various instructional strategies in much the same way the researchers did (Duncan, 1971; Johnson, 1971). Unfortunately, individuals may interpret identical data differently (White, Note 1). Following the development of simple analytical tools, such as a uniform method of summarizing change over time, the reliability of interpretation of visually inspected data improved (Kazdin, 1976; White, Note 1). Even with such analytical tools, however, Liberty (Note 2) found that teachers trained in the use of such analytical tools did not use the data to make instructional changes in ineffective programs.

As a result of these findings, *decision rules* for use with direct performance data were developed to provide information to teachers about when to change an instructional program (Liberty, Note 2; White & Haring, 1976). In order to use these rules, classroom teachers set performance aims and selected a target date by which the aim was to be met. Then, a line was drawn, on a calendar-synchronized chart, from the student's present performance at the current date to the intersection of the desired performance aim and the target date. The line produced on the chart thus described the minimum acceptable change required to move the student from current to desired performance levels. Thereafter, as data were collected and charted, each day of data was compared with the "line" to see if it met the change aim, or "minimum 'celeration line." If performance failed to meet the 'celeration aim for 3 consecutive program days, it was recommended that the teacher change the instructional program.

Studies have tested the effectiveness of these rules when applied to programs for mildly handicapped persons. In these studies, mildly handicapped pupils whose teachers applied minimum 'celeration rules to make instructional strategy decisions generally showed greater progress gains than students whose teachers did not use the rules (Bohannon, 1975; Mirkin, 1978).

The minimum 'celeration rules do not, however, help teachers select the strategy with the highest probability of promoting pupil progress. The minimum 'celeration rules state that a change should be made if the student fails to meet the change aim (line) for 3 consecutive days. What type of strategy change in instructional procedures should be made? Educators have suggested a wide variety of strategies to try when a student's performance falters: moving to a less difficult skill level (e.g., Bricker & Dennison, 1978), changing the prompts and cues (e.g., Panyan, 1972), or changing the setting in which instruction occurs (Panyan, 1972). In addition, an informal examination of several hundred projects involving mildly handicapped students showed that these, and many other types of tactic changes such as changing consequences and schedules of reinforcement, have been employed. In some cases the strategy chosen was successful in promoting learning; in other cases, the tactic failed to facilitate progress.

The first attempt to determine performance-based strategy change rules empirically was based on a post-hoc analysis of several hundred projects with learners labeled mildly handicapped and learning disabled. Several performance variables were examined: the level or frequency of correct performance, the change in correct performance during the period of time in which a particular tactic was in effect, the frequency of error responses, and the change in errors over the same period of time. These variables were compared with the pupils' performance prior to the introduction of a strategy. The informal analysis showed that changes in antecedent events had the highest probability of being successful if they were introduced when correct performance was either showing no growth or was decelerating, the frequency of corrects was less than 20 per minute, and errors were at or about 10 per minute. Antecedent changes introduced when correct performances were higher and error performances were lower did not seem to be as effective. On the other hand, consequent changes were most successful when corrects were either showing no growth or were decelerating, the frequency of corrects was equal to or greater than 20 per minute, and errors were below 10 per minute.

Changes made in the antecedent cues, prompts, demonstrations, and so on, usually were designed to provide information to the learner on how to respond, and thus might be predicted to be more effective at lower performance levels. Consequence changes, which motivate performance, were more likely to be effective when the behaver had acquired the behavior but was not proficient. These results made possible the beginnings of a functional definition of phases of learning. Each phase, theoretically construed in a hierarchy to include acquisition, fluency building, maintenance, generalization, and adaptation, would be differentiated on the basis of the instructional tactics with the highest probability of facilitating learning if learning faltered. Decision rules would permit classroom teachers to identify the stage of learning from pupil performance data and select an intervention strategy accordingly. The first strategy decision rules were based on the informal analysis described above (White & Haring, 1976). No formal test of these strategy rules has been reported, although Sokolov (Note 3) investigated performance data for 3,000 students in regular classrooms K-6 and found supportive evidence for the classification of faltering performances at 20 corrects per minute as consequence problems.

In 1975 the present authors began an investigation designed to determine empirically based strategy decision rules for use by teachers and therapists working with learners labeled severely or profoundly handicapped. A number of specific studies were conducted during the first 2 years. Generally, however, teachers were left on their own. Teachers and research staff collected daily data on a variety of instructional programs to document pupil progress. Data generally included both a measure of accuracy (correct and error) and of time (e.g., rate), although some adjustments in data collection procedures were made to allow for interruption of performance time by manager manipulations and antecedent and consequent events.[1] The data were then charted and teachers were allowed to

---

[1] The most frequently collected data type was rate, either collected in the usual method (cf. White & Haring, 1976) or adjusted. Since then, however, the necessity for collecting the other two principal types of time-based data, latency and duration, has become evident. Currently research on the use of these data types to monitor pupil progress is underway.

determine for themselves if and when each program should be changed and, if a program was changed, the type of change that would be made. It was hoped that, by not restricting the frequency and types of changes teachers made, information concerning a wide range of both successful and unsuccessful program change strategies might be obtained.

During these first 2 years, 20 pupils and 14 teachers participated. The pupils ranged in age from 3 years to 21 years. All had been classified as either severely or profoundly handicapped. Many had secondary handicapping conditions (e.g., cerebral palsy, hearing impairment or deafness, visual impairment or blindness, seizure disorders, motor disorders, motor involvement), and many received regular medication which probably interfered with learning. In short, the subjects under study were in many respects typical of the general populations of severely and profoundly handicapped pupils.

The pupil performance variables examined included the level, or frequency, of correct and incorrect performances, the direction of change in performance over the 5-day period preceding an instructional strategy change, and the variability, or bounce, in correct performance. Together, these variables were considered "learning patterns." Twenty-three different learning patterns were identified from the 247 instructional phases resulting from the first 2 years of project activities (see Figure 1).

Analyses were then conducted to determine the effects of the instructional changes made by the teachers. Any change that produced either an immediate increase in level or an acceleration of correct performance was considered a successful change, as long as errors did not also increase ($\leq \times 2$). Changes that produced no effect or that actually decreased correct performance and/or increased error performances ($\geq \times 2$) were considered unsuccessful.

Learning patterns were then grouped according to the type of strategy change that was generally most successful. For example, with a pattern of corrects decelerating, and errors higher than corrects, and also decelerating, and both performances at 10 or less, the changes that were most successful in improving correct performances were changes designed to provide information to the learner about how to perform the behavior by changing or adding prompts, cues, and so on, or by changing or coding the instructional materials. This particular learning pattern was placed in a category with other patterns in which similar changes were successful in improving performance. Together, these six learning patterns were grouped into a category of learning patterns, which was called "Antecedent Changes" since the beneficial changes were generally changes designed to provide information on how to perform. Learning patterns in this category are shown in Figure 1. Six percent of the instructional phases fell into this category.

Approximately 28% of the learning patterns generally showed high frequencies of correct responses and low frequencies of error responses, with little bounce. In most of these cases, changes in consequences were effective in improving correct performances. However, in some cases other strategies proved

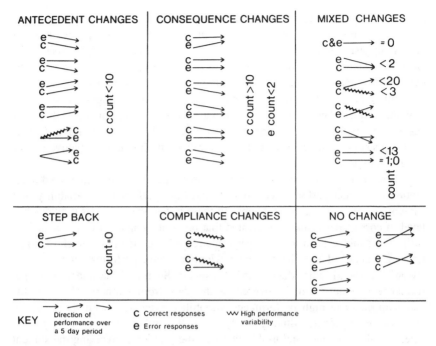

Figure 1. Learning patterns derived from the first 2 project years, utilized for decision making during the third project year.

successful in facilitating fluent responses, including some antecedent changes (e.g., telling the student to "go fast"). Sometimes consequence changes were not successful (e.g., changing from praise to juice as a subsequent event for corrects). In general, however this category was similar to the "Fluency-Building Problems Category" determined from the data on the performance of the mildly handicapped.

Sometimes changes produced an unsuccessful effect. An examination of the patterns involved in these cases showed that changing an instructional program in which corrects were accelerating was likely to produce a deceleration of corrects. In other words, if correct performance was accelerating and was at a higher level than errors, regardless of the frequency and trend of errors, the instructional program should not be changed. If a change were made, it was likely to produce unfortunate results. Five patterns, a total of 48% of the phases, fell into this category, labeled "No Change." Results in this category were similar to the patterns expected from the analysis of performance data of the mildly handicapped.

One learning pattern that had not been identified in the data from mildly handicapped students showed correct responses remaining at zero, and errors higher than corrects and accelerating. The only change in strategy that was successful in improving correct performance in these three cases was to reduce the level of skill difficulty by moving to easier or prerequisite skills. These performance patterns are the only ones that responded to decreasing the required response requirements. Yet moving to a prerequisite skill is a program change that is suggested quite often (e.g., Baldwin, 1976; Bradfield & Heifetz, 1976; Bricker & Dennison, 1976; Fredericks, Riggs, Furey, Grove, Moore, McDonnell, Jordan, Hanson, Baldwin, & Waldow, 1976; Panyan, 1972). This tactic was employed 53 times during the first 2 years of the project, and was successful only three times! These results suggest that moving to a prerequisite skill or to an easier skill level is a change decision that only rarely will be effective. Instead, the results suggest teachers should concentrate on finding more effective instructional strategies.

Ten other instances of two learning patterns that both showed a rapid deceleration of correct performances to zero and high performance variability were categorized as compliance problems. In these cases, the student's previous high level of correct performance indicated that he or she could, in fact, perform the skill. The rapid deterioration of performance gave notice that somehow conditions had changed and the student no longer would perform—an instance of "won't" respond rather than "can't" respond. Such rapid deceleration of performance had not been discovered in the data from learners labeled mildly handicapped. The high performance variability associated with these patterns also was unexpected. Although only a small number of cases fell into this category (4.5% of the total usable phases), the problems involving the students who displayed such patterns were enormous. Generally, the compliance problems were evident in other instructional programs and in the classroom management of these students. Programs designed to improve compliance generally ran into difficulties because of the extensive amount of time involved in implementing successful strategies (e.g., the most successful strategy was to implement contingencies for each command throughout the school day). Because of these problems, a separate investigation of compliance problems and strategies was undertaken (Haring, White, & Liberty, Note 4, Note 5; Liberty, 1977).

The sixth and final category of learning patterns responded to a wide variety of changes—both antecedents and consequences. However, changing the level of the skill (to an easier form of the same skill, or a prerequisite skill) without changing either the antecedents or consequences was not successful in promoting progress in the instructional programs. In these cases, 12% of the total, a high probability strategy change, could not be predicted from the effects obtained.

The most important question is, of course, just how successful teachers were in selecting instructional changes that facilitated pupil progress. During the first project year, 33% of the decisions produced successful results; during the second year, 41% of the decisions resulted in improved pupil progress.

During the next year, teachers applied strategy change rules derived from project results to see if the "success rate" could be improved. In order to implement rules, the teacher collected 5 days of performance data and, looking at the level, direction of trend, and variability of the data, matched the learning pattern of the student with the patterns shown in Figure 1. Then, the "rule" advised the teacher to change (or not to change) the instructional format according to the category of the learning pattern.

These rules were used by teachers and pupils at the Gordon Hauck Special Education Center of the Lake Washington School District, Washington. Six teachers and 20 severely/profoundly handicapped pupils volunteered to test the rules. Data were collected as before, but rather than leaving the teachers to their own devices to determine when and how programs should be changed, special meetings were held on the average of once every 5 days to inspect pupil performance data and to discuss the application of the decision rules to those data collected on the students' individualized instructional programs.

Over the course of the year, 151 change decisions were made. Of those, in 60 cases, the pupil met the teacher's performance aim and moved to the next curriculum step. A total of 192 decisions were made based on pupils' learning patterns. Seventy-four of the patterns (39%) demonstrated acceptable progress, while 18 patterns (4%) fell into the "step back" category; 14% fell into the "compliance change" category; 14% fell into the "change for more information on how to perform" category (shown as "Antecedent Changes" in Figure 1); 42% fell into the "change to motivate fluency" category ("Consequence Changes" in Figure 1); and 26% fell into the "miscellaneous change" category.

Once the pattern of learning was categorized, teachers could choose to change or not change the instructional format as they wished. For learning patterns in the "change to provide more information" category, teachers chose to change in accord with the rule (i.e., by changing the instructional plan to provide more information to the student on how to perform a correct response) nine times and choose to disregard the rules (by changing something else or nothing at all) seven times. The power of the rule was then tested by comparing the effects of the chosen strategy on pupil performance with the effects predicted by the "rule" (i.e., success was predicted when the rule was applied; failure was predicted when the rule was ignored). Predictions proved accurate eight out of the nine times the rule was followed and five out of the seven times the rules were not followed. In short, predictions based on this "rule" were correct a total of 81% of the time.

When learning patterns indicated a problem in the category "change the contingencies or consequences," teachers chose to follow the rule 32 times and chose to ignore the rule 17 times. Predictions of the results (i.e., improved performance if the rule was followed; no improvement if the rule was ignored) proved correct in 30 of the 32 cases where the rule was followed and in 9 of the 17 cases where the rule was ignored. Overall, the "consequence change rule" successfully predicted the outcome in 79% of the cases.

As mentioned earlier, of all types of problems encountered, difficulty in the fluency-building phase of learning appeared most prevalent. The extent of that problem appears even greater, however, when one considers the eventual outcome of "successful no change patterns." According to the rules derived during the first 2 years of research, one is best to leave well enough alone when a pupil's performance appears to be improving from day to day. Any program change implemented while the pupil is progressing is likely to disrupt that progress. In 42% of the 74 cases where pupils appeared to be getting better during the third project year, however, the prediction of continued progress proved to be wrong. In all of those cases, the pupil changed from a pattern of progress to a pattern that would indicate problems in fluency building. Thus, results suggest that many of the programs are successful only while the student is performing at a relatively low level ("acquiring" the skill). Strategies aimed at improving performance of an acquired skill (achieving mastery), when they are effective, have short term impact. More research is needed concerning strategies that facilitate fluency building.

The final question is, of course, whether teachers who used these decision rules have a higher probability of making decisions that improve pupil performance than teachers who do not use decision rules. A total of 192 instances of decisions involving the rules were analyzed to determine the effectiveness of the rules in predicting the success (or failure) of a strategy type. A change made in accord with the rules is, in effect, a prediction that the decision will have a "successful" effect. In 109 of the 148 cases, that prediction proved to be correct; in 39 cases, the prediction was incorrect—the decision did not produce a successful effect. There were 44 decisions that were made "contrary" to the rules (e.g., changing consequences when the student's learning pattern fell into the "antecedent change" category). By extension, the rules would predict such contrary decisions to have an unsuccessful effect on performance. In 28 of the 44 cases, the decision did produce an unsuccessful effect; in 16 cases, the "contrary decision" produced a successful effect. Overall, the rules correctly predicted the effects of the decisions in 137 (71%) of the 192 decisions and incorrectly predicted the effects in 55 (29%) of the cases. So far the rules themselves seemed to hold up fairly well. The major question is, however, whether the use of data-decision rules improved the 33% and 41% "success rates" of the teachers who had not used rules in the first 2 years. During the third project year, teachers using the strategy change decision rules made decisions that improved pupil performance in 65% of the phases.

These results suggest that it is possible to discriminate a pupil's instructional needs on the basis of his or her performance during instructional programs. The learning patterns used to make these discriminations are not as simple or as clear-cut as those observed with normal or mildly handicapped pupils, but they do seem to be extensions of those rules rather than a completely different set of rules. During the final 2 project years, these rules will be refined and tested by other teachers and pupils.

USING DECISION RULES IN THE CLASSROOM

The decision rules can be implemented by teachers, although certain conditions are suggested if the decision rules are to be used effectively. The rules will assist in determining strategy changes in instructional programs designed to teach new behaviors or to improve performance in behaviors the student has previously acquired. Data on the use of the rules in programs designed to decelerate or eliminate behaviors are not available.

Second, the rules have the highest probability of being effective if an instructional program is planned and implemented consistently from trial to trial and from day to day. When teachers change procedures from trial to trial, or from day to day, the rules may not be effective. In addition, pupil progress under continually changing conditions is difficult to determine, perhaps because the continual shifting is "confusing" to the student. Procedures probably should be implemented for approximately 5 to 7 days or instructional sessions in order to determine their effectiveness. Conditions of planned change, as when verbal stimuli are modified for generalization training, can be treated as consistent programs. The instructional program should include a plan for antecedent events, designed to provide the cues and stimuli necessary to signal the student to begin responding, and subsequent events, designed to consequate error or correct responses.

Next, the teacher should provide a minimum of 10 opportunities for independent responding during each instructional session. The more opportunities to perform the skills, the more rapid the acquisition (e.g., Azrin, Shaeffer, & Wesolowski, 1976). White and Haring (1976) have suggested that a minimum of 10 opportunities to perform be given daily. For some self-help skills that minimum may include providing additional opportunities to eat, dress, and so on (Westling & Murden, 1978). If the student is just beginning to learn a response, provide the student with a very short period of time in which to respond independently, and then assist the student to respond if he or she does not respond during the period allowed. Over a period of five to seven sessions, if the response never occurs independently, the decision rules advise moving to a less difficult skill or response. If the student cannot perform a "whole" response, the program may be designed so that the student has the opportunity to perform just a small part of the behavior independently. If the student cannot perform any part of the response independently after five to seven sessions, it may be appropriate to move to a different related skill or to an easier skill level.

Another condition that will facilitate use of the rules in the classroom is the determination of an appropriate performance aim. It is necessary as well as desirable that the teacher define the standard of performance that is the program aim. Usually an accuracy criterion alone, such as 80% correct, will not be sufficient to ensure mastery (White & Haring, 1976). The pupil who can tie his shoe with 100% accuracy still may not have mastered the skill; that is, a student who takes 5 seconds to tie his or her shoe is more fluent at shoe-tying behaviors than the pupil who takes 30 minutes, although both may be 100% accurate. In fact, it is the fluency dimension of performance that has a direct impact on the pupil's environment. Since Mom may not be able to wait for 30 minutes, that pupil cannot functionally tie his shoe—Mom ties it for him instead of waiting. In the case of shoe tying, as with many self-help skills, fluency is measured by duration, and a suitable aim for shoe tying probably would include a statement of duration. Fluency in other types of skills may be related to rate or latency. Rate is the measure that is usually most appropriate to vocational and traditional academic skills, and latency may be of highest concern in teaching compliance, conversation, question answering, labeling, and other communication skills. The performance aim should be set so that the learner will be able to perform as well as his or her nonhandicapped chronologically age-matched peers. Lower aims will ensure retarded performance (Barrett, 1979).

It is also necessary that data on pupil performance be collected and charted. It is necessary to collect information on performance in order to determine if the instructional strategies are effective. The most direct method of collecting data is usually the easiest: count the number of times the correct behavior occurs and the number of times the incorrect behavior occurs. However, this information alone does not provide sufficient information to make adequate instructional decisions (Haring et al., Note 5; White & Haring, 1976; White & Liberty, 1976). Information on the time of the responses is also necessary. Although collecting data on the time of the response may require extra teacher effort, the advantage in making appropriate decisions is worth it. A number of sources are available that describe how to collect time-based data (Snell & Smith, 1978; White & Haring, 1976; White & Liberty, 1976).

Although some data have been collected using duration and latency measures, the rules to date are based primarily on rate data. During the project, teachers have found it necessary to adjust rate data collection procedures to fit program and instructional requirements. These data are collected by starting a stopwatch following the initial cue to respond and then stopping the watch when the pupil has completed the response or the allowable response period has expired. This method is repeated for each trial during the session. Accuracy data can be recorded for each trial, and time data can be accumulated until the end of the session. Rate per minute is then calculated by the formula *count ÷ time*. In this way, the data collected reflect pupil performance only, and do not include teacher time to prepare materials, give cues, and/or administer consequences.

If data are collected during each instructional session, the student has many opportunities to "tell" the teacher, via his or her performance, about the effectiveness of the strategies. If, however, data are collected only occasionally, the information the student can provide about his or her education is limited, and it is also more difficult to determine when a particular strategy is inappropriate for that student. Data should be collected, if possible, during each instructional session.

Finally, in order to interpret more easily the information collected, data should be charted to display graphically the overall changes in performance from day to day (Snell & Smith, 1978; White & Haring, 1976). The decision rules have been designed to be used with charts that utilize a ratio-interval or semi-logarithmic scale for performance on the vertical axis and an equal interval scale for time on the horizontal axis (see *Teaching Exceptional Children,* 1971, *3*(3); White & Haring, 1976).

Once a program and data collection procedure have been implemented, teachers can make decisions by drawing learning pictures for the data approximately every 6 data days. Learning pictures can be drawn by following the steps listed below. The steps are followed once to draw a line for correct performance and once to draw a line for error performance; together with the level of performance these lines form the "learning picture."

1. Use the most recent six or seven data points. Look at the first three of those data points on the chart. Find the second highest data point. Find the second *day* of data. Mark a + at the intersection of the second highest point and the second data day.
2. Look at the last three data points (the three most recent). Find the second highest data point of those three points. Find the sixth day of data. Mark a + at the intersection of the points.
3. Draw a line through the two +'s, from the first point of the 6 or 7 days to the last. These steps are illustrated in Figure 2. Repeat steps 1–3 using the error plots.
4. Look at the level of performance, or the counts of corrects and errors, at the end of the 6-day period.

To determine the type of change that, according to project results, has the highest probability of accelerating pupil performance, compare the derived learning pattern with those shown in Figure 1, and change according to the category designation. Once a decision has been made, the teacher continues conducting the program, charting the data, and making decisions every 6 or 7 data days. An example of data and decisions is shown in Figure 3 and discussed below.

The learning picture for the data shown in the first phase of Figure 3 matches with the picture in Figure 1 for a change to provide additional information. In the first phase, the teacher said, "Give me the penny/nickel" and held out her hand. In the second phase, this was changed to "penny/nickel," which was paired with the gestural cue of the open hand. Also in the second phase, the teacher put a penny or nickel in her own hand before giving the direction. Thus, when the student picked up the coin from the selection of objects on the table and placed it in the teacher's hand, he or she could match his or her selection with the permanent model. As the data during the second phase show, the use of antecedent changes provided sufficient information to reduce errors. The learning picture at the time of the next decision matched the "no change" category, and the teacher continued the format.

Data demonstrate that, in many respects, the learning pictures of severely handicapped students resemble those of mildly handicapped students. Learners with the label of severely handicapped respond to the same general instructional formats, which should include planned antecedent events, a precisely described target behavior, and contingent consequent events. They progress through

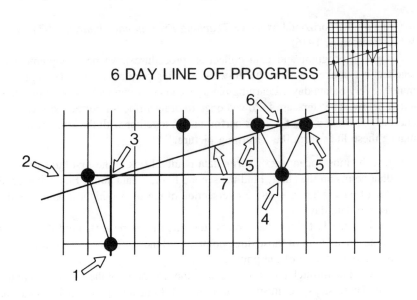

Figure 2.   Method for the calculation of the 6-day line of progress.

acquisition and fluency stages, which may be identified from their performance, and they respond to many of the same instructional strategies. Data may be collected on the performance of severely/profoundly handicapped learners in much the same way that data can be collected on mildly handicapped learners. Those data can then be used to identify when a particular instructional format is not facilitating progress and to identify strategy changes according to the particular individual's performance, as described in this chapter.

STRATEGIES FOR ACQUISITION PROBLEMS

Sometimes, of course, pupils will progress through both "acquisition" and "fluency building" on the strength of a well planned instructional format. In such cases, the designation of a stage of learning is unnecessary. When learning falters, such a designation may be used conveniently to help select strategies that facilitate pupil progress.

The stage of learning called "acquisition" in this chapter has been functionally defined by the research results. Acquisition is the period of learning,

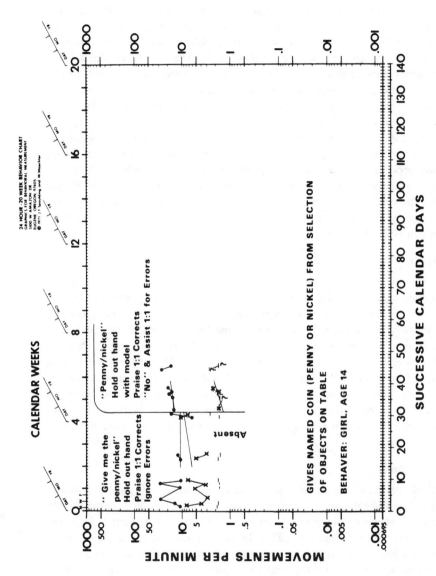

Figure 3. Example of performance data used in making decisions. Learning patterns are shown as drawn on the chart of the data.

when if performance falters, changes designed to provide information to the learner about how to perform the desired response have a higher probability than other strategies of promoting pupil progress. Acquisition problems are currently identified by comparing the data collected on pupil progress in instructional programs over a 5- to 7-day period with the "Antecedent Change" patterns shown in Figure 1. If the patterns match, an acquisition problem is identified, and changes aimed at telling the learner how to respond are likely to be more successful in facilitating success than changes aimed at increasing the motivation of the learner.

Many different strategies can be used in order to inform the learner how better to perform the response. Strategies can be implemented either before or after the response opportunity. If the strategy is implemented as a correction procedure, contingent upon incorrect responses, it will be faded automatically—as the learner makes fewer errors, the procedures will be eliminated. Since whatever procedure is "added" will eventually have to be faded so that conditions of responding are equivalent to those in natural environments, it may be that the correction procedure will be more efficient than providing the information as an antecedent strategy. However, data that bear on this question are not available at this time.

Directions

Directions given to the student can include, for example, verbal directions, signed directions, pictured directions, imitative directions, or gestural directions (Snell & Smith, 1978). Several types of directions may be given at once, as when a teacher says "Give me the toy" (verbal) and holds out his or her hand (gestural). Directions alone will not come to control the behavior unless they are paired with effective reinforcers (Ayllon & Azrin, 1964), but the directions do provide information to the learner about what he or she is supposed to do. Severely handicapped students may have to be taught how to follow directions (e.g., Streifel & Wetherby, 1973) before such directions can be used in instructional programs, as discussed in the section on strategies for compliance problems.

Demonstrations

In general, teacher demonstration (sometimes called *modeling*) has been used as a strategy contingent upon an incorrect response or a failure to respond with severely handicapped students (e.g., Horner & Keilitz, 1975; Lent & McLean, 1976; Nelson, Cone & Hanson, 1975). In those situations, the teacher demonstration is a procedure designed to provide information to the student to "correct" his or her behavior on the next opportunity to perform. Such procedures have not always proved effective with severely handicapped persons (e.g., Nelson, Cone, & Hanson, 1975). York, Williams, and Brown (1976) suggest, however, that imitation training may not only serve to teach severely/profoundly handicapped students how to imitate, but it may also teach them how to learn from a teacher demonstration. In imitation training, the teacher demonstration of the desired behavior is part of the direction (e.g., "Do this"—clap hands), while the requested response is one that is already in the learner's repertoire. Thus, imitation training is designed to establish stimulus control over specific behaviors, rather than to teach new behaviors. Once the student is able to imitate, teacher demonstration may be an effective instructional strategy for new behaviors.

Litrownik, Franzini, and Turner (1976), working with trainable mentally retarded students, found that a demonstration before each trial led to better initial response than did a massed demonstration prior to any opportunity to perform. Smith and Lovitt (1975), working with learning disabled students, found that an antecedent teacher demonstration before the first opportunity to perform, when paired with a permanent model, improved arithmetic performance. Hendrickson, Roberts, and Shores (1978) compared antecedent and contingent demonstrations in teaching learning disabled children basic sight-reading vocabulary reading words. Both procedures were more effective than no demonstration, but the antecedent demonstration was more efficient than contingent demonstration, with fewer trials to criterion.

Physical Guidance

Physically guiding the learner through the behavior has been used frequently and successfully in teaching severely handicapped learners a variety of behaviors, including imitative behaviors (e.g., Streifel & Wetherby, 1973; Waxler & Yarrow, 1970; Whitman, Zakaras, & Chardos, 1971). In most cases, it has been used contingently as a correction procedure following an error response or no response. Nelson et al. (1975) found that the contingent physical guidance procedure was more effective than the contingent teacher demonstration in teaching appropriate utensil use to severely retarded subjects. Physical guidance can also be provided antecedent to the learner's opportunity to respond. The teacher presents the materials, cues, directions, and so forth, and then guides the student through the behavior, prior to the independent response opportunity. Correction procedures may be used in conjunction with the antecedent physical assist. This procedure was sometimes used by instructional managers during the third project year. They provided an "assisted demonstration" before each opportunity to perform.

Prompts

Prompts can also be used to provide information to the learner about how to respond. Prompts can be physical, verbal, signed, or gestural, and can be given antecedent to the opportunity to respond or as part of a correction procedure. A physical prompt is usually a tap or small movement to the pupil's hand (or appropriate body part) designed to get the response started. Verbal (signed or gestural) prompts provide information to the learner in addition to the initial directions. For example, the direction might be "Put blue with blue," a verbal prompt might be "It's next to the red," and a gestural prompt might be pointing to the correct placement. If prompts are given antecedent to the response, the direction and the prompt may both come to control the behavior. It may be necessary to use a stimulus delay procedure (Streifel, Bryan, & Aikins, 1974; Touchette, 1971) in order to fade the prompt so that the verbal direction or presentation of the materials alone becomes the stimulus for the behavior. Risley and Reynolds (1970) found that stressing or emphasizing a key word in an antecedent verbal direction improved verbal imitation with three disadvantaged subjects. The emphasis served as a prompt.

Permanent Models

In addition to prompts, permanent models may show how to respond correctly. The permanent model shows the learner the "finished product" of his or her behavior. A permanent model for a shoe-tying program would be a completely tied shoe. In some discrimination programs, the permanent model may be a necessary part of the program. For example, in sorting pennies and nickles, a penny in one section of a cash register and a nickle in another section serve as models for the placement of the coins and cue the student which is the "penny bin" and which is the "nickle bin." Smith and Lovitt (1975) used teacher demonstration plus a permanent model to teach arithmetic problems successfully to learning disabled students. The authors were unable to locate published research relating to the use of permanent models with severely handicapped students. However, in the current study, permanent models were used antecedent to the response in some discrimination programs.

Materials

Information can be provided to the learner by changing or rearranging the materials. In discrimination training, for example, the "correct" choice can be placed closer to the learner than the incorrect choice (Snell & Smith, 1978), and then the position of the materials is gradually changed to allow a more independent choice. Gold (1972) used color coding of materials to provide information to severely handicapped workers for the assembly of bicycle brakes. The color cues helped the learners acquire the task faster than the cues provided by the materials alone. Azrin, Schaeffer, and Wesolowski (1976) began teaching dressing skills to profoundly retarded learners using clothing two sizes too large, and then gradually reduced this to the appropriate size. Schreibman (1975) used fading procedures to change stimulus figures in a discrimination task.

Verbal Feedback

A final contingent strategy that can provide information to the learner is praise. The efficacy of praise has often been reported. Praise during acquisition should be directed at the specific targeted behavior (e.g., "That's right, blue with blue"; "Hey, you did a great job tying your shoe") rather than toward the individual ("good girl"). This type of directed praise includes verbal feedback to provide information to the learner concerning his or her performance. Verbal feedback may also be provided contingent upon incorrect performance ("No, you put red with blue") but may actually increase incorrect responses (Burleigh & Marholin, 1977). Verbal feedback may be paired with another consequence, such as food, music, hugging, and so on.

Other Strategies

Other contingent strategies, in addition to those described above, can be used to provide information during acquisition. Error drills have been used with learning disabled students (Hansen & Eaton, 1978) to improve accuracy, and were used by instructional managers during the third project year. Generally the student is given repeated trials on those items or responses most frequently missed. Thus, information is increased only for those responses or behaviors where it is needed. Prompts, directions, and models can also be used antecedent to requests for responses previously missed.

Which Strategy?

In this section several different strategies for accelerating progress when acquisition problems are identified have been presented. Which strategy to choose? Currently, performance data that might help in the selection of a particular strategy are not available. In fact, it is likely that such data would be very difficult to collect, since it is probable that the success or failure of a particular strategy when implemented with a particular pupil is dependent on several different characteristics. In addition to the particular learning pattern, the type of behavior being taught may also be important. For example, permanent models may be more effective with self-help skills than with preacademic skills, while physical guidance works best in self-help skills. These types of questions may be empirically answered by future research. Another probable factor is, of course, individuality of performance of both pupil and teacher. One pupil may respond better to gestural cues while another responds better to physical guidance. If the teacher does not feel comfortable using a particular strategy, the implementation of that strategy may not accelerate responding. These questions may be answered by empirical data; until they are, however, the decision rules will help in identifying generic areas for change, but rules to help select a specific strategy are not available.

Teachers may then consider other reasons in the selection of strategies. Since behavior change is directed at preparing students to participate in community and home activities, any "help" required for that student beyond that which can be normally found or provided in community settings will have to be eliminated before full mastery of the behavior can be achieved (Brown, Nietupski, & Hamre-Nietupski, 1976). For example, students must be able to demonstrate shoe tying without permanent models in order to perform comparably to their age peers, or to be able to tie shoes at the bowling alley. Thus, if such models are used, they must eventually be removed. More subtly, verbal cues and other non-natural stimuli must be faded from the instructional setting. Since verbal cues like "Take a bite" are not routinely provided in restaurants, the severely handicapped individual should be taught to respond appropriately in the absence of such cues. How can this be done? Acquisition may be quicker if instruction is provided in an environment as nearly like community and home environments as possible, using natural materials, stimuli, and consequences. Then, if the learner falters, information can be *added* and then faded when the student can perform the response. Another method would be to provide as much information *initially* as might be required to facilitate acquisition and then fade it out. Research may identify which of these methods is the most effective in accelerating learning; currently, however, the individual classroom teacher must choose.

STRATEGIES FOR FLUENCY-BUILDING PROBLEMS

Fluency building is that stage of learning in which changes designed to motivate fluent and efficient performance are most likely to accelerate faltering progress. Increasing efficiency may involve increasing the rate of the behavior, increasing or decreasing the duration of the behavior, or decreasing the latency of responding. Much research has emphasized increasing rate of performance, especially with regard to performance on vocational tasks (Bellamy, Inman, & Schwarz, 1978). Chaffin (1969) reports that production rate is a significant variable in the failure of retarded adolescents in job placements. Barrett (1979) discusses the importance of performance rates in relationship to the goal of community integration and normalization. O'Brien, Azrin, and Bugle (1972) designed a program to increase the duration of walking, while other programs have been designed to decrease the duration of various self-help skills, such as shoe tying (Westling & Murden, 1978). Stimulus-delay procedures are designed to reduce the latency with which the student responds to a stimulus. In each case, the particular time component is a measure of the fluency with which the subject can use the acquired skill. A subject who can correctly name a picture within 1 second (latency) is more "fluent" with that label than a student who needs 10–15 seconds to name the picture correctly. Similarly, a student who can sort at a rate of 30 objects per minute is more fluent with the skills needed for sorting than a student who sorts at a rate of 10 objects per minute, although both may be 100% accurate.

An instructional format, which includes opportunities for practice and consequences for correct and incorrect responses, may prove powerful enough to move the student from acquisition to a specified fluency criterion. When learning falters, however, changes must be made.

Fluency-building problems were identified in the learning patterns of mildly handicapped students as generally beginning at approximately 20 correct responses per minute, with errors at 10 per minute or less, and with correct responses either flat or decelerating (White & Haring, 1976). Data collected on mildly handicapped students generally reflected performance in academic tasks, such as reading and math, as probed during 1-minute performance samples. In many of the severely and profoundly handicapped subjects of this research, those same performance patterns have been identified with fluency-building problems. However, in many cases the fluency-building problems occurred at lower performance rates. The "Consequence Change" patterns shown in Figure 1 include those identified as fluency-building problems during the third project year. The learning patterns that were identified as "fluency-building problems" responded to changes in the instructional format which emphasized the provision of additional practice and/or changes in consequences designed to motivate fluent performance.

Drill and Practice

The traditional method of improving performance is drill and practice in the behavior (e.g., Smith, 1968). However, much of the research in this area has been conducted with mildly handicapped students on paired-associate tasks. O'Brien, Azrin, and Bugle (1972) increased the amount of practice for walking by restraining an alternative behavior, crawling, and increased "locomotion time" spent walking. Mayhall and Jenkins (1977) compared the effects of daily and less-than-daily sessions on the performance of learning disabled children; daily instruction with the associated increase in practice produced superior performances. In general, increases in the amount of practice may result in increases in rate, if appropriate contingencies are available. However, research with severely handicapped persons has not compared the effects of different types or amounts of practice on performance.

Instructions

The most direct tactic aimed at increasing fluency would be to tell the learner to "go fast" (e.g., Loos & Tizard, 1955) or to give the learner specific performance goals (e.g., Zimmerman, Overpeck, Eisenberg, & Garlick, 1969). Instructions may initiate behavior change (Ayllon & Azrin, 1964; Hopkins, 1968), although they may not be sufficient to sustain or further accelerate behavior change. Instructions are probably the most "natural" way of increasing behavior, but they may not be the most effective over the long run. In the results to date, instructions have produced an increase in level of performance when first introduced but have not resulted in continued acceleration of fluent performance.

Manipulation of Consequences

Consequences for correct and/or fluent performance, as well as for incorrect and/or disfluent performance, are a necessary part of every instructional format. When progress falters during a fluency-building phase, however, manipulating the consequences is far more likely to produce progress than the manipulation of antecedents. The pupil does not need more information on how to perform, but reinforcement to continue improving performance on a skill that is probably being practiced over and over again. Although researchers have used a variety of consequences for correct behavior with severely handicapped learners, including food, juice, music, hugs, and vibrators (Bailey & Meyerson, 1969; Bellamy, Inman, & Schwarz, 1978; Snell & Smith, 1978), in most cases paired with verbal or signed praise, it is often difficult to identify potential reinforcers for a specific severely/profoundly handicapped student (Spradlin & Spradlin, 1976). Some authors have suggested "reinforcer" surveys to identify consequences for correct responses (e.g., Snell & Smith, 1978; Williams & York, 1978). From observation of the student, and through presentation of a variety of edibles, toys, and other possible consequences, the manager "decides" what the student "likes" and then uses the consequence contingently during an instructional program. However, these are not very precise methods, and a consequence that the subject may "choose" in one situation may not be effective in increasing his or her behavior in another situation (Haring et al., Note 4); if it is not effective, it is not a reinforcer.

Generally, merely changing from one type of contingency to another will produce only short term effects on performance (Haring et al., Note 5) and perhaps with less dramatic effects than when the consequence change is accompanied by verbal instructions as to the contingencies (Herman & Tramontana, 1971; Van Houten, Hill, & Parsons, 1975).

Once an appropriate consequence has been identified, its delivery is usually made contingent upon the desired response. When the pupil is first learning to perform, consequences are usually delivered for each accurate performance of the desired response. During fluency building and after fluency has been achieved, this "one-to-one" schedule may not be effective for all programs. In programs designed to increase rate, for example, as the rate increases, the number of consequences increases. The learner may become satiated and that consequence may lose its effectiveness. In addition, the consequences scheduled for the instructional environment may not be natural to the community environment in which the behavior will be ultimately performed.

To avoid the possible effects of satiation, to increase the naturalness of the setting, and to build fluency, intermittent schedules may be implemented. Stephens, Pear, Wray, and Jackson (1977) found that, while accuracy remained high throughout, rate of naming pictures for severely handicapped subjects was higher under intermittent fixed-ratio schedules than under one-to-one schedules. In the same article, the authors report another study in which they compared low and high fixed-ratio schedules, and found that intermediate schedules produced the highest rates. Schroeder (1972), in a series of studies, concluded that ratio rather than interval schedules might produce higher rates on simple tasks, although a very high ratio may not produce as large an increase as a lower ratio on difficult tasks.

Another method of changing the schedule is to make the consequences contingent upon a certain response rate (Haring et al., Note 5; Zimmerman, Overpeck, Eisenberg, & Garlick, 1969; Zimmerman, Stuckey, Garlick, & Miller, 1969). However, unless the desire performance increases from day to day (or decreases if that is desired), in a "changing criterion" design, the learner may perform only at the level sufficient to receive the contingency (Hartmann & Hall, 1976). Performance parameters that can be manipulated include rate, duration, and latency. In establishing a "changing criterion" for rate of response, either the required number of responses in a set period of time can be increased, or the amount of time for a set number of responses may be decreased. Ayllon, Garber, and Pisor (1976) found that gradually reducing time limits for task completion from 20 to 15 to 10 and finally to 5 minutes was extremely effective in increasing performance rate for moderately retarded students, while an abrupt decrease in the time limit interfered with task rate. Reducing the time limit for completing a correct response, or a number of correct responses, and then making reinforcement contingent upon that desired performance was effective in increasing severely handicapped subjects' rate on a variety of tasks (Haring et al., Note 5).

Another method of increasing fluency is to provide contingent punishing consequences for low work rates (Zimmerman, Overpeck, Eisenberg, & Garlick, 1969). Such contingent punishing consequences may include time-out from the opportunity to work, or loss of the consequence (e.g., tokens) previously earned for high work rates (response cost). Haring et al. (Note 5) found that having students repeat performances until daily criteria were met resulted in an increase in performance rate. It was not clear whether this increase in rate was due to the extra practice that occurred when the students' performance was low or due to an avoidance response to the repeated practice trails that were contingent on low rates.

Other Strategies

Haughton (Note 6) has suggested that rearranging the instructional environment to allow the student greater opportunity to perform a task may affect the development of fluency. For example, rather than teacher presentation of each item in a "match-to-sample" format, the learner could be given a large number of items to sort independent of any teacher presentation of material. Carnine (1976) found that when teacher presentation of items is necessary, a fast-rate teacher presentation resulted in reduced latency of responding for two first graders when compared to a low-rate presentation of items. Van Houton and Thompson (1976) found that an explicit timing of math performance increased rates of performance in second graders, in comparison with implicit (secret) timings. The accuracy of performance was maintained during the implicit and explicit timings. Van Houten, Hill, and Parsons (1975) found that public posting of performance rates increased performances, while teacher praise for performance had mixed effects. Arranging for work with a more competent peer may also increase work rate through the effect of demonstration (Brown & Pearce, 1972). Although these studies did not involve severely/profoundly handicapped students, the procedures and techniques may have implications for them.

Haring et al. (Note 5) used a "beat the clock" technique to increase rate of performance with severely handicapped subjects. This technique combines a verbal direction ("Go fast, beat the clock"), a statement of the contingencies ("If you beat the clock, you may have this prize"), a set amount of time to complete the task (the clock is set at the amount of time), a daily increasing number of required responses to earn the consequence, feedback on performance ("Oh! The clock went off and you've finished all of your work!"), and a consequence (prize).

Which Strategy?

Which strategy should a classroom teacher choose when a pupil's performance falters during the fluency-building stage of learning? Just as with acquisition problems, it is unlikely that decision rules based on performance patterns will help decide this issue, especially since the reinforcing impact of any consequence is dependent upon the individual pupil. Classroom teachers may be able to decide intuitively between nuts or juice based on their history with a particular behaver; such a choice is currently beyond the decision rules. The classroom teacher may also want to consider such issues as the schedule and type of consequences available in natural environments in selecting strategies during fluency building.

MISCELLANEOUS PROBLEMS WITH INSTRUCTIONAL FORMATS

Learning patterns that fall into the "miscellaneous" category are puzzling, because it seems that the manipulation of consequences or of antecedents has equal probability of improving learning. In most cases where such patterns have been identified, the instructional format provided by the classroom teacher is generally lacking some basic provisions. The most common mistake seems to be providing identical consequences for both correct responses and incorrect responses. In one common problem case, for example, if the student responds correctly, he or she is praised, while if the student responds incorrectly he or she is assisted to respond and then praised. If pupil performance patterns fall into this category, the teacher should reexamine the instructional format. For some basic considerations of instructional formats, the reader is referred to *Exceptional Teaching* (White & Haring, 1976).

INCORRECT SKILL STEP

One of the most frequently used change strategies is to reduce the level of difficulty of the program, usually by requiring an easier version of the skill level or a prerequisite skill. The data available suggest, however, that "stepping back" to an easier version of the skill has the highest probability of being effective in only one given situation (see Figure 1). If such a decision is made in other cases, it not only has a low probability of improving performance, but it may also serve to delay curricular progress and prolong instructional time. The use of the data-based decision rules promotes the modification of instructional settings to facilitate individualized progress, rather than the modification of what is being taught.

STRATEGIES FOR "COMPLIANCE" PROBLEMS

The term *compliance* has become almost a catchword recently. It is typically associated with "minding" behavior: Does the student do what you ask? It has also been referred to as "instruction-following behavior," but instructions with a difference—instructions that classroom teachers *expect* the student to obey. It is known that the pupil is able to respond, and the instruction is given with the expectation that it will be followed. When the student does not follow the instruction, problems occur.

The three general types of problems involve classroom management, skill assessment, and instructional decisions. Often, directions are used to help move students and materials from place to place or from activity to activity. Instructions that might be used to help manage the classroom include: "Pick up your coat," "Come here," "Stand up," "Go to the sink," "Get in line," and so forth. Students who do not obey these instructions may cause problems in general classroom management. Directions and instructions are also used to help determine the appropriate level at which to begin instruction. Initial assessment is used to determine what skills the student already can perform and what skills the student needs to learn. Students are expected to "try" to follow instructions in such situations. A student who does not attempt to follow instructions presents the problem of determining whether he or she can actually do the requested behavior but *won't* or whether he or she really *can't* follow a particular instruction. If he or she cannot respond, the student needs to be taught. If he or she will not respond, the teacher has a compliance problem. But which is it? This problem very often results in placing the student at an instructional level that is too easy. The student may then become bored and display disruptive behaviors, which lead to more problems. Finally, instructions are generally used in teaching new behaviors and skills. For example, in teaching a student to discriminate between a quarter and a penny, the cue might be, "Point to the quarter." If the student does not point to one of the choices, the teacher is faced with the dilemma of whether or not the student just "won't" point, or whether he or she can't choose the correct answer and so just doesn't respond at all. Should the teacher provide more information to help the student learn the discrimination, or should he or she try to improve instruction-following behavior? Which decision should it be?

These three problems may be compounded if instructions are used to "get rid" of various behaviors. Such commands represent a special case of "instruction following."

Using Instructions to Eliminate or Decrease Behavior

Some of the most common instructions we use are those that tell the student *not* to do something (e.g., "Don't lie," "Don't do that"). Generally, such instructions are used to control behavior that is considered inappropriate for some reason. Sometimes such directions are effective, but, more often, they serve only to increase the behavior at which they are aimed, which makes matters worse (Burleigh & Marholin, 1977).

A criticism-trap can develop whereby the teacher's direction serves to reinforce the student for the inappropriate behavior, and, if the student obeys the instruction, the teacher is reinforced for giving the direction, as in this sequence:

Jim gets out of his seat.
Mr. Smith says, "Go back to your seat."
Jim goes back to his seat.

Jim was successful in attracting the teacher's attention (by getting out of his seat) and was probably reinforced by the "admonition." Mr. Smith, on the other hand, was reinforced for giving the instruction by the fact that Jim did go back to his seat. In the future, whenever Jim wants to get Mr. Smith's attention, he can get out of his seat. Mr. Smith can probably avoid this entire problem by giving Jim attention for staying in his seat and doing his schoolwork, rather than attention for getting out of his seat. In this case, misplaced consequences create a trap that can go on and on. In general, it is best to consequate the inappropriate behavior in some other fashion, (e.g., by ignoring Jim and praising Steve for staying in his seat) and continue to provide consequences for the desired behaviors. Using commands to eliminate or decrease behavior may be effective in the short run but usually has the opposite effect in the long run; as a result, such commands are not usually considered to be in the same class as the commands involved in compliance.

Commands included in "instruction following" are those that, in general, ask the student to perform some action (rather than request the student to stop some action) and that are NOT given in response to some inappropriate behavior by the student.

Acquisition of Instruction-Following Behavior

There are two general paths in learning to follow instructions. In one, the instruction is learned at the same time as the behavior. In the other, the instruction is learned after the behavior has been learned.

Teachers do not give commands and expect them to be followed if the pupil cannot perform the required action; instead, the pupil is provided instruction in that behavior. If the student cannot stand, compliance to the instruction "Stand up" is not expected. If the learner is being taught to stand, however, the words "Stand up" may be used as part of the signal to the behaver. As the pupil learned the response, he or she would also learn to associate the signal "Stand up" with the behavior. So, if the pupil is acquiring a behavior, he or she is also learning which set of words, cues, objects, or stimuli signal the performance of the behavior. The student is acquiring the "instruction" at the same time he or she is acquiring the behavior.

In other instances, the behavior is acquired long before the instruction. For example, children may learn to look at adults before they learn to respond to "Look at me." In this case, the "acquisition of instruction following" is simply learning to associate a particular set of words (or other stimuli) with a previously learned behavior.

Whichever the case, learning to follow instructions requires that the pupil learn a discrimination: a particular response (as opposed to another) should follow a particular direction (and not another). This discrimination is learned like any other discrimination, by associating the consequences of a behavior with that response. Consequences for following directions must be different from the consequences for not following the direction. The difference in consequation teaches the student the discrimination.

Generally, a reinforcing consequence must be determined and given following the correct behavior only. The incorrect behavior, either not responding at all to an instruction or responding with some other behavior, should be ignored or followed by some consequence that the student does not "like." Beware of "helping" the student finish the response and then praising him or her for "trying to do it" or for anything else. If the student "likes" being helped, and "likes" being praised, chances are that he or she will "do it wrong" again just so he or she will be helped and praised. Unless there is a difference in consequation, the student may not be able to discriminate what it is he or she is supposed to do in response to your instructions.

The acquisition of instruction-following behavior continues until the student consistently obeys the instruction. Then, consequation is usually reduced to the more natural intermittent schedule. The command-response pairs acquired by the student become the pool for the determination of noncompliance.

Consistency and Compliance

The collection of command-response pairs that has been acquired by the student serves as a compliance "pool." When the student is asked to perform a behavior from his or her pool, it is expected that the student will obey. Compliance 100% of the time is not expected, however. In fact, kindergarteners are compliant roughly 85% of the time (Piat, Sadler, and Vickers, Note 7).

The key word here is *expect*. In order for us to come to expect, or predict, an event, that event must occur "predictably." A great deal of variability will prevent us from making a good prediction. If a student has scored 75%, 80%, 78%, 79%, and 82% on spelling tests in the past, a reasonable prediction or expectation concerning his or her performance on the next test is between 79% and 85%. However, if a student has scored 10%, 95%, 50%, 25%, and 85% on previous tests, it will be difficult to predict the next test score. The compliant student is not only one who will obey but one who will do so consistently, day after day. The consistency of compliance is just as important as the level of compliance.

Noncompliance Noncompliance is "not minding" and "not following instructions," carried out consistently. There are two general ways of being noncompliant: either by not responding to the command at all, or by performing some other, nonrequested, behavior. Noncompliant students usually "don't respond" to commands, as opposed to responding by "doing something else."

There *are* times when some noncompliant students choose to "do something'' rather than to ''do nothing.'' Usually this is in an instructional choice situation. In any choice situation (e.g., matching, sorting), there exists the possibility of getting the correct answer by chance, if responses are random. Thus, we will expect the student who is trying to match prices with advertisements from a choice of five to occasionally succeed just by luck (approximately once every five trials). As the skill is acquired, performance will, of course, improve above chance levels. The noncompliant student, on the other hand, may consistently respond incorrectly, never matching the price to the ad. In choice situations, noncompliant students may consistently—and supiciously—do the ''wrong'' thing.

Since noncompliance is based on not following instructions from the command-response pool, the noncompliant student is generally noncompliant throughout the school day. If noncompliance only occurs during particular situations, it may not be a compliance problem.

Identifying Noncompliance   Noncompliance can only occur if both of the following conditions are met:

1.   The student is able to perform the behavior.
2.   The student has previously performed the behavior in response to the instruction given.

Thus, the two most important aspects in the determination of noncompliance are the behavior and the command. The behavior must be something in the student's response repertoire. He or she must be able to perform the behavior, and, generally, the performance of the behavior should have been observed in the situation in which the command is given.

The command must have elicited the desired response in the past. Thus, the student must know or understand what is being requested. Generally, an appropriate response to the specific command should have been observed in the situation in which the command is to be given.

The following examples illustrate some of the problems in determining noncompliance:

1.   Cherie has cerebral palsy as well as several other handicapping conditions. She is usually either in her wheelchair or on a floor mat. She is unable to stand up. Cherie failed to stand up in response to a ''Stand up'' command. This is NOT an instance of noncompliance, since Cherie is unable to perform the behavior.
2.   John is able to walk and to stand up. John has responded to the command ''Come here'' in the past. He failed to respond appropriately to the direction ''Go to the sink.'' This is NOT an instance of noncompliance, because it is not known if John understands the command ''Go to the sink.''
3.   Later in the day, however, John is asked to ''Come here.'' He does not respond. This is probably an instance of noncompliance.
4.   Mark's mother reported that Mark will say ''mmm'' at home. To get him to

do it she closes her lips and says "mmm." One day at school, Mark's teacher asks him to say "mmm," using the same command that his mother uses. Mark does not respond. This is NOT an instance of noncompliance, since Mark's correct response to this instruction has not been observed at school.

Noncompliance in Instructional Programs   Noncompliance in instructional programs is difficult to determine because, during instructional programs, the failure of the student to respond correctly may be either an indication of noncompliance or an indication of "not knowing" what to do. Noncompliance during an instructional program can usually be distinguished from "not knowing" according to various performance characteristics (see also Figure 1).

Probably the most common indicator of compliance problems is variability in correct performance, the opposite of the predictability common to compliant students. Day-to-day performance of noncompliant students can vary greatly, from 20 correct per minute on one day to 0 correct on the next. Performance variability itself becomes a pattern; one extreme day does not by itself constitute a problem with variability. Noncompliant students often will exhibit performance variability from day to day that is greater than the change over time.

The lack of variability in certain situations may also be an indicator of compliance problems. In programs that require a discrimination, a certain level of corrects and of errors can be determined by chance. If the corrects are consistently below chance levels, determine if there is a "preference" for one position over another (the student always picks the object on the left, for example) or for one object over another (e.g., the student always picks the cup). This can be determined by collecting and analyzing data on each trial, while varying choice commands and positions. If there is not a preference problem, and corrects are consistently below chance levels, the student may be noncompliant.

Another indicator of compliance problems is a decrease in correct performance from a relatively high level to a very low level. Compliance problems may occur at any performance level in a program. However, if performance is at 100% but not at the fluency aim (e.g., 60 per minute), the problem may be a fluency-building problem, which may produce similar changes in level.

These performance characteristics may help understand and identify compliance problems when they occur during instructional programs. Although compliance or noncompliance is not completely understood at this time, there are some program changes that have been effective in correcting these problems. In general, however, compliance problems during instructional programs can be remediated only for a relatively short period of time.

Move to a More Difficult Skill Level   It is often very difficult to determine appropriate instructional levels for noncompliant students. As a result, instruction is sometimes begun at levels that are "too easy." Students consistently required to do work that is too easy may exhibit noncompliant behaviors or seem "bored." This may be especially true when noncompliance is seen during a specific program rather than throughout the school day. If the behavior is very important, and is one that it is critical the student learn to perform consistently at high levels, then it will be necessary to select another strategy. If, however, the skill is at an intermediate level, or is one in a task hierarchy, it may be most expedient to move to a more difficult skill level. It may be necessary to move several times in order to determine an appropriate level.

Students may also exhibit noncompliant behavior when criteria for moving on require consistent performance for 3 or more days (e.g., 100% for 4 consecutive days as a criterion for moving to the next task step). Teachers should examine criteria carefully: Is it really necessary to require 100% for several consecutive days, or does this delay the student? Are such criteria based on previous data, or are they merely a "best guess" about ending levels? Sometimes it may be unnecessary to require a student to remain at criterion for several days, partiularly when the specific skill will be used or incorporated in the next step, or when the step is just one small part of a behavior sequence.

Change or Add a Motivating Consequence for Correct Performance Noncompliance is probably the result of a breakdown in stimulus control, which in turn is the result of a failure of the consequences to continue controlling the behavior. The most easily implemented change is to add or change the "motivating" consequence for the correct behavior.

Change the Schedule for Consequation of Correct Responses Another method of reestablishing stimulus control is to continue using this same consequence but on a "leaner" schedule. For example, if the consequence has been available for every correct response, it could be made available only following two correct responses.

Institute a Response-Cost Procedure In the response-cost procedure, the student gains something for correct responses and loses it for incorrect responses. For example, the student may be praised and given a raisin for each correct response. If the student is prevented from eating the raisins he or she earns until the end of the session, it is then possible to remove a raisin for each incorrect response. Of course, the student can then go into the "hole" and lose raisins that have not been earned. It is generally better to avoid this deficit situation, and to remove consequences only after they have been actually rewarded. If possible, the student should be told that the contingency is in effect at the beginning of each instructional session.

Eliminate Competing Consequences Often, other consequences not immediately discernible may be affecting performance on the program. If, for example, the student is expected to perform for a limited number of trials, or for a limited amount of time, the student may simply be "waiting it out." In this case, either being "released" from the program or having "free time" may be reinforcing the noncompliance. Or, if recess follows the program, or lunch, or something equally as exciting, the Premack principle may be working against compliance.

Such competing consequences can be used by making them contingent upon correct performance. The contingency can involve increasing the number of correct responses or consecutive correct responses required before the termination of the program, for example. In this case, the student would be required to score one correct on the first day, two correct on the second, three correct on the third, and so on. The instructional session would continue until the aim for that day was reached. The student would be informed of the contingency prior to the instructional session.

Sometimes the competing consequence is simply teacher proximity. Data show that students in wheelchairs often will perform noncompliantly simply to increase the session time and consequently the amount of time in which the teacher is present, even if the consequences for noncompliance are painful (Haring et al., Note 5). In these cases, the time-out procedures can be implemented. For example, if the student has not responded within 5 seconds, the manager would leave the setting, returning only when the correct response had been performed.

In other cases, the availability of "chance corrects" may reinforce non-compliance. The student who consistently goes to the left position may be con-sequated for so doing if the left position is occasionally the correct position. The other extreme is the student who makes persistent errors beyond chance levels. In these cases, establish an order of trials that prevents such consequation. For example, in a sorting program, the student may "never" sort items of a particular shape. In such cases, a type of "repeat for error" drill might be effective. Each time the student made an error, that stimulus condition would be repeated until a correct response was obtained. This procedure permits the student to receive the consequation for correct responses only when all types of correct responses are performed. The "repeat for error" procedure may be coupled with an "increasing aim," as described above.

Other Consequences   Aversive contingencies that may be used as a "last resort" include: ignoring the pupil and removing any materials; removing the student from the instructional session for a short period (or leaving the student alone); and a forceful putting-through procedure, or mandate. These consequences would immediately follow any noncompliant response and would not be accompanied by any other feedback, especially a verbal reprimand. Since aversive contingencies may result in harmful side effects, they should be used only in extreme conditions, and only after obtaining parent and school approval, as required. Aversive consequences should only be continued if they demonstrate their effectiveness quickly, and they should be removed as soon as possible.

GENERALIZATION AND ADAPTATION

The strategies presented are those that can be used to facilitate pupil progress through two functionally defined stages of learning: acquisition and fluency building. But what of the learning stages beyond: generalization and adaptation?

Generalization may be said to occur when a learned response is observed to occur in the presence of "untaught" stimuli. Adaptation is said to occur when the topology of a learned response changes in the presence of "untaught" stimuli. What are the environmental conditions that will facilitate generalization and adaptation?

Stokes and Baer (1977) summarized various tactics that have been reported as facilitating generalization. The fact that generalization is not always observed, however, suggests the necessity of developing "a technology of generalization, so that programming will be a fundamental component of any procedures when durability and generalization of behavior change are desirable" (Stokes & Baer, 1977, p. 365). Research can identify exactly what programming procedures are particularly effective with severely/profoundly handicapped persons and how they can be implemented by teachers in classrooms. Perhaps, with sufficient training, severely/profoundly handicapped students can "learn how to generalize," and programming for generalization would not be necessary.

In adaptation training, the student would learn how to modify behaviors to meet the requirements of new situations. For example, if one teaches a student to walk over smooth surfaces, will the pupil be able to adapt his or her walking movements to walk successfully over rough ground without further instruction? That is one step beyond generalization—changing the topology of the response to meet the novel response requirements of the new setting. Adaptation is also a crucial issue in regard to severely/profoundly handicapped persons, since it is certainly impossible to teach students every variation of every behavior/skill necessary to meet the changing requirements of different environments. Essentially, adaptation amounts to problem solving. Guralnick (1976) suggests that to solve problems direct training in the use of effective problem-solving strategies be given, that such strategies may involve cognitive self-guidance, and that they focus attention on the distinctive features of the problem. Guralnick used self-reinforcement, teacher demonstration, verbal directions, verbal mediation (having the subject repeat the directions aloud), and verbal feedback in teaching moderately retarded subjects to solve complex perceptual discrimination problems. Can those procedures be used effectively with severely handicapped students? What skills are prerequisite to problem solving? Until these questions are answered, the behavioral repertoire of severely handicapped students may remain severely limited.

Obviously a great deal of research remains to be done in order to determine effective instructional plans for severely/profoundly handicapped learners. Much of the research to date has not only concentrated on less handicapped individuals, but has also failed to show the appropriateness of various instructional strategies to the total continuum of skill development. The current research shows promise in achieving this discrimination and provides a method, through the use of decision rules, for the appropriate application of strategies to meet the learning needs of individual pupils.

REFERENCES

Ayllon, T., & Azrin, N. H. Reinforcement and instructions with mental patients. *Journal of the Experimental Analysis of Behavior*, 1964, *1*, 327-331.

Ayllon, T., Garber, S., & Pisor, K. Reducing time limits: A means to increase behavior of retardates. *Journal of Applied Behavior Analysis*, 1976, *9*(3), 247-252.

Azrin, N. H., Schaeffer, R. M., & Wesolowski, M. D. A rapid method of teaching profoundly retarded persons to dress. *Mental Retardation*, 1976, *14*, 378-382.

Bailey, J., & Meyerson, L. Vibration as a reinforcer with a profoundly retarded child. *Journal of Applied Behavior Analysis*, 1969, *2*, 135-137.

Baldwin, V. Curriculum concerns. In M. Angele Thomas (ed.), *Hey, don't forget about me*. Reston, Virginia: Council for Exceptional Children, 1976.

Barrett, B. Communication and the measured message of normal behavior. In R. York & E. Edgar (eds.), *Teaching the severely handicapped* (Vol. IV). Seattle: American Association for the Education of the Severely/Profoundly Handicapped, 1979.

Bellamy, G. T., Inman, D. P., & Schwarz, R. H. Vocational training and production supervision: A review of habilitation techniques for the severely and profoundly retarded. In N. G. Haring & D. D. Bricker (eds.), *Teaching the severely handicapped* (Vol. III). Seattle: American Association for the Education of the Severely/Profoundly Handicapped, 1978.

Bohannon, R. M. *Direct and daily measurement procedures in the identification and treatment of reading behaviors of children in special education*. Unpublished doctoral dissertation, College of Education, University of Washington, 1975.

Bradfield, R., & Heifetz, J. Education of the severely and profoundly handicapped. In J. L. Bigge & D. A. O'Donnell (eds.), *Teaching individuals with physical and multiple disabilities*. Columbus, Ohio: Charles E. Merrill Publishing Co., 1976.

Bricker, D. D., & Dennison, L. Training prerequisites to verbal behavior. In M. E. Snell (ed.), *Systematic instruction of the moderately and severely handicapped*. Columbus, Ohio: Charles E. Merrill Publishing Co., 1978.

Brown, L., Nietupski, J., & Hamre-Nietupski, S. *The criterion of ultimate functioning and public school services for severely handicapped students*. Madison, Wisconsin: University of Wisconsin and Madison Public Schools, 1976.

Brown, L., & Pearce, E. Increasing the production rates of trainable retarded students in a public school simulated workshop. *Education and Training of the Mentally Retarded*, 1972, *7*, 74-81.

Burleigh, R. A., & Marholin, D. Don't shoot until you see the whites of his eyes—An analysis of the adverse side effects of verbal prompts. *Behavior Modification*, 1977, *1*(1), 109-122.

Carnine, D. W. Effects of two teacher-presentation rates on off-task behavior, answering correctly, and participation. *Journal of Applied Behavior Analysis*, 1976, *9*, 199-206.

Chaffin, J. D. Production rate as a variable in the job success or failure of educable mentally retarded adolescents. *Exceptional Children*, 1969, 35, 533-538.

Duncan, A. Precision teaching in perspective: An interview with Ogden R. Lindsley. *Teaching Exceptional Children*, 1971, *3*(3), 114-120.

Fredericks, H., Riggs, C., Furey, T., Grove, D., Moore, W., McDonnell, J., Jordan, E., Hanson, W., Baldwin, V., & Wadlow, M. *The teaching research curriculum for moderately and severely handicapped*. Springfield, Illinois: Charles C Thomas, 1976.

Gold, M. W. Stimulus facors in skill training of the retarded on a complex assembly task: Acquisition, transfer and retention. *American Journal of Mental Deficiency*, 1972, *76*, 517-526.

Gurnalick, M. J. Solving complex perceptual discrimination problems: Techniques for the development of problem-solving strategies. *American Journal of Mental Deficiency,* 1976, *81*(1), 18-25.

Hansen, C. L., & Eaton, M. D. Reading. In N. Haring, T. Lovitt, M. Eaton, & C. Hansen (eds.), *The fourth r: Research in the classroom.* Columbus, Ohio: Charles E. Merrill Publishing Co., 1978.

Haring, N. G., & Bricker, D. D. (eds.). *Teaching the severely handicapped* (Vol. III). Seattle: American Association for the Education of the Severely/Profoundly Handicapped, 1978.

Hartmann, D. P., & Hall, R. V. The changing criterion design. *Journal of Applied Behavior Analysis,* 1976, *9,* 527-532.

Hendrickson, J., Roberts, M., & Shores, R. E. Antecedent and contingent modeling to teach basic sight vocabulary to learning disabled children. *Journal of Learning Disabilities,* 1978, *11*(8).

Herman, S., & Tramontana, J. Instructions and group versus individual reinforcement in modifying disruptive group behavior. *Journal of Applied Behavior Analysis,* 1971, *4,* 113-119.

Hersen, M., & Barlow, D. *Single case experimental designs: Strategies for studying behavior change.* New York: Pergamon Press, 1976.

Hopkins, B. L. Effects of candy and social reinforcement of smiling. *Journal of Applied Behavior Analysis,* 1968, *1,* 121-128.

Horner, R. D., & Keilitz, I. Training mentally retarded adolescents to brush their teeth. *Journal of Applied Behavior Analysis,* 1975, *8,* 301-309.

Johnson, E. Precision teaching helps children learn. *Teaching Exceptional Children,* 1971, *3*(3), 106-111.

Kazdin, A. E. Statistical analyses for single-case experimental designs. In M. Hersen and D. Barlow (eds.), *Single-case experimental design: Strategies for studying behavior change.* New York: Pergamon Press, 1976.

Lent, J. R., & McLean, B. M. The trainable retarded: The technology of teaching. In N. G. Haring and R. L. Schiefelbusch (eds.), *Teaching special children.* New York: McGraw-Hill Book Co., 1976.

Liberty, K. *An investigation of two methods of achieving compliance with the severely handicapped in a classroom setting.* Unpublished doctoral dissertation, College of Education, University of Washington, Seattle, 1977.

Lindsley, O. R. Direct measurement and prosthesis of retarded behavior. *Journal of Education,* 1964, *147,* 62-81.

Litrownik, A. J., Franzini, L. R., & Turner, G. L. Acquisition of concepts by TMR children as a function of the type of modeling, rule verbalization, and observer gender. *American Journal of Mental Deficiency,* 1976, *80*(6), 620-628.

Loos, F. M., & Tizard, J. The employment of adult imbeciles in a hospital workshop. *American Journal of Mental Deficiency,* 1955, *59,* 395-403.

Mayhall, W. F., & Jenkins, J. R. Scheduling daily or less-than-daily instruction: Implications for resource programs. *Journal of Learning Disabilities,* 1977, *10*(3), 159-163.

Mirkin, P. *A comparison of the effects of three formative evaluation strategies and contingent consequences on reading performance.* Unpublished doctoral dissertation, College of Education, University of Minnesota, 1978.

Nelson, G., Cone, J., & Hanson, C. Training correct utensil use in retarded children: Modeling vs. physical guidance. *American Journal of Mental Deficiency,* 1975, *80,* 114-122.

O'Brien, F., Azrin, N. H., & Bugle, C. Training profoundly retarded children to stop crawling. *Journal of Applied Behavior Analysis,* 1972, *5*(2), 131-137.

Panyan, M. C. *Managing behavior. Part 4: New ways to teach new skills.* Lawrence, Kansas: H & H Enterprises, 1972.

Risley, T. R., & Reynolds, N. J. Emphasis as a prompt for verbal imitation. *Journal of Applied Behavior Analysis*, 1970, *3*, 185-190.

Schreibman, L. Effects of within-stimulus and extra-stimulus prompting on discrimination learning in autistic children. *Journal of Applied Behavior Analysis*, 1975, *8*(1), 91-112.

Schroeder, S. R. Parametric effects of reinforcement frequency, amount of reinforcement, and required response force on sheltered workshop behavior. *Journal of Applied Behavior Analysis*, 1972, *5*, 431-441.

Sidman, M. *Tactics of scientific research: Evaluating experimental data in psychology.* New York: Basic Books, 1960.

Smith, D., & Lovitt, T. The use of modeling techniques to influence the acquisition of computational arithmetic skills in learning-disabled children. In E. Ramp and G. Semb (eds.), *Behavior analysis: Areas of research and application.* Englewood Cliffs, New Jersey: Prentice-Hall, 1975.

Smith, R. M. *Clinical teaching: Methods of instruction for the retarded.* New York: McGraw-Hill Book Co., 1968.

Snell, M. E. (ed.). *Systematic instruction of the moderately and severely handicapped.* Columbus, Ohio: Charles E. Merrill Publishing Co., 1978.

Snell, M. E., & Smith, D. D. Intervention strategies. In M. E. Snell (ed.), *Systematic instruction of the moderately and severely handicapped.* Columbus, Ohio: Charles E. Merrill Publishing Co., 1978.

Spradlin, J. E., & Spradlin, R. R. Developing necessary skills for entry into classroom teaching arrangements. In N. G. Haring & R. L. Schiefelbusch (eds.), *Teaching special children.* New York: McGraw-Hill Book Co., 1976.

Stephens, C. E., Pear, J. J., Wray, L. D., & Jackson, G. C. Some effects of reinforcement schedules in teaching picture names to retarded children. *Journal of Applied Behavior Analysis*, 1977, *10*, 349-367.

Stokes, T. F., & Baer, D. M. An implicit technology of generalization. *Journal of Applied Behavior Analysis*, 1977, *10*, 349-367.

Streifel, S., Bryan, K., & Aikins, D. Transfer of stimulus control from motor to verbal stimuli. *Journal of Applied Behavior Analysis*, 1974, *7*, 123-135.

Streifel, S., & Wetherby, B. Instruction-following behavior of a retarded child and its controlling stimuli. *Journal of Applied Behavior Analysis*, 1973, *6*, 663-670.

Teaching Exceptional Children, 1971, *3*(3).

Touchette, P. Transfer of stimulus control: Measuring the moment of transfer. *Journal of the Experimental Analysis of Behavior*, 1971, *15*, 347-354.

Van Houten, R., Hill, S., & Parsons, M. An analysis of a performance feedback system: The effects of timing and feedback, public posting, and praise upon academic performance and peer interaction. *Journal of Applied Behavior Analysis*, 1975, *8*, 449-457.

Van Houten, R., & Thompson, C. The effects of explicit timing on math performance. *Journal of Applied Behavior Analysis*, 1976, *9*(2), 227-230.

Waxler, C. Z., & Yarrow, M. R. Factors influencing imitative learning in preschool children. *Journal of Experimental Child Psychology*, 1970, *9*, 115-130.

Westling, D. L., & Murden, L. Self-help skills training: A review of operant studies. *The Journal of Special Education*, 1978, *12*(3), 253-283.

White, O. R., & Haring, N. G. *Exceptional teaching.* Columbus, Ohio: Charles E. Merrill Publishing Co., 1976.

White, O. R., & Liberty, K. A. Behavioral assessment and precise educational measurement. In N. G. Haring & R. L. Schiefelbusch (eds.), *Teaching special children.* New York: McGraw-Hill Book Co., 1976.

Whitman, T. L., Zakaras, M., & Chardos, S. Effects of reinforcement and guidance procedures on instruction-following behavior of severely retarded children. *Journal of Applied Behavior Analysis*, 1971, *4*, 283–290.

Williams, W., & York, R. Developing instructional programs for severely handicapped students. In N. G. Haring & D. D. Bricker (eds.), *Teaching the severely handicapped* (Vol. III). Seattle: American Association for the Education of the Severely/Profoundly Handicapped, 1978.

York, R., & Edgar, E. (eds.). *Teaching the severely handicapped* (Vol. IV). Seattle: American Association for the Education of the Severely/Profoundly Handicapped, 1979.

York, R., Williams, W., & Brown, P. Teaching modeling and student imitation: An instructional procedure and teacher competency. *AAESPH Review*, 1976, *1*(8), 11–15.

Zimmerman, J., Overpeck, C., Eisenberg, H., & Garlick, B. Operant conditioning in a sheltered workshop. *Rehabilitation Literature*, 1969, *30*, 326–334.

Zimmerman, J., Stuckey, T., Garlick, B., & Miller, M. Effects of token reinforcement on productivity in multiply handicapped clients in a sheltered workshop. *Rehabilitation Literature*, 1969, *30*, 34–41.

REFERENCE NOTES

1. White, O. R. *A manual for the calculation and use of the median slope—A technique of progress estimation and prediction in the single case.* Regional Resource Center for Handicapped Children, Clinical Services Building, University of Oregon, Eugene, 1972.

2. Liberty, K. A. *Data decision rules.* Unpublished manuscript, Regional Resource Center, University of Oregon, Eugene, 1972.

3. Sokolov, H. *Report on 3300 Pupils, Project Product, Shawnee Mission School District, Shawnee Mission Kansas.* Letter to Owen White, fall, 1977.

4. Haring, N. G., White, O. R., & Liberty, K. A. *An investigation of phases of learning and facilitating instructional events for the severely handicapped: Annual progress report 1976–77.* Bureau of Education for the Handicapped, Project No. 443CH70564, University of Washington, College of Education, Seattle, 1977.

5. Haring, N. G., White, O. R., & Liberty, K. A. *An investigation of phases of learning and facilitating instructional events for the severely handicapped: Annual progress report 1977–78.* Bureau of Education for the Handicapped, Project No. 443CH70564, University of Washington, College of Education, Seattle, 1978.

6. Haughton, E. *More parameters of pupil freedom: Implications for skill development.* Paper presented at the Fifth Annual Conference, American Association for the Education of the Severely/Profoundly Handicapped, Baltimore, October, 1978.

7. Piat, J., Sadler, O., & Vickers, M. *Command compliance rates in pre-school settings.* Paper presented at meeting of the Southeastern Psychology Association, 1974.

Section III
EVALUATION OF OUTCOME: CURRENT RESEARCH

Chapter 7

Methods in Communication Instruction for Severely Handicapped Persons

Doug Guess

The development of communication skills in severely/multiply handicapped persons represents one of the most technically difficult, challenging and important problems in the design and delivery of effective educational services. The vast literature concerning expressive and receptive speech acquisition and remediation cannot be fully covered in a single chapter or even in a single volume. This chapter is intended to provide a concise overview of current state-of-the-art issues and to delineate some practical considerations that are important when considering language-training programs or procedures for use with severely handicapped persons. Unfortunately, available research does not permit definitive answers for selecting either a program or an appropriate response mode for communication training. To the contrary, the teacher or interventionist working to establish communication skills in a severely handicapped population of children must make many critical decisions in the absence of adequate empirical support. These decisions are further complicated by the flood of training programs now available and by the tendency among educators to exaggerate reports of performance gains resulting from training in certain response modes. The present chapter is an effort to clarify issues and options available to teachers and others in decision-making positions.

Initially, a clear distinction needs to be made between a *language-training program* and a *response mode*. A language-training program provides, for the most part, a sequence for teaching communication skills. Programs, regardless of their theoretical underpinnings, are designed to teach the appropriate semantic and syntactic rules that comprise a particular language system. Simplistically stated, programs are intended to teach a language deficient child *what* and *when* to communicate, while the response mode refers to *how* the child communicates. Oral speech, communication boards, and signing are examples of symbol systems that can be used as response modes. They do not constitute a language-training program. Hollis and Carrier (1978) have recently stressed this point:

> The distinction between language and response mode is a critical one, when considering the development of nonspeech language intervention strategies. Many programs currently in use (e.g., Signing Exact English, Bliss, and others) confound language with symbol systems. In short, if we were dealing with individuals who differed little from the norm, this probably would not be a serious problem (p. 80).

The first section of this chapter discusses some prerequisite skills to speech and language development. This is followed by a short review of existing programs for teaching speech and language skills to severely handicapped persons. A third section is devoted to a discussion of nonspeech communication systems with a special emphasis on signing and communication boards. The final section examines the vital question of communication generalization.

SKILLS PREREQUISITE TO SPEECH AND LANGUAGE DEVELOPMENT

A number of variables and conditions appear to be important to the development of speech as a primary communication response mode. There is general professional agreement that certain skills are necessary before speech can be acquired through either normal development or systematic intervention. Numerous theories and opinions stress the dependence of expressive language skills on prior cognitive and perceptual growth (cf. Schiefelbusch and Lloyd, 1974). However, empirical support for these positions is often absent, and the theories themselves are difficult to translate into intervention strategies for teaching language. A further difficulty is that much of the supporting information that is available comes from literature on normal infant and child development. Because handicapped children often do not follow the same sequence of speech and language development as normal infants and children, there are major implications for intervention efforts (cf. Guess, Sailor, & Baer, 1978a, for a discussion of this issue). This section discusses some of the parameters and conditions that have been identified as important to language acquisition, including sensory acuity, receptive language skills, perceptual and cognitive processes, vocal production, and generalized vocal/verbal imitation.

Sensory Acuity

The development of language skills and the type of response mode selected to express a language competence is directly influenced by how well the child receives stimuli through vision, hearing, touch, taste, and smell. Severely handicapped children frequently have sensory impairments that singly or in combination limit the extent to which they are capable of receiving the environmental input necessary for speech and language acquisition. Studies by Mavilya (Note 1) and Cairns and Butterfield (Note 2), for example, have shown that, compared to nonhandicapped infants, hearing-impaired infants increase their relative proportion of nonspeech sounds in relation to speech sounds over time. Thus, impairment to the hearing system directly affects the type of early vocal productions (speech sounds) that appear to be important to later speech acquisition. One would assume that this effect would be even more devastating to children who have severe to profound mental retardation in addition to a significant hearing loss. Unfortunately, the type of developmental studies conducted by Mavilya and Cairns and Butterfield have not also been done with infants and children manifesting other sensory handicapping conditions. This lack of information may be due in part to the lack of appropriate procedures for measuring sensory acuity in severely handicapped individuals.

Chapter 3 of this volume (Sailor et al.) discusses in detail some recent advances in the assessment of visual and auditory efficiency of severely handicapped individuals. Other sensory channels of severely handicapped children, such as touch and smell, are rarely subjected to objective assessment. However, Hollis and Carrier (1978) advise that these modes should also be considered in establishing functional communication skills.

Essentially, sensory acuity plays an important but somewhat indirect role in speech and language acquisition. Impairment to a sensory mechanism, especially hearing, is important because it affects the development of other speech- and language-related skills and increases the possibility of developing deviant patterns. Intact sensory mechanisms permit speech and language precursors to emerge. Damage to the sensory mechanism may not only impair the ability of the child to learn a language but may also influence the choice of appropriate modes to teach the child, irrespective of the particular language competencies to be acquired.

Receptive Language Skills

It is important for children to develop the skills necessary to understand what is being said or presented to them. It is appropriate to investigate receptive language skills in any sensory modality, although the development of auditory reception skills is particularly central to speech acquisition. These skills range from discriminating between sounds to understanding complex verbal or symbolic instructions.

The experimental literature documents that normally developing infants are able to discriminate a wide variety of speech and nonspeech stimuli before the age of 6 months (Butterfield & Cairns, 1974; Eimas, 1974). Mills and Melhuish (1974) have presented findings that suggest 3-week-old infants have already learned to discriminate characteristics of their mothers' voice, and Butterworth and Costillo (1976) have published results showing that the newborn human infant can make eye movements that are spatially coordinated with the loci of sound. These and numerous other studies (e.g., Moerk, 1977) have amply demonstrated that receptive language skills are rapidly developing during the first year of life and that the infant is an active participant in this development. However, little is known of the relationship between receptive language and productive language during the first year of life. There is also little information on the extent to which the emergence of early receptive language skills interacts with other cognitive, perceptual, and environmental factors to provide the foundation for later speech production in the normally developing child. As one might expect, even less information is available on the influences of early receptive language skills on later speech production among young handicapped children, and there is also virtually no information on the ability of handicapped infants to make auditory discriminations between either speech or nonspeech sounds. Thus, the opinion that at least some degree of existing receptive language skills is necessary for speech production by seriously language-delayed children is extrapolated from available literature on normal language acquisition that has a limited empirical base.

It appears that normally developing infants are capable of making some rather remarkable receptive sound discriminations. The extent to which handicapped, especially severely handicapped, children are capable of making these types of discriminations is not presently known, nor is it known just how these early discriminations affect later speech and language development. Furthermore, disagreement exists concerning the relationship between receptive and productive language skills in the acquisition of grammatical rules. For example, it is questionable if receptive understanding must always precede expressive speech in either normal acquisition or remedial training.

Perceptual and Cognitive Processes

Cairns and Butterfield (Note 2) report that around 1970 a consensus arose that language development could not occur without prior perceptual and conceptual development. This position was based on the theory that linguistic structures are built upon already developed perceptual and conceptual structures. What has evolved, according to Rees (1972), is the "language–cognition" controversy. On the one hand, there are those who have earlier proposed that language influences the development of cognition (Bruner, Goodnow, & Austin, 1956; Kendler & Kendler, 1959). At an applied level, this position would seem to suggest that language-training efforts are important in advancing the cognitive development of the child. On the other hand, the view that language is influenced by cognition (e.g., Inhelder & Piaget, 1964) implies that the language interventionist must identify the child's level of cognitive development in order to determine the nature and complexity of the linguistic structures to be included in the training process. This later position that cognition influences language appears to have had the greatest impact on language remediation programs for severely handicapped children (cf. attempts to base language intervention efforts on the cognitive developmental stages described by Piaget in the work of Bricker, Dennison, & Bricker, 1975). However, there are few empirical demonstrations that show the relationships between cognitive performance and linguistic performance, and, as Cairns and Butterfield (Note 2) point out, most references about cognitive structures are derived from measures of linguistic performance. One notable exception is a naturalistic observational study conducted by Kahn (1975) that showed a direct relationship between measures of Piagetian-based sensorimotor development and speaking ability among profoundly retarded persons. In this case, the observed verbal performance of the subjects corresponded to performance expected from their measured level of cognitive ability, using the standardized scale developed by Uzgiris and Hunt (1975).

A cognitive model such as that proposed by Piaget does suggest a more nativistic interpretation of speech and language acquisition with the assumption that there are certain species-specific invariants that determine both the extent and sequence in which language skills can be acquired. This position has been somewhat at odds with a behaviorally oriented approach that emphasizes the environmental influence on language acquisition (e.g., Waryas, 1979). Specifically, the behaviorists have stressed an operant model of shaping as central to language acquisition. However, Horowitz (Note 3) has pointed out that the cognitive model proposed by Piaget leaves a wide margin for individual differences, and acknowledges the possibility for aberrant or delayed development without involving constitutional factors as the entire explanation. Thus, while behaviorism does not give prominence to predispositions for language acquisition, the cognitive approach does leave room for environmental influences on language acquisition. According to Horowitz:

> Though Piaget and many Piagetians have not been interested in a functional analysis of the process of cognitive development, in fact, an operant model of shaping is not inimical to Piaget's theory (p. 22).

Vocal Production

Theories vary in their descriptions of the progression of infant vocalizations that precede emergence of the first words. Siegal (1969) postulates that the initial vocalizations of infants are general reflexive reactions to external or internal stimulation. These are typically followed by a stage of babbling or word play which evolves from enjoyable sound production into self-generated vocal activity. This latter vocal activity transforms into more stylized utterances that eventually emerge into words.

Cairns and Butterfield (Note 2) have pointed out that no one has clearly described the relationship between early vocal behavior and the development of subsequent language. Some theories have argued that there is no continuity between the early babbling behaviors of infants and language behavior after the first word (McNeil, 1970). This position is based on the differences in the quality of vocal sounds before and after the emergence of the first word. Risley (1977), on the other hand, suggests that an operant model will eventually substantiate the close correspondence between the initial vocal repertoires of infants and the verbal behavior of adults in the culture.

Regardless of whether early infant vocalizations are continuous with later word production, a number of studies have shown that infant vocal rates can be increased with contingent reinforcement (Banikotes & Montgomery, 1972;

Haugan & McIntire, 1972; Ramey & Ourth, 1971). Importantly, the systematic use of reinforcers to increase vocal rate is often described, with success, as an initial step in teaching speech skills to nonverbal, severely handicapped children. Early studies described by Lovaas (1966) used contingent reinforcers to increase vocal rate among autistic children as a preliminary step in verbal imitation training. Guess, Rutherford, and Twichell (1969) increased the vocal rate of a mute, 16-year-old, visually impaired and severely retarded boy as a preliminary phase to training vocal imitation. Certainly, the use of contingent reinforcers to increase vocal production has become a frequently used training procedure when attempting to develop generalized imitative repertoires in nonverbal children.

There remain, however, numerous questions related to the vocal production of severely handicapped, speech deficient children. There seem to be no existing studies that have compared the vocal production rates of severely handicapped infants to nonhandicapped infants, nor have studies been reported that have systematically and longitudinally measured the vocal production rate of severely handicapped infants and children. Questions remain concerning the extent to which severely handicapped children deviate from normal development in both the quality and quantity of vocalizations produced. At best, clinical experience has indicated that nonverbal severely handicapped children with high vocal production rates and a high sound diversity are usually better candidates for vocal and verbal imitation training. This observation, however, is made in the absence of systematically collected supporting data.

Generalized Vocal/Verbal Imitation

The importance of verbal imitation as a prerequisite skill for later language development is widely accepted. Both language trainers and theorists from divergent orientations agree that children who can imitate the sounds and words of their communities are well on their way to becoming effective speech users. The role of imitation is extensive in the cognitively based theory of Piaget (Flavell, 1963), where the progression through various developmental stages during the sensorimotor period can be related to increasingly complex imitation skills. This progression involves the development of "pseudo-imitation" at the 3- to 4-month age level in which adult imitation of the infant's actions (e.g., banging a rattle) is followed by the child again repeating the response. In the next developmental stage, the child is capable of imitating simple gestures that can be observed (e.g., clapping hands), while later the child is capable of imitating responses that cannot be visually observed (e.g., sticking out the tongue or simple vocal sounds). Finally, with the emergence of "deferred imitation," the infant is able to produce a response modeled earlier. Deferred imitation signals the ability to act upon the representation of events, which is necessary for the development of productive language. According to Piagetian theory, children should not be able to speak until they are capable of "deferred imitation." The study cited by Kahn (1975) earlier in this chapter has provided some experimental support for this position with older severely and profoundly retarded subjects. Sailor, Guess,

Goetz, Schuler, Utley, and Baldwin (this volume) present a detailed examination of the issues and research that bear on the role of imitation in language instruction.

COMPREHENSIVE SPEECH AND LANGUAGE DEVELOPMENT PROGRAMS[1]

This section reviews selected comprehensive speech- and language-training programs that are applicable for a severely handicapped population. With the exception of Non-SLIP (Non-speech Language Initiation Program, Carrier & Peak, 1975), these training programs have been designed primarily for the establishment of oral speech as the dominant response mode. A later section describes current efforts to adapt some of these programs to nonspeech response modes.

Most of the language intervention programs and theoretical strategies for intervention reviewed in this section reflect an interaction between psycholinguistic and learning theory. The Guess, Sailor, and Baer program (Guess, Sailor, & Baer, 1976a, 1976b, 1977b, 1978b) comes closest to representing a strict learning theory interpretation of speech and language development. Modeling, imitation, reinforcement, and an operant remedial logic are the cornerstones of the training sequence. Other language-training programs incorporate operant conditioning principles into their interventions, but identify them as effective teaching techniques rather than as theoretical constructs for language acquisition. Applications of these strategies to speech and language remediation represent psycholinguistic approaches (cf. Stremel & Waryas, 1974) and the Piagetian cognitive developmental approach (Bricker, Dennison, & Bricker, 1975).

The Stremel and Waryas Program

Stremel (1972) and Stremel and Waryas (1974) have developed an intervention program that incorporates psycholinguistic theory with operant teaching procedures. Stremel and Waryas's interpretation of previous linguistic analyses embraces the tenet that early language acquisition is best described as a rule-governed system that progresses in sequential stages. The regularities observed in linguistic development on semantic, syntactic, and phonological levels are taken to imply that any language performance level necessarily depends on a prior level of linguistic development. Following the guidelines offered by Bloom (1971, 1974) and other psycholinguists, Stremel and Waryas stress the teaching of grammatical forms (SUBJECT + VERB + OBJECT) to express various semantic relationships. Individual responses within each step of the program are taught by using operant principles such as stimulus control programming and shaping responses through the use of differential reinforcement. Edibles, tokens, and social praise are considered to be viable reinforcers for language performance. The program has been divided into three main sections (Early Language Training, Early-Intermediate Language Training, and Late-Intermediate Lan-

---

[1]The author is grateful to William Keogh of the University of Vermont, who made substantial contributions to the content in this section of the chapter.

guage Training), with placement in the program dependent on a set of entry behaviors. For example, in order to enter Early Language Training a child should be able to attend to the supervising adult, follow simple instructions, and comprehend and label at least 10 pictures or objects.

The Early Language Training phase first teaches the child to express a wide range of nouns and verbs and then trains language structures such as NOUN + VERB ("Mama go") and VERB + NOUN ("Want cookie"). As training progresses, these grammatical structures are expanded to include pronouns, adjectives, prepositions, and Wh-questions. Training emphasizes both the receptive and productive use of these basic structures. After children have mastered most of the grammatical structures of phase I, they are advanced to Early-Intermediate Language Training. During this phase, group instruction may replace one-to-one instruction. Training at this stage focuses on expanding the child's use of a basic grammatical repertoire and teaching the productive and receptive use of auxiliary verbs, negatives, and possessives. The final phase continues to build the child's grammar and use of syntax by teaching plurals and noun/verb tense agreement along with other grammatical forms.

The MacDonald and Horstmeier Program

MacDonald and Horstmeier (1978) have developed a semantics-based assessment and training strategy to teach early expressive language. The major objective of the Environmental Language Intervention Program is to teach children to use language functionally. The specific content is based on psycholinguistic data, particularly the work of Schlesinger (1971). Essentially, eight semantic-grammatical rules identified by Schlesinger serve as the basis for training. All of the eight rules express specific functions similar to those used by Stremel and Waryas (1974). For example, the utterance "Daddy throw" might express the AGENT + ACTION rule function; the utterance "Throw ball" might express the ACTION + OBJECT rules; or "No ball" might express the negation function. Rules that are trained first are those that have been observed to occur most frequently in the child's own language repertoire.

One particular feature that distinguishes this program from others is the manner in which the semantic-grammatical functions are trained. Imitation, conversational, and structured-play training occur concurrently so that the child will begin to use the newly acquired structures functionally as soon as they are mastered imitatively. The purpose of the imitation phase is to teach the child to produce particular semantic-grammatical utterances so that control of the utterances can be more easily shifted to conversational and spontaneous use. The child is asked to imitate a two-word utterance in the presence of two discriminative stimuli. First, the child is given a model, or linguistic cues, such as the instruction, "Say, 'throw ball.' " A second discriminative stimulus is paired with the instruction that is functionally tied to the utterance. An example would be to always throw a ball up into the air each time the child is asked to say "throw ball." The consequences for a correct imitation include the repetition of the original model "throw ball," social praise, and token reinforcement. A brief time-out period follows incorrect imitations by the child before a new trial begins.

Conversational training runs concurrently with imitation training. The discriminative stimuli are slightly altered during this phase so that a more conversation-like response is given. The nonlinguistic cue remains the same (throwing a ball into the air). The verbal cue, however, is changed from "Say, 'throw ball' " to "What am I doing?" Correct approximations are reinforced as in imitation training, and, when necessary, a prompt such as "Say, 'throw ball' " is provided to increase the likelihood of a reinforceable response.

The structured play phase of the training program runs concurrently with the two phases described above. As in the earlier phases, specific discrimination stimuli, expected responses, and programmed consequences are clearly given.

The Bricker, Dennison, and Bricker Program

The Constructive Interaction-Adaptation Approach to Language Training (Bricker, Dennison, & Bricker, 1975) represents the most recent revision of the Brickers' language intervention program. As in some of the previous versions of the Brickers' work, this strategy embraces psycholinguistic theory, operant conditioning principles, and Piagetian thought. It is one of the most comprehensive language intervention programs reviewed. For some users, however, its comprehensiveness might be considered a handicap, especially for those who have little control over the environments where speech deficient students live.

Piagetian principles of cognitive development, especially during the first 2 years of life, served as a model for structuring the Bricker-Dennison-Bricker program. Piaget has described the first 2 years of life as being a *sensorimotor period*. During this period, the infant is almost continually interacting with or exploring the environment. Eventually, the infant learns that objects endure or remain the same even though they are perceived from different angles or are temporarily out of sight. The concept of *object permanence* is held to mark the beginning of a process by which the infant assimilates and organizes new events with those that have been previously learned. Because these events are the referent of communication behavior, this period is seen as critical for language training.

Within the Piagetian framework, 24 language-training phases have been structured and classified under five general headings: Attending Skills, Imitation, Functional Use, Comprehension, and Production. Although the phases are consecutively ordered for convenience, training does not proceed in a linear fashion. Instead, two and possibly three phases might be trained concurrently. For example, phase 22 is designed to teach the initiation of three-word strings such as "Boy eat cookie." Concurrently, but in a different training session, the child is taught to comprehend AGENT + ACTION + OBJECT grammatical relations; "Boy eat cookie" (phase 23) is one such relation. It is conceivable that expressive training on these same forms could also be trained concurrently (phase 24).

Similar concurrent training strategies are seen in all of the programs reviewed so far, especially, the Environmental Language Intervention Program (MacDonald & Horstmeier, 1978) where imitation, conversational, and structured-play training are conducted simultaneously on any target form.

The unique training features of the Bricker-Dennison-Bricker program center around the authors' attempts to utilize the Piagetian framework in training. For example, the goal of phase 10 is to establish different action patterns in which children learn to anticipate the effect their actions have on objects, persons, and events. By this process, the child learns such attributes as weight, texture, color, and so on. According to this approach the children will eventually begin to associate the words and sounds they hear in their environment with the particular action and object with which they are engaged.

The Constructive Interaction-Adaptation Approach attempts to incorporate language training into the more global conceptual developmental process rather than treat it as a separate domain. This approach assumes that the child's total experience contributes substantially to the language-learning aspect of cognitive growth, and suggests that any attempt to teach speech and language include as much of the "natural world" in the training as possible.

The Kent Program

The Language Acquisition Program (Kent, 1974) was developed for institutionalized, severely retarded, nonverbal children from 5 to 20 years old. The 1974 edition evolved after 8 years of work by the author and her colleagues. It is one of the few programs reviewed that targets students who completely lack speech. Language instruction is conducted in a much more structured manner and relies heavily on the use of operant principles. The author stresses the importance of one-to-one instruction throughout, but does suggest that two students could receive training during a single session. Such simultaneous training, however, would only be considered for use with children under good instructional control.

Training is divided into three general stages: Pre-Verbal, Verbal-Receptive, and Verbal Expressive. The Pre-Verbal section teaches attending skills and specific motor imitations that are considered to be prerequisites for performance in later phases of the program. The child is taught to sit in a chair, stereotypic or interfering behaviors (such as rocking, climbing, or gazing) are eliminated using overcorrection procedures, and the child is then taught to look at objects and at the trainer's face in response to commands such as "Look at this" or "Look at me." The final phase in this section teaches specific motor imitations in response to the instruction and model "Do this." The training sequence, definitions of each behavior, and the criterion for advancing from phase to phase are clearly presented. Children are regularly tested throughout training to ensure that they maintain skills that have been previously trained and to guide the trainer in deciding what phases need to be trained next.

The entire second section of the program concentrates on developing a fairly comprehensive, albeit somewhat arbitrary, receptive language repertoire. Initially, the motor responses that were taught imitatively during the previous stage are brought under instructional control. In a successive manner the child gradually learns (via a pointing response or an action) body parts, simple objects, and compliance with simple instructions such as "Sit down." This basic receptive vocabulary is expanded throughout the remaining phases in this stage until the child is able to understand and comply with such instructions as "Make a circle" (with a magic marker), "Make a tower" (with blocks), and so on.

The first phase in the Verbal-Expressive section reverts back to verbal imitation. The early emphasis is devoted to building a generalized verbal repertoire through the use of standard reinforcement and shaping techniques. Once the child has learned to reproduce single-word utterances imitatively, control is then switched to instructions such as "What is this?" or "What is in the box?" The training rationale in this section follows the same "expansion" paradigm used in the previous section but in the verbal mode.

The Guess, Sailor, and Baer Program

Functional Speech and Language Training for the Severely Handicapped (Guess, Sailor, & Baer, 1976a, 1976b, 1977b, 1978b) includes a 60-step training sequence based primarily on a learning theory approach to speech and language development. Several conceptual modifications in the program have been published at various times (Guess, Sailor, & Baer, 1974; Sailor, Guess & Baer, 1973), and performance data from students in the program have also been presented (Firling, 1976; Guess, Sailor, & Baer, 1977a; 1978a; Guess, Sailor, Keogh, & Baer, 1976).

The entire training program has been published in a four-part series: *Part 1: Persons and Things* includes the first nine steps of the program (Guess, Sailor, & Baer, 1976a); *Part 2: Actions with Persons and Things* contains steps 10–29 (Guess, Sailor, & Baer, 1976b); *Part 3: Possession and Color* encompasses steps 30–42 (Guess, Sailor, & Baer, 1977b) and *Part 4: Size, Relation, and Location,* includes steps 43–60 (Guess, Sailor, & Baer, 1978b).

Initial sequencing of the program steps was based on the literature on normal speech and language acquisition. Revisions in that sequence, however, have been based on data collected from severely handicapped persons trained with the program.

The Functional Speech and Language Training for the Severely Handicapped program emphasizes the importance of rapidly bringing children into contact with "communication" as an effective means of controlling the environment. This implies that the speech taught to the child must be *functional* Accordingly, many of the skills taught in the program produce consequences that are naturally reinforcing to the child, thereby reducing the reliance on "artificial" reinforcers as the child progresses through the sequence. Functionality is also used to imply that speech training must be engineered in a way that will allow the children to expand their own repertoires. This might be done, for example, by teaching the children to ask "What's that?" when confronted by a significant environmental event for which they have no label. With function as an overriding principle, the basic framework of the program has been organized along the following five dimensions: reference, control, self-extended control, integration, and reception.

Reference assumes that a fundamental function of language is to symbolize: to learn that certain sounds (words) represent objects and events. Throughout the training program, reference is used in varied contexts, including the basic skill of labeling objects, the description of actions, the designation of ownership (*my, your*), the attribution of color, and the description of relational properties between objects (size, position, location).

The *control* dimension introduces the student to the power of language by teaching various forms of requesting behavior, such as "I want (object or action)," "I want (action-with-object)," and "I want you to (action-with-object)." The primary intent of including the request forms is to emphasize to students the importance of language in managing their environment and to give them the skills necessary to initiate speech in relation to specific needs.

The *self-extended control* dimension, in reality a problem-solving technique, is designed to teach children to request specific information based upon their own determination of what they do not know from that which they already know. This is developed by teaching children to ask questions such as "What is that?" in response to unknown objects, "What are you doing?" in response to unknown actions, "Whose (object)?" when determining ownership, "What size?" to inquire about the largeness or smallness of objects, "What color?" when confronted with novel color stimuli, and "Where is (object/location)?" to establish or identify the relationship between objects or the locations of either objects or persons.

The *integration* dimension builds directly upon self-extended control and attempts to teach children to determine when to seek appropriate information by asking questions and when to respond with appropriate referents when information is already within their existing language repertoire. A second function of the integration dimension is "dialogue" that conceptually requires the students to chain together all or some of the previously learned skills so that they can carry on a simple, but appropriate, conversation centered around a functional activity or theme.

Corresponding to objectives in productive speech, the program also trains concepts in the *receptive* dimension to round out the students' ability to speak and understand. Many receptive skills are taught using a "yes/no" response from the student to indicate comprehension of the concepts. The Guess-Sailor-Baer program differs from previous programs in that a productive skill is taught before the corresponding receptive skill. For example, students are trained to label objects before they are taught to receptively identify these same objects. The teaching of productive skills in the program, following by receptive training (if necessary) of the same skill, is not intended to minimize the importance of receptive training, but is intended to emphasize the purpose of bringing the student rapidly into the speaking community, as contrasted to the nonspeaking but instruction-following community.

A basic criterion for entry into the program is competence as a generalized verbal imitator. The program is designed for use by teachers, language trainers, and parents who have a basic understanding of operant techniques. The program also includes specific instructions in each step for procedures to foster the generalization of acquired skills to other persons and other settings.

NONSPEECH COMMUNICATION SYSTEMS

The Carrier and Peak Program

The Non-SLIP (Non-speech Language Initiation Program) curriculum, designed by Carrier and Peak (1975), is a nonspeech communication system developed specifically for severely and profoundly retarded persons. The authors point out that most language intervention programs in use have failed with this segment of the language deficient population ". . . because most attempts to teach low level retardates have been based on programs or training procedures developed primarily for higher functioning children" (Carrier & Peak, 1975, p. 4).

A major impetus for the development of Non-SLIP came from nonhuman primate research in which various nonspeech symbol systems were used to study communication. Instead of teaching within the speech mode, students in Non-SLIP are taught to manipulate abstract-shaped symbols that represent articles, nouns, verbs, and prepositions. The teaching method employs operant conditioning principles, particularly reinforcement techniques, to shape criterion behavior.

Before grammatical strings are taught, a series of prerequisite skills must be mastered. The student must be able to pick up plastic symbols and place them on a wooden tray. Then, via a match-to-sample paradigm, the student must be taught to discriminate among various symbol shapes, pictures and objects, pictures and their plastic abstract-shaped symbol representations, five colors, and stripes that run across a corner of the symbols. It is apparent to those who have had experience in working with severely and profoundly retarded children that the prerequisite skills required by Non-SLIP are challenging. In fact, more time may be spent teaching the student the Non-SLIP prerequisites than the communication phase of the program.

Like most programs, Non-SLIP is intended to teach only those behaviors judged to be necessary for an individual to perform the basic functions of communication. Once the prerequisite matching skills have been learned, students are taught to string together in sequence seven symbols by placing them on a wooden tray. The seven-component sequence consists of an ARTICLE + NOUN + VERB AUXILIARY + VERB + PREPOSITION + ARTICLE + NOUN. Once this sequence has been mastered, the student is taught that each of the slots in the seven-component string represents specific "symbol classes." For example, the second slot is filled by selecting a plastic symbol from the symbol class "nouns," the fourth slot is for "verbs," and so on. The color and stripe discriminations mastered during prerequisite training serve to distinguish the first appearing nouns and articles from those appearing later in the sequence, thus teaching the child to sequence the symbols "grammatically."

The first phase of Non-SLIP that requires the student to make a conceptual, or abstract, association is the labeling phase. Since the student already has been taught to match symbols with symbols and pictures with pictures, this phase attempts to teach a symbol-to-picture match. That is, the student is shown a picture of a boy, girl, man, lady, baby, dog, cat, cow, or bird, and is required to "label" the picture by selecting the symbol that identifies the particular picture. Other grammatical classes are taught in a similar manner until the student has learned the rudimentary communication system.

Manual Signs and Gestures

Often referred to as manual communication, the nonspeech system of signing is generally characterized by the use of hand and body signs and gestures to convey a message. A number of signing systems are available. Two of the more extensively used signing systems are American Sign Language and Signing Exact English.

American Sign Language (ASL or Ameslan) is descended from the French Sign Language and the Spanish Manual Alphabet and has been the prevalent system among deaf adults in the United States. ASL contains a set of rules that are used to form an infinite number of sentences. The syntactic rules used in ASL are quite different from the English language (e.g., there is no sign for the verb *to be*). Wilbur (1976) has pointed out that ". . . ASL does in fact function as a complete language and fully meets the communicative needs of the deaf among themselves as a linguistic and sociologic community (p. 433)." The fact that the vocabulary, syntax, and morphology of ASL are not congruent with the English language has prompted some to minimize its importance as a viable communication system with the severely handicapped (Hollis & Carrier, 1978; Kopchick & Lloyd, 1976). Accordingly, Signing Exact English is often recommended as a more appropriate manual system for the severely handicapped person.

Signing Exact English, developed by Gustason, Pfetzing, and Zawolkow (1972) includes 2,100 words, 70 affixes, and 7 contractions. The words are divided into basic, complex, and compound words. The same sign is used for two English words if those two words are alike in two or three features (pronunciation, spelling, or meaning). Signing Exact English is word based, in contrast to ASL which is idea or concept based (Hollis & Carrier, 1978). The rationale for Signing Exact English is that the child will use actual English semantics and syntax; thus, his or her language abilities should be more comparable to those of hearing peers.

Surveys of teachers using manual systems with special populations (Fristoe & Lloyd, 1978; Goodman, Wilson, & Bornstein, 1978) indicate a fairly wide-spread confusion among respondents concerning exactly what signing system is being taught. Results from these surveys indicate that many individuals who reported using ASL were actually using signs from ASL in English word order. Regardless of this confusion, manual signing may offer some distinct advantages as a communication mode for some severely handicapped persons. Wilbur (1976) points to visual visibility as an advantage since the learner is able to see the shape of the model's hands and his and her own hands. The fact that signs take advantage of the visual-perceptual system is an important advantage for those individuals who have impairments to the auditory system. Hollis and Carrier (1978) point out, however, that children with neuromuscular involvement of the arms, hands, and fingers—especially cerebral palsied children—may have great difficulty in producing manual signs. Another disadvantage of signed communication is the restricted audience with which the user can communicate. This may pose a special disadvantage in attempts to integrate severely handicapped persons into normal community settings. For this, and other reasons, signing in combination with oral speech ("total communication") has gained wide-spread interest and application as an intervention strategy.

Simultaneous Communication

In a chapter describing a "total communication" approach, Kopchick and Lloyd (1976) state:

> In dealing with the severely language impaired, the oral/aural stimuli (words) and motor/visual stimuli (signs) must always be presented together. Anything less than this truly simultaneous communication can cause confusion and impair effectiveness, resulting in failure to achieve maximal benefit offered by a total communication approach (p. 504).

Certainly one of the most important benefits alluded to by Kopchick and Lloyd (1976) is the prospect that signing, coupled with oral speech training, may serve to enhance the acquisition of speech among severely handicapped individuals. An additional desired result is the development of a communication system through signing even if oral speech fails to emerge. Kopchick and Lloyd (1976) identified as prime candidates for "total communication" those individuals who are nonverbal, noncommunicative, unintelligible, and nonresponsive to oral modification or those individuals who have demonstrated high level receptive skills but very limited expressive skills. They also suggest that "a rule of thumb that is often used for selecting clients for a total communication program is simply the failure to imitate speech" (p. 510).

While a "total communication" approach has great appeal and may be a potentially valuable intervention strategy for nonspeaking severely handicapped individuals, decisions to implement this approach should nevertheless be made with some caution. At present, there are virtually no unequivocal data that establish that "total communication" does, indeed, enhance the development of speech.

At a more theoretical level, there are arguments that "total communication" should logically enhance communication and especially oral speech development. There are also related data that might contraindicate a "total communication" approach for at least some children. Use of "total communication" is theoretically supported by those studies that have provided empirical evidence in support of response class development. Basically, response classes are those behaviors that, by reason of either *functional* or *topographical* similarity, can be manipulated so that intervention efforts directed at a selected exemplar of a response class affect other members of that class even in the absence of direct training. Thus, systematic increases or decreases in target members for instances of a response class may be expected to generalize appropriately to other members of the class that were not the targets of direct intervention. Potentially, "total communication" would lead to the development of the response class since both the oral and manual symbols are functionally related. For example, the word *ball* has the same meaning as the manual sign BALL that is simultaneously presented by the sender or receiver of the message. In essence then, either the manual or oral sign system might be expected to enhance the use of the other within the logic of response class development.

Conversely, a similar position can be used to argue against the effectiveness of "total communication." Koegel, Egel, and Dunlap (this volume) discuss stimulus overselectivity as a learning characteristic of severely handicapped and young nonhandicapped children. Stimulus overselectivity, particularly characteristic of children labeled autistic, refers to the tendency to respond to only one component of a complex stimulus array. Imitation training with autistic children, for example, has shown that these children might respond to only one component of a complex stimulus array.

There is obviously a need for studies that carefully and systematically measure the facilitating effect of a "total communication" program over time with populations of severely handicapped, nonspeaking individuals. Still other investigations are needed to delineate the parameters that might predict the failure or success of this approach.

Communication Aids and Techniques

For some children with severe motor impairments, neither verbal speech nor signing may provide an appropriate response mode, and still other techniques and aids may be necessary to augment the communication process. One class of aid, generally referred to as "communication boards," encompasses prostheses ranging from fairly simple lap boards constructed by a classroom teacher to sophisticated electronic devices that enable the child to produce printed forms of an intended message. Activation of communication can be accomplished through a variety of responses ranging from eye gaze or pointing with the hand and fingers, to pointing with a head stylus, to activating mechanical switches and levers. Undeniably, the technology for communcation aids and techniques is expanding rapidly in the attempt to provide appropriate communication and interaction systems for individuals who might otherwise not have the physical capabilities for expressive communication. However, it is important that these techniques be conceptualized as supplemental systems rather than as means to replace the existing communication systems of the child (Vanderheiden & Harris-Vanderheiden, 1976).

Prerequisite Skills for Communication Aids McDonald (1976) has pointed out that attention to visual stimuli and verbal symbols is a basic prerequisite for children who are to be trained on communication boards. This includes both the ability to identify common objects receptively and the ability to match objects with some type of representation, whether it be pictures, words, drawings, or three-dimensional symbols.

In preparing a child for eventual training on communication boards, the classroom teacher might choose to start with teaching basic visual, tactile, and/or auditory attending skills. Establishment of visual and auditory skills (especially attending to verbal speech) might then extend to object discrimination training using the actual objects or models of the objects. Object identification would then be followed by match-to-sample training where the child is required to match the object to a visual representation of it.

McDonald also emphasizes the need or desire to communicate as an important entry skill for use with communication boards. Harris-Vanderheiden and Vanderheiden (1976) have stressed the importance of teaching children that through communication (e.g., body movement, gestures, pointing) they can control and affect their environments. The controlling aspect of communication for nonverbal children has also been stressed by Guess, Sailor, and Baer (1978a). One of the major points discussed by these authors for teaching speech to nonverbal children is to provide them with the skills to control other significant persons in their environments, emphasizing both the power and utility of language. Guess et al. (1976a) also have pointed out the need for teaching the controlling functions of language at a very early stage in the child's intervention program. Sailor et al. (this volume) present a detailed discussion of basic considerations in the development of communication programs for nonverbal severely handicapped children.

Language Content for Nonspeech Communication Systems

As discussed earlier, it is critical to make the distinction between language and the response mode used to convey that language. This distinction is most important when considering nonspeech communication systems involving either signing or communication boards. Once the appropriate response mode has been selected for a particular child, the problem of exactly what language content to teach the child remains. Unfortunately there are few recommendations, guidelines, or procedures for selecting the language content to be taught to the nonspeech child using an augmented communication mode.

Data from a study by Schlesinger (1972) have indicated that the acquisition of sign language among deaf children parallels the basic milestones of spoken language. A sign language program for severely handicapped persons described by Stremel-Campbell, Cantrell, and Halle (1976) was based on early two-word syntactic constructions normally used to express semantic relations. Additionally, functional and motivating objects were included in the vocabulary that was taught. While there is certainly the temptation to use the structure of normally developing language as the basis for teaching nonspeech modes, there are indications that severely handicapped, language-delayed children do not follow the same sequence of language development observed in nonhandicapped children (Guess, Sailor, Keogh, Baer, 1976).

Hamre-Nietupski, Stoll, Holtz, Fullerton, Ryan-Flottum, and Brown (Note 4) have described seven strategies for determining the initial communicative content appropriate for individuals being taught to sign. Several of these strategies would also be appropriate in selecting language content for communication boards.

A first strategy recommends that training content be based on student preferences for objects, actions, places, and people in the school, home, and other community environments. Vocabulary selection should also consider how frequently the words occur in natural settings. Within practical limits, the teacher should include words in the curriculum that occur frequently in the student's daily life. A third strategy recommends that initial communicative content should be sequenced in a manner similar to normal development to represent recurrence (e.g., "more"), cessation (e.g., "stop"), nonexistence (e.g., "all gone"), and existence (e.g., "this," object labels).

An initial selection of signs that physically approximate the actual actions or the shape of the referent objects may facilitate language learning. In the BALL sign, for example, the hands are cupped as if the persons were actually holding a ball. General learning and programming principles would suggest that signs should be rearranged along a continuum from easy to hard, based upon the complexity of the motor skills required to form the sign. Hamre-Nietupski et al. (Note 4) point out that for some students signs that involve the use of the fingers may be quite difficult or signs involving two hands performing different actions may be especially hard for some students. Touch signs, those that involve one hand touching the other or touching other parts of the body, may be more easily acquired than non-touch signs since touch signs involve tactile feedback while non-touch signs do not. The recommendation to use touch signs to accelerate learning is supported by Stremel-Campbell et al. (1976). A final strategy offered by Hamre-Nietupski et al. recommends using signs that are topographically dissimilar for determining initial communicative content. Topographically dissimilar signs refer to those signs whose physical configurations do not closely approximate the physical configuration of other signs. Signs that are topographically dissimilar may be easier for the student to discriminate visually and produce.

Adaptations of Existing Language Development Programs

There has been some effort to adapt speech and language curricula for severely handicapped children to nonspeech modes. The Language Acquisition Program (Kent, 1974) has been adapted for a signing approach for use with retarded persons with significant hearing impairments. More recent efforts have been made to adapt the Functional Speech and Language Training for the Severely Handicapped program by Guess, Sailor, and Baer (1976a) to both signing (Waldo, Hirsch, & Marshall, Note 5) and communication boards (Waldo, Hirsch, & Marshall, Note 6). Adaptation of the speech version of the Guess-Sailor-Baer program (1967a, 1976b, 1977b, 1978b) to signing in Signing Exact English has produced relatively few problems. Essentially, signing is used in following the 60-step sequence outlined in the oral version of the program. Figure 1, for example, shows the signs used in step 8 of the Guess, Sailor, and Baer (1976a) program. In this example, the teacher asks, "What want?" and the student replies, "I want candy." Other items are, of course, included for the student to request via signs in this particular step of the program. For each step in the training program, the teacher presents the language stimuli first with speech and signs, then with signs alone, and finally with speech alone. Each stimulus mode is trained to criterion separately. Students are expected to respond using both signs and speech (as much as possible). A scoring system allows the teacher to record each response mode both alone and in combination, using a "total communication" approach.

Attempts to adapt the Guess, Sailor, and Baer program (1976a) to a communication board response mode have presented some procedural problems, especially with those steps involving question asked by the student (Guess et al., 1976a). A scoring system worked out for adapting the program to communication boards (Waldo et al., Note 5) allows each response to be scored as a pointing response, speech, or the combination of pointing and speech. Thus, like the signing adaptation, a "total communication" approach is used. Encouraging related data for the adapted programs using communication boards have been reported in Waldo et al. (Note 5) and Guess et al. (1976a).

THE PROBLEM OF GENERALIZATION

The problem of generalization is central to communication intervention efforts with severely handicapped individuals and is equally basic for both speech and nonspeech response modes. Guess, Keogh, and Sailor (1978) have pointed out that "It appears to be easier to *establish* a rudimentary language repertoire in language deficient children than it is to teach the spontaneous use of the skills in nontraining situations" (p. 375). This underscores a common dilemma encountered by the classroom teacher, the speech-language therapist, or others who are providing instruction in communication skills to a severely handicapped population. Simply stated, severely handicapped individuals have difficulty in displaying their newly taught skills in settings different from that found in training, to persons different from the original trainer, and with materials and/or setting events that vary from those present during training.

There are two basic major types of generalization that need to be considered in communication-training efforts. The phenomenon of *stimulus generalization* occurs when language skills are used in an array of stimulus conditions that differ

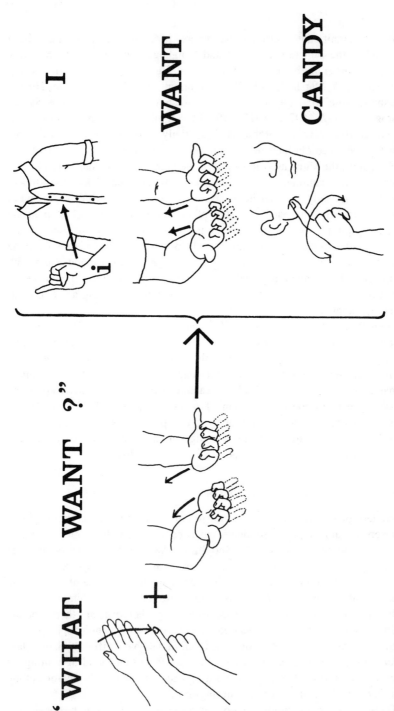

Figure 1. Example showing the use of signing in Signing Exact English with step 8 of the Guess, Sailor, and Baer (1976a) Functional Speech and Language Training for the Severely Handicapped program, as adapted by Waldo, Hirsch, and Marshall (Note 5).

from those present during training. The phenomenon of *response generalization* is observed to occur when language behaviors that are topographically similar to those trained are used in the same or similar settings.

> Traditionally, many theorists have considered generalization to be a *passive* phenomenon. Generalization was not seen as an operant response that could be programmed, but as a description of a "natural" outcome of any behavior change process. That is, a teaching operation repeated over time and trials inevitably involves varying samples of stimuli, rather than the same set every time; in the same way it inevitably evokes and reinforces varying samples of behavior, rather than the same set every time (Stokes & Baer, 1977, p. 349).

Harris (1975) provided a cogent review of literature on speech intervention efforts with nonverbal children using operant techniques and focused on the generalization of various skills developed in language-training programs (e.g., attention training, verbal imitation, functional speech, and receptive language). She found that, in all the studies to date, generalization of responses either failed to occur or was neither programmed to occur nor measured where it might have occurred. Harris speculated from her review that 1) generalization may occur by utilizing more than one person to train students from the outset (see Garcia, 1974), and 2) one of the important factors in facilitating generalization should be repeated training in a wide number of settings and training in the natural environment rather than in the classroom.

Guess, Keogh, and Sailor (1978) support the conclusions of Harris and describe a sociological analysis of the factors that might affect the generalization of communication skills:

> Investigations into the myriad of socioecological variables affecting speech and language must be done to produce a complete technology for producing generalization. The extent to which a child generalizes is as much a function of the socioecological environment in which the child resides as it is of the child's language abilities. Generalization is thus perceived as an interaction that is changing continually as the level of language competency in the child and the loci of environmental variables, which enhance, maintain, or decrease language usage, change (p. 392).

The type of socioecological approach advocated by Guess, Keogh, and Sailor (1978) includes specific recommendations for training generalization among severely handicapped individuals. Additionally, Stokes and Baer (1977) reviewed over 200 articles that pertain to various techniques for producing generalization. Table 1 presents a classification of these techniques according to training procedures and environmental factors that facilitate generalization (Rogers-Warren, Note 7). This latter category is subdivided into person and physical variables.

Training Procedures That Facilitate Generalization

The variety of techniques included under this category generally relate to manipulations of materials, persons, procedures, and settings within training sessions

Table 1. Techniques for producing generalization

Training procedures that facilitate generalization	Environmental factors that facilitate generalization

1. Multiple trainers
2. Sufficient exemplars
3. Varied settings
4. Appropriateness of content
5. Sufficient duration
6. Schedule of reinforcement
	A. Person variables
	  1. Prompts for language
	  2. Reinforcers for language (natural and programmed)
	  3. Models for language
	  4. Person availability
	    a. Ratio adult/child
	    b. Communication skills of persons (peers)
	    c. Rate/content of interactions
	B. Physical variables
	  1. Common stimuli
	  2. Arrangements that facilitate verbal/social interaction

in order to produce better generalization during nontraining periods of the day. These techniques emphasize things done to the student in order to produce greater generalization in contrast to efforts to manipulate environmental variables to achieve the same outcome. Certainly, however, there is considerable overlap between these major approaches.

1. Multiple Trainers This training technique implies that generalization can be enhanced by using a number of different trainers, each of whom is presumably using the same or similar procedures in teaching identified communication skills. Thus, for example, a speech-language therapist, classroom teacher, and parent might all be teaching the same skill to the student at the same time in order to increase the probability that the use of the skill will be generalized to other persons not directly involved in the training program.

2. Sufficient Exemplars According to the review by Stokes and Baer (1977), this is one of the most advanced and widely used techniques of the current technology for teaching generalization. With this technique, the number of exemplars specifically taught is increased until generalization to new stimuli, responses, or settings does occur. Teaching sufficient exemplars was demonstrated in a study by Baer and Guess (1973). Four mentally retarded students were taught to expand verb actions into nouns by applying the -er suffix. Each student was shown a picture of an action while the trainer provided the label, e.g., "This man bakes." The student was then required to complete the final word of a stimulus phrase that involved the correct suffix ending. For example, the trainer would say, "He is a _____?" and the student was required to provide the correct word (e.g., "baker"). Results showed that the students were eventually able to provide the correct -*er* suffix to new and previously untained verbs. Similar studies showing the use of the sufficient exemplar technique to teach generalized responses have been reported for verb tenses (Schumaker & Sherman, 1970), plurals (Guess, Sailor, Rutherford, & Baer, 1968; Sailor, 1971), adjective inflections (Baer & Guess, 1973), subject-verb agreement (Lutzker & Sherman, 1974), and verb inflections (Clark & Sherman, 1975).

3. Varied Settings Teaching the same or a similar skill across a variety of different environments is another basic technique for producing generalization. Garcia (1974), for example, produced generalized conversational skills among two severely handicapped children by systematically training across different settings *and* with a different trainer in each setting.

Training in varied settings is obviously a recommended technique that contrasts with the more traditional therapy model where students are taught communication skills only in the separate "therapy room."

4. Appropriateness of Content It seems obvious that training should focus on those content areas that have the most meaning and function for students in their daily interaction with the environment. Guess, Keogh, and Sailor (1978) have pointed out that generalization is a function of environmental opportunities for expression. This implies that *what* is taught to the child is just as important as the specific procedures that are used in training. Specific communication skills trained should consider variables such as the frequency of opportunity for use of these skills in the natural environment, the age-appropriateness of the content, and the extent to which the skills are likely to be maintained through other programmed or natural contingencies in the environment.

5. Sufficient Duration Generalized use of a communication skill is more likely to occur when the skill has been taught to a stringent criterion. The problem with this technique is determining exactly what criteria can be used to judge the sufficiency of training. Language trainers are familiar with children whose performance declines over time during training. Usually, attempts are made to revive the student's performance level by introducing new reinforcers. Thus, while sufficient duration appears valuable as a technique, consideration must be balanced with the possibility that the student may become "burned out" on the task.

6. Schedule of Reinforcement Stokes and Baer (1977) refer to "indiscriminable contingencies" as a potential tactic for producing generalization. This indicates the need to program training conditions in order to prevent extinction of learned responses, while at the same time arranging a reinforcement schedule that makes it difficult for the student to discriminate among specific instances of "reinforceable" stimuli. An issue is whether or not the tactic of delayed reinforcement can contribute to generalization of a communication response by making the times, places, and other cues in which a reinforcement contingency actually operates less discriminable to the student during training efforts. Thus, not knowing that reinforcement occurs only in setting 1, the student may respond to similar stimuli in settings 2, 3, and so on.

Environmental Factors That Facilitate Generalization

The tactics and techniques discussed in this section focus on those variables (person and physical) that can be manipulated in various settings in order to increase generalized use of communication skills. These techniques thus include the manipulation of numerous sociological and ecological variables in those environments where generalized use of communication skills is desired.

Hart and Rogers-Warren (1978) point to two types of environments (training and talking) that are involved in the acquisition and generalization of communication skills. The *training* environment is often used to provide one-to-one instruction for language deficient children. In this environment, specific procedures are programmed for both the child and trainer in order to teach specific language skills. The previous section has discussed some of the tactics and techniques used to produce generalization during these one-to-one training sessions. The *talking* environment, as discussed by Hart and Rogers-Warren (1978), provides the child with the opportunity to express learned communication skills. Basically, the goal in the talking environment is the functional use of language. The talking environment usually involves a variety of persons, a multiplicity of stimuli, and numerous opportunities for the child to communicate in a functional manner. The authors point out, however, that

> Although a child may learn a great deal of language in a one-to-one training environment, the new language may not be used as a communication tool beyond the training setting. Thus, the child may not communicate much better than before training. Transfer and generalization of newly learned skills may be slow, either because the language repertoire has little reference to the child's talking environment or because the talking environment has not been programmed to provide the appropriate stimulus events (p. 198).

Hart and Rogers-Warren (1978) have consequently proposed a milieu teaching model that integrates and incorporates important features in both the training and talking environments. The milieu teaching model outlined below relies on the communication that occurs in everyday settings and incorporates the persons, events, objects, and contingencies typically present in the setting into the teaching program (Table 1).

A. Person Variables The techniques included in this category all involve attempts by persons in the child's environments to appropriately set the occasions for the use of communication skills.

1. Prompts for Language This category includes a number of techniques that can be used by other persons to enhance language use and generalization among children. Requiring children to ask for things, providing situations requiring children to ask questions, and placing children in situations where they are likely to make comments about ongoing activities are some examples of this training technique. This type of generalization tactic has been referred to as "incidental teaching" (Hart & Risley, 1975) and is based on a process of teaching functional language through environmental arrangement (both through the verbal behavior of attending adults and through the physical arrangements of the environment).

2. *Reinforcers for Language* Providing appropriate positive reinforcers for language behavior in the natural environment is an obvious but frequently neglected factor for generalization. Hart and Rogers-Warren (1978) point out that providing materials and adult attention or reinforcers is a critical factor in milieu teaching. It should be added that the extent to which persons do, indeed, provide reinforcers in the natural environment must not be left to chance. As a tactic for producing generalization, specific training should be provided to persons on how and when to reinforce the child's language behavior. This is especially critical in institutional settings where often impoverished physical environments interact with poorly trained adult staff to produce a climate where language use is punished or virtually becomes extinct.

3. *Models for Language* The use of modeling as a training tactic has experienced wide application in language remediation programs. For example, the majority of language-training programs discussed in the second section of this chapter incorporate some form of adult- or peer-modeling techniques. Modeling can also be an effective training tactic in producing generalization in the natural environment. Procedurally, adults (or other peers) model the language expected of the child. The modeled language may be in part, or totally, a previously learned response by the child. The child is expected to produce the modeled language response in the environment, and under more naturally occurring conditions. Lahey (1971) demonstrated that adult modeling was sufficient to increase the use of both color and size adjectives among a population of environmentally deprived young children. Adjectival use increased through the modeling procedure even though no reinforcers were made contingent on the use of these adjectives when describing common objects.

4. *Person Availability* This factor includes variables such as the adult to child ratio in the environment, the communication skills of both the adults and the peers in the child's environment, and, importantly, the rate and content of the communication interactions. All of these variables are somewhat interrelated and critical to the child's opportunity for expression through some form of communication. Certainly the adult to child ratio in the child's language environment is a central factor in both the rate and content of the communication interactions that are available to the child. If nothing else, the ratio of adults to children is important in the extent to which structured, language-oriented opportunities can occur. Warren, Rogers-Warren, Stremel-Campbell, Longhurst, and McQuarter (Note 7) have systematically measured and analyzed the effects of structured versus nonstructured environments on the verbal behavior of both attending adults and children with severe language delay. Results suggest that structured environments are critical to eliciting and supporting verbal behavior among language-delayed children. When measures of teacher questions, instructions, demands, models, and praise, and child obligatory responses, commentary, and

instruction were compared across free time and academic situations (unstructured vs. structured), much greater rates of all categories of adult and child behavior were observed in the structured environments. The more severely delayed the children were, the greater the quantitative differences in their behavior from structured to unstructured settings. Significantly, children tended to display higher rates of trained language generalization in the structured environment, a finding that further supports the therapeutic benefits afforded by these settings.

B.   Physical Variables   The manipulation of physical variables to produce generalization of language skills can be related to the selection of materials used in the environment, the actual arrangement of furniture and other types of equipment where language behavior is desired, or the architectural design of the teaching setting.

1.   Common Stimuli   This tactic for producing generalization has been described in a small number of studies included in the review by Stokes and Baer (1977). It assumes that generalization is more likely to occur if there are sufficient features common to both training and generalization settings. Rincover and Koegel (1975) have reported a study that exemplifies this training technique. In this study, 10 autistic children were trained to perform one of three target behaviors in a treatment room setting. Six of the 10 children demonstrated generalization of the learned target behavior to another person in another setting outside the building. Four children, however, showed no initial transfer to the generalization setting, but transfer was observed when initial training stimuli were introduced into the generalization setting. These stimuli were almost incidental to the teaching instructions, such as subtle hand prompts and the presence of the table and chair used in the treatment room. The Rincover and Koegel study (1975) indicated that at least some autistic children may require an almost exact duplication of training stimuli in other settings if generalization is to occur. It is not likely that all severely handicapped children will require such an exact duplication of common stimuli in both training and generalization settings. Nevertheless, it is likely that at least the same general class of stimuli should be available in both training and generalization settings in order to enhance the transfer of learned behaviors. Certainly, this is a generalization training tactic that can be easily implemented.

2.   Arrangements That Facilitate Verbal/Social Interaction   There are existing studies that have reported on arrangements in the physical environment that either enhance or impede the generalization of language. Studies by Hart and Risley (1968, 1975) with disadvantaged preschool children have shown that access to materials as part of incidental teaching procedures can be used effectively to increase the use of nouns and descriptive adjectives. Hart and Rogers-Warren (1978), for example, have recommended placing desired objects on shelves in order to increase requesting behavior among language deficient children. This and similar recommendations by Hart and Rogers-Warren (1978) provide guidelines for the arrangement of classroom materials to both teach new language skills and increase the generalized use of existing skills. Warren et al.

(this volume) present the status and implications of current research data on the issue of generalization.

SUMMARY

This chapter has provided an overview of some basic considerations in communication training for severely handicapped students. The fact that there is now considerable information available to the classroom teacher is both significant and encouraging. It is significant because much of the information is relatively new. It is encouraging because teachers now have available to them training programs and techniques that are appropriate to severely handicapped children. One can only hope that the momentum can be continued in the years to come. Obviously, more research is needed in the practical application of communication-training programs in classroom settings. We still need to know what programs and response modes are best for different severely handicapped students who vary so much in their learning, motor, and sensory characteristics. We still need to know how all the bits and pieces of information fit together. And, inevitably, we will need additional information for the new questions that arise as we try to further advance our knowledge in communicative training for severely handicapped persons.

REFERENCES

Baer, D., & Guess, D. Teaching productive noun suffixes to severely retarded children. *American Journal of Mental Deficiency,* 1973, 77, 498-505.

Banikotes, F., & Montgomery, A. Male and female auditory reinforcement of infant vocalization. *Developmental Psychology,* 1972, 6, 476-481.

Bloom, L. Why not a pivot grammar? *Journal of Speech and Hearing Disorders,* 1971, 36, 40-50.

Bloom, L. Talking, understanding, and thinking. In R. L. Schiefelbusch & L. L. Lloyd (eds.), *Language perspectives—Acquisition, retardation, and intervention.* Baltimore: University Park Press, 1974.

Bricker, D., Dennison, L., & Bricker, W. Constructive interaction-adaptation approach to language training. *MCCD Monograph Series, No. 1.* Mailman Center for Child Development, University of Miami, 1975.

Bruner, J., Goodnow, J., & Austin, G. *A study of thinking.* New York: John Wiley & Sons, 1965.

Butterfield, E., & Cairns, G. Discussion summary—Infant reception research. In R. L. Schiefelbusch & L. L. Lloyd (eds.), *Language perspectives—Acquisition, retardation, and intervention.* Baltimore: University Park Press, 1974.

Butterworth, G., & Costillo, M. Coordination of auditory and visual space in newborn human infants. *Perception,* 1976, 5, 155-160.

Carrier, J., & Peak, T. *Non-SLIP (Non-speech Language Initiation Program).* Lawrence, Kansas: H & H Enterprises, Inc., 1975.

Clark, H., & Sherman, J. Teaching generative use of sentence answers to three forms of questions. *Journal of Applied Behavior Analysis,* 1975, 8, 321-330.

Eimas, P. D. Linguistic processing of speech by young infants. In R. L. Schiefelbusch & L. L. Lloyd (eds.), *Language perspectives—Acquisition, retardation, and intervention.* Baltimore: University Park Press, 1974.

Firling, J. Functional language for a severely handicapped child: A case study. *AAESPH Review*, 1976, *1*, 53–74.

Flavell, J. *The developmental psychology of Jean Piaget*. Princeton, New Jersey: Van Nostrand, Co., 1963.

Fristoe, M., & Lloyd, L. A survey of the use of non-speech systems with the severely communication imparied. *Mental Retardation*, 1978, *16*, 99–103.

Garcia, E. The training and generalization of conversational speech form in nonverbal retardates. *Journal of Applied Behavior Analysis*, 1974, *7*, 137–149.

Goodman, L., Wilson, P., & Bornstein, H. Results of the national survey of sign language programs in special education. *Mental Retardation*, 1978, *16*, 104–106.

Guess, D., Keogh, W., & Sailor, W. Generalization of speech and language behavior: Measurement and training tactics. In R. L. Schiefelbusch (ed.), *Bases of language intervention*. Baltimore: University Park Press, 1978.

Guess, D., Rutherford, G., & Twichell, A. Speech acquisition in a mute adolescent male: A case study. *New Outlook for the Blind*, 1969, *63*, 8–14.

Guess, D., Sailor, W., & Baer, D. To teach language to retarded children. In R. L. Schiefelbusch & L. L. Lloyd (eds.), *Language perspectives—Acquisition, retardation, and intervention*. Baltimore: University Park Press, 1974.

Guess, D., Sailor, W., & Baer, D. *Functional speech and language training for the severely handicapped. Part 1: Persons and things*. Lawrence, Kansas: H & H Enterprises, 1976. (a)

Guess, D., Sailor, W., & Baer, D. *Functional speech and language training for the severely handicapped. Part 2: Actions with persons and things*. Lawrence, Kansas: H & H Enterprises, 1976. (b)

Guess, D., Sailor, W., & Baer, D. A behavioral remedial approach to language training for the severely handicapped. In E. Sontag (ed.), *Educational programming for the severely handicapped*. Reston, Virginia: A Special Publication of the Division on Mental Retardation, Council for Exceptional Children, 1977. (a)

Guess, D., Sailor, W., & Baer, D. *Functional speech and language training for the severely handicapped. Part 3: Possession and color*. Lawrence, Kansas: H & H Enterprises, Inc., 1977. (b)

Guess, D., Sailor, W., & Baer, D. Children with limited language. In R. L. Schiefelbusch (ed.), *Language intervention strategies*. Baltimore: University Park Press, 1978. (a)

Guess, D., Sailor, W., & Baer, D. *Functional speech and language training for the severely handicapped. Part 4: Size, relation, and location*. Lawrence, Kansas: H & H Enterprises, Inc., 1978. (b)

Guess, D., Sailor, W., Keogh, W., & Baer, D. Language development programs for severely handicapped children. In N. Haring & L. Brown (eds.), *Teaching the severely handicapped* (Vol. I). New York: Grune & Stratton, 1976.

Guess, D., Sailor, W., Rutherford, G., & Baer, D. An experimental analysis of linguistic development: The productive use of the plural morpheme. *Journal of Applied Behavior Analysis*, 1968, *1*, 297–306.

Gustason, G., Pfetzing, D., & Zawolkow, E. *Signing Exact English*. Rossmoor, California: Modern Signs Press, 1972.

Harris, S. Teaching language to nonverbal children with emphasis on problems of generalization. *Psychological Bulletin*, 1975, *82*, 565–580.

Harris-Vanderheiden, D., and Vanderheiden, G. Basic considerations in the development of communicative and interactive skills for non-vocal severely handicapped children. In E. Sontag (ed.), *Educational programming for the severely and profoundly handicapped*. Reston, Virginia: A Special Publication of the Division on Mental Retardation, Council for Exceptional Children, 1976.

Hart, B., & Risley, T. Establishing use of descriptive adjectives in the spontaneous speech of disadvantaged preschool children. *Journal of Applied Behavior Analysis,* 1968, *1,* 109–120.

Hart, B., & Risley, T. Incidental teaching of language in the preschool. *Journal of Applied Behavior Analysis,* 1975, *8,* 411–420.

Hart, B., & Rogers-Warren, A. A milieu approach to teaching language. In R. L. Schiefelbusch (ed.), *Language intervention strategies.* Baltimore: University Park Press, 1978.

Haugan, G., & McIntire, R. Comparisons of vocal imitation, tactile stimulation, and food reinforcers for infant vocalizations. *Developmental Psychology,* 1972, *6,* 201–209.

Hollis, J., & Carrier, J. Intervention strategies for nonspeech children. In R. L. Schiefelbusch (ed.), *Language intervention strategies.* Baltimore: University Park Press, 1978.

Inhelder, B., & Piaget, J. *The early growth of logic in the child.* London: Toutledge and Kegan Paul, 1964.

Kahn, J. Relationship of Piaget's sensorimotor period to language acquisition of profoundly retarded children. *American Journal of Mental Deficiency,* 1975, *79,* 640–643.

Kendler, H., & Kendler, T. Vertical and horizontal processes in problem solving. *Psychological Review,* 1959, *69,* 1–6.

Kent, L. *Language Acquisition Program for the Severely Retarded.* Champaign, Illinois: Research Press, 1974.

Kopchick, G., & Lloyd, L. L. Total communication programming for the severely impaired: A 24-hour approach. In L. L. Lloyd (ed.), *Communication assessment and intervention strategies.* Baltimore: University Park Press, 1976.

Lahey, B. Modification of the frequency of descriptive adjectives in the speech of Head Start children through modeling without reinforcement. *Journal of Applied Behavior Analysis,* 1971, *4,* 19–22.

Lovaas, O. I. A program for the establishment of speech in psychotic children. In J. K. Wing (ed.), *Childhood autism.* Oxford: Pergamon Press, 1966.

Lutzker, J., & Sherman, J. Producing generative sentence usage by imitation and reinforcement procedures. *Journal of Applied Behavior Analysis,* 1974, *7,* 447–460.

McDonald, E. Design and application of communication boards. In G. Vanderheiden & K. Grilley (eds.), *Non-vocal communication techniques and aids for the severely physically handicapped.* Baltimore: University Park Press, 1976.

MacDonald, J., & Horstmeier, D. *Environmental Language Intervention Program.* Columbus, Ohio: Charles E. Merrill Publishing Co., 1978.

McNeil, P. The development of language. In H. Mussen (ed.), *Carmichael's manual of child psychology.* New York: John Wiley & Sons, 1970.

Mills, M., & Melhuish, E. Recognition of mothers voice in early infancy. *Nature,* 1974, *252,* 123–124.

Moerk, E. L. *Pragmatic and semantic aspects of early language development.* Baltimore: University Park Press, 1977.

Ramey, C., & Ourth, L. Delayed reinforcement and vocalization rates of infants. *Child Development,* 1971, *42,* 291–297.

Rees, N. Bases of decision in language training. *Journal of Speech and Hearing Disorders,* 1972, *37,* 293–304.

Rincover, A., & Koegel, R. Setting generality and stimulus control in autistic children. *Journal of Applied Behavior Analysis,* 1975, *8,* 235–246.

Risley, T. The development and maintenance of language: An operant model. In B. Etzel, J. LeBlanc, & D. Baer (eds.), *New developments in behavioral research: Theory, method, and application.* In Honor of Sidney Bijou. Hillsdale, New Jersey: Lawrence Erlbaum Associates, 1977.

224 / GUESS

Sailor, W. Reinforcement and generalization of productive plural allomorphs in two retarded children. *Journal of Applied Behavior Analysis,* 1971, *4,* 305-310.
Sailor, W., Guess, D., & Baer, D. An experimental program for teaching functional language to verbally deficient children. *Mental Retardation,* 1973, *11,* 27-35.
Schiefelbusch, R. L., and Lloyd, L. L. (eds.). *Language perspectives—Acquisition, retardation, and intervention.* Baltimore: University Park Press, 1974.
Schlesinger, I. Production of utterances in language acquisition. In D. Slobin (ed.), *The ontogenesis of grammar.* New York: Academic Press, 1971.
Schlesinger, H. Language acquisition in four deaf children. In H. Schlesinger & K. Meadows (eds.), *Sound and sign.* Berkeley: University of California Press, 1972.
Schumaker, J., & Sherman, J. Training generative verb usage by imitation and reinforcement procedures. *Journal of Applied Behavior Analysis,* 1970, *3,* 273-287.
Siegal, G. Vocal conditioning in infants. *Journal of Speech and Hearing Disorders,* 1969, *34,* 3-19.
Stokes, T., & Baer, D. An implicit technology of generalization. *Journal of Applied Behavior Analysis,* 1977, *10,* 349-267.
Stremel-Campbell, K., Cantrell, D., & Halle, J. Manual signing as a language system and as a speech initiator for the non-verbal severely handicapped student. In E. Sontag (ed.), *Educational programming for the severely and profoundly handicapped.* Reston, Virginia: A Special Publication of the Division on Mental Retardation, Council for Exceptional Children, 1976.
Stremel, K. Language training: A problem for retarded children. *Mental Retardation,* 1972, *10,* 47-49.
Stremel, K., & Waryas, C. A behavioral-psycholinguistic approach to language training. *American Speech and Hearing Monographs,* 1974, *18,* 96-124.
Uzgiris, J., & Hunt, J. McV. *Assessment in infancy: Ordinal scales of psychological development.* Chicago: University of Illinois Press, 1975.
Vanderheiden, G., and Harris-Vanderheiden, D. Communication techniques and aids for the non-vocal severely handicapped. In L. L. Lloyd (ed.), *Communication assessment and intervention strategies.* Baltimore: University Park Press, 1976.
Waryas, C. Language intervention programming as a revolutionary activity. *Human Communication,* 1979, *3,* 71-83.
Wilbur, R. The linguistics of manual language and manual systems. In L. L. Lloyd (ed.), *Communication assessment and intervention strategies.* Baltimore: University Park Press, 1976.

REFERENCE NOTES

1. Mavilya, M. *Spontaneous vocalization and babbling in hearing impaired infants.* Unpublished doctoral dissertation, Columbia University, 1969.
2. Cairns, G., & Butterfield, E. *Assessing language-related skills of prelinguistic children* (Final Report). United States Office of Education School Systems Branch, Bureau of Education for the Handicapped, 1976.
3. Horowitz, F. *Receptive language development in the first year of life.* Kansas Research Institute for the Early Childhood Education of the Handicapped: Reviews of Literature, University of Kansas, Lawrence, 1978.
4. Hamre-Nietupski, S., Stoll, A., Holtz, K., Fullerton, P., Ryan-Flottum, M., & Brown, L. Curricular strategies for teaching selected nonverbal communication skills to nonverbal and verbal severely handicapped students. In L. Brown, J. Nietupski, S. Lyon, S. Hamre-Nietupski, T. Crowner, & L. Gruenewald (eds.), *Curricular strategies for teaching functional object use, nonverbal communcation, problem*

solving, and mealtime skills to severely handicapped students (Vol. VII, Part I). University of Wisconsin, Madison, 1977.

5. Waldo, L., Hirsch, M., & Marshall, A. *Functional sign training for the severely multihandicapped.* Handicapped Media Services and Captioned Films Program, Bureau of Education for the Handicapped (#446AH70146), 1978.

6. Waldo, L., Hirsch, M., & Marshall, A. *Functional communication board training for the severely multihandicapped.* Handicapped Media Services and Captioned Films Program, Bureau of Education for the Handicapped (#446AH70146), 1978.

7. Warren, S., Rogers-Warren, A., Stremel-Campbell, K., Longhurst, T., & McQuarter, R. *An analysis of the effect of structured and unstructured environments on the verbal behavior of adults and language delayed children.* Unpublished manuscript, University of Kansas, Lawrence, 1978.

Chapter 8

Assessment and Facilitation of Language Generalization

Steven F. Warren, Ann Rogers-Warren,
Donald M. Baer, and Doug Guess

How newly learned behavior generalizes to other appropriate settings, persons, and responses is a familiar though unresolved issue in both basic and applied research. Basic research has documented the phenomenon of generalization in children's learning, but descriptions of the process and the variables that control it are incomplete. The successful use of behavior modification techniques to correct behavior problems and to teach new skills in training settings has made generalization of treatment effects a prominent issue in applied research and education. Successful teaching of new behavior is a two-part process. The first step is to establish a target behavior in a training situation; the second is to establish the day-to-day use of the new behavior in all appropriate circumstances. A technology for the first step has been developed and its application demonstrated across many populations. The task that now remains for both researchers and educators is to develop a technology for ensuring that both new skills and behavior changes extend and maintain outside of training.

Nowhere is the study of generalization more important than in language remediation efforts. The purpose of language training is to teach or improve communication skills. To fulfill this purpose, the trained skills must be used outside the training setting, with persons who are not trainers, and must describe objects and events that are physically different from, but conceptually similar to, those described during training sessions. Thus, failure to produce generalized language in communication contexts is failure of language training to meet its most important goal. Very little is known about generalization of skills taught through typical language-training procedures, despite the frequent use of language-training programs in institutions, special remediation programs, and

The work reported in this chapter was supported in part by grant USOE G0076–05086 from the Bureau of Education for the Handicapped and grant HD00870–13 from NICHD.

public schools. If the evidence from other types of behavior change programs is representative, it seems unlikely that language training alone typically produces sufficient generalization to meet the goal of training communicative competence.

Generalization is an important issue for severely retarded students because they typically do not learn sufficient language skills from the natural environment, have limited communication strategies, and have difficulty generalizing newly learned behavior to other settings, persons, and stimuli. Because of their limited language skills, many retarded children will be enrolled in language-training programs, and thus they represent a large portion of the target population for language intervention. While it has been verified that they can indeed learn language skills in either a vocal or manual modality in training contexts, there has been little assessment of the effects of language training on their day-to-day communication skills.

This chapter focuses on issues relevant to language generalization. Included are a discussion of definitions, a selective review and analysis of previous research, a description of a current research program and findings, an overview of generalization assessment and facilitation techniques designed for use by educators, and a discussion of future research and programming issues.

DEFINITIONS

Defining and measuring generalization from language training is itself a complex task. The common definitions of *stimulus generalization* (generalization across persons, settings, objects, or time) and *response generalization* (the display of topographically different responses that are similar in function to the trained responses) provide only a limited beginning. The successful use of communication requires both stimulus and response generalization, usually concurrently. The language-learning child must be able to produce novel utterances to describe new events in settings removed in time and space from training. Establishing a comprehensive repertoire will require not only thorough training, but also the ability to recombine trained forms, the ability to acquire additional vocabulary from the natural environment, and the ability to generalize across similar events and dissimiliar settings. It is impossible to teach appropriate responses for every example of a stimulus class or to train all possible word combinations that exemplify a syntactic form. The problem for the child is to produce appropriate utterances based on training as the particular environmental conditions become increasingly removed in time and space from the original training setting, and as the stimulus properties of these events increasingly vary.

Stimulus generalizations may be simple or complex depending on the characteristics of the setting in which the generalized response occurs. Generalization across stimuli may occur relatively easily when the stimuli closely resemble those present during training (for example, the correct use of the label "ball" in the classroom setting when the teacher holds up a ball similar to one used in training and says, "What is this?"). The same response in a circumstance less similar to the training format would be more difficult (for example, if the trained child has said "ball" while looking at a picture of a ball, with no accompanying verbal prompt from an adult).

Response generalization may involve simple or complex recombinations of trained and untrained forms into novel utterances. For example, a novel utterance is produced when children combine the verb "want" with trained nouns such as "ball," "cookie," and "hat," or with untrained nouns already in their repertoire or acquired from the natural environment. Typically, students are taught some exemplars of a syntactic form (e.g., pronoun–verb–preposition–noun) and it is assumed that they will generalize by combining other words in their repertoires to form the newly trained syntax. Usually only a small number (10 to 30) of exemplars of a linguistic response class are taught. Unless response generalization occurs, training does not produce a sufficient repertoire to enable communication in more than the few specific instances where those trained examples are appropriate.

Table 1 summarizes a simplified practical generalization gradient. Three types of generalization are described: probe, natural environment, and maintenance (generalization across time). These categories are based on the relative structure of the response opportunity in comparison to the training structure, on the similarity of the language stimulus to the one used in training the initial response, and on the length of time between training and the response opportunity. These categories are focal points on the continuum but do not represent every possible dimension of generalization complexity.

Probe Generalization

Probe generalization is defined as responses to stimulus and response situations structured by the language trainer. In probes, generalization is tested using stimulus and response situations similar to the ones used in training. For example, a trainer first teaches the child to produce statements of the form "want ball," "want milk," and "want cookie," in response to the presentation of these objects. Then a second adult in the same setting holds up a cookie (or other probe item) in front of the child and asks, "What want?" to which the child might respond, "Want cookie." Probes typically differ from training in that they 1) take place in different settings (e.g., the classroom or the home), 2) employ a different trainer (e.g., a teacher or parent), and/or 3) utilize different stimuli (e.g., objects rather than pictures, objects different from those used in training). Most experimental studies reporting measures of generalized language have relied on structured probes of generalization.

Natural Environment Generalization

Natural environment generalization is defined as spontaneous generalization by the child to stimulus and response variations that occur outside the training setting, and is assessed by observing the child in unstructured, nontraining settings. It differs from probe generalization in that no specific attempt is made by

Table 1. Practical generalization gradient

Type of generalization	Definition	Examples	Probable prerequisites for occurrences
Probe	Generalization to *similarly structured* stimulus and/or response situations conducted concurrent with training, arranged by the trainer.	Generalization to other trainers, stimuli, or response forms topographically or functionally related to the training item or to training procedures momentarily conducted in a non-training setting.	Sufficient training.
Natural environment	Generalization outside the training setting to naturally occurring language opportunities roughly concurrent with program training (although not necessarily concurrent with training of this response).	Generalization to other classrooms, homes, or settings across adults and peers.	Probe generalization and opportunities to display responses.
Maintenance	Natural environment generalization that occurs *after* all training has stopped and the treatment program is discontinued. Or, generalization to probes conducted after all training has ceased.	Generalization displayed by the child after transition to the public school program.	Sufficient training, probe and/or natural environment generalization, and opportunities to display responses.

the evaluator to elicit the target response from the child. Natural environment generalization is an extremely important measure because it indicates the extent that the child is using the trained language in the "real world." Measures of generalization to the natural environment have rarely been reported in published language generalization analyses.

Maintenance

Maintenance, the effects of training after all formal intervention has ceased, can be assessed either by probes or natural environment measures. For example, a child may have received language training while residing in a state institution, and then have left the institution for a community setting. To the extent the child displays trained language to the subsequent community setting, maintenance is demonstrated.

RESEARCH ON LANGUAGE GENERALIZATION

Many studies have examined the generalization of trained language behaviors during structured probes. This research has made a significant contribution to current knowledge of generalization as a process, as well as to the development of systematic language-training programs (Guess, Keogh, & Sailor, 1978; Harris, 1975). The majority of these studies have examined some aspect of morphological development or of syntactic development; a few have examined conversational speech. Guess and Baer (1973) trained severely retarded subjects in the receptive and productive use of the plural morphemes -s and -es. They measured generalization to new exemplars and across modalities through interspersed productive and receptive probes. Lutzker and Sherman (1974) trained three retarded subjects and two developmentally normal toddlers to use sentences with correct subject-verb agreement to describe pictures. Generalization was assessed on the basis of the subjects' sentence descriptions of novel pictures presented in interspersed probe trials. Other examples of generalization analysis of morphological training include those by Baer and Guess (1971, 1973), Guess (1969), Guess, Sailor, Rutherford, and Baer (1968), Sailor (1971), and Schumaker and Sherman (1970). Analyses of the generalization of syntactic training include the studies by Bennett and Ling (1972), Clark and Sherman (1975), Garcia, Guess, and Byrnes (1973), Hester and Hendrikson (1977), Jeffree, Wheldall, and Mittler (1973), Stevens-Long and Rasmussen (1974), and Wheeler and Sulzer (1970). Examples of generalization analyses of conversational speech can be found in the work of Garcia (1974) and Tucker, Keilitz, and Horner (1973).

These analyses typically showed considerable generalization by learners. Apparently it is relatively easy to establish generalized responding within a morphological or syntactic response class under controlled conditions. However, these results may not accurately represent the results of comprehensive language training. Previous studies taught language skills ranging from the use of one specific grammatical rule to the chaining together of two or three specific conversational statements. No study taught more than three linguistic elements; thus, these investigations were more limited in content and purpose than the language-training programs that purpose to teach functional language. All but two studies (Hester & Hendrikson, 1977; Jeffree, Wheldall, & Mittler, 1973) assessed generalization in structured probes with no analysis of the transition from probe generalization to natural environment generalization or to maintenance. Clearly, a more extensive assessment of generalization in the natural environment is needed.

GENERALIZATION TO THE NATURAL ENVIRONMENT

Since 1976, the authors and their colleagues[1] at the University of Kansas have been engaged in a program of longitudinal research on the generalization of language training to nontraining environments. This program of research was conceived to accomplish the following objectives:

1. Develop a measurement system to assess the generalized effects of comprehensive language training on children's language use in nontraining environments
2. Determine the effects of training on language use by children with moderate to severe language deficiencies
3. Analyze the ecological variables that set the occasion for language in various environments
4. Manipulate environmental variables in order to facilitate generalized language display

Progress to date is discussed below.

Methodology

The effects of comprehensive language training on 25 children, representing a range of language delays from severe to mild, have been analyzed. These children have been studied at two sites: the Kansas Neurological Institute (KNI), a residential facility for severely and profoundly retarded children, and the Language Project Preschool (LPP), a preschool for language-delayed children located at the University of Kansas. KNI children displayed a range of verbal skills from single-word utterances to five-word sentences. They received systematic training in either the Guess, Sailor, and Baer (1978) language-training program or the Stremel and Waryas (1974) program (discussed in more detail in the previous chapter by Guess) in addition to 6 hours of daily classroom instruction in preacademic, art, vocational, and self-help skills. LPP children were home-living, 3–5-year-olds, enrolled in the preschool for daily, 3-hour sessions. In

---

[1]Collaborators have included Richard Schiefelbusch, Thomas Longhurst, Kathleen Stremel-Campbell, and Ann Marshall.

addition to the regular preschool curriculum, each child received daily language training on the Stremel and Waryas (1974) language program. LPP children typically showed 1–2-year language delays, and the source of these delays varied. Some of the children showed evidence of a general developmental delay resulting from nutritional deficits and lack of environmental stimulation, while determinations of learning disabilities or auditory impairments were made for about half of the children. Language skills varied from the use of one-word utterances to the expression of five-word utterances.

Four to six language samples were collected on all children at both sites each week. In taking each sample, an observer made a verbatim transcription of the child's utterances during a 15-minute period. In addition, a tape recording of the child's language and of the language directed to the child was made. The tape recordings were obtained by having the child wear an apron containing a small wireless microphone. The child's speech was transmitted to a receiver and tape recorder located in an adjacent room. The tape-recorded sample was used to supplement and correct the record made in vivo. The high quality of the recorded sample, in combination with the observer's record, provided highly reliable data (averaging about 90%; Rogers-Warren & Warren, in press).

The completed verbatim samples were entered into the computer to be compared with the child's specific training data for evidence of generalization. The computer program charted the child's production of nontraining words and speech forms and classified all trained and untrained forms syntactically. For example, in the sentence *I want cookie,* the program would classify each word (*I* as a pronoun, *want* as a verb, and *cookie* as a noun) and classify the whole sentence as a pronoun–verb–noun combination. In addition, the program calculated mean length of utterance (MLU) and type-token ratios (the ratio of novel words and forms to all words and forms used), and maintained a dictionary of the child's entire current vocabulary.

Summary of Findings

The application of this system to study natural environment generalization has produced some preliminary findings regarding the effects of language-training programs; however, the research is continuing at the time of this writing and numerous critical questions still remain to be answered. Some recent findings are summarized below.

Word Generalization   Words are the building blocks of language acquisition, and for many children language training begins with learning labels for common objects and actions. Both the Guess, Sailor, and Baer (1978) and the Stremel and Waryas (1974) programs train sets of noun referents to criterion before beginning training on word combinations. In the present study, structured probes and longitudinal natural environment samples were taken and analyzed to determine the generalized effects of object label training for six severely retarded KNI children. The analysis had several purposes: to determine the generalization and maintenance of the labels trained; to determine which *specific* trained labels were most functional (i.e., most likely to generalize) and which *classes* of labels were most likely to generalize (e.g., food labels); and to analyze the differences between generalization measured by structured probes and generalization derived from longitudinal language samples.

The six students included two females and four males who ranged in age from 10.5 to 16.0 years at the conclusion of the longitudinal observations. All six children had resided at KNI for several years. Observations were conducted in four settings at the institution: the children's regular classroom, the art classroom, the dining hall, and the living unit. An average of 15 labels were successfully trained for each child. The labels were chosen on the basis of an initial skill test given by the language trainer. The number of sessions to criterion ranged from 5 (T.F. and S.B.) to 126 (B.Q.), with an average of 43 sessions.

Generalization and maintenance were measured by structured probes and by longitudinal observations of children in their natural environments. Subjects' retention of the trained labels was probed concurrent with the longitudinal observation period. Probes were conducted in the following way: A research assistant took the child aside in the classroom and twice presented each item to the child with the question "What's this?" Correct responses were verbally praised and incorrect answers were ignored. The point at which longitudinal natural environment observations were implemented, the length of the observation period, and the number of observations per setting varied from child to child depending on the child's availability for observation.

The computer program analyzed word generalization by comparing each child's list of trained labels with the spontaneous (non-imitated) words in the child's verbatim samples. Each occurrence of a trained word was counted, and a dictionary of the child's entire vocabulary was compiled. Results for each child are summarized in Table 2. Three children gave correct responses to all probe items (these data are presented in Table 2) while the remaining three showed only partial generalization on the probes. For the longitudinal observations, only those words that children displayed correctly in the probes were considered. This

Table 2. Generalization ratios per child

| Subject | Probe ratio | Longitudinal observations | |
		1 Occasion	2 Occasions
T.F.	9/9 = 100%	7/9 = 78%	6/9 = 67%
S.B.	14/14 = 100%	14/14 = 100%	13/14 = 93%
B.Q.	18/18 = 100%	17/18 = 94%	16/18 = 89%
J.L.	13/16 = 81%	11/13 = 85%	10/13 = 77%
D.M.	15/16 = 94%	9/15 = 60%	6/15 = 40%
B.F.	11/16 = 69%	5/11 = 45%	2/11 = 18%
Mean	80/89 = 90%	63/80 = 79%	53/80 = 66%

The ratios on the longitudinal observations have as their denominators the number of words the child successfully displayed in the probes.

decision was based on the assumption that labels not produced under the optimal structured conditions provided during probes had not been sufficiently trained and, therefore, could not be expected to generalize to the much less structured natural environment. Thus, the probes were considered tests of training adequacy and naturalistic observation tests of the functional use of adequately trained responses. Only words that were shown to be adequately trained (displayed correctly during probes) were tested for functional use.

Table 2 displays the ratio for words observed at least once (non-imitatively) in the natural environment and those occurring at least twice. On the one-occurrence criterion, the subjects ranged from 45% (5/11 by B.F.) to 100% (14/14 by S.B.) correct. At this criterion level, the mean generalization ratio for the group was 79%. When the criterion was made more stringent by requiring that a word be observed on at least two different occasions, the generalization ratios of all the subjects decreased to an overall group mean of 66%.

Correlations between the percentage of one-occurrence generalization by each subject and several other variables were conducted using the Pearson Product Moment Correlation formula. No significant correlations were found between percentage of one-occurrence generalization and the total number of observations per subject, the Peabody Picture Vocabulary Test (Dunn, 1965) scores, the Houston Language Age (Crabtree, 1963) scores, or the number of words trained per child. A 0.85 correlation was found between total vocabulary size of each child and percentage of one-occurrence generalization. This correlation was significant at the 0.05 level.

A total of 36 different words were trained during the study. Sixteen of these words were trained with three or more children. The generalization ratios for each of these words, based on a one-occurrence criterion are presented in Table 3. Six of the 16 words were generalized by all children trained on these words, and only two words were generalized by fewer than half the children. Trained words were grouped by word class (i.e., food labels, toy labels, etc.), and the generalization ratios for each word class, based on a one-occurrence criterion, are presented in Table 4. Of the classes trained, food labels were the most likely to generalize, followed closely by toy labels, eating utensil labels, and clothes labels. Body part labels (e.g., leg, ear, hand) were least likely to generalize. The results of this analysis demonstrate that severely retarded institutionalized children can be taught functional noun labels in one-to-one training and later display generalization of these labels in the natural environment.

The longitudinal measurements evaluated the extent to which trained labels were used in the natural environment. Seventy-nine percent of the labels produced correctly during probes were observed to occur in the natural environment. This finding is based on the most lenient criterion, which required only that a student display a given word once (non-imitatively) during the entire measurement period (which averaged 177 observations per child). When the criterion required display of a given word on at least two separate occasions, the overall percentage of generalization decreased to 66%. One child's (B.F.) generalization ratio was only 18% using the more stringent criterion.

Several factors should be considered in interpreting the generalization data. First, children were observed only about 1 to 1½ hours (4–6 15-minute observations) each week. Assuming they slept an average of 9 hours a day, these observations accounted for only about 1% of the time when they could have used the trained labels. It is possible that, even with the large number of observations across a variety of settings, generalized use of some words may have been missed. If a child used a word during the brief samples, it seems likely that the word may have been used on other unobserved occasions although it is impossible to determine the number of occasions. Further, unlike verbs, prepositions and general types of grammatical structures, a noun label may be used appropriately only under special conditions. For example, the word *cup* refers to that specific object, whereas the verb *eat* or the article *the* may be used in numerous contexts in relation to many other objects. Some trained nouns will be displayed at a low rate even if the child has generalized appropriate use of the word because the context for applying the labels occurs infrequently. If the child was not observed in a context in which the label was appropriate (e.g., *toothbrush* is typically appropriate only in the bathroom), no evidence of generalized use could be expected.

In light of these considerations, the generalization to the natural environment displayed by the children might be considered impressive. Data suggest that much of the training was sufficient for potential generalization and that the vocabulary was functional in the institutional environment. The only variable significantly correlated with differential generalization was the size of the child's vocabulary. This index of the verbal skills may be a better predictor of language generalization than either the Houston or Peabody assessments. Further research on the efficiency of this and other possible generalization predictors is warranted.

Table 3. Generalization ratios of words trained across three or more subjects (one-occurrence criterion)

Label	Number of students trained for	Number of students generalized for	Generalization ratio
Ball	5	5	100%
Shoe	5	5	100%
Car	4	4	100%
Milk	4	4	100%
Pop	3	3	100%
Candy	3	3	100%
Cookie	6	5	83%
Apple	5	4	80%
Cup	5	4	80%
Spoon	5	4	80%
Table	3	2	67%
Hat	6	4	67%
Ear	4	2	50%
Nose	4	2	50%
Chair	3	1	33%
Tummy	3	0	0%

Table 4. Generalization ratios by word class (one-occurrence criterion)

Class	Words trained	Generalized	Percentage
Food	28	24	86%
Toys	12	10	83%
Eating utensils	11	9	82%
Clothes	16	12	75%
Other	5	3	60%
Furniture	6	3	50%
Body parts	13	4	31%

Sixteen words were trained across at least three children, which allowed an analysis of the generalizability of specific labels. The 12 words that were generalized by more than half the children who received training would appear to be highly functional for severely retarded institutionalized children, and therapists and trainers may wish to include them in language training with these populations. Words that represent food, toys, eating utensils, and clothes appear to be highly functional because they are very likely to generalize. Names of body parts did not generalize readily and may have little productive function for severely retarded students. This result mirrors research findings with normal children (Anglin, 1977; Nelson, 1973; Rinsland, 1945). Normal children first learn the names of things they can act on and things that serve important functions in their life (e.g., food, people, toys). At least initially, they do not learn the names of things simply because they are there. The data reported here suggest severely retarded children share this acquisition strategy.

One unresolved problem in assessing generalization of newly trained responses is determining the point at which sufficient generalization has occurred and no further intervention is required. The demand characteristics of the communication episode seldom explicitly require a particular word or phrase. Although there are clearly obligatory response occasions requiring verbalization, most language use is initiated at the speaker's discretion. For these reasons, it is impossible to calculate the number of opportunities for language display and to select a criterion for sufficient generalization based on a ratio between display of language and number of opportunities.

The amount of word generalization observed in the natural environment is encouraging. It suggests that vocabulary training, a critical component of language training, may be very functional, and, hence, represent an important and reasonably successful component of a comprehensive language-training program.

Syntactic Generalization In addition to acquiring labels to refer to objects, events, and actions, the child must learn a set of rules for combining words into sentences. These rules could be based on syntactics, semantics, pragmatics, or a combination of the three. Syntactic rules may be taught by training the child to produce multiple exemplars of each rule. The child's task is to learn the rule for ordering words into similar sentences from these examples, and to demonstrate knowledge of the rule by producing novel, correctly ordered sentences. Generalization from training could take three forms: 1) the child could use the exact sentence taught in training (e.g., "I want a cookie"); 2) the child could use the syntactic structure trained (e.g., pronoun-state-verb[2]-article-noun) and substitute different examples for some of the parts of speech (e.g., "I want a *truck*"); or 3) the child could use the trained syntax and substitute untrained forms for all the parts of speech (e.g., "She needs the pencil"). The analysis of syntactic generalization accepted 1) exact matches, 2) partial matches, and 3) nonmatching exemplars as evidence of syntactic generalization. Children's verbatim transcripts were compared with records of their training to determine if the exact examples or the underlying syntactic organization had generalized.

Language training typically proceeds through a series of steps, each designed to teach a specific syntactic structure. By taking baseline measures of a child's use of each syntactic form prior to training, a multiple baseline experimental analysis is possible in which each trained structure represents a separate baseline. A hypothetical analysis is shown in Figure 1. If a language-training program produced generalized use of trained forms, its effects could be seen in the series of graphs such as those presented. A strong experimental analysis and generalization assessment would require that at least three syntactic forms be trained and measured sequentially and that the subjects' spontaneous language be monitored for a length of time before and after training to demonstrate experimental control.

The majority of the children at both sites (KNI and LPP) displayed syntactic generalization similar to that shown for T.R. in Figure 2. T.R. rapidly progressed through the steps of the Guess, Sailor, and Baer language-training program. She was trained on 12 syntactic forms over a period of 7 months, and quickly reached criterion on nine of these. She did not reach criterion on two forms (pronoun-state-verb-state-verb-noun, Example 7 in Figure 2; pronoun-state-verb-state-verb, Example 5 in Figure 2) but was nevertheless advanced because she showed excellent progress on other steps trained concurrently. Despite T.R.'s rapid progress through the training program, she did not use the trained forms in the natural environment with the exception of the pronoun-state-verb-noun form (e.g., "I want cookie") that did eventually generalize. (Training on the state-verb-noun and pronoun-state-verb-noun forms had been started before measures of generalized language were instituted as part of this research.)

The analysis of syntactic generalization is ongoing. Results for four LPP children and four other KNI children to date have shown a relatively small amount of syntactic generalization as exemplified by T.R.'s data. For the four LPP children, generalization to the natural environment occurred for a mean of 4 of 12 syntactic forms trained (33%), while for KNI children, a mean of 5 of 23

---

[2]The term *state-verb* refers to those verbs that express a state of being (e.g., wanting, liking, knowing) as opposed to an overt action. Common state-verbs include *want, like, love, hate,* and *know.*

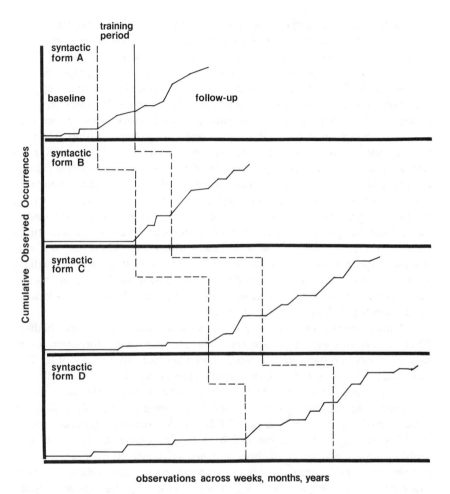

Figure 1. Hypothetical effects of syntactic form training are shown as they might appear in a child's use of a given trained form (e.g., form A) in the natural environment. Experimental control is demonstrated by the fact that, for the most part, the hypothetical child does not begin to use the different forms until they are trained.

trained forms generalized (22%). Less complex syntactic forms eventually generalized, probably as a result of being embedded in more complex syntactic forms taught later. This repetition across structures provides a type of multiple exemplar training for the simpler forms. For example, the form verb-noun may first have been trained by itself, and then trained as an embedded component in pronoun-verb-noun, noun-verb-noun, pronoun-verb-verb-pronoun, and so on.

The amount of syntactic generalization observed suggests that training may not produce generalization of this dimension even though syntax training is emphasized. Changes in the specific syntactic forms selected for training and the manner in which they are trained might produce more generalization to nontraining settings. Another interpretation is also possible. A syntactic analysis may not reveal all the generalized effects of language training since language training also teaches semantic relationships and communication functions. Analyses along these parameters may provide a better account of the effects of language training.

Semantic Generalization Sentences can be described in terms of their underlying relational meanings (semantics). The sentence *He kicks the ball,* characterized syntactically as a pronoun–verb–article–noun string, is semantically described as an example of an agent–action–object relationship. The relationship between syntax and semantics is complex (see Bowerman, 1978, for a review of semantics in current psycholinguistic literature). Training that focuses on syntax simultaneously teaches semantic relationships. The relative importance of each aspect in terms of language development has yet to be articulated beyond the fact that both play a major role. All sentences used in training and found in the verbatim samples can be characterized semantically to determine if language training has generalized along a semantic dimension. However, semantic analyses require knowledge of the communication context, such as intonation, gestures, and objects present, in addition to the actual words used in order to allow an accurate interpretation of semantic relationships found in two- to four-word utterances (Bloom, 1970; Brown, 1973).

A pilot semantic generalization analysis was conducted with three children. Since the analyses were done post hoc, complete contextual information necessary to clarify the meanings of some short utterances was unavailable. This increased the likelihood of errors in classifying some sentences semantically, but these errors may be assumed to be random. The results of this analysis are intriguing. The best example is provided by examining T.R.'s data along the dimension of semantic generalization.[3] T.R. showed almost no generalization of the 12 syntactic forms that she had been taught (Figure 2). Her data were analyzed for generalization of three semantic relationships: state–complement ("want cookies"; trained before generalization observations began), experiencer-state–complement ("I/You want cookies"; nine syntactic forms were trained), and agent–action ("I eat"; two syntactic forms were trained). The results of this analysis are presented in Figure 3. Her display of the three semantic relations in the natural environment during an 8-month period is shown. The graphs chart cumulative types (novel forms only) and tokens (all forms). Where there are two lines on a graph, the lower line represents types; the upper, tokens. Where only one line appears, all occurrences of the form were novel. The state–complement relationship was trained before observations started. The dates of training and criterion are shown on the first graph (TR: 4-5-77; CR: 4-5-77). On the other two graphs, the beginning of training on each exemplar is shown by

---

[3]The descriptive terms used in this discussion include the following: 1) *state,* a term for a state of being (e.g., *want*); 2) *experiencer,* someone having a given experience; 3) *agent,* someone or something that causes an action; 4) *action,* the event that happens; and 5) *complement,* that which is brought into existence by the action. Further discussion of these and other terms commonly used in semantic analyses can be found in Brown (1973).

a solid triangle. Points at which criterion performances were achieved are shown by solid triangles within circles.

No generalized usage of the state-complement form could be attributed to language training. However, T.R. did show a cumulative generalized effect of training on sequentially more complex program steps that included the experiencer-state-complement form. It appears that T.R. learned the state-complement relation in the course of training on experiencer-state-complement. Her use of experiencer-state-complement suggests a strong training effect. Nine exemplars of this relationship were trained, the first before generalization observations began. While T.R. showed generalization on only the first trained syntactic form (pronoun-state-verb-noun), she displayed a strong acceleration in the display of the semantic relationship that the syntactic forms expressed. This generalization appears attributable to training with multiple exemplars across different syntactic structures. The solid triangles on Figure 3 show where training on each of these exemplars commenced.

The third semantic relationship trained, agent-action, also generalized. There was a strong acceleration in T.R.'s use of agent-action statements after criterion was reached on the second exemplar of this relationship (see Figure 3). T.R.'s performance might be explained by the sequential training of numerous examples of one particular semantic relationship. In fact, the training taught progressively more complex ways to express the agent-action relationship.

Data from two additional students were analyzed for semantic generalization. One of these students, a mildly delayed child from the LPP program, showed a pattern similar to T.R.'s semantic generalization data for these two children show strong effects for five of seven relationships trained, an outcome much different from that shown by the syntactic analysis. The third child, a severely retarded KNI student, displayed no syntactic or semantic generalization. However, this child was taught only one syntactic form representing each semantic relationship, while the two children who displayed generalized responding had been trained on multiple exemplars of each semantic relationship. This may represent a critical training difference.

Generalization of Communication Functions   Utterances have syntactic and semantic structure, and they also serve specific purposes and express intent by fulfilling particular pragmatic functions. Utterances function as requests, instructions, descriptions, declaratives, and so on. Most language-training programs do not train pragmatic functions as such, although the format in which training occurs may implicitly train them. However, the Guess, Sailor, and Baer curriculum has been organized to teach four basic production functions: control, self-extended control, reference, and integration. It is thus possible to analyze the spontaneous utterances of students trained on this curriculum for evidence of generalized use of these functions. Any utterances, regardless of form, that serve the same *purpose* as the examples trained for a particular function can be considered a generalized instance of that function. For example, children are trained to control their environment using statements such as "I want cookies." If children

T.R. KNI
Form Generalization

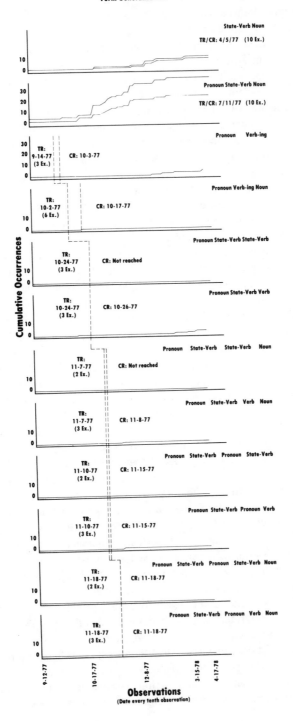

Cumulative Occurrences

Observations
(Date every tenth observation)

request objects using the form "Give me," they can be credited with a generalized use of the control function. Learning the function of language is critical to appropriate language use. Teaching the control function is a primary goal of the Guess, Sailor, and Baer program.

In a pilot analysis, verbatim data on two KNI children whose language had been subjected to syntactic and semantic analysis were analyzed for the presence of control statements. Utterances were classified purely on the basis of wording, in the absence of extensive context data. Because the same sentence, in different contexts, could serve different communication functions, misclassifications were of course possible; however, errors due to the lack of context data were assumed to be random.

T.R. displayed almost no syntactic generalization, but a considerable amount of semantic generalization. Her acquisition and display of "control" were apparent. Figure 4 shows her data over an 8-month period. Cumulative types (novel occurrences) are shown on the lower line, and tokens (all occurrences) are indicated by the upper line across observation blocks (5 observations = 1 block). Training exemplars (forms designed to be used for the control function) are shown by the solid triangle. Figure 4 shows a strong acceleration in T.R.'s use of control statements concurrent with training on nine different exemplars of this function. T.R. did not use any trained syntactic forms in the natural environment, except pronoun-state-verb-noun, which was used with increasing frequency toward the end of the study. Use of that form alone is not sufficient to account for accelerated use of the control function. T.R. used untrained syntactic forms to control the environment at a higher rate after the control exemplars were trained. The second child, the same severely retarded KNI resident who failed to display any syntactic or semantic generalization, did not demonstrate any acceleration in acquisition of the control function as a result of training.

These function analysis data are limited, yet they suggest some interesting possibilities. T.R. appeared to acquire the communication function, control, that was the goal of the program stage. She learned the general function and to express some semantic relations, but did not generalize the specific syntax used to train them. The other pilot child showed minimal acquisition of the control function, failed to generalize either the trained syntax or underlying semantic relationships, and showed no acceleration in use of the control function in conjunction with training.

Figure 2. The cumulative display in the natural environment of 12 sequentially trained syntactic forms by T.R. is shown. Every tenth observation is dated along the bottom axis. The top two forms shown were trained before observations were begun. The dates on which training was started and criterion was reached are shown on the right side of these graphs. The number of exemplars trained for each specific form is also shown. The other forms were trained after the observations began. The date training started, the date criterion was reached, and the number of exemplars trained is shown near the left side of the graphs. Where two lines are shown on a graph, the top represents tokens (all occurrences) and the bottom represents types (novel utterances only). Where only one line is shown, all occurrences were novel (subject had not displayed them before).

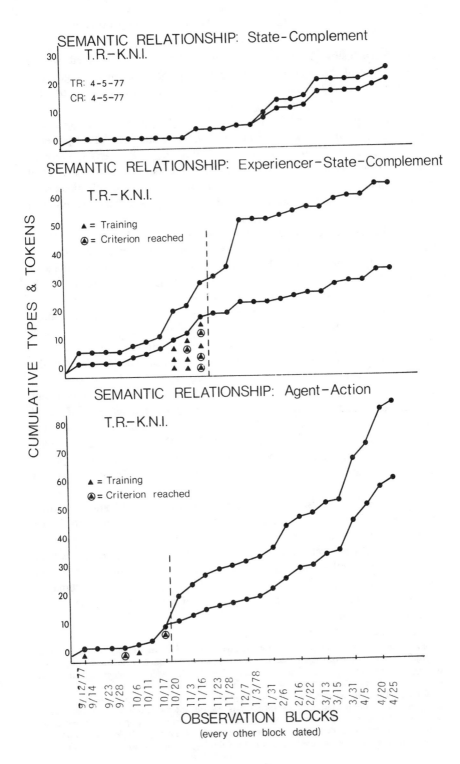

THEORETICAL IMPLICATIONS

The completed work suggests some hypotheses about critical factors in language development and the generalized use of language. Programmatic training can be very successful as indicated by consistent generalization of trained vocabulary. The relative ease with which normal children acquire labels for common objects and events is reflected in the generalization data. Further research is required to explore children's use of newly trained terms as referents and to describe the concept development that accompanies the acquisition of vocabulary. The data suggest that correct use of syntax is a more difficult skill. Only a few students generalized syntactic forms, and usually only after multiple examples of the syntactic form were trained.

To define generalization by common semantic relations supposes a semantically rather than a syntactically based model of language acquisition. Two of three children showed strong semantic generalization. If this finding is a general one that can be replicated across children with varying language skills, it would suggest that semantic relations may be the basis of rule-governed linquistic behavior. Further analyses are needed to contrast semantic and syntactic generalization descriptions, and to determine the exact parameters of semantic generalization. It is possible that the semantic analysis is, to a limited extent, only a broader type of the syntactic analysis, essentially serving to combine syntactic categories rather than representing an independent dimension of students' language.

Perhaps the most intriguing analysis centers on functional communication. The pragmatic aspect of language has emerged recently as a topic of great interest. However, there is little known about the development of functional communication, particularly among language deficient populations. Generalization of vocabulary and syntax across communication functions is probably the most critical dimension of normal language usage. Determining how this generalization occurs, and if it is facilitated by specific training, may provide additional insight into the organization of the linguistic communication system.

The trend in language research has been to consider the components of language in isolation. In the 1960s, language was characterized as a syntactic system, in the early 1970s as a semantic system based in cognitive development, and currently as a pragmatic communication system. The missing theory is the integration of these three representatives of linguistic skill into a cohesive model of child language. The present work is a step toward a data-based analysis of the

Figure 3. The cumulative display of three semantic relationships by T.R. is shown. The relationship shown in the top graph was trained, prior to the start of observation, on the dates shown. The other two relationships were trained while observations were ongoing. The solid triangles indicate when training commenced on a given syntactic exemplar, and the circled triangles indicate when criterion was reached. Where two lines are shown on a graph, the top represents tokens (all occurrences of a form) and the bottom represents types (novel occurrences only). Where only one line is shown, all occurrences were novel. Each individual data point represents the summation of four observations.

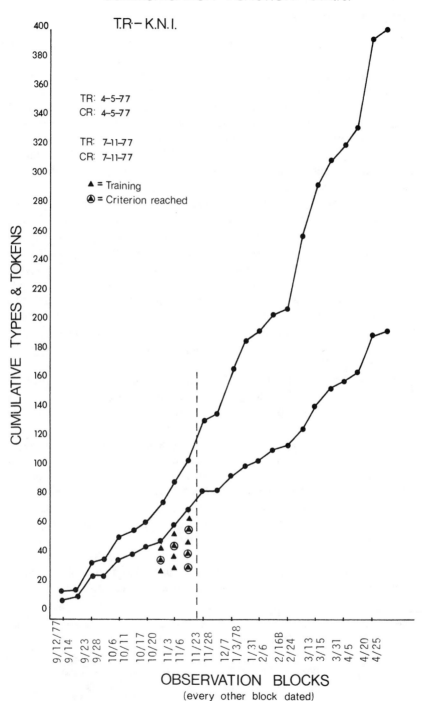

COMMUNICATION FUNCTION: Control

T.R.- K.N.I.

TR: 4–5–77
CR: 4–5–77

TR: 7–11–77
CR: 7–11–77

▲ = Training
◬ = Criterion reached

CUMULATIVE TYPES & TOKENS

OBSERVATION BLOCKS
(every other block dated)

interface between syntax, semantics, and functions in the delayed child's linguistic system. By integrating training items into an emerging language system, and carefully tracking the child's use, it may be possible to identify how the language-learning child organizes linguistic rules and generates new, appropriate utterances to describe a vast array of environmental events. Studying deficient populations requiring specific teaching offers a unique opportunity to develop, at the very least, a well documented analog to the process of language acquisition. There are, of course, practical as well as theoretical implications to language-training research. Findings support a model of teaching that programs generalization via multiple exemplar training strategies rather than waiting for it to occur. Further investigation is needed to identify content and formats for training that are efficient in terms of the teaching time they require.

CLINICAL APPLICATIONS

Some of the potential implications of this research for language remediation are apparent, such as a result of the work completed on probe generalization. Research in progress or in planning will broaden the empirical basis for language intervention. However, for the instructor in the field, the need for strategies to effect language generalization is immediate. Since training must continue in the absence of a complete research base, a discussion of the assessment and facilitation of generalization in an educational context is appropriate here. Recommendations are intended for the therapist or teacher attempting to assess and facilitate language generalization without the aid of observers and research assistants.

Measurement of Generalization

A necessary first decision for the practitioner is what to measure: probe, natural environment generalization, maintenance, or some combination of these? Natural environment generalization and maintenance are the ultimate measures of a program's effectiveness; however, assessment of generalization in structured probes is far easier to conduct. Generalization to structured probes is probably a necessary prerequisite for naturalistic generalization and maintenance, and is easily assessed. A person other than the trainer can conduct unreinforced training trials with the student to assess generalization across persons. Trials with untrained members of the same stimulus class also can be inserted into a training session. For example, a child who has been taught the label "hat" using a brown cowboy hat, could be queried using a number of different hats to determine if the use of the label has generalized to other examples of the stimulus class. Such uses

Figure 4. The cumulative display of the communication function of control by T.R. is shown. Two exemplars were trained before observations began. The dates when training started and criterion was met are shown in the upper left corner of the graph. Other exemplars were trained while observations were being conducted and are represented by the solid triangles (and criterion dates by the circled triangles). Each individual data point represents four observations.

of probes should be standard in language training efforts. Generalization to structured probes is critical and should not be assumed even if the child has easily acquired the skill in training. If generalization does not occur in structured probes, training should be continued until it does.

While the assessment of performance on structured probes in easily accomplished, assessment of performance in the natural environment and maintenance analyses is more difficult. The easiest natural environment check is to observe the child in the classroom or home environment and listen for instances of the trained language. It is not a large step from this informal observation to writing down or tape-recording what the child says in these settings. A permanent written record allows the teacher to measure generalization specifically. The cost of this procedure, in terms of time, depends on how often it is done. Accuracy of the assessment usually increases with more frequent measurements. In the research described above, students were observed at least 1 hour per week (four 15-minute samples). For a teacher, a reasonable goal might be one 15-minute observation period each week, at a time when the child is likely to talk. Even a few observations are better than none at all. The teacher's observations also provide general informal information about when and how the child uses language, in addition to any specific generalization assessments.

In sum, two strategies are recommended. First, any trainer should assess generalization to probes as a part of training. Probes across settings, persons, and stimuli should be included at the end of each training step. Second, the trainer should assess generalization to the natural environment as frequently as possible.

In research, it is advantageous to measure the syntactic, semantic, and communication function generalization of sentence training. In practice, however, monitoring all three dimensions may not be feasible. The overall goal of treatment should be considered in selecting a model for assessing generalization from training. With a severely retarded child, the goal of language training is to assist the child in establishing some degree of control over the environment. For example, the primary goal of the early stages of the Guess, Sailor, and Baer training program is to teach the child the function of control by teaching the child to request actions and things from others. For this population, it may be most reasonable to look for generalization of language functions, with that generalization reflected in an increased use of sentences of the type trained to control the environment by requesting things or actions. With higher level children, it is more difficult to identify the preferred dimension for measurement, and there is little empirical basis for a strong recommendation at this time. In this vacuum perhaps the best approach is to assess on the basis of the expressed goal of the training program being used.

There are three prerequisites to any formal assessment of the generalized effects of training. First, the training procedures must be effective. The student's actual learning of words and sentences, at some satisfactory criterion level, must be verified by probes of the student's performance on each step. If the child cannot produce probe generalizaiton, then more training is needed before an assessment of natural environment generalization is attempted. Second, it is necessary to keep accurate and complete records of trained words and sentences, of the dates when each training step began and ended (or that the child was moved to another training step after repeatedly failing to reach criterion), and of the results of all probes. Third, it is important to keep a written record of those trained responses that do occur in the natural setting. Comparing this record with the training records will show what trained forms are being generalized.

The accuracy of such assessment will be limited by the frequency and duration of the observations. Assessing generalization, particularly in the natural environment, requires considerable time for observation and analysis. Many words and several sentence forms are appropriate only in specific situations, and a child may actually have a specific word or form in his or her repertoire yet fail to display it because the appropriate opportunity has not occurred during the observation. There are several strategies for determining whether a performance discrepancy is a measurement problem or a problem of generalization per se. One might begin by examining the child often and in many circumstances, thereby increasing the representativeness of the observational sample. A second approach would be to compare the child's success on probes to samples obtained in the natural environment. If the discrepancy between probe and natural environment generalization records is very large, it may indicate insufficient observation rather than an actual failure to generalize. A third but difficult strategy is to measure the child's opportunities for displaying specific language in the natural environment and to compare this with the actual rate of display. In some environments, opportunities and support for language may be infrequent, thus making generalization unlikely.

Facilitation of Generalization

In the past, generalization has been regarded as a useful, but typically unplanned outcome of training (Stokes & Baer, 1977). Its occurrence was a passive phenemenon, and the most frequent procedure used to achieve generalization was "train and hope." The research reported here, as well as that reviewed by Stokes and Baer (1977), indicates that generalization is not an automatic outcome of training. Because one hallmark of severely handicapped children is their frequent inability to generalize from teaching situations, a practical approach to environmental facilitation of language generalization may be to assume that in-setting support for generalization will be needed. The following two sections offer some strategies for facilitating generalization of trained language. These strategies are based on considerable research, and most have been tested with severely handicapped populations.

Two considerations should underlie the development and application of generalization facilitation techniques. The first is that the techniques support generalized language in nontraining settings, such as classrooms, the community, and the home. The second is that the techniques should be reasonably efficient. Efficiency in this instance means that they can be used either in the context of language training or in applied settings with a minimal amount of training, and produce obvious, positive effects. Language training is only one of many activities required of the classroom personnel or the parent; thus, any technique or intervention to prompt generalization in natural settings should be compatible with the ongoing activities of the teacher. Not all of the techniques suggested below are equally easy to apply, but all of them are possible.

Training Procedures

The facilitation of generalization begins in the context of training. The manner in which a word or sentence is trained will affect its generalization (Harris, 1975). Four specific training-based procedures to facilitate later generalization are considered below: 1) training sufficient exemplars, 2) programming common stimuli, 3) training loosely, and 4) using indiscriminable contingencies.

Training Sufficient Exemplars In this procedure, the number of exemplars taught is increased until generalization to novel stimuli, responses, or settings occurs. For example, in a study by Baer and Guess (1973), four mentally retarded children were taught to expand actions verbs into nouns by applying the -er suffix (e.g., play–player, sing–singer). After training with a number of exemplars (mean of 4–5 exemplars) the children were able to provide the correct -er suffix during probes with new and previously untrained verbs.

Stokes and Baer (1977) have identified some 60 studies that demonstrate the sufficient exemplars tactic. Generalization of this type has been referred to as "generative response training" in the language development literature. It is the most thoroughly researched component in the current technology for facilitating language generalization (Guess, Keogh, & Sailor, 1978). The number of exemplars needed to produce generalization depends on the target behavior, the child, and stimulus conditions. In the studies reviewed by Stokes and Baer (1977), there was considerable variability in the number of exemplars required for generalization. However, frequently only a small number of exemplars (typically from two to five) had to be trained before generalized performance was observed. The longitudinal research discussed earlier supports the versatility and power of the sufficient exemplars approach. The observed semantic generalization appeared to be the result of training multiple syntactic exemplars of the same semantic relationships. For example, T.R.'s use of the agent–action relationship seemed to generalize as a result of training on pronoun–verb(ing), and pronoun–verb(ing)–noun syntactic forms.

This technique can be incorporated into regular language programming by training with additional exemplars of stimuli (e.g., different types of hats, different trainers, or different environments). The chosen exemplars should reflect the dimensions along which generalization is desired. If a child learns the current training item(s) but does not respond to novel items, then further training is needed. If the child generalizes to new training items but does so only for the teacher who has conducted training so far, then other teachers are required. If a child will generalize to new training items for any teacher, but only in one setting, then new training settings are required. The relative power and efficiency of this technique suggests it as the first choice in efforts to facilitate probe and natural environment generalization. Detailed discussion of the sufficient exemplars technique can be found in the Stokes and Baer article (1977) and in a chapter by Guess, Keogh, and Sailor (1978).

Programming Common Stimuli Programming common stimuli may facilitate performance in the natural environment. Common stimulus components are incorporated in training and in the generalization settings. Optimally, the common stimuli function to cue the subjects to display target behaviors in the nontraining setting.

An example of the use of common stimuli was reported by Rincover and Koegel (1975). They trained 10 autistic children to perform one of three target behaviors (nonverbal motor imitation, touching a body part in response to verbal instruction, or raising either the right or left arm) in response to the appropriate verbal cue. Four subjects initially demonstrated no generalization of the target behavior when tested by another person in another setting. Rincover and Koegel then introduced stimuli from the training setting into the generalization setting. Even though the stimuli used (hand prompts, furniture from the training room) were incidental in the actual training, their presence in the natural environment was sufficient to elicit the trained response.

Only a few studies have deliberately used common stimuli to facilitate generalization. While this technique logically is promising, its potential usefulness, strength, and versatility must be determined by more systematic research.

Training Loosely This tactic reverses the usual procedures employed in discrimination learning. Variability in the range of stimuli presented and in the responses allowed is incorporated into training to maximize the student's sampling of the many dimensions that could mediate transfer to other situations and of the many forms relevant to the *class* of behavior being trained. It is the purpose of a loose training approach to eliminate massed training with repetitive stimuli and precisely stereotyped training formats in favor of a wider sampling of varied stimuli and formats within each class of responses to be trained. Sometimes this prescription is achieved by accident, and usually it is considered unfortunate. Trainers, settings, and training stimuli may vary naturally because of insufficient planning, staff turnover, and changes in client load. Although such unplanned variability is not entirely desirable, it may sometimes function as a "loose training" procedure, and may actually facilitate generalization. However, some severely retarded children have difficulty learning from widely varied stimuli and contexts. It may be safer to begin training with relatively consistent stimuli and procedures and increase variability as the child acquires the skill. Although there has been little applied research on this approach, a trainer might endeavor to vary stimuli, trainers, and settings more or less systematically in the interests of facilitating generalization.

Using Indiscriminable Contingencies By definition, the antithesis of generalization is discrimination. Procedurally, discrimination depends on the correlation of distinctive stimuli with the opportunity for reinforcement. Presumably, generalization may be promoted by making reinforcement indiscriminable, thus preventing extinction of the response in forms and settings in which it will not be reinforced. Specific language responses often are not reinforced directly outside of training. Thus, it is possible that discriminating the contingencies impedes generalization to nontraining settings. Following this logic, there are several ways to make contingencies indiscriminable and thereby enhance generalization. One is to delay reinforcement, thus making the times and places during which the response earns reinforcement unclear. This approach may be useful in promoting generalization but may actually interfere with initial skill acquisition.

A better known approach is to make the contingencies indiscriminable by implementing intermittent schedules of reinforcement. The essential feature of such schedules is their unpredictability, the impossibility of discriminating reinforcement occasions from nonreinforcement occasions until reinforcement occurs. Only a few studies using this strategy to promote generalization have been documented, but the resistance of trained responses to extinction under various reinforcement schedules has been well researched. Varying the schedule and stimulus conditions of reinforcement in training should begin once the subject has acquired the target response.

If the techniques discussed above fail or cannot be implemented, direct training should be introduced in the settings in which the response is desired. The result should not be referred to as generalization because it is an outcome of direct training or a sequential modification.

Possibly the most effective use of these training-based procedures is to combine them with procedures to facilitate generalization in the natural environment. Environmentally based procedures are also useful in promoting overall language development and can be implemented by persons with limited knowledge of children's skills and language-training programs.

Environmental Procedures

Environmentally based techniques are procedures used in nontraining settings to promote generalization to these environments. Three general guidelines form the basis of these techniques: 1) create opportunities for language use, 2) make language functional for the child, and 3) reinforce the use of any language.

Create Opportunities for Language The first step in supporting generalization is to ensure opportunities for language display. Opportunities abound naturally, at least for the competent adult language user. To the language-learning child, however, those opportunities may not be obvious. Thus, the first task is to make apparent to the language-learning child the instances when language is required or desired.

This represents a problem of stimulus control. In training, the stimulus events indicating that language is required are straightforward. Usually the trainer asks a question, holds up a picture or object, and waits for the child to verbalize. In natural environments, however, most language opportunities are not so clearly structured. Descriptive data collected during the last 2½ years suggest that, except during academic instruction, adults ask few questions and demand few verbalizations from language deficient children. Generalization fails to occur because the functional stimuli (both objects and verbal prompts) present in training do not occur in the classroom or in the home. One means of facilitating generalization would be to introduce stimuli in the natural setting that signal that language is required or useful. Two classes of stimuli are particularly important: things to talk about, and people to talk to.

Failure to observe generalization, particularly in the early stages of language training, may result from the limited number of things the child is able to talk about. If the objects or events the child has learned to label or describe in training are not present in the nontraining setting, there are no opportunities for the child to generalize. Simply introducing training stimuli into nontraining settings may be sufficient to prompt generalization. However, it is likely that other training stimuli, such as questions, or holding up the object for the child to see or touch, also may be needed as initial support. A teacher might construct a list of training probes and then structure opportunities for the child to respond to those probes in the classroom. If the object or picture then remains available in the room, both students and staff can be prompted to verbalize about it on other, unstructured occasions.

There is no language stimulus more important than a listener. Descriptions of children's environments have identified two important points: both the number of adults present and the amount that those adults verbalize influence children's language rate and generalization. Initial observations of 20 severely retarded children indicated that as the number of adults increased the rate of child verbalization also increased. In a later study, when rates of adult verbalization were compared with rates of child verbalization and generalization across settings, the same relationship was found. When adults spoke more, children spoke more and generalized more readily. There may be diminishing returns, however. Adult speech rates probably should not exceed moderate levels, or children again will have no opportunities to speak.

Arranging the environment to make listeners more readily available and to prompt interactions may be one time-efficient means of promoting generalization. For example, VanBiervliet, Spangler, and Marshall (Note 1) examined rates of peer-directed verbalizations by severely retarded children in an institution dining hall. They found that residents verbalized more when they served their own meals "family style" than when they picked up individual food trays and seated themselves cafeteria style. Structuring the environment to create opportunities and reasons to talk (requesting food items) and persons to talk to (stable groups at each table) increased language use without continuous staff prompts for verbalizations. Environmental arrangements to facilitate language are particularly attractive because they do not require constant staff involvement, and should be considered whenever possible.

Make Language Functional for the Child   Another way of facilitating generalization is to make language functional for the child. Language must actually change the environment and mediate needed goods and services. In many settings populated by severely handicapped children, language may not be functional. Other ways may be more efficient in changing the environment to get what is needed. Nonverbal behavior such as pointing or grabbing may produce a cookie more quickly than saying "cookie." Thus, the task for the teacher is to make language work uniquely well for the child.

One technique that has been used with moderately skilled children includes a chain of behaviors by the teacher to prompt language display. Use of incidental teaching techniques was first documented by Hart and Risley (1975). The environment is arranged to offer many interesting objects and activities that function as reinforcers. When the child indicates interest in one of these objects, the teacher focuses attention on the child and requests (mands) the child to verbalize (e.g., "Tell me what you want"). If the child does not know the name of the object or needs a model to complete a sentence, the teacher supplies a verbal model. When the child verbalizes, the object, praise, and continued attention are provided as reinforcers. Across many trials, a simple lesson is taught: language, and often only language, can be used to obtain desired objects or activities.

In an experiment with three language-delayed children, Rogers-Warren and Warren (in press) used the mand-model-reinforce strategy to increase overall rates of verbalization. The procedures worked well to increase verbalization and to prompt generalization of specific trained forms. Halle, Marshall, and Spradlin (1979) devised a simpler way to teach this lesson using a brief delay as a stimulus for requests. Six children in a residential treatment center for severely retarded children were taught to ask for their meal trays at breakfast. Training consisted of the staff member calling the child's name, then holding the tray and waiting for the child to verbalize. If the child had not verbalized at the end of 15 seconds, the staff member modeled the verbalization, "Tray please," and prompted the child to imitate. Regardless of the child's response, the tray was delivered. All six children learned to request trays at the breakfast training setting and generalized to a lunch setting where the delay was used without models. Systematic probes across unknown trainers and novel settings demonstrated that most children generalized requesting to other appropriate circumstances.

Daily activities of handicapped children in academic and living settings should offer other opportunities to prompt specific responses. For example, generalization of labels taught in training might be prompted at mealtime, before going outside, or whenever the object is used. Incorporating a language requirement in daily routines requires identification of appropriate responses, a procedure for requesting and prompting the verbalization, and ensuring a reinforcing consequence. However, prompting language in the context of already familiar routines should be relatively easy.

Reinforce the Child for Language Use   Possibly the easiest and the most obvious means of supporting generalized language is simply to reinforce it whenever it occurs. Reinforcing specific responses may be difficult in the ongoing stream of daily activities. The teacher must know what the child had been trained to say, must be sure that the child has opportunities to display the learned response, and must catch the child using it. A more practical approach may be to increase the overall rate of reinforcement for any language use. Reinforcing some members of the broad class of language behavior may be sufficient to maintain the newly trained language responses. To the extent that language works to control the environment, a strong reinforcement base may already exist. Attention, praise for language, and presenting desired objects or services only when they are requested are positive consequences that signal to the child that this is a setting where language is both required and reinforced, just as it is in the training setting.

Environmental facilitation techniques can be categorized into two types: those that rely on arranging the physical environment to prompt language, and those that arrange only the social-verbal environment to prompt language. In many cases, both physical and social arrangements are used to provide opportunities and sufficient natural reinforcers.

Techniques for facilitating generalization by creating opportunities for its use, making it functional for the child, and reinforcing the child's language display are, in general, relatively simple. However, implementing any facilitation procedures will require support from staff, parents, or other individuals in the child's environment. The problem of generalization actually extends to two populations: the children learning language, and the individuals learning to support the children's newly learned language. To maximize generalization, staff need to know specifically what language has been trained. It is not enough to assume that weekly or monthly staffings convey sufficient information. Rather, special steps must be taken to inform everyone about the child's current language-training program. Like the child, the staff will need support in their efforts. Arrangements primarily intended to facilitate child verbalizations may also aid the staff in prompting and reinforcing language. For example, incorporating prompts for language into already existing routines may be a means of reminding staff to require language, as well as an opportunity to teach specific language functions to students. Staff and parents may need some initial practice with prompting or reinforcement to be comfortable doing it and to integrate it into their repertoires. Reinforcers, such as graphs of their performance, regular feedback, evidence of child progress (i.e., graphs or verbatim transcripts of child utterances) should be programmed for generalization facilitators as well as for target child populations.

Both training-based and environment-based facilitation techniques may be needed to ensure generalization. No research has shown either approach to be superior, and, in fact, the distinction between the training setting and the natural environment is an arbitrary one. In reality, a continuum exists across all the settings the child enters.

FUTURE RESEARCH DIRECTIONS

Research on language generalization to date has been modest, although significant attention has been devoted to studies of performance on structured probes. There have been few investigations of generalization to the natural environment or of language maintenance, which may be the most important outcomes of language training.

Longitudinal investigations of natural environment generalization and maintenance are expensive. However, the further development of successful language remediation strategies would seem to depend on them, because they offer systematic analyses of the effectiveness of training curricula in settings where communication skills are functional and necessary. Information from such analyses can provide the basis for developing improved curricula.

The investigation of natural environment language generalization should parallel research to develop a technology of language generalization. Considerable work remains. Of the four specific approaches discussed above, three (loose training, common stimuli, and indiscriminable contingencies) have received little or no systematic investigation relative to language generalization. Very little work has been done on procedures to be used in the natural environment independent of formal training.

Language is a critical behavior. A language-delayed individual is severely, but not necessarily permanently, impaired. Curriculum developers have formulated programs to teach language based on their "best guesses" about how language works and how it can be taught (see Guess, this volume, for a related discussion). The longitudinal analysis of language generalization provides an opportunity to improve on these guesses and to develop effective programs incorporating content that has a reasonable probability of generalizing to the natural environment. Concurrent research on techniques to promote generalization can provide a comprehensive and effective technology for remediating language delays.

The critical need for language training, its possible role as an experimental test of current theoretical analyses of language systems and acquisition strategies, should make evaluation a research priority. This priority is further supported by the applied value of successful language-training programs. A *successful* language-training program, especially one that brings previously nonlinguistic children to some appreciable level of language use, shows that the pattern of experiences it provides is at least a sufficient set of conditions for the emergence of some language skills. It is exceptionally difficult to test different theories of language acquisition against one another. Language-training programs represent less than ideal but nonetheless important attempts to determine sufficient conditions for language acquisition. When training succeeds, it validates theories positing training conditions as functional for language acquisition and invalidates theories arguing that language acquisition is impossible without some condition manifestly absent in the program in question. Certainly, the success of such programs does not establish the *necessary* conditions of language acquisition, but in the present state of theory in this area, contributions toward the definition of *sufficient* conditions are immensely valuable.

REFERENCES

Anglin, J. M. *Word, object, and conceptual development*. New York: W. W. Norton & Co., Inc., 1977.

Baer, D. M., & Guess, D. Receptive training of adjectival inflections in mental retardates. *Journal of Applied Behavior Analysis*, 1971, *4*, 129–139.

Baer, D. M., & Guess, D. Teaching productive noun suffixes to severely retarded children. *American Journal of Mental Deficiency*, 1973, *77*, 498–505.

Bennett, C. W., & Ling, D. Teaching a complex verbal response to a hearing impaired girl. *Journal of Applied Behavior Analysis*, 1972, *5*, 321–327.

Bloom, L. *Language development: Form and function in emerging grammars*. Cambridge, Massachusetts: The MIT Press, 1970.

Bowerman, M. Semantic and syntactic development: A review of what, when and how in language acquisition. In R. L. Schiefelbusch (ed.), *Bases of language intervention*. Baltimore: University Park Press, 1978.

Brown, R. *A first language: The early stages*. Cambridge: Harvard University Press, 1973.

Clark, H. B., & Sherman, J. A. Teaching generative use of sentence answers. *Journal of Applied Behavior Analysis*, 1975, *8*, 321–330.

Crabtree, M. *Houston test for language development*. Chicago: Stoelting Co., 1963.

Dunn, L. M. *Peabody picture vocabulary test*. Circle Pines, Minnesota: American Guidance Services, Inc., 1965.

Garcia, E. The training and generalization of a conversational speech form in nonverbal retardates. *Journal of Applied Behavior Analysis*, 1974, *7*, 137–149.

Garcia, E., Guess, D., & Byrnes, J. Development of syntax in a retarded girl using procedures of imitation, reinforcement, and modeling. *Journal of Applied Behavior Analysis*, 1973, *6*, 299–310.

Guess, D. A functional analysis of receptive language and productive speech: Acquisition of the plural morpheme. *Journal of Applied Behavior Analysis*, 1969, *2*, 55–64.

Guess, D., & Baer, D. M. An analysis of individual differences in generalization between receptive and productive language in retarded children. *Journal of Applied Behavior Analysis*, 1973, *6*, 311–329.

Guess, D., Keogh, W., & Sailor, W. Generalization of speech and language behavior. In R. L. Schiefelbusch (ed.), *Bases of language intervention*. Baltimore: University Park Press, 1978.

Guess, D., Sailor, W., & Baer, D. *Functional speech and language training for the severely handicapped*. Lawrence, Kansas: H & H Enterprises, Inc., 1978.

Guess, D., Sailor, W., Rutherford, G., & Baer, D. M. An experimental analysis of linguistic development: The productive use of the plural morpheme. *Journal of Applied Behavior Analysis*, 1968, *1*, 225–235.

Halle, J., Marshall, A., & Spradlin, J. Time delay: A technique to increase language use and facilitate generalization in retarded children. *Journal of Applied Behavior Analysis*, 1979, *12*, 95–103.

Harris, S. L. Teaching language to nonverbal children—with emphasis on problems of generalization. *Psychological Record*, 1975, *82*, 565–580.

Hart, B., & Risley, T. R. Incidental teaching of language in the preschool. *Journal of Applied Behavior Analysis*, 1975, *8*, 411–420.

Hester, P., & Hendrikson, J. Training functional expressive language: The acquisition and generalization of five-element syntactic responses. *Journal of Applied Behavior Analysis*, 1977, *10*, 316.

Jeffree, D., Wheldall, K., & Mittler, P. Facilitating two-word utterances in two Down's syndrome boys. *American Journal of Mental Deficiency*, 1973, *78*, 117–122.

Lutzker, J. R., & Sherman, J. A. Producing generative sentence usage by imitation and reinforcement procedures. *Journal of Applied Behavior Analysis*, 1974, *7*, 447–460.

Nelson, K. Structure and strategy in learning to talk. *Society for Research in Child Development Monographs*, 1973, *38*.

Rincover, A., & Koegel, R. L. A treatment of psychotic children in a classroom environment: I. Learning in a large group. *Journal of Applied Behavior Analysis*, 1975, *8*, 45–60.

Rinsland, H. D. *A basic vocabulary of elementary school children.* New York: Macmillan Co., 1945.

Rogers-Warren, A., & Warren, S. F. Mands for verbalization: Facilitating the display of newly-taught language in children. *Behavior Modification*, in press.

Sailor, W. Reinforcement and generalization of productive plural allomorphs in two retarded children. *Journal of Applied Behavior Analysis*, 1971, *4*, 305–310.

Schroeder, G. L., & Baer, D. M. Effects of concurrent and serial training on generalized vocal imitation in retarded children. *Developmental Psychology*, 1972, *6*, 293–301.

Schumaker, J., & Sherman, J. A. Training generative verb usage by imitation and reinforcement procedures. *Journal of Applied Behavior Analysis*, 1970, *3*, 273–287.

Stremel, K., & Waryas, C. A behavioral-psycholinguistic approach to language training. *American Speech and Hearing Monographs*, 1974, *18*, 96–124.

Stevens-Long, J., & Rasmussen, M. The acquisition of simple and compound sentence structure in an autistic child. *Journal of Applied Behavior Analysis*, 1974, *7*, 473–479.

Stokes, T. F., & Baer, D. M. An implicit technology of generalization. *Journal of Applied Behavior Analysis*, 1977, *10*, 349–367.

Tucker, D. J., Keilitz, I., & Horner, R. D. Increasing mentally retarded adolescents' verbalizations about current events. *Journal of Applied Behavior Analysis*, 1973, *6*, 621–630.

Wheeler, A. J., & Sulzer, B. Operant training and generalization of a verbal response form in a speech deficient child. *Journal of Applied Behavior Analysis*, 1970, *3*, 139–147.

REFERENCE NOTE

1. VanBiervliet, A., Spangler, P., & Marshall, A. *The effects of family dining on the verbal behavior of institutionalized children.* Unpublished manuscript, University of Kansas, Lawrence, 1979.

Chapter 9

Learning Characteristics of Autistic Children

Robert L. Koegel, Andrew L. Egel, and Glen Dunlap

The recent proliferation of behavior modification procedures for educating autistic children has produced one of the most significant changes in the treatment of autism. The technology that is being developed has resulted in an increased interest in providing treatment opportunities. This is especially evident from the advent of state and federal legislation mandating public education of handicapped, including autistic, children. However, many educators are unaware of the progress that is being made, or even what is meant by the term *autism*. Therefore, this chapter begins with a description of what is usually meant by *autism*.

DESCRIPTION OF AUTISM

Autism was first described as a distinctive disorder by Leo Kanner in 1943. Various elaborations of his definition have followed (e.g., Ferster, 1961; Goldfarb, 1961; Kanner, 1973; Ornitz & Ritvo, 1968; Rutter, 1978; Schopler, 1978), including the current definition adopted by the National Society for Autistic Children (Ritvo & Freeman, 1978). In general, autism is described as a severe form of mental disorder that has profound effects not only upon the lives of the children afflicted, but upon the lives of their parents and members of their community as well. Approximately one child in every 2,500 births is likely to be labeled autistic. Typically, the disorder is not diagnosed until the child reaches the age of 2 to 5 years; however, there is a general consensus among researchers that the disorder is probably present from birth.

Portions of the research described in this article were supported by U. S. Public Health Service research grants MH28210 and MH28231 from the National Institute of Mental Health, and U. S. Office of Education Research grant G007802084 from the Bureau of Education for the Handicapped. Correspondence regarding this article should be addressed to Robert L. Koegel, Social Process Research Institute, University of California, Santa Barbara, California 93106.

When people refer to autism they are typically describing children who display a majority of the following symptoms:

1. *A lack of appropriate speech:* The children are usually nonverbal or echolalic (parroting phrases spoken to them, but unable to use them meaningfully in other contexts).
2. *Lack of appropriate social behavior:* They either appear oblivious to other people's presence or relate to people in a bizarre manner.
3. *Apparent sensory deficit:* The children are often incorrectly suspected of being blind or deaf.
4. *Lack of appropriate play:* They usually ignore toys or interact inappropriately with them (for example, throwing or mouthing a toy truck).
5. *Inappropriate and out-of-context emotional behavior:* Extreme tantrums or outbursts of hysterical laughter may be common, or, on the other hand, the children may display a virtual absence of emotional responding.
6. *Self-stimulation:* The children typically engage in high rates of stereotyped, repetitive behaviors, such as flapping fingers or rhythmically rocking for hours without pause.
7. *Isolated areas of high level functioning ("splinter skills"):* Some of the children are especially proficient in a particular area such as music, number configurations, or manipulation of mechanical instruments, yet demonstrate otherwise low level intellectual functioning (Rimland, 1978).

Another frequently cited characteristic is their normal physical appearance. As children, they present no associated physical deformities (although years of untreated autistic responding may eventually lead to physical abnormalities in posture, teeth, etc); indeed, they are often cute and physically attractive.

Major Problems in the Diagnosis of Autism

When one attempts to define *autism,* it immediately becomes apparent that one is faced with tremendous heterogeneity (cf. Schreibman & Koegel, in press). First, there is more than one definition, and these definitions are not in complete agreement (cf. Churchill, Alpern, & DeMyer, 1971; Ritvo & Freeman, 1978; Rutter, 1978; Schopler, 1978). Second, within any one of the proposed definitions, there is still great variability in the application of the diagnosis. That is, the term *autism* refers to a "syndrome," in which all of the symptoms need not be present in each case. As a result, one "autistic" child may exhibit a set of behaviors almost totally different from that of another child.

The heterogeneity represented by children considered autistic leads to at least three major problems. First, the diagnosis does not facilitate communication. Even when professionals agree on a given definition, that definition still only summarizes the behaviors of the group and does not specify the behaviors of any individual. Second, the diagnosis of autism per se does not imply a treatment procedure. There is no consensus among professionals as to how to treat autism. Where there is occasional agreement on a specific treatment technique, the technique is usually for a particular symptom (e.g., self-destructive behavior), not for the syndrome as a whole. Third, the term *autism* does not suggest a prognosis. It is true that without treatment most autistic children do not improve; however, a few autistic children do improve without treatment (Rutter, 1968). With treatment, some autistic children improve a great deal, while others show little change at all (Lovaas, Koegel, Simmons, & Long, 1973).

Behavioral Assessment

In an attempt to resolve some of the above problems, many investigators have deemphasized the importance of defining autism, and have instead focused on assessing individual behaviors. There is still an attempt to classify or group, but in this case it is toward clustering *behaviors* according to those that covary and/or have common controlling variables. According to this approach, a functional definition of autism is gradually developed as each of the individual behaviors accompanying the disorder becomes understood and can be treated.

In general, the approach proceeds as follows. In the first step, individual behaviors are operationally defined. For example, instead of simply saying that autistic children exhibit self-stimulatory behavior, this behavior is spelled out in such a way that independent observers can reliably record it regardless of the child's overall diagnosis. For example, in Table 1, self-stimulatory behavior has been defined for each of two children in terms of the exact behaviors each child exhibited (from wiggling toes inside of tennis shoes to swishing saliva in the mouth, etc.).

The second step in a behavioral assessment involves identifying the variables that control the behavior. This may involve a library search for research articles dealing with each behavior. For example, Carr (1977) has reviewed an extensive body of research dealing with self-destructive behavior, and has identified the major variables known to control this behavior (descriptions of several of these variables are provided later in this chapter). While literature reviews are a common and quite valuable process for identifying controlling variables, it should be pointed out that direct functional analyses of individual behaviors continue to represent the most accurate method.

The third step in a behavioral assessment is to *group the behaviors* according to common controlling variables. Note that this is *different from grouping children* according to similarities in behaviors. In a behavioral assessment, the label is not applied to the child or to a group of children. Just as one would not refer to broken-leg children or measles children since there is no reason to assume that these children are similar with respect to any of their other behaviors, so one should not refer to self-stimulatory children. Rather, the labeling process is applied to behaviors and groups of behaviors. Relatively large numbers of behaviors can be grouped. For example, in Table 1, individual behaviors can easily be grouped together and referred to by the same name since they all appear to be controlled, as a group, by the same variables. Future research may reveal that subcategories and/or larger, more comprehensive categories of behaviors

Table 1. Complete list of self-stimulatory responses for subject 1 and subject 2

subject 1
1. Eye crossing
2. Finger manipulations (moving the hands with continuous flexion and extension)
3. Repetitive vocalizations (excluding recognizable words)
4. Feet contortions (tight, sustained flexions)
5. Leg contortions (tight, sustained flexions)
6. Rhythmic manipulation of objects (repeatedly rubbing, rotating, or tapping objects with fingers)
7. Grimacing (corners of mouth drawn out and down, revealing the upper set of teeth)
8. Staring or gazing (a fixed glassy-eyed look lasting more than 3 sec.)
9. Hands repetitively rubbing mouth
10. Hands repetitively rubbing face
11. Mouthing objects (holding non-edible objects in contact with the mouth)
12. Locking hands behind head
13. Hands pressing on or twisting ears

subject 2
1. Staring or gazing (a fixed glassy-eyed look lasting more than 3 sec.)
2. Grimacing (corners of mouth drawn out and down, revealing the upper set of teeth)
3. Hand waving vertically or horizontally with fingers outstretched in front of eyes
4. Hands vigorously and repetitively rubbing eyes
5. Hands vigorously and repetitively rubbing nose
6. Hands vigorously and repetitively rubbing mouth
7. Hands vigorously and repetitively rubbing ears
8. Hands vigorously and repetitively rubbing hair
9. Hands vigorously and repetitively rubbing clothes
10. Hands vigorously and repetitively rubbing objects
11. Hand flapping in air
12. Hand wringing (alternately rubbing and clutching hands)
13. Finger contortions (tight, sustained flexions)
14. Tapping fingers against part of body or an object
15. Tapping whole hand against part of body or object
16. Mouthing objects (holding non-edible objects in contact with the mouth)
17. Rocking (moving the trunk at the hips rhythmically back and forth or from side to side)
18. Head weaving (moving head from side to side in a figure 8 pattern)
19. Body contortions (sustained flexions or extensions of the torso)
20. Repetitive vocalizations (excluding recognizable words)
21. Teeth clicking (audibly and rapidly closing teeth together)
22. Tongue rolling and clicking
23. Audible saliva swishing in mouth
24. Repetitively tapping feet on floor
25. Repetitively tapping toes inside shoes (visible through canvas tennis shoes)
26. Leg contortions (tight, sustained flexions)
27. Repetitively knocking knees against each other
28. Repetitively knocking ankles against each other
29. Tensing legs and suspending feet above the ground
30. Head shaking (rapid small movements from side to side)
31. Tensing whole body and shaking

This table was first published in *Journal of Applied Behavior Analysis*, 1974, 7, 523. Reprinted here by permission.

may be identified. For example, Lovaas, Varni, Koegel, and Lorsch (1977) have argued that certain self-stimulatory behaviors and certain types of delayed echolalia may be controlled by the same variables, e.g., a need for sensory input (cf., also, Koegel & Felsenfeld, 1977). Eventually with this approach an empirically defined limit is reached, where all of the behaviors controlled by a given set of variables have been identified. At that time, one of these sets of behaviors (which perhaps most closely fits one of the existing global definitions of autism) could be adopted as a functional definition of autism.

That definition of autism would be a useful one. First, it would facilitate communication. Any two independent observers recording the self-stimulatory behavior of the children described in Table 1, for example, would come up with essentially the same numbers. Phrased differently, it may be easy to read the definition and then visualize the behavior, although probably not to visualize the entire child. Second, the definition suggests a treatment (when the variables controlling the behavior are known). The teacher can manipulate the controlling variables and accordingly change the behavior in a desirable and predictable direction. The treatment procedure can frequently be taken directly from the methods section of a journal article, where treatments are described in detail (followed by a detailed description of the results produced by those procedures). Third, the definition suggests a prognosis. If most of the variables controlling the behavior are known (as appears to be the case with self-destructive behavior), then the prognosis for that behavior is extremely favorable. On the other hand, when many of the variables controlling a behavior are unknown (as appears to be the case with many self-stimulatory behaviors), then the prognosis for that behavior is guarded.

In summary, the behavioral approach to assessment 1) is immediately useful for the treatment of individual behaviors across children regardless of their overall diagnosis, and 2) has the potential to provide a means of gradually evolving a functional overall definition of autism. Naturally, since the behavior modification approach to the treatment of "autism" has dealt with changing behaviors, both individually and in covarying groups, it has relied heavily on the behavioral method of assessment.

Among the first targets addressed by behavior modifiers was the teaching of appropriate verbal repertoires. Hewett (1965), Lovaas (1966, 1969), and Lovaas, Berberich, Perloff, and Schaeffer (1966) used imitation and shaping procedures to establish speech in mute autistic children. Similar procedures were then applied to the modification of echolalic speech (Carr, Schreibman, & Lovaas, 1975; Risley & Wolf, 1967). Behavioral researchers have also considered more sophisticated verbal behaviors, such as prepositional usage (Sailor & Taman, 1972), complex sentence forms (Wheeler & Sulzer, 1970), and compound sentence structure (Stevens-Long & Rasmussen, 1974). Several language programs now incorporate these early studies with more recent findings into comprehensive regimes for language development in autistic children (e.g., Lovaas, 1977). A number of comprehensive treatment programs have shown that the application of such programs to individual children can result in marked generalized improvement such that the children no longer exhibit many autistic behaviors (cf. Lovaas et al., 1973; Wetzel, Baker, Roney, & Martin, 1966; Wolf, Risley, Johnston, Harris, & Allen, 1967; Wolf, Risley, & Mees, 1964).

Given, then, that major changes can be produced in the behaviors of "autistic children," are they still autistic? Given current definitions, probably not. The remainder of this chapter is devoted to a discussion of the issues involved in using the educational system to produce those changes. The review of the literature is divided into two categories: 1) problem areas that can interfere with the teaching process in general (as well as solutions to those problems), and 2) the application of these teaching techniques to the classroom environment.

GENERAL TEACHING PROBLEMS AND SOLUTIONS

Reviews of the literature on the development of teaching procedures for autistic children have pointed to five major problem areas that can interfere with the educational process: 1) physically disruptive behavior, such as tantrums and aggression, 2) self-stimulatory behavior, 3) lack of motivation, 4) stimulus overselectivity, and 5) absence of generalization and maintenance of treatment gains. The following sections provide detailed discussion of these problems and suggest effective procedures for solving them.

Physically Disruptive Behavior

One of the most salient problems with which an educator of autistic children must be prepared to deal concerns frequent outbursts of temper and other disruptive behavior. Since tantrums are characteristic of many autistic and other severely handicapped children, a large body of research has been devoted to the development of effective techniques for eliminating such behavior. *Extinction* is an effective and frequently used procedure for reducing undesirable behavior. Typically, in an extinction procedure a teacher withholds a reinforcer contingent on a particular behavior. For example, if a child's tantrums are maintained by the reinforcer of teacher attention, ceasing to provide that attention eliminates the tantrums. While extinction is an effective procedure, research has demonstrated several possible drawbacks to its use. First, there is usually a gradual reduction in the strength of the behavior, rather than a sharp, dramatic drop (cf. Lovaas & Simmons, 1969). Second, there is usually an initial (temporary) increase in the strength of the behavior. For example, once the attention maintaining a child's tantrum is no longer present, the intensity of the tantrum may increase as the child attempts to "recover" the lost attention.

Punishment has also been shown to be an effective treatment procedure for behaviors that have not been successfully treated by other methods such as extinction (Lichstein & Schreibman, 1976; Lovaas & Simmons, 1969; Tate & Baroff, 1966). Punishment refers to the presentation of a stimulus contingent upon a particular behavior with the result of reducing the frequency of the behavior. A review of the literature indicates that a wide variety of effective techniques are available. Many times a mild verbal "no" is sufficient to reduce the undesirable behavior, while in other cases physical punishment in the form of a quick slap on the hand or even contingent electric shock may be necessary. However, clinicians and teachers may find the use of physical punishment too extreme for a particular behavior, or such severe punishment may be inappropriate in certain situations.

It is important for teachers to note that punishment may serve only to suppress behavior temporarily. Consequently, it appears necessary for the teacher to teach the child concurrently a new, appropriate behavior that can be used in place of the undesirable behaviors. Schreibman and Koegel (in press) have noted several considerations that should determine whether punishment procedures are appropriate. The first consideration is the nature of the response suppression desired. For example, punishment might be the treatment of choice for a severely self-abusive or highly aggressive child. Second, punishment may be chosen when other procedures such as extinction have failed. Finally, the teacher should select the mildest punisher that will effectively reduce the disruptive behavior.

One relatively mild, yet effective, procedure for dealing with outbursts is *time-out*. White, Nielsen, and Johnson (1972) have defined time-out as an "arrangement in which the occurrence of a response is followed by a period of time in which a variety of reinforcers are no longer available." In a classroom situation, this may involve placing the child in a small bare room for a specific time following the undesirable behavior, or it may merely involve the teacher looking away from the child (if the reinforcers are primarily social). Time-out has been used extensively for eliminating behavior across a wide variety of children and in varying situations. One of the earliest empirical demonstrations of its effectiveness was completed by Wolf, Risley, and Mees (1964), who demonstrated that tantrums and self-destructive behavior in an autistic child can be reduced effectively by placing the child alone in a room each time the behavior occurs. The authors also suggested that it is desirable to positively reinforce incompatible nondeviant behavior in combination with time-out. Time-out has also been used effectively to control the aggressive behavior of retarded children (Bostow & Bailey, 1969; Hamilton, Stephens, & Allen, 1967; White et al., 1972) and delinquents (Tyler & Brown, 1967).

While time-out has been shown to be an extremely effective punishment technique for reducing undesirable behavior, there are several important parameters to consider when implementing the procedure. One consideration is the optimum duration of a time-out episode for a child. While the literature suggests that time-out intervals ranging from 2 minutes (Bostow & Bailey, 1969) to 3 hours (Burchard & Tyler, 1965) have been used successfully, White et al. (1972) have pointed out that a majority of investigators have reported successful results using time-out durations in the range of 5 to 20 minutes. However, it also can be inferred from the above studies that there is no consensus on an "optimum" duration for time-out. Duration appears to be dependent on the child and the particular behavior that is to be reduced. An effective time-out period for one child may be completely ineffective for another.

Recent research has pointed out that this is also true of the time-out procedure in general. Solnick, Rincover, and Peterson (1977) have suggested that there is no "standard" time-out procedure that will effectively reduce problem behavior for all children. In a study designed to examine both the possible punishing and reinforcing effects of time-out, the authors found that when time-out was employed to suppress tantrums, it had the opposite effect; that is, time-out resulted in a substantial *increase* in the frequency of tantrums. Upon further analysis, it was shown that the child used the time-out period to engage in self-stimulatory behavior. In other words, the increase in the number of tantrums appeared to be a function of increased sensory reinforcement resulting from the opportunity to engage in self-stimulation. These results suggest that teachers using time-out should ensure that the child is not engaging in preferred behaviors during the time-out period.

A related finding from the Solnick et al. (1977) study suggested that the effectiveness of a time-out procedure also may be influenced by the nature of the "time-in" setting. The authors found that when the time-in setting was not highly reinforcing (i.e., "impoverished"), time-out was ineffective in reducing the frequency of spitting and self-injurious behavior. In a situation such as this, time-out may serve as a negative reinforcer in that the child's behavior removes him or her from an undesirable situation or deficient environment. However, when the *time-in* environment was highly reinforcing (i.e., "enriched"), the same time-out procedure was effective in reducing the undesirable behavior (Carr, Newsom, & Binkoff, 1976; Solnick et al., 1977).

Additional techniques for reducing tantrums and other undesirable behaviors have also been developed, and may be employed when time-out is undesirable, inappropriate, or ineffective. For example, Plummer, Baer, and LeBlanc (1977) found that, in situations where time-out had the effect of negatively reinforcing inappropriate behavior, the use of *paced instructions* (instructions presented regardless of the child's behavior) was an effective alternative to time-out. In considering alternatives to time-out, another point to note is that time-out may be costly in terms of available teaching time, since it requires that the child be removed from the teaching environment each time the inappropriate behavior occurs. Clark, Rowbury, Baer, and Baer (1973) have suggested that the use of an intermittent schedule of time-out will reduce inappropriate behavior while allowing for more teaching time. Their results indicate that time-out used as a consequence for every third or fourth occurrence of an inappropriate act can be almost as effective as a schedule in which time-out is applied for every occurrence of the disruptive behavior.

Another punishment is that referred to as *restitution* or *overcorrection* (Foxx & Azrin, 1972). The restitution procedure proposed by Foxx and Azrin has two objectives: 1) to overcorrect the environmental effects of an inappropriate act, and 2) to require the disruptor to practice thoroughly overly correct forms of appropriate behavior. The first objective is achieved through the use of *restitutional overcorrection*. This procedure requires the disruptive individual to return the disturbed situation to a greatly improved state, thus providing an instructive situation in which the individual is required to assume personal responsibility for the disruptive act. For example, a child who smeared paint on a floor might be required to clean up the mess and then vacuum and wax the area. The second objective is achieved through *positive practice overcorrection*. Using this procedure, the child who smeared the paint on the floor might be required to paint repeatedly on paper. When no environmental disruption occurs, the restitutional overcorrection is not applicable and only the positive practice is used. The effectiveness of overcorrection as a procedure for eliminating aggressive disruptive behavior was clearly demonstrated by Foxx and Azrin (1972). They employed an overcorrection procedure to reduce aggressive behavior (e.g., physical assault, property damage, tantrums, and biting). The results showed that while time-out and social disapproval had been ineffective in eliminating the above behaviors, overcorrection reduced the disruptive behaviors to a near zero level within 1 to 2 weeks. Overcorrection thus appears to be a viable means for reducing aggressive behavior. In addition, the procedure (as described by its proponents) may minimize some of the negative properties of other punishment procedures; it may also educate the individual in appropriate behavior; and it appears to require relatively little staff training (Foxx & Azrin, 1972). Further research, however, appears necessary in order to substantiate these latter points. Axelrod, Brantner, and Meddock (1978), in a review of overcorrection research, note that possible side effects have yet to be carefully examined, that the importance of maintaining topographical similarity between the response and its consequence is unclear, and that many parameters (such as duration of consequence) of maximally efficient administration of overcorrection are still unknown. These authors also point out that component analyses of the procedure may, in the future, serve to relate overcorrection more explicitly to punishment per se.

The procedures discussed above are punishment methods that are widely used to reduce and/or eliminate disruptive behaviors. For many teachers this may be a necessary first step in preparing an effective learning environment for the autistic child. However, if an educator decides to use any punishment procedure, it is important to realize that punishment only suppresses undesirable behavior. As long as the reinforcer (e.g., attention) is still available, the child will want to obtain it. Therefore, teachers should concurrently provide that reinforcer for other desirable behaviors in order to expand the child's behavioral repertoire in a more appropriate direction.

Self-Stimulatory Behavior

One type of disruptive behavior that warrants special attention is self-stimulatory behavior. Self-stimulatory behavior is the persistent stereotyped-repetitive behavior that is considered to be one of the most defining characteristics of autistic children (Rimland, 1964) and one of the most formidable obstacles to educating them. Lovaas, Litrownik, and Mann (1971) observed that responding was disrupted when a child engaged in self-stimulatory behavior, yet recovered when self-stimulation was absent. They suggested that when children are engaged in self-stimulation they may not be able to attend to more relevant stimuli. With this issue in mind, Koegel and Covert (1972) attempted to teach a simple discrimination task to three autistic children with high levels of self-stimulatory behavior. Their results clearly established that self-stimulatory behavior can interfere with the acquisition of a new discriminative stimulus. They found that, although the children continued responding, none of them learned the discrimination during episodes of self-stimulation. However, when self-stimulation was suppressed, the children acquired the discrimination. This apparent inverse relationship between self-stimulation and the acquisition of new, appropriate behaviors has been repeatedly demonstrated. Risley (1968) and Foxx and Azrin (1973) found that various pro-social and attentional behaviors increased when self-stimulation was suppressed, while other researchers have pointed to increases in spontaneous unreinforced behaviors, such as appropriate play (Epstein, Doke, Sajwaj, Sorrell, & Rimmer, 1974; Koegel, Firestone, Kramme, & Dunlap, 1974).

Therapeutic procedures utilized in attempts to suppress self-stimulation have varied, as have the results. One procedure involved *reinforcing responses incompatible with self-stimulation.* For example, Mulhern and Baumeister (1969) employed reinforcement for sitting still to reduce rocking behavior in two retardates. They found that this procedure reduced the inappropriate rocking behavior by about one-third. Others (e.g., Deitz & Repp, 1973; Herendeen, Jeffrey, & Graham, 1974) have also employed differential reinforcement to reduce self-stimulatory behavior substantially. Despite the demonstrated effectiveness of reinforcing incompatible behavior to reduce self-stimulation, the procedure has not been successful in completely suppressing self-stimulatory behavior nor in universally producing decreases of the magnitude previously reported (e.g., Foxx & Azrin, 1973).

A second procedure that has been used effectively to reduce and eliminate self-stimulatory behavior employs physical punishment in the form of contingent electric shock (Lovaas, Schaeffer, & Simmons, 1965; Risley, 1968) or contingent slaps on the hand or thigh (Bucher & Lovaas, 1968; Foxx & Azrin, 1973; Koegel & Covert, 1972; Koegel et al., 1974). Each of these studies has demonstrated that contingent physical punishment is a highly effective method for suppressing self-stimulation. However, as noted above, such severe punishment procedures can have many problems, and time-out probably will increase the behavior. As a result, other investigators have developed alternative punishment techniques that also are effective in suppressing self-stimulatory behavior. For example, Robinson, Hughes, Wilson, Lahey, and Haynes (1974) found that the use of response-contingent *water squirts* was effective in reducing self-stimulatory behavior and noted the relative ease with which this procedure was applied. Furthermore, it required very little time (1-3 seconds) to deliver the punishment and, therefore, did not require the teacher to leave one child in order to deliver punishment to another. Despite these benefits, the complete and enduring elimination of self-stimulatory behavior was not achieved. In addition, the authors indicated that the reduced levels of self-stimulation did not generalize beyond the classroom environment.

Another "mild" punishment procedure that has been shown to be extremely effective in suppressing self-stimulation is *overcorrection* (Foxx & Azrin, 1973). Foxx and Azrin (1973) compared several techniques used to suppress self-stimulation (including punishment by a slap and reinforcement for not engaging in self-stimulation) with positive practice overcorrection. Their results show that the only procedure that eliminated self-stimulatory behavior in the experimental session and during the entire school day was the positive practice overcorrection procedure. The treatment was effective across several types of self-stimulatory behavior including head weaving, object mouthing, hand clapping, and hand mouthing. Furthermore, the results suggested that a verbal reprimand in conjunction with an occasional application of the overcorrection procedure was sufficient to maintain reduced levels of self-stimulation. Other investigators (e.g., Azrin, Kaplan, & Foxx, 1973; Epstein et al., 1974; Herendeen et al., 1974) have confirmed and extended the above findings. Thus, overcorrection appears to be a viable method for substantially reducing self-stimulatory behaviors. While positive practice overcorrection offers an effective alternative to intense physical punishment and reinforcement of incompatible responses, its practicality in applied settings may be limited due to the demand on therapist time and energy. The technique demands more attention (in some settings) to a particular individual than classroom teachers may be able to afford.

Despite some successes with the above procedures in reducing self-stimulatory behavior, the generalized, durable *elimination* of self-stimulatory behaviors has not been achieved (Rincover & Koegel, 1977b). Recently, investigators have suggested that the difficulty in eliminating self-stimulation may be a function of its internal reinforcing properties. That is, self-stimulation may be viewed as operant behavior maintained by its sensory consequences (Rincover, Newsom, Lovaas, & Koegel, 1977). For example, a behavior such as finger flapping may be maintained by the resulting proprioceptive feedback. The conceptualization of self-stimulatory behavior as behavior maintained by its auditory, proprioceptive, or visual consequences has led to the development of a new procedure for eliminating self-stimulation. The procedure of *sensory extinction* is based on the notion that self-stimulatory behavior should extinguish when the reinforcing (sensory) consequences are removed. Rincover (1978a) has demonstrated the effectiveness of sensory extinction for eliminating self-stimulation. He found that self-stimulation was reliably extinguished when specific sensory consequences were removed, and increased when those consequences were permitted. For example, one child's incessant spinning of plates was extinguished when a carpet was placed on the spinning surface (a table), thereby eliminating the auditory feedback provided by the spinning plate. The failure of other sensory extinction manipulations (i.e., visual and proprioceptive) to produce similar decreases in plate spinning suggested that the auditory stimulation was, in fact, the functional reinforcer maintaining the self-stimulatory behavior. In general, Rincover (1978a) found that the sensory reinforcers maintaining the self-stimulation were unique to individual children and that different sensory extinction procedures were required for different self-stimulatory behaviors. This finding could pose some problems with children who engage in numerous self-stimulatory behaviors since it may be difficult to concurrently program sensory extinction procedures across modalities. Nevertheless, the results of this procedure have far-ranging clinical implications. The data suggest that sensory extinction may be a convenient and effective procedure for eliminating self-stimulatory behavior when compared to procedures such as physical punishment, overcorrection, or reinforcement of incompatible behaviors. Rincover (1978a) suggested that the procedure requires very little staff training or child surveillance, has an immediate effect, and should require relatively little effort to program the generalization and maintenance of treatment gains.

While additional research is needed to establish more concretely the parameters involved in the durable elimination of self-stimulation, the procedures reviewed above may help the educator increase the effectiveness of the learning environment by reducing the levels of self-stimulatory behavior the child may exhibit.

Lack of Motivation

A common problem encountered by educators is the autistic child's characteristic lack of motivation. Many investigators (e.g., Mittler, 1966; Rincover, Newsom, Lovaas, & Koegel, 1977) have described these children as showing little curiosity or interest in any but a very small portion of their environment. Consequently, investigators have attempted to develop various methods for motivating autistic children. Several promising lines of research include: 1) the influence of correct vs. incorrect task completion on autistic children's motivation to respond to learning tasks, and 2) the effect of contingent sensory stimulation on the motivation of autistic children.

Influence of Correct vs. Incorrect Task Completion on Motivation   When autistic children are presented with a learning task, they frequently make many incorrect attempts, thus lessening the availability of reinforcement for responding per se. This is particularly true with complex tasks that require some amount of time to complete. For example, when an adult attempts to teach an autistic child to get dressed, the child typically makes many errors and takes so long to complete the task that the adult often discontinues training and dresses the child just to finish the task. Relating this to the notion of availability of reinforcers, the child makes many on-task responses but is never rewarded for on-task responding, or receives so few and such delayed rewards that it may be difficult to relate them to correct responses occurring in the original task. Therefore, one might expect the overall number of attempts to respond to decrease (e.g., Rincover & Koegel, 1977a). Phrased differently, one might say that the child appears very unmotivated to continue responding.

Following this line of thought, Koegel and Egel (1979) designed a study to assess the influence of correct vs. incorrect task completion on autistic children's motivation to respond to learning tasks. For this study, motivation was defined in terms of the proportion of the time the children spent attempting to complete the task. Initially, the children in the study were presented specific tasks and instructed to complete them. The amount of on-task responding and the number of correct responses made were recorded for each child. The results demonstrated that during this condition the children were generally incorrect, and showed low and decreasing levels of responding to those tasks. Koegel and Egel conceptualized this finding in relation to the research on "learned helplessness." This research has defined learned helplessness as a "state" in which the subject has learned that responding and reinforcement are independent (e.g., Miller & Seligman, 1975; Overmeier & Seligman, 1967; Seligman & Maier, 1967). Learning that responding and reinforcement are independent has two basic effects on subjects' behavior. First, the subjects are slower to initiate responses and may not respond at all. Second, subjects have greater difficulty learning the response-reinforcement contingency even when they initiate responses that produce reinforcement because the percentage of reinforced responses is so low (e.g., Seligman, Klein, & Miller, 1976). As previously described, the behavior of the autistic children in the Koegel and Egel study, and of autistic children in general (Ferster, 1974), is strikingly similar to the behavior exhibited by subjects in the learned helplessness studies.

As a result of these findings, Koegel and Egel (1979) developed a treatment procedure designed to increase the child's level of correct responding. For each task, verbal and manual prompts were used in an attempt to keep the children working until they correctly completed the task and received a reward. The results of this treatment procedure showed that prompting the children to complete the task correctly led to improved and increased levels of both on-task responding and the general level of enthusiasm. Furthermore, the results demonstrated that after prompting was discontinued on-task responding remained high *only* if the children continued to complete the task correctly. The implications of these findings for educators are two-fold. First, the autistic children's typically low level of correct responding may result in coincidental low levels of rewards for on-task behavior, thus decreasing their attempts to respond to the task at all. Second, treatment procedures designed to increase the children's receipt of reinforcement for correct responding may result in coincidental reinforcement for "perseverance," increasing the children's overall motivation to respond to those tasks.

Effect of Contingent Sensory Stimulation on Motivation Many investigators consider the characteristic lack of motivation noted in autistic children to be related to the potency or desirability of available reinforcers (e.g., Ferster,

1961; Lovaas & Newsom, 1976). Most educators of autistic children rely on primary (e.g., food) and/or social (e.g., praise) reinforcers. A number of investigators (e.g., Ferster, 1961; Lovaas & Newsom, 1976; Lovaas, Schaeffer, & Simmons, 1965) have noted the difficulty involved in establishing meaningful social rewards for many autistic children. As a result of these difficulties, most teachers must depend on primary rewards to motivate and maintain the children's behavior. However, reliance on primary rewards can create serious problems. Lovaas and Newsom (1976) point out that these rewards may become artificial for older children since they exist only in limited settings such as treatment environments. Second, they suggest that reliance on food rewards results in limited generalization because other environments in which the child interacts may not prescribe primary rewards. An additional problem that can arise is that the children may become satiated and as a result refuse to continue working. These issues can represent severe difficulties for an educator attempting to teach and motivate autistic children.

Some investigators have attempted to help solve these difficulties by investigating alternative forms of reinforcement. Recently, investigations have been conducted to assess the motivational properties of sensory stimulation. As suggested previously (see section on self-stimulatory behavior), one can conceptualize self-stimulation as behavior being maintained by the sensory feedback it produces. This form of sensory stimulation may be inferred to be highly reinforcing since autistic children characteristically spend hours engaged in self-stimulatory behavior (Hung, 1978; Lovaas et al., 1971; Rimland, 1964). Rincover et al. (1977) designed a study to investigate the reinforcing properties of sensory stimulation for autistic children. They initially determined preferred sensory stimuli for each child and then attempted to motivate the children to respond using those sensory stimuli as reinforcers. In other words, brief presentations of the child's preferred sensory event (e.g., a low frequency strobe light or popular music) were presented contingent on correct responses. Their results clearly demonstrated that sensory stimulation could be used as an effective consequence to produce high levels of responding that were relatively durable over time. The authors noted that, while the use of primary reinforcers such as food tended to result in problems of satiation and lack of generalization, the autistic children in this study never did satiate in the general area of their preferred sensory stimulation. Furthermore, when the children did become satiated on a specific event (e.g., a particular song), a minor change in the sensory event led to a recovery of the original high rate of responding.

These findings are very encouraging in light of their therapeutic implications. Rincover and Koegel (1977b) have pointed out that treatment gains might be enhanced if sensory reinforcers were used in educational settings. This is especially true since these types of reinforcers are relatively easy to identify and provide, and because their use may facilitate the generalization of treatment gains from the classroom to other situations since sensory reinforcers are not necessarily limited to a particular setting.

The results of studies in these two areas suggest numerous methods for enhancing the motivation of autistic children. Both approaches lend themselves to relatively easy application in a classroom setting and, taken together, may provide educators with an effective means for motivating an autistic child.

Stimulus Overselectivity

Characteristic of many autistic children (and other children, see Lovaas, Koegel, & Schreibman, 1979) is a tendency to respond to only a very restricted part of their environment. Researchers investigating the learning abilities of autistic children have become increasingly concerned about this problem, which has been labeled *stimulus overselectivity* (Lovaas, Schreibman, Koegel, & Rehm, 1971). Specifically, it appears that when autistic children are presented with a learning situation that requires responding to complex stimuli their behavior comes under the control of a very limited portion of the stimuli. In the first experimental demonstration of this problem, Lovaas et al. (1971) trained normal, retarded, and autistic children to make a response in the presence of a complex stimulus consisting of visual, auditory, and tactile cues. When the components of the stimulus complex were then presented individually, the authors found that the normal children responded equally to all three component cues, while the autistic children responded primarily to only one (auditory or visual) of the component cues. Additionally, the authors found that the autistic children could be taught to respond to the nonfunctional cues when these cues were presented alone. Thus, the study suggested that the deficit was not a function of a specific sensory impairment, but was a problem in responding to a component cue in the context of other cues. Since the original demonstration by Lovaas et al., this finding has been replicated in a two-cue situation (Lovaas & Schreibman, 1971), with all-visual cues (Koegel & Wilhelm, 1973), and with cues presented auditorially (Reynolds, Newsom, & Lovaas, 1974). A comprehensive review of these and other studies related to stimulus overselectivity has been provided by Lovaas, Koegel, and Schreibman (1979) and by Schreibman and Koegel (in press).

The implications of these findings for educational settings become obvious when one examines the number of situations encountered that require the ability to respond on the basis of multiple cues. One implication centers on the autistic child's language deficits. Lovaas et al. (1971) have speculated that, since acquisition of meaningful speech requires attending to simultaneous presentations of multiple auditory and visual cues, a child who responded on the basis of only one of the cues would have a difficult time acquiring meaningful language. This speculation has been given additional support by Reynolds et al. (1974). In a study designed to investigate auditory discrimination learning, the authors found evidence of auditory overselectivity among the autistic children. In other words, the autistic children (in contrast to the normal children) responded primarily on the basis of one component of a two-component auditory stimulus. The authors suggested that since speech perception requires attention to multiple auditory cues (i.e., intensity, duration, and frequency), overselectivity to any one specific auditory cue might interfere with language perception and acquisition.

The autistic child's failure to develop appropriate *social behavior* and the difficulties encountered in attempting to teach social behavior may also be related to selective responding (Schreibman & Lovaas, 1973). Specifically, Schreibman and Lovaas taught normal and autistic children to discriminate between life-like male and female figures. Follow-up probes demonstrated that, while the normal children distinguished between the figures on the basis of a number of cues, the autistic children used minor or irrelevant cues to make the discrimination. For example, if, after the child had learned to respond differentially to the two human figures, the shoes were removed, the child suddenly began to respond incorrectly to the two figures. With subsequent training the autistic child regained the discrimination. However, subsequent data showed that again the child was using some other irrelevant cue. Thus, it is possible to conceive that the autistic child's social deficits may be a result of the child's responding to a limited set of stimuli. A child who recognized people solely on the basis of irrelevant cues such as hair length, presence or absence of eyeglasses, and so on, would be at a severe disadvantage in learning socially appropriate behavior.

An important variable influencing social development and the learning of other complex behaviors is *observational learning* (Bandura, 1969). It seems likely that a child who responded on the basis of a limited number of cues would learn very little through observation. Varni, Lovaas, Koegel, and Everett (1979) obtained evidence suggesting that, in fact, overselectivity may prevent or severely limit observational learning. They found that when autistic children observed a situation in which a teacher gave a command and then rewarded a model for some appropriate response, they usually learned only part of the response chain they observed. For example, in response to the command "phone" (for which the modeled response was to pick up the telephone receiver), the autistic child might touch the phone rather than pick it up. Those children that did learn the complete response failed to associate it with the teacher's instruction, so that the child might pick up the phone regardless of whether the instruction pertained to the phone or some other stimulus (e.g., a toy truck).

The stimulus overselectivity of autistic children also has implications for the use of certain *prompts* in instructional programming. Prompting is a technique commonly used in classrooms to facilitate teaching handicapped children. Prompts are typically "extra-stimuli that are added to the learning environment to ensure correct responding" (Koegel & Rincover, 1976). For example, if a teacher wanted to teach a color discrimination, he or she might follow the initial instruction (e.g., "Give me red") by pointing to a red object. If the child is to learn the discrimination successfully, the prompt (pointing) eventually must be removed so that the child is responding on his or her own. While the removal of a prompt may seem to be a relatively simple procedure, many studies have shown that autistic children have a particularly difficult time shifting from the prompt stimuli (e.g., finger pointing) to the training stimuli (red object). In a study designed to assess the effectiveness of using prompts for teaching normal and autistic children, Koegel and Rincover (1976) demonstrated that the use of extra cues in an attempt to guide learning seriously impaired learning for the autistic children.

They pretrained autistic and normal children on a color discrimination. Once this discrimination was learned, the colors were used as prompts to teach four new discriminations (e.g., a low pitched tone presented concurrently with the color red, and a high pitched tone with the color green). The colors were then gradually eliminated until only the auditory stimuli were present. The results clearly showed that, while normal children successfully used the prompts to learn the auditory discrimination, the autistic children continued to respond only on the basis of the color prompt. In other words, the autistic children only maintained the auditory discrimination until the color prompt was completely removed; they failed to transfer from the color prompt to the training stimulus. The finding that prompts can, in fact, interfere with learning was further supported when the investigators demonstrated that the autistic children learned the auditory discrimination when prompts were not used. Similar results have also been found in other investigations (cf. Rincover, 1978b; Schreibman, 1975) and are not surprising when examined in light of what is known about stimulus overselectivity. Since most prompt procedures introduce multiple cues (prompt and training stimulus) into the learning environment, the overselectivity hypothesis would predict that the autistic child would respond on the basis of a limited number of the cues presented.

An important aspect of teaching new skills to autistic children is ensuring that the new skills taught in the classroom generalize to outside environments. If an autistic child's behavior comes under control of a limited number of stimuli, it may limit the extent to which a behavior learned in the classroom transfers to other environments. The problem of limited *generalization of treatment gains* and the role overselectivity may play was demonstrated in a study by Rincover and Koegel (1975). In this study one teacher taught autistic children a simple response to command (e.g., "Touch your nose"). As soon as each child had learned this response, a second teacher took the child into another environment and made the same request. Four of the 10 children did not perform the behavior in the new environment. It was shown that these children failed to generalize to the new situation because they had initially learned the response on the basis of irrelevant cues. For example, one child's responding was controlled by incidental hand movements (which happened by chance to have accompanied the therapist's instructions in the original treatment environment). Thus, if anyone moved their hands in that manner, the child would respond appropriately. However, the child never responded appropriately to the verbal cue. This study suggested that the amount of generalization may, in some cases, vary with the number of relevant cues that controlled the behavior initially. The more restricted and idiosyncratic the stimuli that originally controlled the behavior, the less generalization there will be.

Remediation of Overselectivity Deficits It is now apparent that the autistic child's tendency to respond to environmental events on the basis of a very limited number of cues can severely impair efforts to teach skills ranging from the simplest discrimination to complex social behavior. As a result, research has been undertaken to discover methods for dealing with this problem. The research has focused on two main types of procedures: 1) those designed to avoid the overselectivity problem by constructing special situations in which the child can learn appropriate skills, and 2) those that work directly on the overselectivity itself.

The most extensive work in the first area has been conducted by Schreibman (1975) and Rincover (1978b). Schreibman developed a method for working "around" the selective responding, using prompts that were contained within the training stimulus (within-stimulus prompt). This procedure did not require the child to respond to multiple cues because the prompt was not extraneous to the training stimulus but was part of it. In comparing the within-stimulus prompt with extra-stimulus prompts, Schreibman found that the children learned the discrimination only when the within-stimulus prompt was employed. The within-stimulus prompting procedure can be illustrated with the following example. In teaching a child to recognize the difference between a *p* and a *b,* a teacher might emphasize (through exaggeration) the "stems" of the letters. The direction of the stems is considered the relevant component of the discrimination since the other components of the letters are redundant. The exaggerated component is then gradually faded until the child is discriminating between the appropriate-sized letters. Since the prompt is contained within the final stimulus, it requires the child to respond only on the basis of this stimulus and not other additional cues.

Rincover (1978b) has extended Schreibman's work, by examining four treatment procedures designed to facilitate prompt fading. Of the four (within-stimulus distinctive feature, within-stimulus nondistinctive feature, extra-stimulus distinctive feature, and extra-stimulus nondistinctive feature), the most effective technique was the within-stimulus distinctive feature prompting procedure (WSDF). In the WSDF procedure, a child is pretrained to respond to a feature of one stimulus that is not a part of the other stimulus (i.e., a distinctive feature). For example, in an *E* vs. *F* discrimination, the bottom line of the *E* is the distinctive feature that would be emphasized. During pretraining this feature is exaggerated and presented alone. Subsequently, the stimuli are presented with the pretrained feature superimposed on the correct choice. At that point, the exaggerated feature is gradually faded until the stimulus takes its normal form. This procedure, a special form of within-stimulus prompting, appears to be the most effective prompting procedure known for autistic children at this time. Both Schreibman's and Rincover's work suggests that methods for teaching autistic children can be devised despite the children's tendency to respond selectively. These procedures offer one optimistic picture for dealing with stimulus overselectivity.

The second area of research has dealt with treating the overselectivity itself, by teaching autistic children to respond on the basis of multiple cues. It was noted in some of the earlier investigations of overselectivity that a few of the children eventually used the extra-stimulus prompt to learn the discrimination being taught. In other words, some of the children learned to respond on the basis of more than one cue. This observation has led to research that has investigated techniques for working directly on the overselectivity problem. In one study, Schover and Newsom (1976) attempted to teach autistic children to respond to multiple cues by overtraining an already learned discrimination. Their results indicated that through overtraining they were able to increase the number of cues to which the children responded. Schreibman, Koegel, and Craig (1977), further investigating the overtraining procedure, found that overtraining per se (just exposure) did not increase the number of cues to which the child responded. Instead, they found that prolonged interspersing of unreinforced trials with component cues among reinforced trials with the stimulus complex eliminated overselectivity (in 13 out of 16 autistic children who were initially overselective). Koegel and Schreibman (1977) carried this line of research one step further. They taught four autistic and four normal children a conditional discrimination requiring a response to multiple cross-modality (auditory and visual) cues. Their results showed that the autistic children learned the discriminations, although they did not learn them with ease, nor did they learn them in the same manner as normal children. The autistic children persistently tended to respond at a higher level to one of the component cues and only after many (typically hundreds of) trials did they learn to respond on the basis of both cues. This was, however, optimistic in that they *did* learn to respond to multiple cues. Furthermore, in one case, when an autistic child was taught a series of successive conditional discriminations, the child eventually learned a generalized set to respond to new discriminations on the basis of both component cues. The results of these studies suggest that the selective responding characteristic of many autistic children is a problem that is modifiable. The implication, and hope, is that such an approach might eventually teach autistic children to respond to their environment in a more normal manner, and enable them to learn through approaches regularly used in normal classrooms.

Absence of Generalization and Maintenance of Treatment Gains

Classrooms for autistic children are designed to establish or increase a wide variety of appropriate skills. Unfortunately, it is often noted that, while the child may perform a particular skill quite well in the classroom/treatment setting, the skill does not maintain in other environments. This was clearly shown by Lovaas, Koegel, Simmons, and Long (1973), who found that, despite dramatic gains made by autistic children during treatment, those children who were institutionalized following therapy regressed significantly. Other investigators have also noted the failure of treatment to generalize to other situations without special intervention in the extra-therapy environment (e.g., Baer, Wolf, & Risley, 1968; Birnbrauer, 1968; Kale, Kaye, Whelan, & Hopkins, 1968; Kazdin & Bootzin, 1972; Stokes & Baer, 1977; Stokes, Baer, & Jackson, 1974; Wahler, 1969; Walker & Buckley, 1972).

The failure of treatment gains to generalize has led investigators to examine the variables that might limit generalization and to develop various procedures for promoting generalization.

Variables Influencing Generalization One variable that may limit the extent to which a behavior learned in a classroom generalizes to other environments is the number and type of relevant stimuli that control the behavior. The Rincover and Koegel (1975) study discussed earlier (see the section on overselectivity) demonstrated that the failure of four autistic children to generalize a response learned in one setting to another was due to the acquisition of stimulus control by irrelevant stimuli that were not present in the extra-therapy environment. In order to bring about the generalization of treatment gains to extra-therapy settings, it was necessary to introduce into the extra-therapy setting the stimuli that came to control responding in the treatment environment. The authors pointed out that a therapist working with autistic children must be sure that new behaviors are learned on the basis of relevant stimuli both intended to achieve control and likely to be present in extra-treatment environments.

It is interesting to note, however, that the above results did not hold true for all of the children in the study. Six children showed some transfer of treatment gains across settings without special intervention. These children apparently learned to respond to a stimulus that was functional in both the therapy and extra-therapy settings. Rincover and Koegel suggested that in cases where the children do initially transfer (which may be the more common phenomenon), it may be beneficial to emphasize methodologies for *maintaining* treatment gains in other settings rather than for producing transfer. Koegel and Rincover (1977) designed a study to assess possible differences between variables affecting the *transfer* and *maintenance* of treatment gains across settings. Initially, the authors continuously recorded responding to a particular instruction (e.g., "Touch your nose") in both a therapy and an extra-therapy setting. The results showed that while one child's responding failed to generalize to the extra-therapy environment, the responding of two other children did generalize. However, further testing demonstrated that responding in the extra-therapy setting was not maintained. Koegel and Rincover suggested that the lack of response maintenance in the extra-therapy setting may be a result of the child forming a discrimination between an environment in which contingent rewards are given and one where few contingent rewards are provided.

In order to reduce the discriminability of the reinforcement schedules, Koegel and Rincover manipulated two variables: 1) the schedule of reinforcement in the treatment setting, and 2) the presence of noncontingent reinforcement in the extra-therapy environment. The results showed that extra-therapy responding extinguished within a very short number of trials when a continuous reinforcement schedule was employed in the treatment. As the schedule of reinforcement in the therapy was gradually thinned to reinforcement for every fifth correct response, responding in the extra-therapy environment was maintained over longer and longer periods of time. The presentations of noncontingent reinforcement

(NCR) in the extra-therapy setting had a similar effect on the durability of responding. Furthermore, the results showed that a thin schedule of reinforcement in the treatment environment in conjunction with the periodic use of NCR in the extra-therapy setting produced the greatest response maintenance. Koegel and Rincover (1977) pointed out that these results suggest that teachers may be able to program specifically for maintenance of behavior change for extended periods of time after treatment is terminated. The authors noted that programming extra-therapy maintenance from within the classroom may resolve some of the problems that can occur when autistic children are placed in different classrooms with a new teacher and with new peers.

Other procedures for promoting generalization of treatment gains have been reported throughout the behavioral literature (for an extensive review, refer to Stokes & Baer, 1977). Several procedures can be adapted quite easily for use in a classroom situation. Investigations have shown that *multiple teachers* can be employed to facilitate generalization from the original teacher to others in the child's environment. Stokes, Baer, and Jackson (1974) found that a greeting response taught to four retarded children by one adult did not generalize to other staff members. However, high levels of generalization and maintenance of the response were noted after a second adult taught and maintained the response in conjunction with the first. Lovaas and Simmons (1969) also found it necessary to use multiple teachers to ensure generalized suppression of self-destructive behavior. Similarly, additional research has found that generalization is enhanced if instruction takes place in a *number of settings* beyond the original environment (e.g., Griffiths & Craighead, 1972; Lovaas & Simmons, 1969). Thus, the research has pointed out that in order to program generalization it may be necessary to continue the training with other people in a variety of settings. A convenient method that incorporates both of these approaches is available to the educator of autistic children; training parents in the use of behavioral techniques. Lovaas et al. (1973) and Schreibman and Koegel (1975) have found that treatment gains were maintained for those children who went from treatment to homes in which the parents had received training in behavioral techniques. This is not surprising in light of the research cited above. Trained parents satisfy the need for multiple therapists discussed by Stokes et al. (1974), and parents are also likely to work with the child in a vast number of settings (e.g., grocery store, restaurant) outside of the classroom. Furthermore, parent training clearly provides a mechanism for maintaining treatment gains that are displayed outside of the treatment setting. Obviously the impact of parent training on the education of autistic children is potentially tremendous.

Investigations have also been conducted to determine if generalization of behavior change can be programmed from within the clinic. Most of these investigations have focused on the type of reinforcers used and the nature of the treatment setting.

The problems encountered in using primary (food) rewards with autistic children have already been discussed; their use leads to rapid satiation and a lack of generalization because such reinforcers are not universally available outside the treatment setting. Thus, it is conceivable that generalization would be enhanced if reinforcers that were also present in the ''natural'' environment were used (Stokes & Baer, 1977). The research conducted by Rincover et al. (1977) suggests that the use of sensory reinforcement may facilitate generalization of treatment gains since many sensory reinforcers may be considered ''natural'' (e.g., ''hugs'') or ''universal'' in that they occur frequently in settings other than the treatment environment.

Rincover et al. (1977) have also suggested that the use of sensory reinforcers during treatment or in the classroom environment could significantly enhance the children's motivation to participate in learning tasks. The relationship between high levels of motivation within the treatment setting and the generalization of treatment gains was demonstrated by Turner (1978), who found that children who showed high levels of motivation (as measured by level of interest) in a language remediation program were more likely to generalize the use of target language structures to a nonremediation environment.

Behavioral Contrast All of the studies reported above have examined behavior change in terms of generalization, no generalization, or a lack of maintenance. However, there may be another aspect of behavior change that warrants scrutiny. Anecdotally, it is common for teachers to complain that the behavior a child demonstrates in school deteriorates when the child goes home. It has also been noted that occasionally when two teachers work on the same behavior at different times of the day, each teacher may complain that the other is having an adverse effect on the child. In these situations the problem may be more than a lack of generalization: the child is actually described as getting worse in one environment while improving in another setting.

From the point of view of assessing treatment changes across environments, it is possible that these examples might result from the child discriminating a difference in the reward schedules for the same behavior performed in different environments. This effect has been reported extensively in analog studies in operant research with animals and has been labeled ''behavioral contrast'' (Reynolds, 1961b). The phenomenon occurs when an organism alters its responding during the presentation of *one* stimulus (analogous to the extratreatment environment) as a function of changing only the reinforcement during the presentation of *another* stimulus (analogous to the treatment setting) (Brethower & Reynolds, 1962; Hanson, 1959; Reynolds, 1961a, 1961c, 1961d). Similar results have been reported with children, using a lever press apparatus for responding and pilot lights as discriminative stimuli (O'Brien, 1968; Waite & Osborne, 1972). Johnson, Bolstad, and Lobitz (1976) have also reported contrast effects in an examination of deviant behavior in school and home settings. They found the *improved* behavior in the classroom resulted in *increased* deviant behavior in the home.

A study was recently conducted at the University of California at Santa Barbara Autism Laboratory in order to examine possible contrast effects and to better understand the variables influencing generalization of treatment gains

(Koegel, Egel, & Williams, in press). The results demonstrated that when very different reinforcement contingencies (primary rewards or punishments in treatment settings, and no rewards or punishments in extra-treatment settings) were in effect, the children showed behavior changes, opposite to the treatment results, in the untreated extra-therapy environments. For example, one child's responding in the extra-therapy setting decreased from an average of 50% correct responses to an average of 16% correct responses following the introduction of treatment in the therapy setting. As previously noted, contrast effects may be due to the discriminability of the reinforcement schedules in each environment. Based on this, and the findings of Koegel and Rincover (1977), an attempt was made to reverse the contrast effect. It was found that undesirable trends in responding could be reversed, resulting in generalization of treatment gains, if the reinforcement procedures (rewards or punishments) were made relatively similar in the two settings, even if the maintenance procedures consisted essentially of noncontingent reinforcement. The results of this study and others (e.g., Johnson et al., 1976) should alert teachers and clinicians to the fact that in some instances contrast effects can occur and that they are probably due to the child's discrimination of different reinforcement procedures in different environments.

APPLICATION OF TEACHING
TECHNIQUES TO CLASSROOM ENVIRONMENTS

Thus far, a number of variables influencing the general teaching of autistic children have been discussed. These variables are pertinent in all environments including the home, clinic, and school. The remainder of this chapter discusses those variables that pertain more specifically to the education of autistic children in schools. In this section the following research areas are considered: 1) teaching such children to respond appropriately in the presence of numerous other children (group instruction), 2) teaching the children to work on a task independent of direct supervision, and 3) integrating autistic children into normal classrooms, and 4) training teachers and parents to work effectively with autistic children.

Group Instruction

In order to perform successfully in a classroom setting, children need to acquire a set of skills that is quite independent of successful functioning in a one-to-one environment. Among the necessary skills is the ability to attend, respond, and learn when numerous other children are also involved in the activities. For autistic children, whose ability to learn at all was (until recently) questioned by many, this is a big step. Without question, it is a step prerequisite to functioning in a normal classroom.

Although little research has been reported on the management of group activities for autistic children, a great corpus of data now exists regarding other populations. Successful strategies for managing the classroom behavior of normal, culturally deprived, and retarded children in groups include the utilization of token economies (cf. Kazdin & Bootzin, 1972; O'Leary & Drabman, 1971), contingent teacher attention (Kazdin & Klock, 1973; Madsen, Becker, & Thomas, 1968; Schutte & Hopkins, 1970; Scott & Bushell, 1974; Thomas, Becker, & Armstrong, 1968), and group contingencies (Barrish, Saunders, & Wolf, 1969; Bushell, Wrobel, & Michaelis, 1968; Greenwood, Hops, Delquadri, & Guild, 1974; Packard, 1970). O'Leary and O'Leary (1976) offer a comprehensive and insightful review of behavior modification in school settings. Dunlap, Koegel, and Egel (1979) provide a survey and discussion of this literature as it applies to autistics.

The above studies typically describe behavior management programs for increasing work productivity or decreasing disruptive behavior in previously established groups. Many children (e.g., autistics), however, require specialized training in order to begin to perform successfully in classroom settings at all. Peterson, Cox, and Bijou (1971) conducted an experiment in which they trained preschool children and children with school-adjustment problems to work productively in groups. In the first phase of this study, shaping procedures (with teacher attention as the reinforcer) were used to establish on-task school behavior in a group of two boys. In the second phase, children were gradually added to a dyad of preschool children until a total of eight were successfully working at one time. The Peterson et al. study presented perhaps the first suggestion of a technology for establishing on-task responding in school groups where no group previously existed.

Until recently the major reports of autistic children in group situations were primarily anecdotal, but served to provide a set of general guidelines (cf. Elgar, 1966; Fenichel, 1974; Goldman & May, 1967; Halpern, 1970; Rabb & Hewett, 1967). Hamblin, Buckholdt, Ferritor, Kozloff, and Blackwell (1971) described a three-tiered systematic approach for gradually teaching autistic students to work in a classroom setting. With the use of tokens, shaping procedures, and specified criteria for advancement, their children progressed from participating in the classroom under one-to-one (1:1) instructional arrangements to responding in turn as part of a small group (1:4) to the final stage of preparation for public school integration, which involved thinning reinforcement schedules and remediating developmental deficits. While this work is attractive in its systematization, unfortunately there are no accompanying data to testify to its efficacy. Another example of teaching autistic children to function in groups is reported by Martin, England, Kaprowy, Kilgour, and Pilek (1968). While the emphasis of this investigation concerned the establishment of kindergarten behaviors (such as matching and tracing), the researchers concurrently increased the teacher-student ratio for most of the children and found no appreciable deterioration in performance. Again, however, no systematic data accompanied this aspect of their report.

An experimental demonstration of treating autistic children in a classroom setting was provided by Koegel and Rincover (1974). They first taught eight autistic children certain basic classroom behaviors (including attending to the teacher, imitation, and rudimentary communication responses) in traditional one-to-one sessions. They found, however, that the children rarely performed the responses in a large group, and only occasionally performed them in 2:1 sessions even when they continued to respond consistently in 1:1 sessions. Furthermore, over a 4-week period, the children learned virtually no new behaviors in the classroom-size (8:1) group. The second phase of Koegel and Rincover's study introduced a treatment package designed to "fade in" the classroom stimulus situation from the one-to-one settings. As the children had already achieved criterion performance in 1:1 sessions, they were initially placed in 2:1 sessions with an additional aide seated behind the children. In the 2:1 session, the teacher presented an instruction (e.g., "Touch your nose") and the aide prompted the child to touch his or her nose and then gave the child a reward. When the prompts were faded and both children in the dyad were again responding at criterion level (80%), the reinforcement schedule was reduced to a fixed ratio (FR) of 2, one reward after performing two correct responses. At this point, the children were responding quite successfully in a small group (2:1). This dyad was then merged with another trained group of two children to form a class of four children, one teacher, and two teacher's aides. The same procedures of prompting, prompt fading, and thinning of the reinforcement schedule were again employed. When criterion performance was again achieved (without prompts) and the schedule thinned to FR 4, a functioning class of four autistic children resulted. These four children were then combined with four others, the same procedures were followed, and the product was a class of eight autistic children. The schedule was finally modified to a VR of 8 and the aides were removed from the room. The results of this study showed successful transfer from 1:1 to 8:1 sessions for seven of the eight children; that is, all but one of the children continued to respond appropriately in a class of eight children with one teacher. In addition, all of the children showed acquisition of new behaviors taught only in the large group. The teacher was soon able to introduce a standard preschool curriculum and present a variety of activities such as telling time, social interactions, and rudimentary reading and arithmetic exercises. This experiment documented the feasibility of teaching autistic children in a classroom setting.

Personalized Instruction in a Group

The establishment of productive responding by autistic children in large groups proved that the teacher-child ratio could be successfully reduced. However, the heterogeneity of the autistic population suggests that continuous activity in one group would benefit some children to the effective exclusion of the others. That is, there would be very few group activities that would provide maximal benefit for each individual child's needs. The next goal, then, was to devise procedures for providing individualized instruction for each child without providing additional instructors. An approach to this problem, suggested in previous research in classrooms for retarded children, would be to incorporate individualized (programmed) instruction (Bijou, Birnbrauer, Kidder, & Tague, 1966; Birnbrauer, Kidder, & Tague, 1964) into the group instruction. However, in order to work individually, the autistic children would have to be taught to engage in at least moderately long sequences of responding with only intermittent teacher supervision.

Rincover and Koegel (1977a) incorporated two components into a strategy for establishing individualized instruction in a group: 1) the preparation of programmed materials that were specially designed for each child's level of functioning and pace of learning, and 2) prompting and shaping procedures to increase the duration of independent work. The programmed materials in this study were sheets of paper upon which a permanent *record* of the child's written responses would be recorded (during the teacher's absence). For example, one task was tracing alphabet letters with the lines progressively faded until the child could write the letter without the assistance of the printed guidance.

The children were taught to respond without continuous supervision in the following manner. Initially, a child was handed a worksheet and the teacher instructed the child to "trace the lines." The child was then rewarded for tracing one line (or part of a line, depending on the child's level). When the child reliably performed one response following an instruction, a second response was prompted before a reward was given, and then the prompt was faded. When two responses consistently followed an instruction, the reward contingency was increased to three responses, and so on. With this gradual increase of the response requirement, each child learned to produce at least 12 written responses per teacher instruction. In this manner the teacher was able to remove her presence gradually as each child learned to work alone for periods exceeding 15 minutes. Thus, the teacher could circulate among the children, providing instructions and reinforcers while the children worked steadily and productively throughout the session (see Rincover & Koegel, 1977a, for the details of this procedure).

This study introduced a method for maintaining a manageable teacher-child ratio while the autistic children worked productively at tasks geared to their own rate and level of functioning. When combined with the methods of the earlier classroom study (Koegel & Rincover, 1974), the core procedures are available for designing a flexible classroom structure for autistic children. A teacher and one teacher's aide can relatively easily conduct a class of eight autistic children with a flexible arrangement of group and individual activities, best designed to meet the idiosyncratic needs of the children. For the reader interested in more detail, the procedures for accomplishing the above classroom objectives have been illustrated in videotape format (Koegel, 1978).

Mainstreaming

The availability of procedures for teaching classroom skills to autistic children, along with the recent legislative mandates for provision of public school education, invites the serious consideration of integrating autistic children into the education mainstream. Many authors have written on this topic (Johnson, 1962; Pappanikou & Paul, 1977; Quay, 1968; Rutter, 1970), but the literature is still far from a consensus on the desirability of placing autistic children in normal, or even near-normal, classrooms.

Until educators are equipped with detailed studies describing the strengths, the weaknesses, and above all, the procedures for mainstreaming, one can only speculate about the possible outcomes. For example, one might guess that non-verbal autistic children who are insensitive to their social environments might derive relatively little benefit from immersion in a class of appropriate peer models. Such children would probably be unmanageable in environments not totally structured for the remediation of autistic behaviors (Koegel & Covert, 1972; Rutter, 1970). On the other hand, placing such children in a normal classroom may continuously and clearly point out the most productive target behaviors for their successful development. It is also reasonable to suggest that higher functioning children, with skills not terribly discrepant from their normal peers, might progress appreciably with exposure to the normal social and academic conduct of their classmates. Among other variables, one key to determining the appropriateness of mainstreaming an autistic child may be the child's ability to learn through observation (Bandura, 1969; Egel, Richman, & Koegel, in press).

Addressing the basic question of whether or not an autistic child could learn *productively* in a normal classroom, Russo and Koegel (1977) attempted an experimental placement of five autistic children in public school classes of one teacher and 20 to 30 normal children. Initially, the therapists established appropriate levels of social and verbal responses and reduced self-stimulatory behavior in the classroom setting. These advances were maintained in the classroom by training the kindergarten teacher in the pertinent behavior modification techniques. A follow-up phase of this experiment indicated that for one child subsequent training of the first-grade teacher was required in order to maintain appropriate responding over the following year. While this study does not answer the great number of questions concerning the desirability of regular class placements, it does demonstrate a method for using professional intervention and teacher training to integrate autistic children into normal public school classes. Furthermore, it suggests that many autistic children have the potential to function within regular classrooms. As such, it may be a moral obligation to pursue intensively this approach to treatment.

Parent and Teacher Training

The classroom studies described above attest to the important advances that have occurred in educating autistic children. None of this progress, however, could have been realized if treatment procedures had remained solely in the hands of any single child development professional, or for that matter, solely in the hands of professionals. One of the most significant contributions of behavior modification has been the expansion of the role of the therapeutic agent through the training of persons in the child's natural environment in the principles and procedures of behavioral intervention. This extension of the therapeutic environment has unquestionably facilitated the transfer and maintenance of treatment gains.

A wealth of studies has shown the feasibility and productivity of training teachers and parents to work effectively with normal and retarded children (e.g., Clark & Macrae, 1976; Hall, Panyan, Rabon, & Broden, 1968; Kazdin & Moyer, 1976; Miller & Sloane, 1976; Wahler, Winkel, Peterson, & Morrison, 1965; Zeilberger, Sampen, & Sloane, 1968) as well as specifically with autistic children (e.g., Davison, 1964; Freeman & Ritvo, 1976; Hamblin et al., 1971; Lovaas et al., 1973; Nordquist & Wahler, 1973; Risley, 1968). Such studies have resulted in a number of books and manuals designed to instruct teachers and caregivers to work successfully with their children (e.g., Becker, 1971; Becker & Becker, 1974; Bernal & North, 1978; Hall, 1971a, 1971b, 1971c; Kozloff, 1973; Panyan, 1971; Patterson & Guillon, 1968).

Recent research has also demonstrated the need to train the teachers of autistic children (Koegel, Russo, & Rincover, 1977; Russo & Koegel, 1977). Koegel et al. (1977) designed and assessed procedures for training teachers of autistic children in generalized behavior modification skills. Initially, observers evaluated teachers' performance and found low scores in use of behavior modification procedures with an associated lack of improvement in child behavior. They then provided a week-long training program consisting of written materials, videotaped illustrations, in vivo modeling, and practice with feedback. The teachers were trained to use five behavior modification skills that were considered essential for teaching autistic children. The five skills were: 1) appropriate presentation of S^Ds, 2) effective use of prompts and prompt fading, 3) shaping successive approximations to the target behavior, 4) delivery of contingent and effective consequences, and 5) inclusion of distinct intertrial intervals. After training, each teacher correctly used all of the five skills at least 90% of the time, regardless of the child or task involved, and all of the children made progress on the target behaviors assigned during these sessions. The authors concluded that the training package was effective and produced generalization, and that teachers, in general, require training in order to work effectively with autistic children.

Given that training is essential, or at least strongly recommended, it behooves investigators to evaluate training programs in terms of their diverse effects upon child, adult, and family behavior (cf. Kazdin & Moyer, 1976). Two general areas of training effects demand consideration. The first area concerns the effects of training components and packages upon trainee-child interaction. It is important to know the aspects of training programs that are critical (or dispensable) in terms of their instructional impact and whether they produce durable and generalized results. A number of studies have shown that particular instructional methods are effective in changing specific trainee behaviors (e.g., Bricker, Morgan, & Grabowski, 1972; Cossairt, Hall, & Hopkins, 1973; Herbert & Baer, 1972; McNamara, 1971; Panyan, Boozer, & Morris, 1970). Fewer studies, however, have considered the durability of change produced by training programs (cf. Kazdin & Moyer, 1976) and even fewer have addressed the issues of generalization. The question of whether training results will transfer to novel behaviors and situations is critical since it is easy to visualize the enormous range of teaching interactions typically encountered by the parents and teachers of deviant children. Koegel, Glahn, and Nieminen (1978) conducted two studies that were designed to shed some light on the question of training program generalization. In the first experiment, they compared two training approaches in terms of their differential effects in teaching parents to instruct children on a variety of target behaviors. The first approach consisted of a brief demonstration of the techniques for teaching a specific target behavior. The second approach contained essentially the same components as described in Koegel, Russo, and Rincover (1977) (and in the preceding paragraph) and was not directed toward any of the particular child target behaviors considered in the study, but rather toward general principles of behavior modification. The authors found that the first approach was successful only in its application to the specific target behaviors trained and did not produce a generalized ability to deal effectively with other behaviors or children; the second training approach was successful in teaching a generalized set of procedures that was effective across children and target behaviors. In the second experiment, the authors sought to determine the effect of a training procedure that employed only videotaped examples with no feedback, in vivo modeling, or lectures. They also evaluated the effect of employing only those portions of the videotapes that pertained to antecedent stimuli or consequent stimuli. They found that the full videotaped package was sufficient to train individuals to work effectively with different autistic children and across behaviors, and that exposure to just the antecedent stimuli or consequent stimuli portions of the tape produced training in those areas only. Furthermore, although the teacher's behavior changed with both types of training, it was necessary to have training in both the antecedent and consequent areas in order to improve the behavior of the autistic children.

A second general area that is beginning to attract considerable interest pertains to the possible effects that parent and teacher training may have on the diverse and global aspects of attitudes, adjustments, and interactions of family members. While collateral or "side" effects of behavior modification procedures in the target subject have been noted for some time (e.g., Buell, Stoddard, Harris, & Baer, 1968; Risley, 1968; Sajwaj, Twardosz, & Burke, 1972; Wahler, Sperling, Thomas, Teeter, & Loper, 1970), very little data have thus far been collected on the collateral effects of parent training (cf. Hemsley, Howlin, Berger, Hersov, Holbrook, Rutter, & Yule, 1978; Karoly & Rosenthal, 1977). The present authors have recently initiated, in collaboration with Laura Schreibman and her colleagues, a research project aimed at determining the differential effects of parent training and clinic treatment upon a wide variety of child and family variables (U.S. Public Health Service research grants MH28210 and MH28231). It is expected that the resultant data will contribute to the formulation of a maximally effective combination of parent training and clinic intervention in the treatment of autistic children.

The meticulous methodologies (i.e., procedures) reported in the early attempts to teach autistic children attest to the need for teachers of these children to adopt a highly systematic and empirical approach. Such systematization is one of the hallmarks and advantages of behavior modification and, to a large extent, explains the superiority of behavior modification over many other orientations in achieving educational success with autistic children (Leff, 1968; Lovaas & Newsom, 1976; Lovaas, Schreibman, & Koegel, 1974). Behaviorally oriented teachers invariably include the following components in their teaching programs:

1. *A clear, operational definition of the target behavior:*   A behavioral definition involves describing the target behavior in terms that are clear, objective, and measurable. Specifying the topographical and temporal parameters of the behavioral objective typically serves to distinguish both the correctness of a particular response and the pathway to the desired end for both the teacher and the child.

2. *Specification of a performance criterion:*   Such criteria provide teachers with predetermined indications of success, ensuring that programs are neither prematurely terminated nor drawn out to the point of unproductive boredom. A common criterion for tasks such as color labeling is 9 correct out of 10 opportunities.

3. *Measurement:*   It is quite important for programs to include some means of objectively measuring child performance in order to detect deviations from expected acquisition, error strategies, and target acquisition. Many authors have described numerous and efficient techniques for measuring and plotting child-performance data (e.g., Hall, 1971c).

4. *Procedural description:*   It is useful for teachers to conceptualize their strategies in terms of the various procedural operations for increasing behavior (e.g., positive reinforcement), decreasing behavior (e.g., extinction), or establishing new behavior (e.g., shaping, chaining, prompting).

Others have described these strategies in great detail (cf. Ferster, Culbertson, & Boren, 1975; Schreibman & Koegel, in press; Sulzer & Mayer, 1972).

A convenient procedure for ordering these components to maximize control and efficiency is the *discrete trial format*. A discrete trial is, essentially, a careful ordering of the basic elements of the learning process: stimulus (instruction) → response → consequence. In addition, an extra-stimulus (or prompt) may be inserted between the instruction and the child's response. These are referred to as "discrete" trials because, in teaching a new behavior, it appears to be important to include a distinct intertrial interval (ITI) between one trial's consequence and the next trial's instruction. Thus, a discrete trial contains: 1) the teacher's *instruction,* 2) an optional *prompt,* followed by 3) the child's *response,* 4) the teacher's *consequence,* and finally, 5) the *intertrial interval.*

Instruction (S^D) The teacher's instruction may take the form of a command (e.g., "Touch your nose") or a question (e.g., "Where is your elbow?"). It is a cue to which the teacher wants to give meaning for the child; that is, the instruction is to be established as discriminative for the child to respond and, thus, is referred to as a discriminative stimulus (S^D). In order for the child to associate the S^D with a particular response, that is, in order for the child to learn, the S^D should be salient and easily discriminable, appropriate to the task, and presented only when the child is attending.

The importance of requiring the child's attention before presenting an S^D is supported empirically by the literature pertaining to the interaction of autistic self-stimulation and learning (Koegel & Covert, 1972; Risley, 1968). As noted previously in this chapter, self-stimulation interferes with the acquisition of new behaviors. Also, it is commonplace to perceive off-task responding in general (such as crying, foot tapping, or gazing out the window) as incompatible with the teacher's objective. Finally, it is possible that the attention provided by an instruction may in itself serve secondarily to reinforce inattentiveness.

For an S^D to be salient and easily discriminable means that it should stand out from everything else. It is the only cue that is to acquire meaning for the child through its association with reinforced responses. Therefore, it is critical that the appropriate S^D, and no other stimuli, be perceived by the child just prior to responding. The literature on stimulus overselectivity (see the previous section in this chapter) suggests that providing a salient and easily discriminable S^D is especially important for autistic children. If the S^D does not stand apart, it is unlikely that the child will readily select the relevant stimulus; instead, the child may learn to respond to irrelevant cues (Rincover & Koegel, 1975). In order to ensure an appropriate (productive) S^D presentation, teachers should employ short instructions with clear beginnings and endings that are consistent across trials and that are maximally relevant to the response.

Prompts   A prompt is defined as a cue that is presented with the S^D and that serves to guarantee correct responding. Prompts often take the form of manual guidance (for example, a teacher may manually move the child's hand to the doorknob when presenting the S^D, ''Open the door'') or verbal assistance (a teacher may say, ''What color is this?... Red,'' in order to evoke the desired response, ''Red''). In the behavior modification literature, prompts have been popularly and successfully used to teach many behaviors to normal and retarded children (e.g., Cheney & Stein, 1974; Sidman & Stoddard, 1966, 1967; Taber & Glaser, 1962; Touchette, 1968, 1969, 1971) and autistic children (e.g., Koegel & Rincover, 1974; Metz, 1965). However, some recent research has described particular difficulty in fading prompts with autistic children (e.g., Koegel & Rincover, 1976; Schreibman, 1975). A discussion of these difficulties and recent effort to overcome them has been provided above in the section on overselectivity.

A prompt can only be considered useful if it: 1) is successful in occasioning the desired response (a prompt is of no value—and is probably a hindrance—if it does not guarantee a correct response), and 2) can be eventually removed or faded. Only when a prompt is completely removed and the child is responding to the S^D alone can functional learning be said to have occurred. In light of the earlier discussion of the difficulties in fading extra-stimulus prompts, teachers may be well advised to use within-stimulus prompts whenever possible.

Consequences   A consequence is the teacher-administered stimulus that immediately follows the child's response. This, in many respects, is the most important component of the learning process in that it determines the probability of the response reoccurring. There are two facets of consequences that must be carefully considered in teaching autistic children: the nature of the consequences (positive reinforcer vs. punisher, etc.), and the nature of its delivery (cf. Schreibman & Koegel, in press).

In noting the nature or type of consequation, we must emphasize the need to rely on a functional, rather than descriptive, definition. That is, the type of consequence is defined entirely by the effect its contingent presentation has on the behavior immediately preceding it (Ferster & Skinner, 1957; Skinner, 1938). This distinction is a particularly important one for autistic children, a population whose motivational characteristics are only now beginning to be understood. As noted above, it is by no means safe to assume that food, praise, or hugs will serve as reinforcers. Similarly, there is no guarantee that time-out or even slaps on the thigh will serve as punishers (cf. Carr, 1977). A teacher's first task, then, is to identify truly functional reinforcers and punishers in order to have much chance of successfully modifying an autistic child's behavior.

The manner in which the consequence is delivered is as important as the nature of the consequence. In order to be maximally effective, the delivery of consequences should adhere to four rules. The delivery should be:

1. *Contingent*—that is, the prescribed consequence should immediately follow each occurrence of the specified behavior and it should follow only that particular behavior
2. *Consistent*—unless a reinforcement schedule is being systematically thinned, a consequence should be presented contingent upon each occurrence of the target behavior
3. *Unambiguous*—the consequence must be clear in every respect to the child
4. *Easily discriminable*—the consequence should be distinct from all other surrounding stimuli

Intertrial Interval (ITI) In order to ensure the discriminability of one trial's consequence and the following trial's S^D, a distinct break between trials should occur. Although there is little data to suggest an optimal length for an ITI, there are recent indications that an optimal length of ITI may exist. In assessing matching-to-sample performance in pigeons, Holt and Shafer (1973) found that an ITI above zero seconds was necessary for learning to occur and that relatively long ITIs produced faster acquisition than shorter ITIs. However, once stable, ITIs could successfully be decreased to as low as 1 second to maintain accurate responding. Carnine (1976) then studied the effects of two presentation rates (which were created by manipulation of delays between trials) upon correct responding, off-task behavior, and participation in a group reading task with low achieving, first-grade children. He found that the faster rate of presentation resulted in higher percentages of correct responding and participation and less off-task behavior.

To assess the impact of this variable on the learning of autistic children, Koegel, Dunlap, and Dyer (1980) systematically varied ITI duration (rate of

S^D presentation) with several children working on a variety of discrimination tasks. The data showed a relationship between ITI duration and correct responding. For these children a shorter duration (1–3 seconds) was superior. While the variables determining optimal duration of ITI are unknown, the above studies strongly suggest that optimal durations do exist, even though they may be peculiar to the child, to the behavior being taught, and/or to whether the behavior is under acquisition or maintenance. The implication of these findings is that teachers may benefit by systematically altering their rates of instruction until they find a rate best suited to progress.

While the discrete trial format may seem primarily applicable to one-to-one, structured teaching settings, it is important to note that the components S^D → (prompt) → response → consequence are present and instrumental in all learning environments. The guidelines presented above apply to education in the home, at the beach, and in the car, as well as in the structured school or clinic. The more closely a teacher or parent adheres to the guidelines presented above, the more successful he or she will be in teaching the autistic child.

Curriculum

While some authors have suggested various curriculum guides for autistic children (e.g., Elgar, 1966; Hamblin et al., 1971) and for other severely handicapped populations (e.g., Guess, Sailor, & Baer, 1977; Hamre-Nietupski & Williams, 1976; Williams & Gotts, 1977), there is no one curriculum that is (or has been) popularly adopted. The problems in constructing a general curriculum for autistic children relate to both the heterogeneity and the uneven development of the population. These observations emphasize the need for individualized curricula, which can be constructed on the basis of the behavioral assessment described earlier in this chapter. Thus, it is possible to roughly group individual characteristics into behavioral excesses (e.g., self-stimulation) and behavioral deficits (e.g., lack of speech). From such a framework, it is easy to identify pressing target behaviors and long-range goals. This process is briefly illustrated below.

A first step in beginning work with autistic children almost invariably involves reduction or elimination of off-task behaviors such as self-destruction, tantrums, and self-stimulation. These excesses need to be addressed first because their presence significantly interferes with the establishment of adaptive behaviors. Concurrent with the removal of these disruptions, one must establish alternative responses such as rudimentary attending behaviors (eye contact, sitting in a chair, etc.) and simple instruction following. Once the behavioral excesses are brought under control and attention is established, a child's most glaring deficits are considered. Imitation is a response class that is usually taught quite early in a child's curriculum because it can be used to facilitate the establishment of many additional skills. For example, self-help repertoires frequently are built with the assistance of nonverbal imitative prompts. Speech is also considered very early because 1) deficits in language are often considered the autistic child's most severe problem, 2) it appears to be easier to teach verbal skills to the young child, and 3) language acquisition may involve very extensive shaping and chaining over periods of several years. Basically, the authors' approach has been to teach first those skills in which a child is notably deficient and to eliminate behavioral excesses (such as tantrums). As a child's deviance is progressively overcome, curricular options become more diverse and normalized. With mastery of rudimentary "readiness" skills comes training in the areas of preacademic, academic, and social functioning. Eventually, an autistic child's curriculum may parallel those of the child's normal peers. Many people prefer to be more systematic in approaching target behavior selection. However, at this point the authors have not found any curriculum that has been empirically validated as superior to any other curriculum. It is quite likely that in the future a curriculum more efficient than the ones used by the authors in the past (cf. Rincover & Koegel, 1977b) will be developed. The reader interested in examples of the authors' curricula is referred to Koegel and Rincover (1974), Schriebman and Koegel (in press), and Koegel, Rincover, and Egel (in press).

SUMMARY

The studies reported in this chapter provide compelling documentation that autistic children can be taught a great variety of important behaviors. This progress, all occurring within the past 15 years, has coincided with a concurrent (and necessary) development and dissemination of a teaching technology. While this research into teaching techniques would have proceeded independent of the autistic population, the demanding presence of these hard-to-teach children has spurred the necessary refinement of teaching practice. The simple, now historic, reason for calling autistic children "uneducable" was our ignorance about how to teach. The lessons we have learned from the above-cited studies are not that "autistic children can now learn X behaviors," but rather "we now know how to teach autistic children X behaviors." This distinction is, perhaps, a subtle one, but it underscores a very important point: we have acquired (and are still acquiring) a great deal of knowledge about the variables that influence learning by autistic children. This knowledge has dramatically increased our abilities to teach them. As we continue to advance, we can predict additional gains in our understanding of teaching techniques, curriculum design, and the learning characteristics of autistic children.

REFERENCES

Axelrod, S., Brantner, J. P., & Meddock, T. D. Overcorrection: A review and critical analysis. *The Journal of Special Education*, 1978, *12*, 367-391.

Azrin, N. H., Kaplan, S. J., & Foxx, R. M. Autism reversal: Eliminating stereotyped self-stimulation of retarded individuals. *American Journal of Mental Deficiency*, 1973, *18*, 241-248.

Baer, D. M., Wolf, M. M., & Risley, T. Some current dimensions of applied behavior analysis. *Journal of Applied Behavior Analysis*, 1968, *1*, 91-97.

Bandura, A. *Principles of behavior modification.* New York: Holt, Rinehart & Winston, 1969.

Barrish, H. H., Saunders, M., & Wolf, M. M. Good behavior game: Effects of individual contingencies for group consequences on disruptive behavior in a classroom. *Journal of Applied Behavior Analysis,* 1969, *2,* 119-124.

Becker, W. C. *Parents are teachers.* Champaign, Illinois: Research Press, 1971.

Becker, W. C., & Becker, J. W. *Successful parenthood.* Chicago: Follett Publishing Company, 1974.

Bernal, M. E., & North, J. A. A survey of parent training manuals. *Journal of Applied Behavior Analysis,* 1978, *4,* 533-544.

Bijou, S. W., Birnbrauer, J. S., Kidder, J. D., & Tague, C. Programmed instruction as an approach to the teaching of reading, writing, and arithmetic to retarded children. *Psychological Record,* 1966, *16,* 505-522.

Birnbrauer, J. S. Generalization of punishment effects: A case study. *Journal of Applied Behavior Analysis,* 1968, 1, 201-211.

Birnbrauer, J. S., Kidder, J. D., & Tague, C. Programming reading from the teachers' point of view. *Programmed Instruction,* 1964, *3,* 1-2.

Bostow, D. L., & Bailey, J. B. Modification of severe disruptive and aggressive behavior using brief timeout and reinforcement procedures. *Journal of Applied Behavior Analysis,* 1969, *2,* 31-38.

Brethower, D. M., & Reynolds, G. S. A facilitative effect of punishment on unpunished behavior. *Journal of the Experimental Analysis of Behavior,* 1962, *5,* 191-199.

Bricker, W. A., Morgan, D. G., & Grabowski, J. G. Development and maintenance of a behavior modification repertoire of cottage attendants through T.V. feedback. *American Journal of Mental Deficiency,* 1972, *77,* 128-136.

Bucher, B., & Lovaas, O. I. Use of aversive stimulation in behavior modification. In M. R. Jones (ed.), *Miami symposium on the prediction of behavior, 1967: Aversive stimulation.* Coral Gables, Florida: University of Miami Press, 1968.

Buell, J., Stoddard, P., Harris, F., & Baer, D. M. Collateral social development accompanying reinforcement of outdoor play in a pre-school child. *Journal of Applied Behavior Analysis,* 1968, *1,* 167-173.

Burchard, J. D., & Tyler, V. O., Jr. The modification of delinquent behavior through operant conditioning. *Behaviour Research and Therapy,* 1965, *2,* 245-250.

Bushell, D., Jr., Wrobel, P. A., & Michaelis, M. L. Applying "group" contingencies to the classroom study behavior of pre-school children. *Journal of Applied Behavior Analysis,* 1968, *1,* 55-62.

Carnine, D. W. Effects of two teacher-presentation rates on off-task behavior, answering correctly, and participation. *Journal of Applied Behavior Analysis,* 1976, *9,* 199-206.

Carr, E. G. The motivation of self-injurious behavior: A review of some hypotheses. *Psychological Bulletin,* 1977, *84,* 800-816.

Carr, E. G., Newsom, C. D., & Binkoff, J. A. Stimulus control of self-destructive behavior in a psychotic child. *Journal of Abnormal Child Psychology,* 1976, *4,* 139-153.

Carr, E. G., Schreibman, L., & Lovaas, O. I. Control of echolalic speech in psychotic children. *Journal of Abnormal Child Psychology,* 1975, *3,* 331-351.

Cheney, T., & Stein, N. Fading procedures and oddity learning in kindergarten children. *Journal of Experimental Child Psychology,* 1974, *17,* 313-321.

Churchill, D. W., Alpern, G. D., & DeMyer, M. K. (eds.). *Infantile autism.* Springfield, Illinois: Charles C Thomas, 1971.

Clark, H. B., & Macrae, J. W. The use of imposed and self-selected training packages to establish classroom teaching skills. *Journal of Applied Behavior Analysis,* 1976, *9,* 105.

Clark, H. B., Rowbury, T., Baer, A. M., & Baer, D. M. Timeout as a punishing stimulus in continuous and intermittent schedules. *Journal of Applied Behavior Analysis*, 1973, *6*, 443-455.

Cossairt, A., Hall, R. V., & Hopkins, B. L. The effects of experimenter's instructions, feedback, and praise on teacher praise and student attending behavior. *Journal of Applied Behavior Analysis*, 1973, *6*, 89-100.

Davison, G. C. A social learning therapy programme with an autistic child. *Behaviour Research and Therapy*, 1964, *2*, 149-159.

Dietz, S. M., & Repp, A. L. Decreasing classroom misbehavior through the use of DRL schedules of reinforcement. *Journal of Applied Behavior Analysis*, 1973, *6*, 457-463.

Dunlap, G., Koegel, R. L., & Egel, A. L. Autistic children in school. *Exceptional Children*, 1979, *45*, 552-558.

Egel, A. L., Richman, G., & Koegel, R. L. Normal peer models and autistic children's learning. *Journal of Applied Behavior Analysis*, in press.

Elgar, S. The autistic child. *The Australian Journal on the Slow Learning Child*, 1966, *13*, 91-102.

Epstein, L. H., Doke, L. A., Sajwaj, T. E., Sorrell, S., & Rimmer, B. Generality and side effects of overcorrection. *Journal of Applied Behavior Analysis*, 1974, *7*, 385-390.

Fenichel, C. Special education as the basic therapeutic tool in treatment of severely disturbed children. *Journal of Autism and Childhood Schizophrenia*, 1974, *4*, 177-186.

Ferster, C. B. Positive reinforcement and behavioral deficits of autistic children. *Child Development*, 1961, *32*, 437-456.

Ferster, C. B. Discussion. In R. J. Friedman & M. M. Katz (eds.), *The psychology of depression: Contemporary theory and research*. Washington, D.C.: Winston-Wiley, 1974 (p. 115).

Ferster, C. B., Culbertson, S., & Boren, M. C. P. *Behavior principles*. 2nd ed. Englewood Cliffs, New Jersey: Prentice-Hall, 1975.

Ferster, C. B., & Skinner, B. F. *Schedules of reinforcement*. New York: Appleton-Century-Crofts, 1957.

Foxx, R. M., & Azrin, N. H. Restitution: A method of eliminating aggressive-disruptive behavior of retarded and brain-damaged patients. *Behaviour Research and Therapy*, 1972, *10*, 15-27.

Foxx, R. M., & Azrin, N. H. The elimination of autistic self-stimulatory behavior by overcorrection. *Journal of Applied Behavior Analysis*, 1973, *6*, 1-14.

Freeman, B. J., & Ritvo, E. R. Parents as paraprofessionals. In E. R. Ritvo (ed.), *Autism: Diagnosis, current research and management*. New York: Spectrum Publications, 1976.

Goldfarb, W. *Childhood schizophrenia*. Cambridge: Harvard University Press, 1961.

Goldman, W. S., & May, M. A. Dynamics of classroom structure for emotionally disturbed children. *The Journal of School Health*, 1967, *37*, 200-202.

Greenwood, C. R., Hops, H., Delquadri, J., & Guild, J. Group contingencies for group consequences in classroom management; a further analysis. *Journal of Applied Behavior Analysis*, 1974, *7*, 413-426.

Griffiths, H., & Craighead, W. E. Generalization in operant speech therapy for misarticulation. *Journal of Speech and Hearing Disorders*, 1972, *37*, 457-468.

Guess, D., Sailor, W., & Baer, D. M. A behavioral remedial approach to language training for the severely handicapped. In E. Sontag, N. Certo, & J. Smith (eds.), *Educational programming for the severely and profoundly handicapped*. Reston, Virginia: Council for Exceptional Children, 1977.

Hall, R. V. *Behavior modification: Applications in school and home*. Lawrence, Kansas: H & H Enterprises, Inc., 1971. (a)

Hall, R. V. *Behavior modification: Basic principles.* Lawrence, Kansas: H & H Enterprises, Inc., 1971. (b)

Hall, R. V. *Behavior modification: The measurement of behavior.* Lawrence, Kansas: H & H Enterprises, Inc., 1971. (c)

Hall, R. V., Panyan, M., Rabon, D., & Broden, M. Instructing beginning teachers in reinforcement procedures which improve classroom control. *Journal of Applied Behavior Analysis,* 1968, *1,* 315-322.

Halpern, W. I. The schooling of autistic children: Preliminary findings. *American Journal of Orthopsychiatry,* 1970, *40,* 665-671.

Hamblin, R. L., Buckholdt, D., Ferritor, D. E., Kozloff, M. A., & Blackwell, L. J. *The humanization process.* New York: John Wiley & Sons, 1971.

Hamilton, J., Stephens, L., & Allen, P. Controlling aggressive and destructive behavior in severely retarded institutionalized residents. *American Journal of Mental Deficiency,* 1967, *71,* 852-856.

Hamre-Nietupski, S., & Williams, W. Teaching selected sex education and social skills to severely handicapped students. In L. Brown, N. Certo, K. Belmore, & T. Crowner (eds.), *Madison's alternative for zero exclusion: Papers and programs related to public school services for secondary age severely handicapped students* (Vol. VI, Part 1). Madison, Wisconsin: Madison Public Schools, 1976.

Hanson, H. Effects of discrimination training on stimulus generalization. *Journal of Experimental Psychology,* 1959, *58,* 321-335.

Hemsley, R., Howlin, P., Berger, M., Hersov, L., Holbrook, D., Rutter, M., & Yule, W. Treating autistic children in a family context. In M. Rutter & E. Schopler (eds.), *Autism: A reappraisal of concepts and treatment.* New York: Plenum Press, 1978.

Herbert, E. W., & Baer, D. M. Training parents as behavior modifiers: Self-recording of contingent attention. *Journal of Applied Behavior Analysis,* 1972, *5,* 139-149.

Herendeen, D. L., Jeffrey, D. B., & Graham, M. C. *Reduction of self-stimulation in institutionalized children: Overcorrection and reinforcement of non-responding.* Paper presented at the 8th Annual Meeting of the Association for the Advancement of Behavior Therapy, Chicago, November, 1974.

Hewett, F. M. Teaching speech to autistic children through operant conditioning. *American Journal of Orthopsychiatry,* 1965, *35,* 927-936.

Holt, G. L., & Shafer, J. N. Function of intertrial interval in matching-to-sample. *Journal of the Experimental Analysis of Behavior,* 1973, *19,* 181-186.

Hung, D. W. Using self-stimulation as reinforcement for autistic children. *Journal of Autism and Childhood Schizophrenia,* 1978, *8,* 355-366.

Johnson, G. O. Special education for the mentally handicapped—A paradox. *Exceptional Children,* 1962, *29,* 62-69.

Johnson, S. M., Bolstad, D. D., & Lobitz, G. K. Generalization and contrast phenomena in behavior modification with children. In E. J. Mash, L. A. Hammerlynk, & L. C. Handy (eds.), *Behavior modification and families.* New York: Brunner/Mazel, 1976.

Kale, R. J., Kaye, J. H., Whelan, P. A., & Hopkins, B. L. The effects of reinforcement on the modification, maintenance, and generalization of social reponses of mental patients. *Journal of Applied Behavior Analysis,* 1968, *1,* 307-314.

Kanner, L. Autistic disturbances of affective contact. *The Nervous Child,* 1943, *3,* 217-250.

Kanner, L. *Childhood psychosis: Initial studies and new insights.* Washington, D.C.: V. H. Winston & Sons, Inc., 1973.

Karoly, P., & Rosenthal, M. Training parents in behavior modification: Effects on perceptions of family interaction and deviant child behavior. *Behavior Therapy,* 1977, *8,* 406-410.

Kazdin, A. E., & Bootzin, R. R. The token economy: An evaluative review. *Journal of Applied Behavior Analysis,* 1972, *5,* 343-372.

Kazdin, A. E., & Klock, J. The effects of non-verbal teacher approval on student attentive behavior. *Journal of Applied Behavior Analysis*, 1973, *6*, 643-654.

Kazdin, A. E., & Moyer, W. Training teachers to use behavior modification. In S. Yen & R. McIntire (eds.), *Teaching behavior modification*. Kalamazoo, Michigan: Behaviordelia, 1976.

Koegel, R. L. *Classroom management*. Parts I & II. (Color videotape, 50 min.) Camarillo State Hospital, Camarillo, California: California Department of Health, 1978.

Koegel, R. L., & Covert, A. The relationship of self-stimulation to learning in autistic children. *Journal of Applied Behavior Analysis*, 1972, *5*, 381-387.

Koegel, R. L., Dunlap, G., & Dyer, K. Intertrial interval duration and learning in autistic children. *Journal of Applied Behavior Analysis*, 1980, *13*, 91-99.

Koegel, R. L., & Egel, A. L. Motivating autistic children. *Journal of Abnormal Psychology*, 1979, *88*, 418-426.

Koegel, R. L., Egel, A. L., & Williams, J. A. Behavioral contrast and transfer across settings in teaching autistic children. *Journal of Experimental Child Psychology*, in press.

Koegel, R. L., & Felsenfeld, S. Sensory deprivation. In S. Gerber (ed.), *Audiometry in infancy*. New York: Grune & Stratton, 1977.

Koegel, R. L., Firestone, P. B., Kramme, K. W., & Dunlap, G. Increasing spontaneous play by suppressing self-stimulation in autistic children. *Journal of Applied Behavior Analysis*, 1974, *7*, 521-528.

Koegel, R. L., Glahn, T. J., & Nieminen, G. S. Generalization of parent-training results. *Journal of Applied Behavior Analysis*, 1978, *11*, 95-109.

Koegel, R. L., & Rincover, A. Treatment of psychotic children in a classroom environment: I. Learning in a large group. *Journal of Applied Behavior Analysis*, 1974, *7*, 45-59.

Koegel, R. L., & Rincover, A. Some detrimental effects of using extra stimuli to guide learning in normal and autistic children. *Journal of Abnormal Child Psychology*, 1976, *4*, 59-71.

Koegel, R. L., & Rincover, A. Research on the difference between generalization and maintenance in extra-therapy responding. *Journal of Applied Behavior Analysis*, 1977, *10*, 1-12.

Koegel, R. L., Rincover, A., & Egel, A. L. *Classroom treatment of autistic children*. Houston: College Hill Press, in press.

Koegel, R. L., Russo, D. C., & Rincover, A. Assessing and training teachers in the generalized use of behavior modification with autistic children. *Journal of Applied Behavior Analysis*, 1977, *10*, 197-205.

Koegel, R. L., & Schreibman, L. Teaching autistic children to respond to simultaneous multiple cues. *Journal of Experimental Child Psychology*, 1977, *24*, 299-311.

Koegel, R. L., & Wilhelm, H. Selective responding to the components of multiple visual cues by autistic children. *Journal of Experimental Child Psychology*, 1973, *15*, 442-453.

Kozloff, M. *Reaching the autistic child*. Champaign, Illinois: Research Press, 1973.

Leff, R. Behavior modification and the psychoses of childhood: A review. *Psychological Bulletin*, 1968, *69*, 396-409.

Lichstein, K. L., & Schreibman, L. Employing electric shock with autistic children: A review of the side effects. *Journal of Autism and Childhood Schizophrenia*, 1976, *6*, 163-174.

Lovaas, O. I. Program for establishment of speech in schizophrenic and autistic children. In J. K. Wing (ed.), *Early childhood autism: Clinical, educational, and social aspects*. London: Pergamon Press, 1966.

Lovaas, O. I. *Behavior modification: Teaching language to psychotic children.* (Instructional film, 45 min, 16-mm sound.) New York: Appleton-Century-Crofts, 1969.

Lovaas, O. I. *The autistic child.* New York: Irvington Publishers, Inc., 1977.

Lovaas, O. I., Berberich, J. P., Perloff, B. F., & Schaeffer, B. Acquisition of imitative speech in schizophrenic children. *Science,* 1966, *151,* 705-707.

Lovass, O. I., Koegel, R. L., & Schreibman, L. Stimulus overselectivity in autism: A review of research. *Psychological Bulletin,* 1979, *86,* 1236-1254.

Lovaas, O. I., Koegel, R. L., & Simmons, J. Q., & Long, J. S. Some generalization and follow-up measures on autistic children in behavior therapy. *Journal of Applied Behavior Analysis,* 1973, *6,* 131-166.

Lovaas, O. I., Litrownik, A., & Mann, R. Response latencies to auditory stimuli in autistic children engaged in self-stimulatory behavior. *Behaviour Research and Therapy,* 1971, *9,* 39-49.

Lovaas, O. I., & Newsom, C. D. Behavior modification with psychotic children. In H. Leitenberg (ed.), *Handbook of behavior modification and behavior therapy.* Englewood Cliffs, New Jersey: Prentice-Hall, 1976.

Lovaas, O. I., Schaeffer, B., & Simmons, J. O. Experimental studies in childhood schizophrenia: Building social behaviors by use of electric shock. *Journal of Experimental Research in Personality,* 1965, *1,* 99-109.

Lovaas, O. I., & Schreibman, L. Stimulus overselectivity of autistic children in a two stimulus situation. *Behaviour Research and Therapy,* 1971, *9,* 305-310.

Lovaas, O. I., Schreibman, L., & Koegel, R. L. A behavior modification approach to the treatment of autistic children. *Journal of Autism and Childhood Schizophrenia,* 1974, *4,* 111-129.

Lovaas, O. I., Schreibman, L., Koegel, R. L., & Rehm, R. Selective responding by autistic children to multiple sensory input. *Journal of Abnormal Psychology,* 1971, *77,* 211-222.

Lovaas, O. I., & Simmons, J. Q. Manipulation of self-destruction in three retarded children. *Journal of Applied Behavior Analysis,* 1969, *2,* 143-157.

Lovaas, O. I., Varni, J. W., Koegel, R. L., & Lorsch, N. Some observations on the nonextinguishability of children's speech. *Child Development,* 1977, *48,* 1121-1127.

McNamara, J. R. Teacher and students as a source of behavior modification in the classroom. *Behavior Therapy,* 1971, *2,* 205-213.

Madsen, C. H., Jr., Becker, W. C., & Thomas, D. R. Rules, praise, and ignoring: Elements of elementary classroom control. *Journal of Applied Behavior Analysis,* 1968, *1,* 139-150.

Martin. G. L., England, G., Kaprowy, E., Kilgour, K., & Pilek, V. Operant conditioning of kindergarten class behavior on autistic children. *Behaviour Research and Therapy,* 1968, *6,* 281-294.

Metz, J. R. Conditioning generalized imitation in autistic children. *Journal of Experimental Child Psychology,* 1965, *2,* 389-399.

Miller, S. J., & Sloane, H. W., Jr. The generalization effects of parent training across stimulus settings. *Journal of Applied Behavior Analysis,* 1976, *9,* 355-370.

Miller, W. R., & Seligman, M. E. P. Depression and learned helplessness in man. *Journal of Abnormal Psychology,* 1975, *84,* 228-238.

Mittler, P. The psychological assessment of autistic children. In J. K. Wing (ed.), *Early childhood autism: Clinical, educational, and social aspects.* London: Pergamon Press, 1966.

Mulhern, I., & Baumeister, A. A. An experimental attempt to reduce stereotypy by reinforcement procedures. *American Journal of Mental Deficiency,* 1969, *74,* 69-74.

Nordquist, V. M., & Wahler, R. G. Naturalistic treatment of an autistic child. *Journal of Applied Behavior Analysis,* 1973, *6,* 79-87.

O'Brien, F. Sequential contrast effects with human subjects. *Journal of the Experimental Analysis of Behavior*, 1968, *11*, 537–542.

O'Leary, K. D., & Drabman, R. Token reinforcement programs in the classroom: A review. *Psychological Bulletin*, 1971, *75*, 379–398.

O'Leary, S. G., & O'Leary, K. D. Behavior modification in the school. In H. Leitenberg (ed.), *Handbook of behavior modification and behavior therapy*. Englewood Cliffs, New Jersey: Prentice-Hall, 1976.

Ornitz, E. M., & Ritvo, E. R. Perceptual inconstancy in early infantile autism. *Archives of General Psychiatry*, 1968, *18*, 76–98.

Overmeir, J. B., & Seligman, M. E. P. Effects of inescapable shock upon subsequent escape and avoidance learning. *Journal of Comparative and Physiological Psychology*, 1967, *63*, 28–33.

Packard, R. G. The control of "classroom attention": A group contingency for complex behavior. *Journal of Applied Behavior Analysis*, 1970, *3*, 13–28.

Panyan, M. C. *Behavior modification: New ways to teach old skills*. Lawrence, Kansas: H & H Enterprises, Inc., 1971.

Panyan, M., Boozer, H., & Morris, N. Feedback to attendants as a reinforcer for applying operant techniques. *Journal of Applied Behavior Analysis*, 1970, *3*, 1–4.

Pappanikou, A. J., & Paul, J. L. (eds.). *Mainstreaming emotionally disturbed children*. Syracuse, New York: Syracuse University Press, 1977.

Patterson, G. R., & Guillon, M. E. *Living with children*. Champaign, Illinois: Research Press, 1968.

Peterson, R. F., Cox, M. A., & Bijou, S. W. Training children to work productively in classroom groups. *Exceptional Children*, 1971, *37*, 491–500.

Plummer, S., Baer, D. M., & LeBlanc, J. M. Functional considerations in the use of procedural timeout and an effective alternative. *Journal of Applied Behavior Analysis*, 1977, *10*, 689–706.

Quay, H. C. The facets of educational exceptionality: A conceptual framework for assessment, grouping, and instruction. *Exceptional Children*, 1968, *35*, 25–32.

Rabb, E., & Hewett, F. M. Development of appropriate classroom behaviors in a severely disturbed group of institutionalized children with a behavior modification model. *American Journal of Orthopsychiatry*, 1967, *37*, 313–314.

Reynolds, B. S., Newsom, C. D., & Lovaas, O. I. Auditory overselectivity in autistic children. *Journal of Abnormal Child Psychology*, 1974, *2*, 253–263.

Reynolds, G. S. An analysis of interaction in a multiple schedule. *Journal of the Experimental Analysis of Behavior*, 1961, *4*, 107–117. (a)

Reynolds, G. S. Behavioral contrast. *Journal of the Experimental Analysis of Behavior*, 1961, *4*, 57–71. (b)

Reynolds, G. S. Contrast, generalization, and the process of discrimination. *Journal of the Experimental Analysis of Behavior*, 1961, *4*, 289–294. (c)

Reynolds, G. S. Relativity of response and reinforcement in a multiple schedule. *Journal of the Experimental Analysis of Behavior*, 1961, *4*, 179–184. (d)

Rimland, B. *Infantile autism*. New York: Appleton-Century-Crofts, 1964.

Rimland, B. Inside the mind of an autistic savant. *Psychology Today*, 1978, *12*, 68–80.

Rincover, A. Sensory extinction: A procedure for eliminating self-stimulatory behavior in developmentally disabled children. *Journal of Abnormal Child Psychology*, 1978, *6*, 299–310. (a)

Rincover, A. Variables affecting stimulus-fading and discriminative responding in psychotic children. *Journal of Abnormal Psychology*, 1978, *87*, 541–553. (b)

Rincover, A., & Koegel, R. L. Classroom treatment of autistic children: II. Individualized instruction in a group. *Journal of Abnormal Child Psychology*, 1977, *5*, 113–126. (a)

Rincover, A., & Koegel, R. L. Research on the education of autistic children: Recent Advances and future directions. In B. B. Lahey & A. E. Kazdin (eds.), *Advances in clinical child psychology* (Vol. 1). New York: Plenum Press, 1977. (b)

Rincover, A., & Koegel, R. L. Setting generality and stimulus control in autistic children. *Journal of Applied Behavior Analysis*, 1975, *8*, 235-246.

Rincover, A., Newsom, C. D., Lovaas, O. I., & Koegel, R. L. Some motivational properties of sensory stimulation in psychotic children. *Journal of Experimental Child Psychology*, 1977, *24*, 312-323.

Risley, T. R. The effects and side effects of punishing the autistic behaviors of a deviant child. *Journal of Applied Behavior Analysis*, 1968, *1*, 21-34.

Risley, T. R., & Wolf, M. M. Establishing functional speech in echolalic children. *Behaviour Research and Therapy*, 1967, *5*, 73-88.

Ritvo, E. R., & Freeman, B. J. National Society for Autistic Children definition of the syndrome of autism. *Journal of Autism and Childhood Schizophrenia*, 1978, *8*, 162-167.

Robinson, E., Hughes, H., Wilson, D., Lahey, B. B., & Haynes, S. *Modification of stereotyped behaviors of "autistic" children through response-contingent water squirts.* Paper presented at the 8th Annual Convention of the Association for the Advancement of Behavior Therapy, Chicago, November, 1974.

Russo, D. C., & Koegel, R. L. A method for integrating an autistic child into a normal public-school classroom. *Journal of Applied Behavior Analysis*, 1977, *10*, 579-590.

Rutter, M. Concepts of autism: A review of research. *Journal of Child Psychology and Psychiatry*, 1968, *9*, 1-25.

Rutter, M. Autism: Educational issues. *Special Education*, 1970, *59*, 6-10.

Rutter, M. Diagnosis and definition of childhood autism. *Journal of Autism and Childhood Schizophrenia*, 1978, *8*, 139-161.

Sailor, W., & Taman, T. Stimulus factors in the training of prepositional usage in three autistic children. *Journal of Applied Behavior Analysis*, 1972, *5*, 183-192.

Sajwaj, T., Twardosz, S., & Burke, M. Side effects of extinction procedures in a remedial pre-school. *Journal of Applied Behavior Analysis*, 1972, *5*, 163-176.

Schopler, E. On confusion in the diagnosis of autism. *Journal of Autism and Childhood Schizophrenia*, 1978, *8*, 137-138.

Schover, L. R., & Newsom, C. D. Overselectivity, developmental level and overtraining in autistic and normal children. *Journal of Abnormal Child Psychology*, 1976, *4*, 289-298.

Schreibman, L. Effects of within-stimulus and extra-stimulus prompting on discrimination learning in autistic children. *Journal of Applied Behavior Analysis*, 1975, *8*, 91-112.

Schreibman, L., & Koegel, R. L. Autism: A defeatable horror. *Psychology Today*, 1975, *8*, 61-67.

Schreibman, L., & Koegel, R. A guideline for planning behavior modification programs for autistic children. In S. M. Turner, K. S. Calhoun, & M. E. Adams (eds.), *Handbook of clinical behavior therapy*. New York: John Wiley & Sons, in press.

Schreibman, L., Koegel, R. L., & Craig, M. S. Reducing stimulus overselectivity in autistic children. *Journal of Abnormal Child Psychology*, 1977, *5*, 425-436.

Schreibman, L., & Lovaas, O. I. Overselective response to social stimuli by autistic children. *Journal of Abnormal Child Psychology*, 1973, *1*, 152-168.

Schutte, R. C., & Hopkins, B. L. The effects of teacher attention on following instructions in a kindergarten class. *Journal of Applied Behavior Analysis*, 1970, *3*, 117-122.

Scott, J. W., & Bushell, D., Jr. The length of teacher contacts and students' off-task behavior. *Journal of Applied Behavior Analysis*, 1974, *7*, 39-44.

Seligman, M. E. P., Klein, D. C., & Miller, W. R. Depression. In H. Leitenberg (ed.), *Handbook of behavior modification*. New York: Appleton-Century-Crofts, 1976.

Seligman, M. E. P., & Maier, S. F. Failure to escape traumatic shock. *Journal of Experimental Psychology*, 1967, *74*, 1–9.

Sidman, M., & Stoddard, L. T. Programming perception and learning for retarded children. In N. R. Ellis (ed.), *International review of research in mental retardation* (Vol. 2). New York: Academic Press, 1966.

Sidman, M., & Stoddard, L. T. The effectiveness of fading in programming a simultaneous form discrimination for retarded children. *Journal of the Experimental Analysis of Behavior*, 1967, *10*, 3–15.

Skinner, B. F. *The behavior of organisms: An experimental analysis.* New York: Appleton-Century-Crofts, 1938.

Solnick, J. V., Rincover, A., & Peterson, C. R. Determinants of the reinforcing and punishing effects of time-out. *Journal of Applied Behavior Analysis*, 1977, *10*, 415–428.

Stevens-Long, J., & Rasmussen, M. The acquisition of simple and compound sentence structure in an autistic child. *Journal of Applied Behavior Analysis*, 1974, *7*, 473–480.

Stokes, T. F., & Baer, D. M. An implicit technology of generalization. *Journal of Applied Behavior Analysis*, 1977, *10*, 349–368.

Stokes, T. F., Baer, D. M., & Jackson, R. L. Programming the generalization of a greeting response in four retarded children. *Journal of Applied Behavior Analysis*, 1974, *7*, 599–610.

Sulzer, B., & Mayer, G. R. *Behavior modification procedures for school personnel.* Hinsdale: Dryden Press, 1972.

Taber, J. I., & Glaser, R. An exploratory evaluation of a discriminative transfer program using literal prompts. *Journal of Educational Research*, 1962, *55*, 508–512.

Tate, B. G., & Baroff, G. S. Aversive control of self-injurious behavior in a psychotic boy. *Behaviour Research and Therapy*, 1966, *4*, 281–287.

Thomas, D. R., Becker, W. C., & Armstrong, M. Production and elimination of disruptive classroom behavior by systematically varying teacher's behavior. *Journal of Applied Behavior Analysis*, 1968, *1*, 35–46.

Touchette, P. E. The effects of graduated stimulus change on the acquisition of a simple discrimination in severely retarded boys. *Journal of the Experimental Analysis of Behavior*, 1968, *11*, 39–48.

Touchette, P. E. Tilted lines as complex stimuli. *Journal of the Experimental Analysis of Behavior*, 1969, *12*, 211–214.

Touchette, P. E. Transfer of stimulus control: Measuring the moment of transfer. *Journal of the Experimental Analysis of Behavior*, 1971, *15*, 347–364.

Turner, B. L. *The effects of choice of stimulus materials on interest in the remediation process and the generalized case of language training.* Unpublished master's thesis, University of California, Santa Barbara, 1978.

Tyler, V. O., & Brown, G. D. The use of swift, brief isolation as a group control device for institutionalized delinquents. *Behaviour Research and Therapy*, 1967, *5*, 1–9.

Varni, J., Lovaas, O. I., Koegel, R. L., & Everett, N. L. An analysis of observational learning in autistic and normal children. *Journal of Abnormal Child Psychology*, 1979, *7*, 31–43.

Wahler, R. G. Setting generality: Some specific and general effects of child behavior therapy. *Journal of Applied Behavior Analysis*, 1969, *2*, 239–246.

Wahler, R. G., Sperling, F. A., Thomas, M. R., Teeter, N. C., & Loper, H. L. The modification of childhood stuttering. Some response-response relationships. *Journal of Experimental Child Psychology*, 1970, *9*, 411–428.

Wahler, R. G., Winkel, G. H., Peterson, R. F., & Morrison, D. C. Mothers as behavior therapists for their own children. *Behaviour Research and Therapy*, 1965, *3*, 113–124.

Waite, W. W., & Osborne, J. G. Sustained behavioral contrast in children. *Journal of the Experimental Analysis of Behavior*, 1972, *18*, 113–117.

Walker, H. M., & Buckley, N. K. Programming generalization and maintenance of treatment effects across time and across settings. *Journal of Applied Behavior Analysis*, 1972, *5*, 209-224.

Wetzel, R., Baker, I., Roney, M., & Martin, M. Out-patient treatment of autistic behavior. *Behaviour Research and Therapy*, 1966, *4*, 166-177.

Wheeler, A. J., & Sulzer, B. Operant training and generalization of a verbal response form in a speech-deficient child. *Journal of Applied Behavior Analysis*, 1970, *3*, 139-148.

White, G. D., Nielsen, G., & Johnson, S. M. Timeout duration and the suppression of deviant behavior in children. *Journal of Applied Behavior Analysis*, 1972, *5*, 111-120.

Williams, W. & Gotts A. E. Selected considerations on developing curriculum for severely handicapped students. In E. Sontag, N. Certo, & J. Smith (eds.), *Educational programming for the severely and profoundly handicapped*. Reston, Virginia: Council for Exceptional Children, 1977.

Wolf, M. M., Risley, T., Johnston, M., Harris, F., & Allen, E. Application of operant conditioning procedures to the behavior problems of an autistic child: A follow-up and extension. *Behaviour Research and Therapy*, 1967, *5*, 103-111.

Wolf, M. M., Risley, T., & Mees, H. Application of operant conditioning procedures to the behaviour problems of an autistic child. *Behaviour Research and Therapy*, 1964, *1*, 305-312.

Zeilberger, J., Sampen, S. E., & Sloane, H. N., Jr. Modification of a child's problem behaviors in the home with the mother as therapist. *Journal of Applied Behavior Analysis*, 1968, *1*, 47-54.

Chapter 10

Program Evaluation and Curriculum Development in Early Childhood/Special Education
Criteria of the Next Environment

Lisbeth J. Vincent, Christine Salisbury, Gail Walter, Pansy Brown, Lee J. Gruenewald, and Michael Powers

Although Public Law 94-142, the Education for All Handicapped Children Act, does not mandate that all preschool-age handicapped children receive a free appropriate public education, many such children are receiving service within public school programs. Kenowitz, Zweibel, and Edgar (1978) reported that 77% of the local educational agencies who responded to their survey of programs available for severely handicapped children indicated that they provided services for preschool-age severely handicapped students. Currently six states have passed legislative mandates to provide service to handicapped children from the point of diagnosis, and approximately half of the states mandate some services for handicapped children below 5 years of age. As Beck (1977) has indicated, those students identified as handicapped during the preschool years are more likely to show severe handicaps than those children identified during the school-age years. Thus, the public school programs that are being implemented for children under 5 years of age need to be designed to provide high quality services to severely handicapped students. These programs need to avoid repeating the past mistakes of other special educational services and instead must focus on innovative services and the documentation of their effectiveness (Bricker, 1978).

The purpose of this chapter is to outline an approach to evaluating the quality and impact of early childhood/special education services. The approach is based on analyzing handicapped childrens' success in educational environments after the preschool years and then feeding this information back into early childhood curriculum design and programming. The approach can best be labeled identification of the *criteria of the next educational environment*.

EARLY CHILDHOOD/SPECIAL EDUCATION:
WHAT SHOULD THE PURPOSE BE?

Brown, Nietupski, and Hamre-Nietupski (1976) have discussed a criterion of ultimate functioning which focuses on those skills that severely handicapped adolescents and adults need to function productively and independently in social, vocational, and domestic community environments. They advocate judging the goals set for severely handicapped students against this criterion of usefulness for future adult life and community functioning. Furthermore, they advocate judging the instructional methodology and curriculum content against the cues and correction procedures that will exist in the natural adult environment. While determining that a 2-year-old severely handicapped student will need dishwashing skills and then teaching those skills would be ludicrous, applying the principle to early childhood curriculum design would not be. That is, the principle could be translated to mean, what skills does the student need in order to function in the maximal number and variety of normal preschool environments and what skills will the child need to function in the next set of environments he or she will enter?

LeBlanc, Etzel, and Domash (1978), in discussing relevant curriculum goals for the preschool-age handicapped student, state that the goals chosen should be comprised of skills that will "ensure success in a child's current preschool setting and . . . ensure successful transitions to other current settings, as well as into future academic and social learning situations" (p. 333).

Taken together, writings of Brown and LeBlanc and their colleagues point to the importance of the future environment when designing curriculum and service delivery models in early childhood/special education. The most common future environment entered by children, both normal and handicapped, after the preschool years is the public school kindergarten classroom. For this reason Vincent and Broome (1977) identified normal kindergarten placement as the overriding goal of early childhood/special education.

Choosing to focus on the future environment of preschool-age handicapped students rather than on current environments has several justifications. Children under 5 years of age do not function in one common environment. Some are at home all day, some in nursery schools, others in day care centers, and others are at babysitters' homes. Parents of young children have varying expectancies in terms of degree of independence/dependence, noisiness/quietness, and so on. In a sense, the demands placed on a child under 5 years of age are idiosyncratic to the individual family. Thus, developing a set of functional skills that would be appropriate to all children would be difficult if not impossible. However, upon entering the public school system all children face at least some commonalities in needed skills. Furthermore, the focus on future educational environments is consistent with the mandates of Public Law 94-142. While school districts often do not have to provide services to preschool-age handicapped children, they must provide "least restrictive" programs for handicapped children when they reach school age.

While a common professionally agreed upon definition does not exist for the term *least restrictive educational environment,* professionals generally agree that this implies that services will be provided to the greatest extent possible in environments that include normal peers (Brown, Wilcox, Sontag, Vincent, Dodd, & Gruenewald, 1977). Kenowitz et al. (1978) indicate that physical location and proximity to normal peers are not the only factors to be considered when determining if a program provides the least restrictive educational opportunity. The appropriateness of the educational programming provided must also be analyzed. Included here is an evaluation of whether or not realistic and appropriate goals are being established for each child and whether or not instructional programming is being implemented in such a way as to meet these goals.

Within the field of early childhood/special education, the provision of services in classrooms that also include normal peers is becoming more and more prevalent. Guralnick (1978) has edited an excellent book, *Early Intervention and the Integration of Handicapped and Nonhandicapped Children,* which serves as an outstanding reference for a state-of-the-art review of integrated preschool programming. Several of the chapters concern the integration of young, severely handicapped students. Based on these chapters and a recent research article by Guralnick (1980), the conclusion that receiving educational services in environments that include less handicapped and normal children is not detrimental to the severely handicapped child and, in fact, may be beneficial appears to be justified. Since ample social/ethical and psychological/educational arguments (Bricker, 1978) also exist for providing integrated programming, increasingly greater provision of this type of service to the severely handicapped preschool-age child seems probable.

However, the questions raised by Kenowitz et al. (1978) related to appropriate goals and instructional methodology still remain to be answered. That is, given that young, severely handicapped students will be educated in environments that include less handicapped and nonhandicapped peers, what will the purpose and method of instruction be? What will educational specialists attempt to teach these children and why? How will they know that the programs they have provided are effective?

Currently, most of the evaluative research on the impact of early childhood/special education programs has been based on the measurement of developmental progress as indicated by measurements taken using standardized developmental assessments or checklists. As such, "success" is translated as a the display of norm-based skills by the child in an isolated testing situation. Pefley and Smith (1976), for example, have summarized the structure and results of 25 federally funded model preschool projects for "at risk" and handicapped preschool-age children. The majority of these programs in presenting data on their effectiveness either offer a count of the number of objectives that children achieved during a given year or list months gained on a standardized or in-house developed checklist.

Reliance on such standardized measures does not allow an accurate assessment of a child's progress. Although a handicapped child may show a dramatic skill gain (e.g., 18 months on the Bayley Scales of Infant Development in 12 months' time), two other factors may lead to the child still being labeled by teachers, parents, relatives, and day care center workers as severely handicapped. First, the acquisition of developmental skills is only a limited aspect of the criterion by which the family child care personnel see a child as handicapped. Even normal children show wide variability in the age of acquisition of major developmental milestones. Thus, a child's performance on the milestones is not necessarily an indicator of the presence or absence of a handicapping condition. Most often families and child care workers label a child as different because his or her *overall functioning* in the natural, ambiguous, complex, unstructured early childhood environment is deviant from that of his or her peers. While it is true that the more severely handicapped child is recognizable because of a lack of acquisition of major developmental milestones, the teaching of these isolated milestones may not make the child nonhandicapped. Second, the skill gains seen on the developmental checklist or assessment may not be carried over into the child's natural environment. The isolated testing situation of the developmental checklists, and even the classroom, do not resemble the natural environment where children are expected to display the learned skills. Thus, even with great developmental progress recorded on the assessment, if the child is unable to transfer those skills to other environments he or she may still be labeled severely retarded. Stokes and Baer (1977) present an excellent summary of the research in generalization of skills by mentally retarded individuals. The basic conclusion that can be reached is that generalization usually does not occur without systematic programming.

As Stufflebeam, Foley, Gephart, Guba, Hammong, Merriman, and Provas (1971) have indicated, in designing evaluation systems considerable attention should be given to the relevance and importance of the information gathered. In the case of early childhood/special education this could be translated into two basic questions: 1) will this information be useful in documenting that the services provided have really made a substantial difference on the educational opportunities or environments that are open to the students served, and 2) will this information lead to program changes and innovation that are shown to be even more beneficial for future handicapped children?

A basic assumption of early intervention is that by providing education in the preschool years, many of the children identified as handicapped could avoid later placement in categorical special education programs. Thus, the important evaluation task is to gather information that indicates whether early intervention in fact decreases the probability of segregated special education placement. The goal for early childhood/special educators becomes not just teaching children developmental milestones but also instructing children in the skills necessary to function in the environments that were predicted to be failure/inappropriate environments for them. Thus, the most successful outcome of early intervention programs would be to prevent the handicapped child from entering the same special education program at age 5 that he or she would have typically entered without remediation. By definition, then, early intervention programs attempt to keep children out of special education when they turn age 5. Ideally, the goal of an early intervention program is to ensure that children in the program enter regular kindergarten placements with age-level peers when they reach school age. At the very least, children given some kind of early intervention should enter a program that is "less restrictive," or more normal, in terms of experiences provided and types of peers present, than the program they would have entered with no intervention. Given that many handicapped children, even the severely handicapped, are being appropriately educated with normal peers during their preschool years, several of the more prevalent school-age special education options can be automaticlly viewed as restrictive, including the segregated schools and totally segregated classrooms.

In summary, the major purpose of early childhood/special education services should be to teach all handicapped children the skills necessary to function in as many as possible of the current and, more importantly, the future environments that are available to normal children. This goal should serve to direct curriculum development, instructional methodology, and program evaluation. Implementing this goal implies that the skills necessary to succeed in the normal school-age environments are objectively documented. Implementing this goal also implies that changes in early childhood/special education and in school-age environments will be undertaken.

FUTURE ENVIRONMENTS: WHAT DO THEY REQUIRE?

Handicapped students are expected to function in a wide variety of academic, community, and domestic environments. The demands of these environments vary in terms of supervision, degree of independence, and complexity of tasks involved, among many other variables. It is not within the scope of this chapter to examine all environments that 5- and 6-year-old students might enter. Thus, as authors and educators we have chosen to focus on the major school environment available to this population: the regular kindergarten classroom.

Early intervention programs that have as their goal the preparation of children for regular kindergarten are faced with the problems of: 1) determining what skills the children are expected to display in kindergarten, and 2) demonstrating that the children are, in fact, ready to enter kindergarten (as opposed to a special education program). Once a child is placed in special education it may become extremely difficult to get the child back into the regular education mainstream (Grosenick, 1972). In order to do so, the child's teacher must demonstrate or prove that the child is capable of kindergarten level work and has the skills necessary for kindergarten. Kindergarten screening tests are often used to help make this determination, and many school districts administer a screening test to all children to determine their skill level and kindergarten readiness and to make decisions about placing children in kindergarten programs.

Numerous screening tests are available. Zeitlin (1976) describes more than 20 screening tests used nationwide. All of these screening tests focus on the child's performance in the usual developmental areas: language skills, cognitive skills, fine and gross motor skills, pre-writing skills, and so on. The screening test of the Madison Metropolitan School District, Madison, Wisconsin, is typical of these tests. The following skills are assessed: color and shape discrimination; cutting, coloring, name writing, and shape copying; classification; seriation; counting; alphabet and numeral recognition; one-to-one correspondence; sight word reading; and language production. Screening tests at the kindergarten level are based upon the skills that a child is presumed to need to function in kindergarten (Boehm, 1971). It is assumed that if the child does well on these tests he or she is ready and has the skills necessary for kindergarten.

Special education preschool teachers who accept this assumption and who want to prepare children for kindergarten may attempt, in turn, to use the items from a screening test as the basis for the special education preschool curriculum. In doing so, they hope to prepare their students to "pass" the screening requirements and enter regular kindergarten.

The assumption that these are the primary skills necessary for kindergarten is, however, open to serious challenge. Anastasiow (1978), for example, refers to the dominant school curriculum as being the socialization and reinforcement of certain personal behaviors. Kindergarten curriculum has as its core the acquisition of social control (turn taking, sitting quietly, listening to directions). Hops and Cobb (1973) also describe several behavioral skills that are prerequisites to academic success. They call these skills survival skills in the sense that they are behaviors children must display in order to "survive" or function successfully in the classroom environment. Hops and Cobb (1973) define kindergarten survival skills as behaviors that are prerequisites to academic responding, or the first components in a chain of academic behaviors such as attending, volunteering, compliance, and direction following.

Not only are survival skills important and necessary, but failure to demonstrate these skills may in itself be viewed as a sign of abnormality. Cohen and Rudolph (1977) describe several "danger signs" that is, behaviors that may indicate a child is in need of special help (presumably special education). These include inability to remember tasks, inability to follow directions, inability to learn from experience or follow models, avoidance of contact with teacher and peers, and need for continual teacher attention. These danger signs can be viewed as simply deficits in, or the inability to display, appropriate survival skills. Clearly, then, a focus solely on preacademic skills may overlook other critical skills that a child is expected to display in kindergarten. Any attempt to identify a child's ability to function in a kindergarten must therefore include an assessment of his or her kindergarten survival skills.

The traditional kindergarten screening tests, while accurately measuring developmental and preacademic skills, do not include assessments of the vital kindergarten survival skills. Furthermore, since the tests are administered in artificial one-to-one or group test settings, they may present a distorted view of the child's typical behavior in a group or classroom setting. Results of screening tests, therefore, may not serve as good indicators or predictors of a child's survival skills. A child may display all the preacademic prerequisites on a screening test, but may lack the social interaction, attending, and direction following skills necessary for successful performance in a kindergarten classroom. Such a child may do very poorly in the large group setting in kindergarten and may become a behavior problem. On the other hand, a child who lacks some preacademic skills, such as knowledge of colors and rational counting, but who is able to imitate peers, attend in groups, and work independently may perform well in kindergarten.

A few studies have been done to establish the importance of survival skills for academic functioning. Lahaderne (1968) and Meyers, Atwell, and Orpet (1968) demonstrated that attending is correlated with achievement in math and reading in fifth and sixth graders. Cobb (1972) correlated 19 specific classroom behaviors (e.g., attending, compliance, volunteering, and talking to peers about academics) with math and reading achievement in first graders. He also found that changing children's survival skills performance changed their achievement scores.

This research provides support for the importance of the concept of survival skills for child success in school as well as the potential to teach these skills, but it does not provide enough information to be useful to a special education teacher preparing children for the transition to regular kindergarten. The special education preschool teacher must have specific information about the demands of a regular kindergarten environment in order to plan for the smooth transition of handicapped children into kindergarten.

Special education teachers are not usually familiar with the typical kindergarten environment and the behavioral requirements of kindergarten (Grosenick, 1972). Because special educators and regular educators receive different kinds of training, they will probably have different methods of organizing their classrooms and structuring learning environments. Thus, special education teachers do not necessarily have the experience or training to prepare children to function in kindergarten in terms of survival skills as well as academic skills. They also may provide children with a learning environment in preschool that is markedly different from that in regular education (Brown, Nietupski, & Hamre-Nietupski, 1976). Children in early education may receive training in school skills that are incompatible with (or at least unrelated to) skills that may be necessary in kindergarten. The discrepancy that can be anticipated between these two different learning environments is predicted to increase the likelihood of behavior problems and/or lack of generalization of skills as a child moves from special to regular education.

In summary, while the dual forces of Public Law 94-142 and early intervention programming have significantly influenced community-based service delivery systems and enhanced the probability that handicapped students will enter regular kindergarten classes, the children's success in such placements will depend not only on the acquisition of developmental skills but also on the acquisition of "survival" skills, that is, social/behavioral skills necessary to function successfully in a regular classroom. In addition, the structure of the early childhood classroom and the content of its curriculum will influence the degree of success a child experiences in a regular school placement. As such, programming that emphasizes the teaching of developmental skills (e.g., developmental milestones) to the exclusion of critical, functional skills may not be as effective for integrating children into kindergarten programming as a program that includes both skill areas. Therefore, the preschool teacher of handicapped students should formulate instructional goals for each child that lead to the development of those competencies that are necessary for the child to function successfully in the next environment.

DETERMINING SURVIVAL SKILLS

The question still remains, however, as to what exactly are the survival skills. As LeBlanc et al. (1978) and Brown et al. (1976) indicate, the most objective way to document these skills is to take an inventory of the environment of concern. Within the Madison Metropolitan School District, the present authors have employed a variety of strategies to complete such inventories.

In that provision of educational services to handicapped children from the point of diagnosis is unique for a public school system, a brief introduction to the school district where this research is taking place seems in order. In July of 1975, the Madison Metropolitan School District received a grant from the Bureau of Education for the Handicapped under the auspicies of the Handicapped Children's Early Education Program. The purpose of this grant was to develop a model system for child find, referral, and service delivery within the context of a community-based public school system. The target population for the grant was all handicapped children between birth and 5 years of age residing in the city of Madison, Wisconsin.

Since July of 1975 approximately 400 children have received services through the school district's Early Childhood Program. The program is housed in three regular elementary schools geographically distributed throughout the city. The program offers both home- and center-based services and is based on a transdisciplinary staff model. The various disciplines involved in the program include parents, early childhood/special education teachers, speech-language therapists, occupational therapists, physical therapists, school psychologists, social workers, school nurses, and pediatricians. The classroom-based portion of the program begins for children as young as 12 months of age. Children are grouped heterogeneously in classrooms, and all classrooms include at least two normal peer models. Children involved in the program follow all state-mandated multidisciplinary team assessment procedures as well as all federally mandated individualized education program (IEP) procedures. Approximately one-half of the preschool-age group also participates in community day care programs. (For further description of the variety of services offered to children and their families by the Madison Metropolitan School District, the reader is referred to an article by Vincent and Broome, 1977.)

A variety of strategies are available to the early childhood/special educator who wants to document the survival skills required in kindergarten programs. The strategies vary in terms of degree of objectivity and time required to implement them, and the information obtained varies in terms of generalizability and usefulness in generating early childhood/special education curricula that focus on survival skills. The present authors have been involved in implementing four such strategies.

Strategy 1: Kindergarten Tryouts

The first strategy implemented by the early childhood/special education teachers within the Madison schools involved selecting the 4-year-old children they believed might be appropriate for kindergarten placement and then negotiating with the kindergarten teacher in their elementary school building to ''take a look'' at these children. Usually this involved the child spending some time in the kindergarten classroom between January and May. The amount of time varied from 1 hour a week for a month to 2 weeks full-time. The kindergarten teacher was to determine whether or not he or she believed the child would be ready for kindergarten in the fall. This proved to be quite difficult for a number of reasons. Usually the child would not be entering the teacher's kindergarten class in the fall. Thus, the teacher had to assess the child against an unknown or at best an unreal ''average'' kindergarten class. Second, the other children in the teacher's classroom were a year older than the target child and the skills for which they were being programmed were not entry level kindergarten skills. Third, the regular kindergarten teacher did not know what skills could be taught in the early childhood/special education classroom or what deficits could be corrected by the following fall.

Despite these difficulties, however, this strategy was successful with a small number of children each year. The kindergarten teachers were able to pinpoint specific strengths and weaknesses of the target children. However, this strategy could not be employed with all 4-year-olds enrolled in early childhood/special education classes. Also, information on needed skills was obtained only about 4 months before a child graduated from early childhood/special education. If a special education teacher wished to make program changes he or she was faced with doing so for only one or two students in a very short period of time. Nevertheless, the strategy was very successful at increasing the amount of contact between special education and regular education staff. This resulted in the early childhood/special education students being included in more activities with the regular kindergarten students, such as physical education and music.

As an initial strategy to begin the process of interfacing early childhood/special education services with traditional school-age services, this strategy represents little investment in terms of time and planning costs while at the same being very effective. Its usefulness for curriculum development and program change in early childhood/special education, however, is limited.

Strategy 2: Follow-Up

The second strategy employed by early childhood/special education teachers involved information exchange between the early childhood/special education teacher and the kindergarten teacher after students from special education preschools were enrolled in regular kindergarten at the beginning of the year. If a child experienced difficulty in academic or behavioral areas, the kindergarten teacher contacted the previous teacher to discuss what skills the student needed in order to function more successfully and any inappropriate behavior displayed by the student that the kindergarten teacher considered intolerable. This is a post-hoc strategy in that the special education teacher finds out after advancing the student what skills should have been taught. One of the rationales underlying this approach is that, when the student encounters problems in kindergarten, some help will be provided for the student. This help often consists of advice to the kindergarten teacher concerning changes that need to be made in his or her classroom. Since this strategy is completed on a student by student basis, the feedback information is difficult to incorporate generally into the curriculum. In order to make the information more useful this strategy would need to be implemented for all students who graduate from early childhood/special education programs.

Such a follow-up study was conducted by one of the present authors for all graduates of the Madison Early Childhood Program between 1975 and 1977 (Brown, 1979). The purposes of the study were to:

1. Follow up on the children who had been involved in an early intervention program to identify which children went into what type of program.
2. Gather impressions from the children's subsequent teachers regarding the children's strengths and weaknesses.
3. Gather impressions from parents regarding the type of program their child was currently in and the type and degree of involvement the parents were having in that current program.

Forty children of kindergarten entry age were graduated from the early childhood/special education program between 1975 and 1977. Twenty-two of the children were placed in regular kindergarten classrooms. The other 18 children were placed in a variety of special education programs ranging from segregated classrooms for the multiply handicapped to a special kindergarten classroom that focused on speech and language skills. Seven of these 18 children were being considered for less restrictive future programs. As a whole, these 40 children spent an average of 66% of their school time with normal peers.

Each of the children's teachers was interviewed and asked questions about the child's strengths and weaknesses upon entering his or her classroom. These statements were then categorized as pertaining to preacademic, language, motor, or social-survival skills. The results of these interviews for the program graduates in 1976 are summarized in Table 1. Generally, equal numbers of strengths and weaknesses were pinpointed by the teachers. The greatest numbers of both strengths and weaknesses were indicated in the social-survival skills category for the first year of the follow-up study. During the second year, specific questions related to survival skills were included on the interview questionnaire. These questions were asked in order to obtain more specific information on how early childhood/special education graduates performed in this domain. Thus, the totals for this category during year two are inflated as a result of specific questions. These data are presented in Table 2.

The next environment teachers were also asked to list skills they thought the children should have been able to display upon entering their classroom but did not display. The skills were also subdivided into the areas of preacademic, language, social-survival, and motor skills. Table 3 summarizes these results. Again, the largest numbers of skill deficiencies were reported in the social-survival category. In fact, more than twice as many social-survival skills were listed as were listed in language or preacademic skills.

Overall the results of the follow-up interviews with the next environment teachers and the children's parents pointed to the importance of social-survival skills rather than the developmental targets measured on developmental checklists or kindergarten screening tools. These results are supportive of Anastasiow's (1978) contention that the major focus of early public schooling is socialization. Several additional findings of interest were that the "guesstimates" made by early childhood/special educators in conjunction with the kindergarten teachers as a result of kindergarten tryouts were generally correct. The children who were recommended for at least a 50% placement in normal kindergarten were succeeding in that environment and being recommended for future regular educational environments in most cases. The children recommended for

Table 1.   Statements of children's strengths and weaknesses made by follow-up teachers

Skill area	Strengths	Weaknesses	Total
Preacademic	24	12	36
Language	6	28	34
Social-Survival	43	34	77
Motor	0	0	0
TOTAL	73	74	

Table 2. Statements of children's strengths and weaknesses by follow-up teachers

Skill area	Strengths	Weaknesses	Total
Preacademic	23	19	42
Language	17	19	36
Social-Survival	142	82	224
Motor	12	14	26
TOTAL	194	134	

5-year-old special educational environments were being recommended for future special educational environments. This finding was in concert with the work of Grosenick (1972) cited earlier, and added even more weight to the need to document critical survival skills objectively and to develop survival skills curricula for early childhood/special education programs.

While a list of approximately 300 statements pertaining to survival skills was obtained from the follow-up research, these statements could not be translated directly into curriculum or instructional goals. Generally, they were not stated in behavioral/measurable terms and no indication of their relative importance was obtained. Thus, the follow-up study served as an initial evaluation tool of how successfully the district's early intervention services upset the prediction/assumption that special educational services would be needed at 5 years of age for these handicapped students. However, it did not lead to systematic assessment or curriculum and programmatic changes that would have a high probability of resulting in more program graduates entering regular educational environments.

The information generated from the follow-up strategy did lead to the implementation of two additional strategies. These strategies were designed to

Table 3. Next environment teachers' view of skills Early Childhood Program graduates should have displayed upon entering their classroom

Skill area	Skills child should have had
First Year Graduates	
Preacademic	10
Language	11
Social-Survival	25
Motor	0
Total	46
Second Year Graduates	
Preacademic	1
Language	0
Social-Survival	6
Perceptual-Motor	1
Total	8

provide specific listings of skills that could be incorporated into early childhood/ special education curricula.

Strategy 3: Kindergarten Teachers Generate Skills

As an outgrowth of the follow-up study, several groups of kindergarten teachers were presented the preliminary information on social-survival skills and asked to generate lists of the most important skills which fit this category that they saw as critical for success. Thirty-seven teachers who were enrolled in a summer workshop with the first author were sampled for this information at Indiana University. Presented in Table 4 are the skills they listed. The majority of skills in this list are not tested during kindergarten screening or during a standardized developmental assessment. Rather, they are skills that occur in group situations and relate primarily to functioning independently in a large group classroom situation where a minimum of adult attention and direction is available. While not stated in objective terms, they could serve as the beginning of a global list of curriculum goals.

Two workshops were sponsored by the Wisconsin Department of Public Instruction for kindergarten and early childhood/special education in the summer of 1979. The workshops focused on concerns and issues related to mainstreaming young, exceptional children. The charge to the workshop participants by the first author was to generate a list of survival skills needed by children to "make it" in the normal school environment. The results of the two groups' work has been summarized in the publication *Out of the Nest: Instructional Strategies to Pre-*

Table 4. Selected kindergarten survival competencies obtained in interviews with kindergarten teachers

1. Initiates interactions with adults and peers
2. Interacts with adults and peers when not the initiator
3. Demonstrates appropriate isolated play skills
4. Makes choices from visible and invisible referents
5. Executes at least one task from start to finish
6. Listens and attends to a speaker in a large group
7. Follows at least a one-component direction
8. Demonstrates turn taking in a small group
9. Demonstrates mobility from place to place
10. Manipulates small and large objects
11. Demonstrates appropriate attention-getting strategies
12. Adapts to working in more than one room with more than one adult
13. Demonstrates simple dressing and undressing skills
14. Attends to task for minimum of 15 minutes
15. Adapts to transitions between activities across the day
16. Expresses ideas to others
17. Communicates with peers and adults
18. Toilets independently
19. Responds to social reinforcement
20. Asks questions of others

pare Young, Exceptional Children for the Mainstream (Lange, 1979). The teachers divided the skills into five broad categories: 1) understanding self and others, 2) communicating, 3) task-related, 4) school and class rules and routines, and 5) self-help. While all of the skills listed are appropriate and necessary for successful functioning in the mainstream, the 16 skills listed under task-related and school and classroom rules and routines are particularly relevant to "surviving" in the regular classroom. These skills are presented in Table 5. Again, the teachers featured the ability to complete tasks without adult direction, supervision, or reinforcement, a skill necessitated by the large group nature of regular kindergarten classes.

The workshops with the kindergarten teachers from Indiana and Wisconsin confirmed the results of the follow-up study. Succeeding in the regular educational environment rested as much with the ability to function in a large group environment as it did with specific isolated behavioral or developmental skills such as "knows colors or numbers." This information would be very useful in building appropriate early childhood/special education curricula. However, the problems of identifying common survival skills across kindergarten classrooms and identifying discrepancies with early childhood/special education programs still remained. An observational study (Strategy 4) was undertaken in response to these problems (Walter, 1979).

Table 5. Skills generated by kindergarten and early childhood/ special education teachers as critical for successful functioning in the normal school environment

Task-Related

1. Holds and/or manipulates materials
2. Follows a three-part direction related to task
3. Makes choices
4. Finds materials needed for task
5. Works on assigned task for 15 minutes
6. Completes task of ability level independently
7. Self-corrects errors
8. Recalls and completes task demonstrated previously

School and Classroom Rules and Routines

1. Can "line up" and stay in line
2. Raises hand and/or gets teacher attention when necessary
3. Replaces materials and "cleans up" work space
4. Moves through routine transitioning smoothly
5. Waits to take turn and shares
6. Controls voice in classroom
7. Stays in "own space" for activity
8. Knows way around school and playground

Strategy 4: Objective Measurement

During the fall and winter of 1978-1979, an observatonal study was undertaken in nine regular kindergarten classrooms, six special education kindergarten level classrooms, and nine early childhood/special education classrooms. The purpose of the study was to obtain information on the nonacademic behaviors (survival skills) that children were expected to display in order to succeed in the various classrooms. This information was to be used to compare the environmental demands of the various classrooms and to analyze areas of needed change in the services available to preschool-age handicapped children. Furthermore, the information would be useful in making smoother for the child, family, and program personnel the transition from early childhood/special education programming to kindergarten level programming. Finally, it was anticipated that this information would lead to the specification of a survival skills curriculum that when successfully implemented would result in a larger percentage of students graduating to regular kindergarten classrooms.

While reporting all of the methods employed and the results of this investigation is not possible in this chapter, the general procedures employed and the results that will have the greatest impact on curriculum development are summarized below.

For each classroom included in the study the following types of information were gathered. An anecdotal recording system was employed to record the classroom schedule, the length of various activities, and survival skills displayed by the children. In addition, a time sampling procedure was employed to measure the classroom structure. This procedure allowed the observer to record whether the activity being observed was teacher directed, teacher guided, or child guided. A teacher-directed activity was any activity in which the teacher supervised throughout the entire activity. A teacher-guided activity was any activity in which the teacher set up the activity requirements but then provided only intermittent supervision. A child-guided activity was any activity in which the child selected the task and worked on it without teacher supervision. Also recorded during the time sampling procedure was the size of instructional groups operating in the classroom. Number of children in an instructional group was classified as single child, small group (2-7 children), or large group (8 or more children). This time sampling system allowed for the acquisition of data on the proportion of time in the various classrooms that children worked on their own or with their peers and whether this work was supervised continuously or intermittently by an adult.

Approximately 60% of the time in normal kindergarten classrooms was spent in teacher-directed activities, with 50% of this time also being spent in large group activities and only 1% in single child activities. In contrast, approximately 70% of the time in special education kindergarten level programs was spent in teacher-directed activities, with approximatelfy 30% of this time spent in small group activities and 30% in large group activities. Early childhood/special education classrooms were also characterized by 70% of time spent in teacher-directed activities. However, 50% of this time was spent in small group activities and 15% in large group activities.

Thus, both levels of special education programs provide approximately 10% more teacher-directed activities than regular kindergarten classes. More striking than this figure is the discrepancy in the amount of activity time conducted in large group settings: regular kindergarten, 50%; special education kindergarten, 30%; and early childhood/special education, 15%.

A similar discrepancy was noted in the use of teacher-guided activities. Regular kindergarten programs were comprised of 20% teacher-guided activities, with half of these activities occurring in large groups. Kindergarten level special education classrooms had approximately the same level of teacher-guided activities but less than 1% was spent in a large group situation. In fact, half of this time (10%) was spent with only one child, whereas in the regular kindergarten classes only 1% of the time was spent this way. Early childhood/special education programs spent only 10% of their time in teacher-guided activities, and none of this was conducted in a large group. Thus, the discrepancy in the way teacher-guided activities are used in various programs is great.

The classes also differed in how child-guided activities were employed. Approximately 20% percent of the time in regular kindergarten classrooms was spent in small group child-guided activities. Only 1% is spent in one child, child-guided activity. This level was also recorded in the special education level kindergarten classrooms. However, only 10% of the time was spent in child-guided small group activities. The early childhood/special education classrooms were characterized by 10% of time spent in one child, child-guided activities and 10% in small group activities.

In summary, the regular kindergartens studied were characterized by greater use of teacher-directed large group activities than either level of special education programs. The regular kindergarten teacher used less teacher-directed small group and one child activities and more child-guided small group activities than special education teachers. As one might expect, the regular kindergarten classroom provided less one-to-one instruction than special education classes and demanded that children perform and learn with less adult supervision and reinforcement.

One interesting finding was the wide variation in kind of activities used in kindergarten classrooms. Summarized in Table 6 are the results from the kindergarten activities survey. Included are the frequency of occurrence of the various activities, the length of time they generally lasted, and the type of survival skills necessary to complete the activities. The only activities that occurred in at least 75% of the kindergartens sampled were snack, teacher-directed or guided large group, teacher-directed or guided small group, free play, show and tell, songs or finger plays, story, and special activities. Thus, in terms of general curriculum development for handicapped preschool children, skills necessary to succeed in a

Table 6. The behavioral requirements and frequency of occurrence of typical kindergarten classroom activities

Activity	Skills[a]	Duration of activity in minutes (Average and Range)	Percentage of classrooms observed that displayed these activities
Free play	I,K,D,E	30 (20–50)	89%
Show and tell	B,C,D,E	10 (5–20)	78%
Calendar-Weather	B,C,D,E	8 (5–10)	56%
Songs, Finger plays	B,C,D,E	7 (5–13)	78%
Musical games	B,C,H,J,D,E	10 (5–20)	67%
Snack	D,E,G	10 (5–15)	100%
Film strip	B,D,E	10	33%
Teacher-directed or guided large group	A,B,C,H,F,D,E	20 (10–30)	100%
Teacher-directed or guided small group	A,B,C,H,F,D,E	25 (20–30)	100%
Movie	B,D,E	10	33%
Games	B,C,H,J,D,E	8	22%
Learning centers	A,D,E,F,H,K	30 (22–40)	33%
Rest	D,E	7 (5–15)	44%
Story	B,C,D,E	10 (5–15)	78%
Independent reading	A,D,E	10	33%
Art	A,B,D,E,F,G,H	20	67%
Recess	I,J,G,D,E,K	15 (15–20)	22%
Motor	B,C,E,H,D,J	20	11%
Chart Story	B,C,D,E	3	22%
Specials			
Art	A,B,D,E,F,G,H	30	89%
Physical education	B,C,E,H,J,G,D	30	89%
Music	B,C,D,E	20	89%
IMC	A,B,C,D,E	30	67%

[a] A, Independent task work; B, Group attending; C, Group participation; D, Following class routines; E, Appropriate classroom behavior; F, Problem solving; G, Self-care; H, Direction following; I, Social/play skills; J, Game-playing skills; K, Functional communication.

variety of activities, rather than in specific activities themselves, will need to be the focus. The most prevalent survival skills were in the areas of following classroom routines and rules, group attending and participation, and direction following. Interestingly enough, functional communication was not critical for many of the activities nor were social/play skills. These are the skills that often form the basis of early childhood/special education programs. While they may be necessary for the child to direct or guide his or her own activities, they may not be essential for the child to blend and function as part of the kindergarten group.

These survival skill areas have been translated into a checklist that contains specific skill items. The checklist is currently being field tested in two special education programs in the Madison schools. The research plan is to finalize a checklist that will become part of the ongoing assessment in the early childhood/special education classrooms in the fall of 1980 and for the utility of the checklist to be tested during the 1980–1981 school year.

The curriculum development plans growing out of this research relate mainly to designing goals, activities, and instructional procedures that correspond to the survival skills. These procedures would then be implemented in the early childhoood/special education classrooms and evaluated based on a higher percentage of children graduating to and succeeding in regular kindergarten environments.

EARLY CHILDHOOD/SPECIAL EDUCATION: WHERE WE NEED TO GO

The major outgrowth of the work so far in the Madison Metropolitan School District is to point out the need for extensive continued research on future environments. While Public Law 94-142 specifies that the current learning characteristics of the child should comprise part of the child's individualized education program (IEP), adequate instruments or procedures for documenting under what conditions a child acquires needed skills and at what rate are not available. Since the variety of environments examined indicated the importance of independent, nondirected and non-teacher-reinforced performance, assessment of these skills with the young, handicapped child becomes a must. Certainly this area in itself could be the focus for a number of research investigations and the development of several instruments and processes for gathering objective data on learner characteristics.

At present with severely handicapped children the tendency is to develop alternative, generally segregated programs, rather than to examine adaptations that could be made in existing nonsegregated programs. Most professionals accept as a given the isolated classroom placement for the severely handicapped child. This is true among both regular and special educational staff. One area of needed research is the degree to which materials, resources, and goals of least restrictive programs can be adapted to meet the needs of a more severely handicapped student. The present authors contend that placing the child in a different setting should be the last alternative chosen rather than the first. Future research will need to be longitudinal in nature and conducted in a wide variety of environments. Through such study, researchers will be forced to document the demands of the environment in which the child is placed and the ways that the child meets, partially meets, or does not meet those demands. Thus, learner style must be an inherent part of research concerning environmental adaptations.

Another area of needed research relates to the use of normal child development data in establishing programming priorities for the preschool-age handicapped child. Thus far in the field of early childhood/special education, assessment, curriculum, and program focus has been developmental in nature. That is, the handicapped child is assessed in relation to the major developmental skills acquired by normal children, and areas of deficit are selected for special programming. The general procedure is to start the child at the point in the developmental sequence where the skill performance breaks down and then to teach the skills in the order acquired by normal children. The assumption that must be made to accept this approach is that normal children acquire skills in the most efficient or at least in a maximally functional manner. The data base that exists for child development is not extensive enough to support such an assumption. It may be that in acquiring skills during the first 5 years of life under extremely varied, nonsystematic conditions normal children show the least efficient sequence of skill acquisition. It may also be that the general pattern of development demonstrated by normal children is not the most effective way to succeed in *teaching* people to function as capable, productive adults. These authors are not suggesting that the data generated on normal child development be disregarded. Rather, the normal skill sequence should be analyzed against the demands of future environments.

One problem faced by all special education teachers is identifying priorities or choosing the most important areas on which to work with a child. The normal development approach sets many skills as equally important at any point in time. Yet the data base on what is necessary to succeed in school-age programs would indicate that some skills are more important than others. An interesting finding from the research reported above is that communication and play skills may not be as important for success in normal kindergarten classrooms as performing without adult direction, supervision, or reinforcement. However, communication and play skills may be more important in environments outside of the classroom. Thus, research must be undertaken to document the demands of community and domestic environments as well as the school environment. The ecological inventory strategy presented in detail by Brown, Branston-McClean, Baumgart, Vincent, Falvey, and Schroeder (1979) could be used for this purpose.

Within the area of classroom survival skills the work conducted to date in the Madison Metropolitan School District generates several future activities and raises many unanswered questions. In order to be used as a programming tool, a survival skills checklist would need to be written with specific criteria for acceptable performance of each skill specified. This could be accomplished by collecting data on several kindergarten children who are doing well in terms of the survival skills and then averaging the rate, duration, and/or quality of their performance. The children could be selected from one classroom or a representative sample of classes. To determine variations in the criteria over time, the procedure for establishing criteria would need to be repeated at several intervals (e.g., the beginning, middle, and end of the school year).

The inventory of survival skills generated by the research conducted to date is assumed to list behavior that is critical to a child's successful functioning in a typical kindergarten classroom. However, the assumption that these skills are, in fact, critical skills must be verified. If the survival skill checklist contains the critical skills, using it would discriminate children who experience social, behavioral, and academic difficulties in kindergarten from those who do not. Several studies could be conducted to answer this question. Two groups of children in the same classroom, one group doing well in terms of academics, social interaction, and behavior, and another group not doing well, could be identified. The performance of each group on the checklist of survival skills could be obtained and then compared. If each checklist skill is truly a "critical" skill, the performance of the two groups on each skill would be different. Skills that are not actually critical could then be eliminated from the list.

A second study would involve using the checklist for predictive purposes. The performance of children on the survival skills checklist could be compared to measures of their later school success. Any predictive study would require longitudinal data over at least 1 year, and preferably several years, of school performance. The data from a predictive study of this type could be used 1) to pinpoint the most critical survival skills, 2) to provide target children with training in survival skills before failure experiences in school occurred, and 3) to supplement traditional screening information for placement decisions.

The checklist of survival skills generated from the research to date is based on performance expected of typical kindergarten children by mid-year. Behavioral expectations for kindergarteners may, however, be different depending on the time of year. Similarly, time sampling data of classroom structure in the study reported above were collected at mid-year. Additional time samples need to be collected at the beginning and end of the year to determine the changes in typical classroom structure during the year.

Although the anecdotal inventory and time sampling information did result in an initial version of a behavioral checklist of survival skills, they did not reveal the typical pattern of contact and interaction between a child and teacher and peers. Additional data collection methods are needed to gather information on this interaction. Questions that should be addressed relate to the frequency and duration of interactions between individual children and their teachers and whether these exchanges are initiated by the child or the teacher. Similar data should be gathered on peer-peer interactions.

Answers to the above questions about child-teacher interaction could be used to determine the degree of independence from teacher control, direction, and reinforcement that a child might be expected to display during various activities. Information on peer-peer interaction could be used to determine the ability of the child to interact socially with peers (both initiating and responding) and the ability of the child to use peers as resources during tasks.

In summary, in order for the research conducted to date to fill the role of being useful evaluative research, investigations on critical survival skills must be continued and investigations on specific child-learning and interaction styles must be initiated. The research completed thus far, while not generating a specific curriculum proposal for early childhood/special education, does lead to several specific programming and service delivery implications.

Given that the acquisition of survival skills is crucial for a child's effective performance in kindergarten, teaching children the survival skills that they do not display becomes the responsibility of preschool educators (in both regular and special education). Ideally, this teaching process would be initiated several years before the children enter kindergarten. In this way, children would not be "held back" a year or placed in a categorical special education program (e.g., an EMR classroom) because they lack adequate training in survival skills. Since it is often neither desirable nor possible to predict 1 or 2 years in advance which children will and will not have sufficient skills to enter kindergarten when they reach 5 years of age, the process of teaching survival skills should be initiated with all children who are enrolled in early childhood/special education programs, even the most severely handicapped. Once children are enrolled in a special education school-age program, obtaining their re-entry into a regular education program is difficult (Brown, 1979). Since many severely handicapped children are served by preschool programs that also include less handicapped and nonhandicapped children, if data reveal that the child has some of the survival skills necessary for kindergarten, it may be possible for educators to document the appropriateness of at least partial integration with nonhandicapped kindergarten-age children.

The terminal objective for teaching any survival skill should be that the child attain the level or mastery criterion of the skill expected of regular kindergarten children by mid-year. This ensures that the child is prepared to function for at least several months in kindergarten without a sense of failure before behavioral expectations increase. This also ensures the child is prepared to function in a kindergarten environment that may have stricter requirements than those stated in the checklist. With severely handicapped students, even achievement of skills not at criterion level would probably ensure that the child would at least be placed in a program that was generally designed for less handicapped students.

Methods for teaching survival need to be delineated carefully. Children may be taught survival skills in one environment but will need to apply these skills in a different environment (the actual kindergarten classroom). A child's success in kindergarten therefore is dependent on his or her ability to generalize from the special education preschool environment to the regular kindergarten environment. However, as the data previously discussed indicate, there are major differences in the classroom structure of kindergarten and special education programs. These differences may make it difficult for the child to generalize skills learned in a special education classroom to the later kindergarten environment. Strategies for teaching survival skills thus will need to minimize this difference and increase the ability of the child to make the transition to the kindergarten environment smoothly.

However, special education is distinguished in part from regular educational environments by teacher behavior and group size. Children who are are considered to display exceptional educational needs are determined to require a higher intensity of programming than normal children. This higher intensity is usually translated as more direct contact between teacher and student and more specific setting of objectives for the student involved. The setting of specific objectives usually entails the delineation of a specific behavior to be taught. This delineation includes under what conditions the child should learn to exhibit the skill. As many authors have indicated, a well developed behavioral objective will include a specific statement as to what the child is to do, under what teacher cues, models, or prompts. Also included will be a proficiency, fluency, or consistency statement related to the child's response. Thus, the writing of behavioral objectives implies a degree of specifity related to instruction that does not exist generally in classrooms for normal children.

Special education teachers translate behavioral objectives into instructional activities and lesson plans. This translation process implies that the teacher most often will be an active participant in the learning situation. He or she will not simply indicate verbally what he or she wants the child to do, but rather through the use of a highly sophisticated technology will ensure that the child completes the response.

The technology available to the special educator has been well documented to result in change in child performance. However, the literature also serves to overwhelmingly document that the change in child behavior displayed under the specific conditions listed in the behavioral objective most often does not generalize to more natural, ambiguous environments (Stokes & Baer, 1977). In a sense, the child may be learning to produce a behavior only under very specified antecedent and consequent conditions. These specified conditions are the very ones that do not exist in regular educational environments. Basically this can result in a vicious circle for handicapped children. They are removed from regular educational services because they do not learn rapidly enough or perform accurately enough under large group, ambiguous instruction. They are placed in a special education environment where greater consistency and individualized instruction are provided. They learn more rapidly and perform more accurately in this environment, but most often this change will not generalize back to the normal environment.

While the application of highly specialized technology may be necessary for handicapped children to learn, the focus of special education should be on the removal of this technology with the continued maintenance of the child response. While certainly almost all special education teachers will indicate that this is part of their plan, the actual special education environment and the mandates for ongoing assessment and program change go against this taking place. Simply the decreased number of children involved in the program results in greater levels of teacher-child contact than can be provided in regular education. The data gathered on early childhood/special education classrooms presented earlier in this chapter highlight the structural results of small class size. In order to decrease this difference, early childhood/special education teachers must implement changes in instructional arrangements. This is particularly true for severely handicapped students who are more likely to receive one-to-one instruction. Several alternatives need to be explored for doing this.

The early childhood/special educator can teach survival skills by gradually approximating the structure of the regular kindergarten environment. If this is undertaken, the following dimensions will need to be analyzed and adapted: class size, adult-child ratio, duration of activities, and opportunity to work in child-guided activities.

A second strategy for teaching survival skills would involve teachers manipulating their own behavior rather than working with environmental context. In this strategy, teachers would alter their interaction patterns with children to more closely approximate that of kindergarten teachers. Although, as indicated earlier, additional research needs to be conducted on teacher-child interactions, several parameters of manipulation can currently be identified. The prime ones relate to teacher reinforcement and amount and duration of direct instructional or supervisory contact with students. This would probably require that special education teachers have someone develop a monitoring system for their interaction and that they be involved in monitoring the behavior of the often large numbers of ancillary personnel who interact with their children.

While the above suggestions do not indicate a specific sequence for teacher and classroom structure changes, they can serve as a beginning in the analysis process for any early childhood/special educator who is concerned with the future functioning of his or her students. Continued research, it is hoped, will lead to a better delineation of a specific sequence and a system for evaluating its implementation and long term effectiveness.

SUMMARY AND CONCLUSIONS

Increasingly, even the most severely handicapped, preschool-age children are receiving educational services in environments that include less handicapped and nonhandicapped peers. Frequently upon reaching traditional school age, these children are then placed in more restrictive programs. Thus, the effect of intensive early intervention may be viewed as nominal in relation to future educational functioning even if significant developmental skill gain has been documented as a result of such efforts. The goal of early childhood/special education must be to provide programs in which children acquire the skills necessary to continue or begin to function in less restrictive environments. Curriculum design and assessment in early childhood/special education need to be expanded to include a focus on survival skills.

Using survival skills as a basis for programming, the educator should devote some instructional time to teaching handicapped students systematically those skills that are necessary for them to function as independently as possible in a complex environment where normally functioning students are the majority. Although these skills may be considered "developmentally" beyond the level of the student, or outside the language, social, motor, or cognitive curriculum areas, their absence from the curriculum may be detrimental when attempting to enroll students in less restrictive programs. The argument for the inclusion of survival skills, then, rests upon a pragmatic, behavioral foundation, a base that reflects systematic planning for the next environment and employs child progress and child success at meeting environmental/behavioral expectations as the ultimate measure of programmatic value.

In a sense, the results of the present authors' research on the demands of the next environment would indicate that traditional special education programming may be incompatible with child success in least restrictive programs. The technology base in the field of special education is very sophisticated and this technology has been well documented to produce child change. Yet this very technology is based on precision of cues, precision in definition of acceptable child responses, and precision and consistency in reinforcement of child responses. As the present authors examined the data from the next environment classrooms, the general trend was for the least restrictive programs to have the least degree of precision and consistency; particularly in the areas of adult supervision and adult reinforcement the least restrictive programs were very discrepant from the main line technology of special education. Therefore, children graduating from special education classrooms may in a sense be dependent on the technology used, and unable to learn in a least restrictive program.

While severely handicapped students will not acquire skills at the same rate as nonhandicapped students, if just placed in a normal classroom, the intensity with which special education technology must be applied in order to get skill gain is not known. Professionals often assume that, the more handicapped the child, the more precise and consistent instruction must be. The present authors believe that this is, however, an assumption and not necessarily a fact. Instructional precision and consistency may rest in the structuring of the environment, including the use of a child's peers, as much as it does in the actions of the teacher. The present authors have no doubt that the formulation of a curriculum for handicapped children under 5 years of age cannot be completed if the demands of future environments are not considered. Accepting as a given that these future environments will be segregated programs for the school-age severely handicapped child is not realistic. In fact, Public Law 94-142 specifies that all children must be educated in normal environments to the maximum extent possible. Unless early childhood/special educators survey and study the future environments of their students, they will train and teach handicapped children in a way that maximizes the probability of placement in restrictive programs. All goals set for young, severely handicapped children must be analyzed not only in terms of developmental appropriateness but also in terms of future utility and functionality.

REFERENCES

Anastasiow, N. Strategies and models for early childhood intervention programs in integrated settings. In M. Guralnick (ed.), *Early intervention and the integration of handicapped and nonhandicapped children*. Baltimore: University Park Press, 1978.

Beck, R. Interdisciplinary model: Planning distribution and ancillary input to classrooms for the severely/profoundly handicapped. In E. Sontag, J. Smith, & N. Certo (eds.), *Educational programming for the severely and profoundly handicapped*. Reston, Virginia: Division on Mental Retardation, Council for Exceptional Children, 1977.

Boehm, A. One model for developing a prekindergarten assessment procedure. *Exceptional Children*, 1971, *37*(7), 372–380.

Bricker, D. A rationale for the integration of handicapped and nonhandicapped preschool children. In M. Guralnick (ed.), *Early intervention and the integration of handicapped and nonhandicapped children*. Baltimore: University Park Press, 1978.

Brown, L., Branston-McClean, M. B., Baumgart, D., Vincent, L., Falvey, M., & Schroeder, J. Using the characteristics of current and subsequent least restrictive environments as factors in the development of curricular content for severely handicapped students. *TASH Review*, 1979, *4*(4), 407–424.

Brown, L., Nietupski, J., & Hamre-Nietupski, S. The criterion of ultimate functioning and public school services for the severely handicapped student. In A. Thomas (ed.), *Hey, don't forget about me: Education's investment in the severely, profoundly and multiply handicapped*. Reston, Virginia: Council for Exceptional Children, 1976.

Brown, L., Wilcox, B., Sontag, E., Vincent, B., Dodd, N., & Gruenewald, L. Toward the realization of the least restrictive educational environment for severely handicapped students. *AAESPH Review*, 1977, *2*(4), 195–201.

Brown, P. *Measuring the success of a pre-school special education program using follow-up data*. Unpublished master's thesis, University of Wisconsin, Madison, 1979.

Cobb, J. Academic survival skills and elementary academic achievement. In E. Meyer (ed.), *Strategies for teaching exceptional children*. Denver: Love Publishing Co., 1972.

Cohen, D., & Rudolph, M. *Kindergarten and early schooling*. Englewood Cliffs, New Jersey: Prentice Hall, 1977.

Grosenick, J. Integration of exceptional children into regular classes: Research and procedure. In E. Meyen (ed.), *Strategies for teaching exceptional children*. Denver: Love Publishing Co., 1972.

Guralnick, M. (ed.). *Early intervention and the integration of handicapped and nonhandicapped children*. Baltimore: University Park Press, 1978.

Guralnick, M. Social interactions among preschool children. *Exceptional Children*, 1980, *46*(4), 248–255.

Hops, H., & Cobb, J. Survival behaviors in the educational setting: Their implications for research and intervention. In L. Hamerlynck, L. Hany, & E. Mash (eds.), *Behavior change: Methodology, concepts and practice*. Champaign, Illinois: Research Press, 1973.

Kenowitz, L. A., Zweibel, S., & Edgar, E. Determining the least restrictive educational opportunity for the severely and profoundly handicapped. In N. Haring & D. Bricker (eds.), *Teaching the severely handicapped* (Vol. III). Columbus, Ohio: Special Press, 1978.

Lahaderne, H. Attitudinal and intellectual correlates of attention: A study of fourth-grade classrooms. *Journal of Educational Psychology*, 1968, *59*, 320-324.

Lange, J. *Out of the nest: Instructional strategies to prepare young, exceptional children for the mainstream*. Madison, Wisconsin: Wisconsin Department of Public Instruction, 1979.

LeBlanc, J. M., Etzel, B. C., & Domash, M. A. A functional curriculum for early intervention. In K. E. Allen, V. A. Holm, & R. L. Schiefelbusch (eds.), *Early intervention—A team approach*. Baltimore: University Park Press, 1978.

Meyers, D., Atwell, A., & Orpet, R. Prediction of fifth-grade achievement from kindergarten test and rating data. *Educational and Psychological Measurement*, 1968, *28*, 457-463.

Pefley, D., & Smith, H. *It's Monday morning*. Chapel Hill, North Carolina: Technical Assistance Development System/University of North Carolina, 1976.

Stokes, T. F., & Baer, D. M. An implicit technology of generalization. *Journal of Applied Behavior Analysis*, 1977, *10*, 349-367.

Stufflebeam, D. L., Foley, W. J., Gephart, W. J., Guba, E. G., Hammond, R. L., Merriman, H. D., & Provas, M. M. *Educational evaluation and decision making*. Itasca, Illinois: Peacock, 1971.

Vincent, L., & Broome, K. A public school service delivery model for handicapped children between birth and five years of age. In E. Sontag, J. Smith, & N. Certo (eds.), *Educational programming for the severely and profoundly handicapped*. Reston, Virginia: Division on Mental Retardation, Council for Exceptional Children, 1977.

Walter, G. *The "survival skills" displayed by kindergarteners and the structure of the regular kindergarten environment*. Unpublished master's thesis, University of Wisconsin, Madison, 1979.

Zeitlin, S. *Kindergarten screening: Early identification of potential high risk learners*. Springfield, Illinois: Charles C Thomas, 1976.

Index